D1247190

The Logic of Perception

Bradford Books

Edward C. T. Walker, Editor. Explorations in THE BIOLOGY OF LAN-GUAGE. 1979.

Daniel C. Dennett. BRAINSTORMS. 1979.

Charles Marks. COMMISSUROTOMY, CONSCIOUSNESS AND UNITY OF MIND. 1980.

John Haugeland, Editor. MIND DESIGN. 1981.

Fred I. Dretske. KNOWLEDGE AND THE FLOW OF INFORMATION. 1981.

Jerry A. Fodor. REPRESENTATIONS. 1981.

Ned Block, Editor. IMAGERY. 1981.

Roger N. Shepard and Lynn A. Cooper. MENTAL IMAGES AND THEIR TRANSFORMATIONS. 1982.

Hubert L. Dreyfus, Editor, in collaboration with Harrison Hall. HUSSERL, INTENTIONALITY AND COGNITIVE SCIENCE. 1982.

John Macnamara. NAMES FOR THINGS. 1982.

Natalie Abrams and Michael D. Buckner, Editors. MEDICAL ETHICS. 1983.

Morris Halle and G. N. Clements. PROBLEM BOOK IN PHONOLOGY. 1983.

Jon Barwise and John Perry. SITUATIONS AND ATTITUDES. 1983.

Jerry A. Fodor. MODULARITY OF MIND. 1983.

George D. Romanos. QUINE AND ANALYTIC PHILOSOPHY. 1983.

Robert Cummins. THE NATURE OF PSYCHOLOGICAL EXPLANA-TION. 1983.

Irvin Rock. THE LOGIC OF PERCEPTION. 1983.

THE LOGIC
OF PERCEPTION

IRVIN ROCK

A Bradford Book

The MIT Press
Cambridge, Massachusetts
London, England

Library of Congress Cataloging in Publication Data

Rock, Irvin.
    The logic of perception.

    "A Bradford book."
    Bibliography: p.
    Includes index.
    1. Perception. 2. Thought and thinking. I. Title.
[DNLM: 1. Perception. 2. Intelligence. 3. Logic. BF
311 R682L]
BF311.R555 1983   153.7   82-24911
ISBN 0-262-18109-6

Typographic design by David Horne.
Composition by Horne Associates, Inc.,
West Lebanon, New Hampshire.
This book was printed and bound
in the United States of America.

To Sylvia

Contents

Preface

IF SOME OF MY FORMER STUDENTS with whom I have lost touch should happen to come across this book, they may find it hard to believe it was written by me. Originally an ardent advocate of the Gestalt point of view, I here defend—and try to expand upon—a viewpoint that constitutes the very essence of what the Gestaltists so effectively criticized. Koffka in his *Principles of Gestalt Psychology* summed up the kind of theory against which the Gestalt movement was aimed as the "network of traditional hypotheses." These included the distinction between sensation and perception and the notion that we unconsciously interpret the sensation on the basis of past experience in arriving at the perception. The ideas in that "network" will be reconsidered in this book.

What accounts for such a compete about-face in theoretical outlook? For a number of reasons, I don't believe it is, entirely, an about-face. First, Gestalt Psychology contains a wealth of ideas, and many of them stand today as correct descriptions of perception and cognition. They have been incorporated into contemporary theorizing and into this book. Indeed some of the Gestalt findings and arguments actually run counter to the core Gestalt thesis that spontaneous neural interactions account for our perceptions. For example, Koffka argued that size perception entails an invariant relation between visual angle and perceived distance, a formulation that is much closer in spirit to an unconscious inference than it is to a hypothetical, interactive brain event based on a ratio of visual angle of object to context in the field, or the like. So one might say that part of what I have tried to do here is to emphasize certain ideas latent in the Gestalt writings instead of other, better-known Gestalt ideas.

Second, I have not resurrected the sensation-perception doctrine, although I have argued that perception can often be understood as the result of a dual-stage process in which the first stage is a representation highly correlated with the proximal input, what I call the proximal mode of perception or literal solution. One might say that there is a sense in which the constancy hypothesis that the Gestaltists so strongly criticized is correct. They went too far in their argument that the proximal stimulus was not in correspondence with the percept.

Third, while I have sought to give a rightful place to past experience as a determining factor in perception, I have not done what the Gestaltists so rightly criticized about some of their predecessors—that is, I have not simply equated explanation with the alleged working of prior experience and overlooked the theoretical difficulties of such a glib assumption. (Contrary to belief, the Gestaltists did not maintain that experience played no role in perception. In fact, Wertheimer included past experience as one factor governing perceptual organization.) Inference may often be based on premises that derive from past experience, but that does not mean that the process of inference reduces to the utilization of experience. Moreover, I have grappled with the central problem of the role of past experience in perception —one to which the Gestaltists called attention—namely, how experience can enter when to do so first requires "bottom-up" processing. So anyone who reads this book as essentially an extension of the Helmholtzian or Transactionalist *empiricism* is, to say the least, misunderstanding what I am attempting to do.

Some of my own research findings have driven me in the direction of a theory that gives more weight to intelligent operations in perception than did the Gestalt theory. Chief among these was the finding that the perceived orientation of a figure very much affects its perceived shape even when the orientation of the figure's retinal image remains unchanged, a finding, I might add, that runs exactly counter to what Köhler inferred when he analyzed the same question of ambiguity in the meaning of the term "orientation." Rightly or wrongly I concluded that this fact implicates "description" in form perception, and that conclusion has shaken me loose from a set of assumptions that had guided my earlier thinking. This finding led me and my associates to ask whether certain other perceptual effects were based on phenomenal rather than retinal properties, such as location in apparent movement, proximity in grouping, and even geometry in form perception itself. In all these cases the finding was that one perception was based upon a prior perception, a fact not directly compatible with the Gestalt approach—nor, I might add with the approach taken by those like J. J. Gibson in expanding upon a stimulus theory of perception.

So much for an attempt to explain how and why my own thinking has changed so radically.

This is a rather speculative book, and at times I feel uncomfortable about it. Since at heart I am an experimentalist who prefers to put hypothesis to rigorous test, speculation on a level remote from the possibility of direct disconfirmation makes me uneasy. In this respect I assure the reader that I am my own severest critic. It seems to me, however, that the point of view advanced here *is* subject to tests of predictions that follow from it. During the writing of the book many facts and phenomena gave me pause—as possibly in contradiction of the thesis being advanced—which suggests that in principle the theory is indeed disconfirmable. Certainly the theory is subject to the longer-range test of its fruitfulness. If not fruitful, it will soon wither and die. Against the unpalatability of theoretical speculation, however, is the potential good it can do in advancing our knowledge. Since I firmly believe that progress in science depends upon the advancement of theory, I have (to be frank) summoned up my courage to speculate. I argue (in the second chapter) that there are only a limited number of kinds of theory of perception that are possible—three, to be specific. If, as I argue further, two of these, the spontaneous interaction and the stimulus theory, are inadequate, then in the resulting theoretical vacuum it is essential that someone undertake the task of elaborating the third, the cognitive theory, so that it can be given its chance in the market place of theoretical ideas. So I elected myself to do the job by marshaling a good deal of evidence in support of it and setting forth some ideas that are perhaps idiosyncratic to my way of thinking. Others, of course, have advocated and are advocating this kind of theory in their own way.

To whom am I addressing this book? To a wide audience I hope, not only to advanced students of perception, but to beginners and to those in other disciplines such as philosophy who, I know, are interested in the subject. Toward this end I have tried to avoid technical language, to define terms with which some readers may not be familiar, and to explain experiments clearly (with the help of illustrations wherever possible). Despite these efforts, should readers with little background in perception find certain points unclear, they can take comfort in knowing that source books are available. My own textbook, *An Introduction to Perception*, may be helpful, and others exist. The bibliography at the back of the book gives many such titles, as well as references to the original source of the finding under discussion. I hope that the more advanced students of perception will be tolerant of the fact that I often go over the ground of phenomena, findings, and explanations with which they are already familiar.

In three places in the book I took the liberty of paraphrasing some of my own previous writing since I was unable to say it better now than I had earlier. I therefore acknowledge these sources: In Chapter 8, the section on anorthoscopic form perception borrows from my article Anorthoscopic perception in *Scientific American*, March 1981, *244*, No. 3, and the section on kinetic stimulus transformations borrows from my article with Deborah Smith, Alternative solutions to kinetic stimulus transformations, *Journal of Experimental Psychology: Human Perception and Performance*, 1981, 7, 19–29. Chapter 9, on unconsious inference, borrows substantially from my chapter In defense of unconscious inference, in W. Epstein, ed., *Stability and Constancy in Visual Perception: Mechanisms and Processes*, New York: Wiley-Interscience, 1977.

I am indebted to the many authors and publishers who have permitted me to reproduce their illustrations or modifications of them. In most cases these are specifically acknowledged in the legend for each figure but in addition I hereby acknowledge with gratitude and give credit to the Macmillan Publishing Company, for permitting me to reproduce the following illustrations from my book *An Introduction to Perception*, 1975; Figures 1-1b, 3-22d, 3-25, 6-8, 6-24, 7-1, 8-1a and b, 8-5, 9-3 and 10-1a; to *Scientific American*, for permitting me to use Figure 3-23 from the article "Vision and touch" by myself and Charles Harris, 1967, *216*, 96–104, and Figures 7-10 and 7-17 from my article "Anorthoscopic perception," 1981, *244*, 145–153. The illustration "giraffe passing a window," Figure 12b, page 131, is from *A Droodle* by Roger Price, copyright 1953, 1954, 1955, 1964, 1966. By permission of the publisher, Price/Stern/Sloan Publishers, Inc. Figures 12a and 12c on page 131 are redrawn from Price.

There remains the pleasure of acknowledging the help that many have given me with this undertaking. The first to read an earlier version of the manuscript, to encourage me to proceed and to suggest revisions, was Robert Schindler. Following that, Stephen Palmer rendered monumental aid in reading critically and discussing with me each chapter during my stay at Berkeley in the Spring of 1981 (and I take this occasion to thank the members of the Department of Psychology at Berkeley, chaired by Stephen Glickman, for their gracious hospitality during that semester). A later draft of the book was then read and very constructively criticized by William Epstein. At the same time, the manuscript was reviewed chapter by chapter by colleagues at Rutgers University, and the penetrating questions raised by Michael Kubovy, Deborah Wheeler, and John Ceraso forced me to rethink virtually every argument. I also appreciate the reactions of members of a seminar at the New School for Social Research chaired by Arien Mack. I acknowledge the thoughtful objections to my theoretical deviationism of my friend of many years, Carl Zuckerman.

I thank Stanley Anton for help of many kinds, including the preparation of the bibliography. As with all my previous books and manuscripts, I am grateful to Sylvia Rock for her support, both abstract and concrete, and I dedicate this book to her with love, appreciation, and admiration.

Once again I want to express my deep indebtedness to and affection for my teachers, Martin Scheerer (whose physical death hasn't diminished his influence on me), Solomon Asch, and Hans Wallach, who are still teaching me by their example of continued dedication to psychology and by their intellectual integrity.

I.R.

Highland Park, New Jersey
March 1983

The Logic of Perception

1 ⬜

Introduction

THE THESIS OF THIS BOOK is that perception is intelligent in that it is based on operations similar to those that characterize thought. (I will consider thoughtlike operations to be intelligent by definition, even though thought itself might not always be considered to be intelligent.) However, the dependence of perception on sensory information makes for certain differences between it and "higher" cognitive functions such as imagination and thinking. Therefore, I will try to make a convincing case for the claim that perception is indeed the result of thoughtlike processes, and I will examine how perception nonetheless differs in certain respects from nonperceptual cognitive processes. I should say at the outset that a serious difficulty for this enterprise is our very limited knowledge of the nature of thought itself. But even if we know little about the nature of thought, a demonstration that perception results from cognitive-like operations does constitute an explanation. Others seek to explain perception in very different ways.

To turn the problem around, so to speak, it is entirely possible that we may learn about the operations of thinking by studying perception. Perception might be the evolutionary link between low-level sensory processes that mediated simple detection of environmental changes in phylogenetically primitive organisms and high-level cognitive processes in more complex forms of life. If the stimulus impinging upon sense organs such as the eye is at best an ambiguous and distortion-prone representation of the external object or object-event producing it, some mechanism had to evolve to yield reliable, veridical apprehension of such an object or event. One possible mechanism to achieve this end entails inferential processing. Therefore, intelligent operations may have evolved in the service of perception. Once they emerged, they may have undergone further elaboration so as to become autonomous and no longer to be necessarily linked to sensory input.

Perception seems to be shot through with intelligence. It is hardly necessary to illustrate this fact for students of perception, but for others, it will be important to give some examples.

Example 1: The first example concerns the phenomenon in which observers have the illusory experience that they are moving although they are stationary. Most people have experienced this effect when sitting in a stationary train or automobile while the adjacent train or automobile is moving. This phenomenon, referred to as induced movement of the self (Duncker, 1929) or more recently as visual kinesthesis (Gibson, 1966) or vection (Brandt, et al., 1973), can be studied in the laboratory by placing an observer inside a rotating drum lined with vertical stripes. Ideally, only the drum is visible; i.e., the stationary floor or ceiling is not visible. After a short period the drum appears to have stopped turning and observers experience themselves as rotating in the opposite direction. There is generally a transitional period in which the drum appears to be slowing down and observers experience themselves as beginning to turn slowly.

The information available to the observer under such conditions is ambiguous. The angular displacement of the stripes of the drum with respect to the observer could result from either their actual motion or the rotation of the observer within a stationary drum. The same is true in cases in daily life where the induced self-motion is linear rather than rotary. Unless acceleration enters in, there would be no proprioceptive information or signal from the vestibular apparatus of the inner ear indicative of body motion were the observer in motion, so that their absence is not unequivocal information that the body is stationary. Still, since observers who are sitting or standing in the dark will not experience themselves in motion—although there too the situation is ambiguous—we must assume there is some "force" at work when the moving scene *is* visible to induce self-motion. Such perceived motion of the self is the preferred outcome and will always occur after some latency period.

I would argue that the "force" yielding induced motion of the self is the tendency to assume that the surrounding environment is stationary. The drum in the experiment is a surrogate of the environment. If this interpretation is correct, the percept can be thought of as the result of a process much like reasoning. The assumption in question is analogous to an implicit axiom. Given the acceptance of it by the perceptual system, the angular displacement of the drum is inferred to result from self-motion.[1]

Another interesting effect can be observed in this kind of situation. Consider what happens when a stationary spot is placed directly in front of the observer, just inside the surface of the drum. At the beginning, the spot will appear to be more or less stationary in front of the rotating drum. But the moment motion is induced in the self, the spot also appears to be moving around with one's body. We have observed this transition in our laboratory. This outcome "makes sense," and some would say it could hardly be otherwise. We say this is because (1) observers experience themselves as rotating and (2) the spot appears straight ahead of the observer.[2] Given 1 and 2 as perceptual facts, it "follows" that the spot must be rotating along with the observer. But don't we mean by follows that it is an inference from 1 and 2, which essentially serve as premises? The outcome could be otherwise if and only if the perceptual system were not governed by logical operations.[3]

The Case against Perceptual Intelligence

Not all students of perception, however, believe that this outcome is actually the result of an intelligent process analogous to reasoning. A phenomenon may appear to be intelligent, but the mechanism underlying it may have no common ground with the mechanisms underlying reasoning, logical thought, or problem solving. Thus, for example, the web of a spider is certainly a remarkable feat of engineering, but that does not mean that the spider reasons or solves a problem in constructing it the way it does or knows what the purpose of the web is, and therefore that anything analogous to thought is operating here. I want to emphasize that while most students of perception

1. At the moment the drum begins to turn, the absence of any signal corresponding to intended self-motion or of proprioceptive feedback of passively imposed self-motion probably opposes the illusory effect because such initial movement would entail acceleration. This may explain why the illusory effect is not always immediate. With the passage of time, however, this constraint seems to disappear or the motion of the self can develop very gradually such that the transition from stationary to rotating would be assumed to be below threshold.

2. The basis of 2 is that the spot yields an image in the center of the retina, the fovea, assuming the observer is fixating it, and the eyes are aimed straight ahead with respect to the head. These two conditions together are known to produce the experience that an object viewed is straight ahead of one's head.

3. Some students of perception might say that the perceived motion of the spot is based on induced motion of objects (not of the self), as in the case of the moon appearing to move in a direction opposite to that of clouds passing in

are aware of the many cases where perception seems to be intelligent, only some have regarded these as resulting from intelligent internal operations (see, for example, Ames, 1951; Arnheim, 1969; Bregman, 1977; Bruner, 1957; Brunswick, 1947; Epstein, 1973, 1982; Gregory, 1970; Helmholtz, 1967; Hochberg, 1970, 1978; Neisser, 1967; Oatley, 1978).

It is fair to say there are good reasons for rejecting the view that perception is the result of intelligent, thoughtlike operations.

First, perception seems to be instantaneous. While it is true that it can hardly be otherwise, i.e., it can hardly be the case that we would perceive either nothing or something quite fuzzy until the percept in question materialized, still the more or less immediate achievement of perceptions suggests a rapid process at odds with the more discursive process we usually associate with thought.

Second, there is no awareness of any thought taking place. Therefore, if it is occurring, it must be unconscious thought, and to many, that has seemed to be a contradiction of terms.

Third, perception is usually independent of or autonomous with respect to what we know on a conceptual level about the prevailing objective state of affairs. Geometrical and other kinds of illusions make this clear. In that sense we might even say that perception is inflexible and stupid, not intelligent, because we continue to perceive erroneously in spite of knowledge to the contrary.

Fourth, there is evidence that the perception of some object or spatial properties is innately determined and not dependent upon past experience. But reasoning has been assumed to be closely linked to prior learning and experience. Therefore, the argument goes, innately determined perception cannot be based upon reasoning-like operations.

Fifth, there is good reason for believing that many animal species and young children perceive the world in much the way we do. For example, all animals that perceive movement when objects *are* moving undoubtedly do not perceive movement when the objects are stationary and they themselves are moving. Otherwise animals could not survive. Since similar stimulation occurs in the two cases, e.g., displacement of the retinal image or eye movement, it has been maintained by some that the perception of the world as stationary during movement of the observer is an achievement, analogous to inference, and such perception has been referred to as position constancy. Can

---

front of it (see Chapter 8, pp. 212-218). But that explanation cannot be correct here, because the motion of the spot begins only when observers begin to feel they are rotating. The conditions for induced motion of the spot prevailed from the beginning but generally do not seem to yield it in this case, probably because the drum is moving at too fast a rate.

we seriously believe that a fish achieves these perceptions on the basis of a process that parallels those that mediate reasoning in human beings?

Sixth, it does not seem appropriate to characterize many kinds of perception as intelligent as, for example, the perception of sensory qualities such as hues, tastes, and smells. Is it not then parsimonious to believe that other kinds of perception can be accounted for without invoking such farfetched cognitive-like explanations?

All this leads to a seventh reason, a deeply ingrained assumption in the psychology of this century. It stems from Lloyd Morgan's canon according to which the scientist should never seek to explain a psychological fact by a mechanism at a higher level if it can be explained by one at a lower level (Morgan, 1894). I too would subscribe to this prescription.

Clearly, then, the burden of proof is entirely on those who do claim that perception results from cognitive mental operations. And all the arguments cited above will have to be countered satisfactorily. In the remainder of this chapter, I will give additional examples that seem to suggest that perception *is* intelligent, primarily to give the reader an appreciation of the phenomena with which we are here dealing. However, I will also give some hints as to why these phenomena are difficult to understand if one assumes they *do not* result from a reasoning-like process (but will postpone a more critical discussion of this).

The Case for Perceptional Intelligence: Other Examples

Example 2: The next example is somewhat more complicated. The effect is the outcome of an anomalous combination of stereoscopic depth information and the motion of the observer. Suppose one is viewing a three-dimensional scene with two eyes. One source of information concerning depth within the scene is retinal disparity, the slightly different images that the two eyes receive by virtue of their slightly different positions vis-à-vis the objects in the scene. In viewing Fig. 1-1 stereoscopically, we know, because the picture is in fact flat, that we have isolated stereopsis as the source of depth perception. After looking at this figure for a while, the reader should experience a strong, realistic depth. The small rectangle should appear to be floating in space well behind the larger one.[4]

So much for these preconditions. Now ordinarily, in viewing a real three-dimensional display, if the observer's head were moved from side to side, the images of contours at different distances would

---

4. The reader can achieve the effect by viewing a stereogram such as the one illustrated in Fig. 1-1.

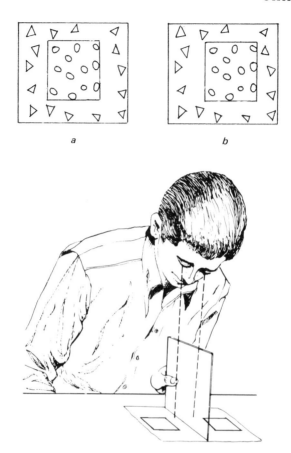

1-1. (a) Stereogram for observing motion parallax illusion. (b) There are several methods for viewing the figures so that one stimulates only the left eye and the other only the right eye. Hold a cardboard between the two views at right angles to the page as shown. Then try to view each half by imagining you are looking through the page at some distance behind it or by crossing the eyes in front of the figures. In the latter case the depth is reversed and the small rectangle will appear to be in front of the large one.

move relative to one another. This can, of course, be achieved with only one eye and can be observed by looking at any scene. One can become aware of this fact as follows: Hold up a finger so that it is in front of an object in the background, and view it with only one eye open. Now move your head from side to side. It can be seen that the lateral "separation" between the finger and some object in the background alternately diminishes and increases as a function of this head motion. In perception this kind of information is referred to as head-movement parallax or simply parallax. The relative change in the location of the images of the objects is based on optics, not psychology, since the direction of the light rays from the objects to the eye changes with changes of head position. Normally we do not attend to this retinal shift directly, but instead it is thought to be transmuted into an impression of depth, and this effect *is* psychology. Thus we speak of parallax as information (a "cue") for depth perception.

What happens when we view Fig. 1-1 binocularly and move the head? As readers should be able to verify for themselves, the object that appears behind, the small rectangle, seems to move in the direction opposite to that of the head (see Fig. 1-2). Although a few authors have referred to this effect or one like it from time to time and it is known to most experts in the field, it remains an essentially unexplained phenomenon (Lindsay and Norman, 1972; Gogel, 1979). Yet it is not so mysterious if one considers the situation carefully. If, normally, parallax changes occur during head motion in viewing three-dimensional things or scenes, what should we expect when there is zero parallax change during head motion, as is the case here (because there is no real depth)? This anomalous condition must lead to an impression of object motion if the perceptual system is governed in its operations by certain rules. In point of fact, an object moving at just the right speed could nullify the parallax change that would ordinarily occur with a certain speed of head motion. If an object were made to do this, we would not be surprised if the observer perceived it doing so. We would no longer call it an illusion but rather a case of veridical perception. But the conditions of stimulation in our example are exactly the same as would be the case if there were an object moving at an appropriate speed; and since perception is (at least in part) a function of the incoming sensory stimulation, it is not at all surprising that we experience the illusion. However, the illusion effect makes very clear that the system is following rules or at least deducing from rules what must be the case under these novel conditions of stimulation. It is worth emphasizing here that this effect will undoubtedly occur even though these particular conditions may never have been encountered before.

There are several other points of importance about this example. For reasons not fully understood by students of perception, depth based on stereopsis alone as given by viewing stereograms takes time to emerge. Thus there may be a period of 15 or 30 seconds before depth is experienced in viewing Fig. 1-1. What happens if during this period one moves one's head? We have demonstrated in our laboratory that the motion illusion is then not experienced. This makes intuitive "sense," because the perceptual system expects parallax

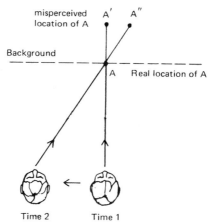

1-2. Rationale for the motion parallax illusion. Point A represents the small rectangle misperceived to be located behind the large one at Point A'. When the head moves to the left, a point that had been at A' would have to have moved to A" if there is no parallax change in its position relative to the large rectangle.

change only during head motion in viewing a three-dimensional display. This simple finding creates grave difficulties for those who would like to explain the illusion in terms other than intelligent rule following. The reason I say this is that the appropriate retinal images and the fusing of them into one unified percept are given right from the start. Thus it would seem that there is no change in stimulation as one passes from the experience of the display as two- to three-dimensional. This fact, if correct, has enormous theoretical significance because, as will be discussed later, some theorists believe that perception can be accounted for entirely in terms of the stimulus reaching the sense organs. Since I do not want to defend the proposition that disembodied subjective experience, so to speak, can play a causal role in perception, I will assume that there is some change in the neural events in the brain that accounts for (or underlies) the transition from two- to three-dimensional experience in viewing the stereogram despite the absence of any change in incoming stimulation from the retina. But even so, the fact remains that it is crucial for the illusion that the perceptual system first produce the impression of depth. Then and only then is zero parallax change with head movement a stimulus event that would logically contradict the perceived depth if the object were stationary. Therefore, the assumption that the perceptual system is engaging in a reasoning-like process becomes all the more compelling. Precisely what is meant by "thoughtlike" or "reasoning-like" process will become clearer in subsequent chapters.

The illusion under discussion should not be thought to depend uniquely upon stereoscopic depth. In principle, we should predict that any conditions that *falsely* lead to a vivid, realistic impression of depth by any source of information (other than parallax itself, of course) should produce the same illusion with head motion. In other words, any two-dimensional display that can lead to a vivid depth impression will also yield zero parallax change with head movement, and so the same illusion should occur.

We can summarize the effect under discussion by saying that given false information about depth, the zero parallax change that obtains during head movement (or locomotion of the observer in space, for that matter) results in the illusory impression that the object that appears behind the three-dimensional arrangement displaces in the direction opposite to that of the observer's movement. Conversely the object that appears in front displaces in the direction of the observer's movement. The reader can observe this by reversing the stereoscopic depth by viewing Fig. 1–1 with eyes crossed. We can now ask whether any parallax change other than the one which should occur on the basis of optics and which therefore typically does occur will produce an illusion of motion in a stationary object. The answer is yes. The zero-parallax illusion is but one of a whole family of such possible illusions. The best-known example is based on viewing a stationary three-dimensional wire object such as a cube. If one views such a cube with one eye, it is possible to achieve a reversal of its depth (Fig. 1-3), so that elements that are in front and had appeared in front (e.g., a, b, c, d) now appear in back, and of course elements that had appeared in back (e.g., e, f, g, h) now appear in front. The reader can reverse the line drawing in the illustration but unfortunately cannot experience the effect that we are about to describe without constructing the three-dimensional cube. If now one can mentally "hold" the reversal while at the same time turning one's head, the cube will appear to be turning in the same direction as the head.

To explain why this occurs, consider the two vertical sides c and f in the figure. Since c is in fact in front of f, when we move to the right, the normal optical change is for the separation between the retinal images of these two contours to increase. This is because we are moving toward the point in space where these two contours would both be in a frontal plane, and we would then be seeing that face of the cube head on, so to speak. From any other position in space we would be seeing that face at an angle, the extreme opposite case being when the eye and contours c and f are all aligned and the retinal separation between c and f would be zero. If, however, f were in front of c, our movement to the right should lead to the opposite change, of decreased separation between these images. Therefore,

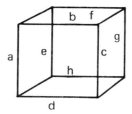

1-3. Drawing of a three-dimensional wire cube; *a*, *b*, *c*, *d* are the sides of one vertical face of the cube and *d*, *e*, *f*, *g* the sides of another face.

when it is (erroneously) seen in front of *c* and we move rightward, the wrong parallax change occurs. To explain how this can be occurring given the depth perceived, the perceptual system arrives at the "inference" that the cube is spinning around at just the rate that could lead to the increased parallax separation for that rate of head movement. In this case the illusion is based not on zero parallax change but on the incorrect parallax change.

It has been claimed that there is another way of accounting for effects of this kind (Gogel, 1979). To reduce the problem to the simplest case, consider a simple object *A* that appears to be located in a particular direction and at a particular distance, at time 1 (see Fig. 1-2). If *A* is stationary and the observer moves, at time 2 it would be in a different direction with respect to the observer. But suppose at time 1 the distance to *A* is misperceived so that it appears to be at *A'*. Then at time 2 in order for it to be along the direction of the ray of light from *A*, it would have had to be in location *A''*. Thus it must appear to move. In fact it has been argued that any perceived motion of the stationary object during observer motion can be taken as an index of the misperception of its distance and thus is an extremely useful tool (Gogel, 1981). But this analysis does not challenge the interpretation offered here that the perceived illusory motion is indicative of a process of intelligent rule following. The observer must interpret three perceptual givens, namely, that at time 2 the object is in a particular direction, that it is at a particular distance, and that the head has moved by a particular amount. For the amount by which the head has moved, the rule for the change in the direction of a stationary object for each distance is apparently known. Were the object seen at *A*, the rule would be satisfied, but for location A^1, it is not. Therefore, the object must have moved.

It would seem that the perceptual system "knows" certain laws of optics that normally obtain and then "interprets" seeming departures from these laws in such a way as to be compatible with them. In doing so, it invents or constructs environmental events that logically would have to be occurring to account for the unexpected stimulus change or lack of change. It does not seem necessary, therefore, to assume that these anomalies have ever been encountered before, and it is doubtful that they have. I am not implying anything about whether knowledge of the laws themselves is or is not acquired on the basis of prior experience (a question I will come back to later) but only that given knowledge of them, novel situations will be interpreted on the basis of them. It is interesting to realize just how powerful the tendency is to perceive in a manner that is inconsistent with the laws. Rather than give them up or momentarily suspend them, the perceptual system will invent an unlikely environmental event that will be compatible with them.

The usefulness for theory of these examples is that they make dramatically clear that the system "knows" and applies certain rules in normal perception. There is an interesting parallel here between perceptual anomalies and the errors of speech children make which reveal so clearly that the child "knows" and is applying certain grammatical or syntactical rules, and in both cases, the knowledge is obviously not consciously represented (Berko, 1958). For example, a child who erroneously refers to "sheeps" evidences knowledge of the rule that plural nouns add an s. Certainly the child has not seen or heard this word, so that the error must stem from the intelligent misapplication of a general rule.

One can consider the effects in these examples as the result of a problem-solving process rather than simply an inference process. But unlike problem-solving in thinking, the solutions here are more or less immediate and achieved all the time by observers. Given the stimulus input and the rules invoked, there is no difficulty and there are no options or alternative solutions. In the next example, however, the situation is different, so that "problem solving" seems a more apt description.

Example 3: Unless the reader is familiar with it, Fig. 1-4 will look like an unidentifiable pattern of black and white regions. Given the instruction to try to identify what it is, observers will sometimes succeed unaided, although they may take a long time to do so. Those who still fail to identify it will usually succeed with some clue, e.g., being told that it is a horse or if necessary precisely what it is, in this case a bugler on horseback. Some may say that all that this example demonstrates is delayed recognition based on the inadequate similarity of the stimulus to the memory of such objects. But this misses a very important point about the example, namely, that when recognition occurs, the percept changes as well. Normally, recognition and identification follow upon perception and the percept is no different before or after recognition (except that phenomenally it now is also

1-4. A figure that at first looks like a meaningless array of fragments but looks entirely different when recognized. After Verville and Cameron, 1946.

familiar and meaningful). But here is a case where the process of identification seems to affect the percept itself. Therefore, the effect is not merely one of successful identification or categorization. In the current jargon this example illustrates top-down processing as well as bottom-up processing. Something about the stimulus must lead to identification (bottom-up, or processing from a lower to a higher level), but identification (memory trace or schema arousal) must serve to modify the percept (top-down, or processing from a higher to a lower level).

How can we describe the manner in which the figure looks different once it is recognized? By referring to the object. The figure now looks three-dimensional and has the three-dimensional shape of a horse and rider. Prior to recognition we would describe the figure very differently. To characterize this kind of effect, I have elsewhere suggested the term "recognition perception" (Rock, 1975). Given recognition, organization is different, e.g., white regions that were background become figure and parts that did not belong together now do or parts that did belong together now do not. Certain regions are now seen in depth that prior to recognition were not. But all these perceptual changes boil down to the fact that the pattern now looks the way the object it stands for looks. As noted above, recognition generally does not lead to perceptual change of this kind but only to the addition of familiarity and identification to the phenomenal experience of a shape. Thus, for example, we can presume that an eighth note looks the same qua shape to those who know what it is as to those who have no knowledge or experience with musical notation.

It seems right to describe the process here as one of problem solving. People looking at Fig. 1-4 quite consciously attempt to discover what the pattern represents. They search actively for a solution both within the pattern and within memory. They become stymied, blocked, or fixated. When the solution occurs, it is usually based on unconscious events; it is sudden and insightful and even pleasurable. It then seems impossible to revert to the presolution percept and difficult to understand why the pattern could not be identified immediately.

The initial difficulty with this figure is that it is first perceived on the basis of certain principles of organization (see Chapter 3, pp. 71–76) that do not yield a whole that is in any way familiar. Thus it tends to be seen as a two-dimensional patchwork. How we manage to make the initial link-up with a memory schema is a problem we will take up later. But once we have succeeded in doing so we have little difficulty when the same figure is seen again (see Leeper, 1935). The process of re-recognition is clearly something different and indicates how we can profit from prior experience in a manner different from the role of experience in the original exposure to this kind of figure.

The searching for and finding of a solution in this example are clearly among the hallmarks of intelligence, and the same can be said about the appropriate utilization of past experience in the construction of the percept that cannot be explained simply in terms of the contents of the stimulus. But there is a more subtle respect in which the perceptual process here can be said to be "thoughtlike." As was noted, the final percept looks different from the initial one in that it would be described very differently. This suggests that the percept has the form of a description. Initially it is "a two-dimensional array of black fragments or streaks," but subsequently it is "a three-dimensional horse and rider in a three-quarter view." I will argue that the description is essentially a proposition that asserts that the object has certain properties, and this is in principle knowledge of the kind that is potentially verifiable. The "language" of the propositional description, i.e., the properties referred to, is conceptual. If this conclusion is correct, the "language" of perception and of thought is much the same.

Some might say that this example is little more than a case of identification or categorization—in spite of my argument that it is more than that—and that once we get to that level of the perceptual process, by definition we are talking about cognitive events. Therefore, the question arises as to whether it is possible to characterize perception in terms of problem solving when we consider properties such as form, size, depth, and motion. Here many would argue that we can deal with perception either in terms of the stimulus input alone or in terms of neural processing that need have nothing to do with cognition or intelligence. This brings me to the next and final example.

Example 4: As is well known, successive stimulation of the retina by entities in slightly different locations will, under appropriate temporal and spatial conditions, yield a vivid impression of motion. Moving pictures and television are based on this fact. In the laboratory, apparent motion, as it is called, is typically studied by presenting stimulus objects as in Fig. 1-5. First *a* is visible for a short duration, following which there is a brief interval, and following that, *b* is visible for a short duration. The cycle then is continuously repeated, and one sees the object moving back and forth. While there is no accepted explanation of this effect, many students of perception now lean toward the hypothesis that there is a neural mechanism that "detects" the discontinuous change of retinal location similar to one that detects continuous change of retinal location (Barlow and Levick, 1965). Presumably, the activation of this mechanism is the necessary and sufficient basis for the perception of apparent motion. If so, there is nothing thoughtlike about the process. Indeed animals, even at birth, and human infants probably perceive motion via such stroboscopic input (Rock, Tauber, and Heller, 1965; Tauber and Koffler, 1966).

a   b

1-5. Successively presented stimulus objects yielding apparent movement.

However, it is at least possible to think of the perception of motion here as the solution to the problem of what is occurring in the world that might yield this unusual sequence of stimulation. The sudden, unexplained disappearance of *a* followed by the sudden, unexplained appearance of *b* elsewhere is elegantly accounted for by the "solution" that *a* has rapidly moved to *b*. I will assemble some evidence in favor of this view in Chapter 7 but will here preview it with one finding. Suppose the stimulus sequence on the retina is achieved by two continuously present objects that are alternately covered and uncovered by an apparently opaque object moving back and forth in front of them (see Fig. 1-6) (Stoper, 1964; Sigman and Rock, 1974). Under these conditions one does not perceive the apparent motion but instead perceives *a* and *b* as permanently present, undergoing covering and uncovering. We have offered the perceptual system an alternative solution that seems to be preferred.

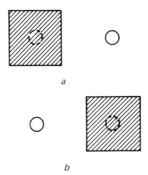

1-6. A different method for presenting two objects (the small circles) successively which might be expected to yield apparent motion. An opaque rectangle alternately covers and uncovers the circles as it moves back and forth.

The abolition of the motion percept poses difficulties for theories that stress the kind of neural explanation outlined above according to which the outcome ought to be inexorable. Thus the outcome under these novel conditions suggests that the perception of motion under the more typical conditions may indeed be best conceptualized as the preferred solution to the stroboscopic stimulus sequence. Of course, the critical reader will not be satisfied with this evidence, and I will return to the topic in Chapter 7.

By way of summary, we can extract from these several examples the following characteristics of perception that seem to suggest intelligence:

1. External objects and events are represented mentally in the form of propositional knowledge. The very essence of intelligence in living creatures, in my opinion, is the capacity to "know," to represent objects, events, and relations in a form that is subject to confirmation or disconfirmation. The claim, then, is that perception also is based on this form of representation.

2. Perception utilizes prior experience to identify things and to modify what is perceived under certain conditions. Rapid "learning" often occurs. Certainly the utilization of past experience, or in short learning, is another hallmark of intelligence.

3. Perception makes use of assumptions and of internalized rules and applies these to novel situations. Computations and inferences occur on the basis of such rules. "Rule following" means more than "lawful." An object in a free fall follows the law of gravitational attraction, but it does not "know" any law. Perception, on the other

hand—or any mental or behavioral act for that matter—that is based on a rule implies that some lawful relation is "known" or internally represented. If so, perception in such cases is intelligent.

4. Perception sometimes is the end result of problem solving in the sense of searching for and finding a good solution to what the stimulus represents. Here we see perception as more generative than simply making deductions from known premises. This is the analog to thinking in its most creative form.

An Overview of the Theory Advocated

In closing this chapter, it may be helpful if I give a summary statement of the kind of theory I propose to advance in the remainder of the book. My view follows Helmholtz's (1867) that perceptual processing is guided by the effort or search to interpret the proximal stimulus, i.e., the stimulus impinging on the sense organ, in terms of what object or event in the world it represents, what others have referred to as the "effort after meaning." In other words, the goal of processing is to arrive at a description of the outer object or event. This way of describing perception should not be taken to mean that the perceptual system distinguishes internal from external events or is self-consciously seeking to interpret internally registered stimuli in terms of external happenings. The "effort after meaning" is not a *consciously* goal-oriented process, and the motivation for it must be the result of evolutionary adaptation.

This *description* of the object or event is cognitive in the sense that its "language" is conceptual and it has the formal status of a proposition. While the description is guided by and must conform to the features of the proximal stimulus, that does not mean it is nothing more than a copy or literal statement of the features of that stimulus. It may contain less or more than can be said to be physically represented in the stimulus. In some cases little in the way of reasoning is involved in arriving at the description. Thus, for example, in most cases of form perception, the description may be based upon factors such as the internal geometry of the stimulating pattern plus information concerning the location of its top, bottom, and sides and so forth. Therefore, it would seem inappropriate to speak of problem-solving or even rule-following processing in such cases. Nevertheless, even here, the description which I take to be the correlate of the percept is a cognitive event.

In other cases, as in Examples 1 and 2, the stimulus is evaluated and interpreted on the basis of assumptions or other information or rules so that the ultimate description is based upon a process very much like inference. By and large perceptual constancies fall under this category (see Chapter 9). In these cases, while the local stimulus may be ambiguous, it does not seem as if the system must search for the appropriate rule to bring to bear on it. Thus, for example, information about distance is immediately "known" to be what is relevant for interpretations of the visual angle of the retinal image (i.e., the size of the retinal image of an object measured angularly), so that such an interpretation occurs without further ado on the basis of "knowledge" of certain rules relating distance to visual angle. "Inference" seems an apt description of what is going on here because the system must infer or deduce a conclusion given certain premises. As in syllogistic reasoning (or general predicate logic) the terms in different premises are related to one another. Yet even in such cases it would not seem appropriate to describe the process as creative problem solving any more than it would when we draw the conclusion based on transitivity that if $a > b$ and $b > c$, then $a > c$.

But there are cases where "problem solving" does seem to be the proper analogy, and Examples 3 and 4 are of this kind. In these cases, the proximal stimulus is ambiguous in the sense that it can be interpreted in more ways than one, although there is usually a preference for one solution over another. Moreover, in some cases the final perception is delayed. The chain of events may include a particular perception that then poses a further problem. In these cases it is as if the "solution" is not so immediately obvious and something must elicit or suggest it. These are the same kinds of features that lead us to distinguish problem solving from other cases of less creative thought.

There are thus four different kinds of cognitive process that I will discuss in the book:

Form construction, which has as its phenomenal outcome the perception of shape and which I will argue is based on a process of unconscious description (see Chapter 3).

Problem solving, which has as its phenomenal outcome the perception of objects, arrays, or events and which I will argue is based on a process of hypothesis generation and testing culminating in a description (see Chapters 4, 5, 6, and 7).

Relational determination, which has as its phenomenal outcome the perception of objects, arrays, or events and which I will argue is based on a process of interpreting relational stimulus information culminating in a description (see Chapter 8).

Inference, which has as its phenomenal outcome the perception of objects, arrays, or events and which I will argue is based on a process of deduction from rules and premises culminating in a description (see Chapter 9). These categories are summarized in Table 1-1.

In the case of problem solving and inference, I will argue that an executive agency, utilizing the information available at a lower level,

Table 1-1

Categories of perceptual process	*Examples*	*Underlying determinative process*		*Phenomenal outcome*
Form construction (Chapter 3)	Perception of shape		Description of figure	Perceived shape of object
Problem solving (Chapters 4, 5, 6, 7)	Kinetic depth effect	Hypothesis generation and testing $\longrightarrow$	Description of object or event	Perceived object, array, or event
Relational determination (Chapter 8)	Induced motion	Interpretation of relational information $\longrightarrow$	Description of object or event	Perceived object, array, or event
Inference (Chapter 9)	Constancy	Deduction from premises based on rules $\longrightarrow$	Description of object or event	Perceived object, array, or event

engages in a sequence of hierarchically based levels of description each tending to supersede and dominate the lower levels of description. At the lowest level the executive makes decisions about what belongs with what in the field, about what is figure and what is ground, and describes the proximal input as representing a two-dimensional object, array of objects, or event in the world (the literal description or solution). As will be made clear in later chapters, this stage of perception is highly correlated with the proximal stimulus, as if it were based on a literal description of it. Generally this level of description will be superseded by a three-dimensional description of the object, array, or event in the world (the constancy, preferred or constructed solution). Finally, the two- or three-dimensional description will generally lead to a description of what the object or event represents based on recognition, the interpretive mode of description. Here the interpretive description accompanies and enriches the object or event description but does not replace it. While the highest level of description achieved is dominant or salient and the lower levels are in the background of awareness, the lower levels are nonetheless more or less simultaneously present. Understandably these distinctions will not be fully clear to the reader in this brief outline.

In discussing perceptual problem solving, I will distinguish that phase of it in which a "solution" is elicited or comes to mind from a second phase in which the viability of that "solution" is tested or checked against all relevant features of the stimulus. This second phase of "testing" is equally applicable to all cases of description, not merely to those in which we speak of problem solving. That is, whether referring to a description of a form or of an object's size, or to other object properties that arise in perceptual problem-solving situations, the description must do justice to, conform to, not be in contradiction of, and be supported by, or in short "match," the proximal stimulus. What this match implies will be discussed in a separate chapter.

This meshing of the solution, which comes from within, with the stimulus, which comes from without, is the distinguishing hallmark of perception as a cognitive process. Imagination, dreaming, and thinking in general are not so constrained. Obviously, then, the characteristics of the stimulus are crucial (albeit not sufficient) for the final perceptual outcome. Although perception is the outcome of a cognitive process very much like the solution of a problem in thought, it is largely autonomous and different from thought as such in various important respects which we will discuss. The processing underlying perception culminating in the description which leads to particular perceptual experiences is obviously neither verbal nor conscious, and generally occurs so rapidly that the perceptual outcome is experienced as instantaneous. By and large perception is not affected by, is insulated from, knowledge about the situation such as is available on a conscious conceptual, ideational level, although under certain conditions such knowledge can play a role. But to say that knowledge defined in this way generally does not affect perception is by no means the same as saying that past experience does not affect perception. This entire problem will require an extended discussion, but I would like to emphasize in concluding this summary statement that in my view a cognitive theory entailing reasoning-like processes is certainly not synonymous with an empiricist theory. For Helmholtz, unconscious inference simply meant the unconscious application of inductively achieved premises. It is a mistake to identify reasoning and problem-solving processes as such with the source of the premises utilized in such processes.

To fully appreciate and understand the kind of theory advocated here, one must contrast it with other possible theories of perception. In the next chapter I argue that there are in fact three different kinds of theories that can be advanced to explain the phenomena of perception. After outlining certain general characteristics of perception, I briefly consider the relative capabilities and limitations of these theories.

2 ⬛

Characteristics and Theories
of Perception

IN THE FIRST CHAPTER I outlined the theory I will try to develop and support in the remainder of the book. I assume readers will keep it in mind as they proceed. I gave some examples to illustrate perceptual phenomena that seem to suggest the occurrence of intelligent processing. However, those with little background in the field have no way of assessing the typicality or representativeness of these examples. Such readers need a somewhat better grasp of what perception is like in order to critically assess any theory that might be advanced. Therefore, in this chapter I will begin by listing what, in my opinion, are the central characteristics of perception. Following that, I describe what I consider to be the three possible theories of perception, indicating how each deals with the phenomena and features of perception outlined in the listing. The point of doing this is primarily to bring into sharper focus, by contrast with entirely different kinds of approaches, precisely what is meant by a cognitively oriented theory such as the one I here put forth. A secondary purpose is to enable the reader to glimpse the strengths and weakness of these differing approaches.

I suggest that the theories can be divided into two categories, those that deem it sufficient to specify attributes of the stimulus correlated with different aspects of perception (stimulus theory) and those that consider it necessary to postulate constructive processes within the organism acting upon the stimulus (constructive theory). For theories of the latter type, I further suggest that such internal construction can be of two kinds, one based on the interaction of the representations of stimuli (spontaneous interaction theory) and another based on inference or similar cognitive processes (cognitive theory).

Characteristics of Perception

I will first attempt to abstract the general features that seem to characterize all perception of objects and events. Some of these features refer to logical considerations about the nature of the stimulus, some to the phenomenological character of perception, and some to more theoretical conclusions that seem to be so obvious as to have the status of facts that any general theory must encompass.

AMBIGUITY AND PREFERENCE

Logically, a given local stimulus is only an ambiguous indicator of the relevant property of the object producing it. For example, an image of a given size, measured by the visual angle that an object subtends at the eye, will be produced by a whole family of objects of varying sizes, each at a different distance (Fig. 2-1a). Thus the perceptual system could never determine from an image's visual angle alone what the size of the object that produced it is. The same is true analogously for image shape with respect to object shape (Fig. 2-1b) (because the slant of the object can vary), image velocity with respect to object velocity (because the distance of the moving object can vary), image intensity (or luminance) with respect to surface color (because illumination can vary), and so forth. Yet perception of such properties is generally not ambiguous. We tend to perceive objects of definite size, shape, and the like.

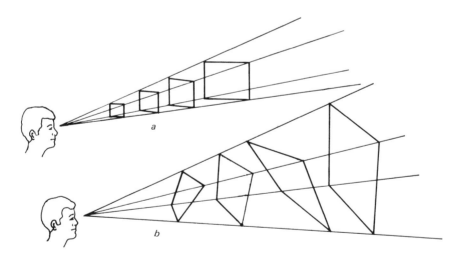

2-1. (a) A family of objects of differing sizes all subtending the same visual angle at the eye. (b) A family of objects of differing shapes yielding the same-shaped image on the retina.

We might refer to the kind of ambiguity described here as *dimensional*, meaning that the specific value along a dimension is logically indeterminate on the basis of the local stimulus alone. By "local stimulus" I mean only the stimulus representing the object property under consideration. But there is another kind of ambiguity of the stimulus that concerns the qualitative character of the percept. The same proximal stimulus can represent different shapes, two- or three-dimensional, or different familiar objects or different events. This second kind of ambiguity might be called *qualitative*. Many examples of it will be given throughout the book. Usually, however, of the two or more qualitatively different percepts to which the stimulus can give rise, one is preferred in that observers will tend to perceive it that way rather than another way and do so more or less every time the stimulus occurs. Therefore, the question arises as to the basis of such preference. Finally in some cases of qualitative ambiguity the stimulus is such that it can as well represent different objects or events; and where the perception *is* ambiguous in that given the same stimulus one may perceive it differently at different times, different observers may perceive it differently at the same time and, for a given observer, the perception may change from one moment to the next. In the latter case we say the stimulus pattern or sequence is *reversible* and speak of *reversible figures*. Well-known examples of it are Rubin's vase-face figure (Fig. 2-2) and reversible perspective patterns such as the Necker cube (Fig. 1-3). Even here there may be individual or population preferences to perceive the stimulus one way or the other, but such preference, if it exists, does not necessarily preclude change of perception or reversal.

2-2. Rubin's well known ambiguous figure of a vase or two face profiles.

So there are several important facts about ambiguity, namely, that different perceptions from the same stimulus are possible but do not ordinarily occur (dimensional ambiguity), that different perceptions are possible and can occur (but one tends to be strongly preferred), that different perceptions can and do occur in certain other cases (qualitative ambiguity), and finally that perceptions may actually change over time for an observer (reversal). Reversal has been shown to occur when the image is stabilized (as in the case of an afterimage) so that not even subtle changes of stimulation such as of retinal locus can be claimed to be responsible for the perceptual change.

CONSTANCY AND VERIDICALITY

A very central fact about perception is the all-pervasive tendency toward constancy of object properties despite variation of or differences between the proximal stimuli. By "proximal stimulus" is meant the stimulus that impinges upon the sense organ rather than the distal stimulus, the external object or event. Such variation of stimulation is of course brought about by the fact that in vision distance and orientation in the third dimension affect image formation in accordance with the principles of optics, or by the fact that our own movement affects image location and its stability, or by the fact that illumination changes affect the luminance from a surface reaching the eye. If perception remains constant and does not mirror proximal stimulus variation, it is correlated with the external object, the distal stimulus. Therefore, to the extent that constancy holds, perception achieves veridicality.[1] Since we know that the achievement of constancy is based on other available sensory information, some might be inclined to reduce this feature of perception to that of context, which I discuss next. But I believe the two should be kept separate, at least for now. To say that size constancy is a function of taking account of distance (via "cues" such as accommodation and convergence) is not the same as saying that the context of neighboring visual images accounts for such constancy. These are, in fact, different hypotheses about the basis of size constancy. Constancy is of course closely related to the fact of dimensional stimulus ambiguity. Logically, the local stimulus is ambiguous concerning object properties, but the outcome is typically determinate, invariant, and veridical. Where ambiguity implies that the same local stimulus can lead to various perceptions, constancy refers to the achievement of the same perception from various local stimuli.

CONTEXTUAL EFFECTS

It is a commonplace by now that perception is very much a function of context, i.e., of the effect of neighboring stimuli (in space,

---

1. Strictly speaking, constancy need not imply veridicality but only that an object will look *the same* regardless of proximal stimulus variations of it brought about by changes of viewing conditions. But if a distant object looks as large as a nearby one of the same size or an object slanted off the frontal plane appears to have the same shape as one of that shape *in* the frontal plane, and further if under these optimum conditions, i.e., near or in the frontal plane, objects *are* seen accurately, then to all intents and purposes, constancy does imply veridicality.

but also to some extent in time). All the geometrical illusions attest to this fact, but perception in general is characterized by contextual effects: whether something appears stationary or moving, how it appears oriented in the environment, its phenomenal color (achromatic or chromatic), its size, shape, distance, and direction. Thus the same triangular outline shown in Fig. 2-2 can look like many different things, from outline perimeter to solid surface, from a surface in a vertical plane to one sloped backward in depth, from figure to ground, from triangular to conical, depending entirely on what else is present (Oatley, 1978).

2-3. A triangular outline that can be perceived in many different ways as a function of context. After Oatley, 1978.

ORGANIZATION

The perceptual world is generally an organized one consisting of distinct and segregated entities, but that is an achievement that can hardly be held to be "given" by the stimulus array. The latter must again be considered to be logically ambiguous as far as "what goes with what" is concerned, but only in certain cases is the outcome ambiguous. One fundamental example of organization is the belongingness of a contour to one region rather than another, thereby rendering it as figure and the other region as ground (see the discussion on pp. 72–74 and Fig. 3-25). But other examples abound in both vision and audition, where principles such as proximity, similarity, "good" continuation, and common fate are operating (see pp. 71–76).

There is a different meaning of "organization" than that of achieving figures, units, and groupings. If an entity such as a form or a melody is thought of in terms of the parts that make it up, the organization of these parts results in a structure with emergent properties. Thus the perceived shape or melody is a quality that exists psychologically only by virtue of the relationship of the parts to one another. In perception, the whole is different from the sum of the parts.

ENRICHMENT AND COMPLETION

While a point of contention in contemporary psychology, the fact can hardly be denied that what we perceive is in certain respects en-riched by mental contents *not* given in the present stimulus. For example, by definition, the phenomenal experience of familiarity (recognition) and meaning (identification) derives from past experi-ence. Here, while other perceptual properties remain unchanged, most objects do appear familiar and we do have an immediate sense of what they are or what their function is. The first time we encoun-tered them, this was not the case. But other object properties may also be affected by prior experience. As brought out by Example 3 in Chapter 1, it is evident that fragmented figures such as the one shown in Fig. 1-4 look different once they are identified than they do prior to that moment. They take on the perceptual properties of the object they represent—such as three-dimensionality—and they are organized differently. Clearly there is an enrichment of perception here based on a contribution from memory. A more debatable case is the cube drawing shown in Fig. 1-3, but it is plausible that its three-dimensional appearance is a function of prior experience with real cubes. If so, the attribute in memory is somehow entering into the overall perceptual experience. Therefore, the stimulus alone does not do justice to the perception.

Related to enrichment is another category that is not necessarily based upon past experience. In some cases one might say that there is *more* in the percept than is logically predictable from the stimulus. One such example is the case of illusory (subjective or cognitive) contour (Kanizsa, 1955, 1974) (Fig. 2-4a). There is no physical con-tour, i.e., no corresponding sharp transition of luminance on the retina for parts of the contours seen in these figures. Since the same kind of effect occurs for unfamiliar shapes (Fig. 2-4b), we have no reason yet to regard this phenomenon as reducible to the effect of past experience. Another example we might include here is that of apparent movement perception. While the stimulus consists only of spatially separate stationary contours that alternately appear and dis-appear at a certain rate, the experience consists of motion of the con-tour from one location to the other. Therefore, logically, there is more in the percept than there is in the stimulus (or at least there is a dimension of experience that has no directly corresponding stimulus counterpart). The term "completion" may be useful to designate effects of this kind.

DELAYED PERCEPTION

A percept sometimes takes some appreciable time to emerge; i.e., it is delayed. Some examples of this fact have already been mentioned such as depth based on stereopsis under stereoscopic laboratory conditions. But there are many other examples. The reorganization

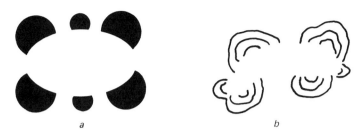

2-4. Illusory contour figures: (a) An ellipse; (b) an unfamiliar shape. After Kanizsa, 1955, 1974.

of fragmented figures often takes quite a while before it occurs. The experience of induced movement of oneself often has a latency period that can be quite long. An illusory contour generally does seem immediate, but conditions can easily be altered so that it is not (for example, in Fig. 2-5). An observer who is naive to the fact that such an illusory percept is potentially achievable in this figure and who is therefore not searching for it may not perceive it for quite a while.

2-5. Illusory contour figures of triangles not seen as readily by naive observers as those in Figure 2-4. After Rock and Anson, 1979.

PERCEPTUAL INTERDEPENDENCIES

Sometimes the only way to understand a perceptual outcome is in terms of the prior emergence of another perception. Example 2 in Chapter 1 demonstrates the illusory effect of object motion based on parallax when, via stereopsis or other cues, the display is first perceived as three-dimensional. Without that prior perception, the para-doxical illusion does not occur. Effects of this kind clearly reveal a chain of events in which the stimulus is not the immediate causal factor.

So much for a brief survey of the general characteristics of percep-tion. At this point we are ready to consider how the theory advocated here deals with these kinds of fact, but to sharpen our understanding of the theory, I will contrast it with other theoretical approaches that have been advanced.

The Three Theories of Perception

What distinguishes perception from other modes of cognition (such as imagination or dreaming or thought) is that perception is the mental representation of external objects and events that is based upon or in some way corresponds to the stimulation reaching our sense organs. It seems to me that a priori there are only a limited number of theories that can explain perception, in fact, three distinct kinds. Varieties of each of these are of course possible, and one might develop an overall theory that combines features of each. Each kind of theory has its champions both past and present, but I believe it will be more useful in order to get at their essence to describe each in the most general way as a possible kind of theory than to empha-size how they in fact emerged in the hands of particular theorists or particular schools of thought.

One can first separate theories of perception into *two* major cate-gories depending upon whether specification of the relevant stimulus for every perception is deemed sufficient (stimulus theory) or it is not and some major contribution of the organism by means of in-ternal processing to transform the stimulus is considered necessary (constructive theory).

STIMULUS THEORY

The basic idea here is that for every distinct kind of perceptual property—of color, size, depth, movement, and the like—there is a unique stimulus (or type of stimulus information) reaching the sense organ. We may or may not know what that stimulus is, but if we do not, it is in principle discoverable. We may choose to call this correla-tion between stimulus and percept the explanation, or we may choose to probe deeper and ascertain the sensory processes that transduce the physical stimulus, encode it neurally, and transmit it deeper into the brain. But as long as the latter processes remain perfectly correlated with the sensory input and simply account for the transmission of the latter from sense organ to the higher, determining, brain event, I believe it is appropriate to subsume such further explanation under the category of "stimulus theory." That is because what is alleged to be going on internally is a direct function of the incoming stimulus; i.e., nothing more is considered necessary by way of explanation of perception than to isolate the relevant stimulus or the neural representation of it in the sense organ or brain.

Obviously, by the very definition of perception, there *is* some unique stimulus that enters into the chain of events that leads to any particular percept. Therefore, one might fairly say that a particular stimulus is at the very least a necessary determinant of a particular perception. When at some point in history it is not known what that stimulus is and it is then isolated, this is a great step forward and certainly explains a great deal about a particular kind of perception that previously had been a complete mystery. For example, when Newton discovered that sunlight was a mixture of various components of light, each with its own frequency of vibration, we could understand that the perception of a given hue was a function of stimulation of the retina by light of varying frequencies. The same point can be made with respect to other sensory qualities. Moreover discoveries about the anatomy, structure, and function of sense organs such as the eye and about the nature of optics led to knowledge about the size, shape, location, and motion of the retinal image. Thus we can now understand at least some of the correlations that obtain between such features of the image and corresponding perceptions. Yet, as should already be clear from the discussion above of the characteristics of perception, the isolation of the relevant stimulus does not provide a sufficient account of perception.

In other words, if the term stimulus in stimulus theory is defined locally, it is evident from the discussion of the list of characteristics of perception that such a theory is totally inadequate. To recapitulate, the local stimulus does not predict what is perceived because precisely what it represents is ambiguous, because it is subject to variability given the same outer object or event, because its effect depends upon context and not only upon its own properties, because it does not do justice to the phenomena of organization, enrichment, completion, delay, and the dependency of one perception upon another.

However, it is possible to redefine the stimulus. It might be argued that it was naive in the first place to believe that the stimulus for object or event perception is merely that local feature of the stimulus that seems to be the relevant one. For example, if we abandon the simpleminded idea that the stimulus for perceived size is solely the size of the object's visual angle subtended at the eye, many of the difficulties listed above disappear. Suppose instead that the true stimulus for phenomenal size is the relationship (i.e., proportion or ratio) of the visual angle of the object to that of other neighboring objects. Thus, for example, it is possible that it is not the absolute size of the image of a man measured in a visual angle that determines how large he will appear but the size of his image relative to the image of the tree he is standing next to that determines his apparent size. Such a size relationship might be said to be a feature of the stimulus just as much as absolute visual angle, although it is based upon a higher-order and more abstract analysis of the stimulus input. The reformulation of stimulus theory along these lines, with emphasis on higher-order features of the stimulus, derives from the work of J.J. Gibson and his associates (Gibson, 1950). [2]

Many of the characteristics of perception given in our list seem to be accounted for by this change of definition of the stimulus. For example, the problem of dimensional ambiguity associated with visual angle alone seems to be resolved. Variations of distance no longer affect the stimulus as redefined because the proportionality of man size to tree size will remain constant. The facts of veridicality and constancy might also be said to be explained. The proportionality does not change with the distance of the pair of objects from the observer, and if that proportionality is the stimulus attribute determining perceived size, the latter should not change as a function of distance change. Contextual effects are no longer a special problem because the new definition of the stimulus is based upon the entire stimulus array or at least much more than just the local stimulus of a single object.

Although this is not the place for a thoroughgoing critical analysis, some real difficulties for such a modified stimulus theory can be briefly mentioned here. One is its incapability of dealing with the fact of perceptual organization if one believes that organization is not anything that is simply "given" by the stimulus. Another is that enrichment defined in terms of effects of past experiences, such as recognition and identification, and the perceptual reorganization of patterns on the basis of representations stored in memory (Example 3 in Chapter 1, the perception of a fragmented figure) are not easily dealt with. These examples seem to be directly counter to the requirement of a stimulus theory if the latter is intended to provide an all-inclusive and sufficient account of perception. For in these cases it is simply not possible to explain the outcome solely on the basis

2. As noted at the beginning of this chapter, the intent here is not so much to do justice to historical developments or to the specific views of particular individuals as to distinguish certain possible kinds of theories from one another. In the case of Gibson, his ideas changed a good deal in the thirty years that spanned his three books (Gibson, 1950, 1966, 1979), and the more radical ideas in his last book are not really discussed here at all.

of the stimulus or of incoming information, no matter how the latter are defined. Still another difficulty concerns the fact of qualitative ambiguity, with all those cases where logically the stimulus represents more than one object or event but where there is a clear preference to perceive one particular object or event or with those cases where the same stimulus actually gives rise to different percepts at different times.

CONSTRUCTIVE THEORIES

The modification of stimulus theory as outlined above grew out of the obvious difficulty with the simpleminded version of it, which can be summarized as follows: There is a lack of one-to-one correlation between local stimulus and percept. The same stimulus can, depending upon other conditions, produce different percepts (e.g., dimensional or qualitative ambiguity), and conversely, different stimuli can produce the same percept (e.g., constancy). Since other stimuli (or the neural events to which they give rise) or possibly central processes of some other kind can affect what is perceived with respect to the given stimulus, a simple stimulus theory seems inadequate. One answer to these difficulties is a modified stimulus theory. But another is to seek an explanation based on certain kinds of processing within the organism. The common ground of any such theory is that some internal constructive process is held to occur that mediates between the incoming stimulus and the percept. Something gets added to the stimulus. It seems to me, however, that historically there have been and logically there are only two distinct kinds of such constructive theories. [3]

One way of resolving the dilemma posed by a lack of a one-to-one correlation between local stimulus and percept is to maintain that the determinant of a perception is not the stimulus but spontaneous interactions between the representations of several stimuli or interaction between the stimulus and more central representations. Such interaction could take any form consistent with the known principles

---

3. Others may disagree with this classification, on two counts. They may feel that the main subdivision should be between constructive (or cognitive) and nonconstructive theories rather than between stimulus and constructive theories, and they may feel that the spontaneous interaction theory is not an example of a constructive theory. The present classification is based on my belief that the most important difference among theories is whether or not it is felt that something must be contributed by the organism of the nature of adding to or transforming the proximal input. It is perfectly true, however, that the spontaneous interaction theory postulates a very different kind of "construction" than the cognitive theory and that the term "constructive" has been reserved for a theory emphasizing the contribution of past experience to perception.

of neurophysiology. The essence of this kind of theory is that the correlate of a percept is not simply (and perhaps is never) the representation of the stimulus in question but rather more complex interactive events that ensue following stimulation and that can allow for known effects such as those of context, constancy, contrast, perceptual changes without stimulus changes, illusions, and the like. But this is not a cognitive theory any more than is the stimulus theory, since no reference is made or need be made to thoughtlike processes such as description, rule following, inference, or problem solving. I will refer to this approach as the spontaneous interaction theory.

The only other way of dealing with the limitations of stimulus theory is to maintain that the correlate of perception is not the stimulus per se but interpretations or inferences made from it concerning what the object or event is in the world that produced it. As is true of the spontaneous interaction theory, here too sensory information other than the focal one under consideration can become relevant, but in addition, more central content (memories, schemata, "assumptions," "decisions," "rules," "hypotheses," "constructions," and the like) enters in. I will refer to this approach as the cognitive theory. It is important to be clear that I am not including under cognitive theory the kind proposed by Berkeley (1709) or Titchener (1926). Koffka (1935) referred to this view as the classical sensation-interpretation theory, by which he meant that the sensory experience (sensation) was held to be perfectly correlated with the stimulus (thus, according to my view, making it a stimulus theory). The interpretation of the sensation was thus *not perceptual* at all but judgmental. Therefore, when I speak of "interpretations" made from the stimulus as a feature of cognitive theory, I mean nonconscious interpretations that lead to *perceptions*, not merely to conscious judgments. Helmholtz (1867) advocated this kind of theory.

The spontaneous interaction theory was developed and elaborated by the Gestalt psychologists (for the most explicit and detailed statement of it, see Koffka, 1935). The interaction which they postulated to underlie perception was of course neural interaction, either between the neural representation of one or more stimuli or between the stimulus and the neural representation of a memory, and these interactions, occurring as they do in a neural medium, were held to be affected by the state of that medium. Given limited knowledge of neurophysiology, it was not possible for the Gestaltists to spell out precisely the kind of neural interaction that was presumed to underlie various kinds of perception. It was simply an assumption that such neural events were the correlates of psychological effects that clearly depended upon stimulus relationships or interactions.

However, in order to consider the kind of theory in its more general form, it is preferable not to equate it with neural interaction. For were we to do so, the implication would be that such a theory is a neurophysiological one in contradistinction to stimulus and cognitive theories. Yet all theories of perception must ultimately be translatable to or reducible to neurophysiological events, at least if one subscribes to the belief that brain events are the ultimate determinants of mental phenomena, as most contemporary investigators in psychology including myself do. In fact it is likely that the kinds of brain events would be different for the three theories. For a stimulus theory, as I have already pointed out, the critical brain event would be nothing more than the terminal representation of the proximal stimulus after the latter is transmitted through the brain to the appropriate "center"; for a spontaneous interaction theory, it would be the kind of neurophysiological event I have been describing here, namely, an event representing the interaction of several stimulus representations or of stimulus representation and trace or stimulus representation and neural medium. We have no idea what kind of brain event would underlie cognitive processing, but presumably it would be very different and probably far more complex than those that have been suggested as noncognitive explanations.

Therefore, what most generally distinguishes interaction theory from the other two theories is not its neurophysiological underpinnings but the kind of process alleged to occur. A good illustration of an interaction approach is the attempt by von Holst (1954) to deal with phenomena such as position constancy. The neural signal from motion of the retinal image is held to be nullified or canceled by the neural signal responsible for the movement of the organism's eye, head, or body, the efferent "command" (or the central representation of that efferent signal). If the two signals match quantitatively, no motion is perceived (constancy), but if they do not, illusory motion will be perceived. Thus the anomalous case of perceived motion of an afterimage during eye movement is also explained by the same mechanism. It is an interesting example because it shows how one might deal with effects that seem to be the result of intelligent processing without invoking such processing as explanation. I cite it as an example of spontaneous interaction because that is what von Holst's hypothesis seems to imply: two internal events interact or summate algebraically with certain consequences.

To cite a better-known example, it was once suggested by Wertheimer (1912) that apparent movement perception results from a flow of electrical energy back and forth from the loci in the brain where the signals from the separately flashing stimuli terminate. While this hypothesis is no longer seriously entertained, it does capture the flavor and intent of this kind of theory better perhaps than any other example. The motion perceived that has no representation in the stimulus (emergent property) is explained by a spontaneous interaction. At a later time it was hypothesized that the degree of interaction between direct electric currents generated in the cortex by projected contours determines the apparent spatial separation between the objects producing these neural contours (Köhler and Wallach, 1944). Since the flow of current is also affected by the state of the neural medium, prior stimulation by other contours in the same vicinity was said to raise the resistance of the medium to such flow of current (satiation). This satiation would then explain the illusory aftereffects wherein contours appeared displaced, tilted, or curved.

But for the most part the Gestalt investigators favoring the neural-interaction view simply uncovered psychological effects that seemed to require that kind of explanation. What these effects had in common was the obvious influence or dependency of one object or unit upon another. Thus, for example, a stationary object appears to move if it is surrounded by a moving one (induced movement); a vertical line appears tilted if it is seen within a rectangle or room that is tilted (rod and frame effect); the speed of a moving object is a function of the size of aperture in which it is seen (velocity transposition effect). In all these examples of contextual effects the surrounding object was considered as a frame of reference on the basis of which the surrounded object's properties were determined.

Interestingly enough, there is a great deal of similarity between the modified stimulus theory and the spontaneous interaction theory. Consider the problem of the perception of lightness of surface color. The problem is to find the correlate or representation of a particular phenomenal shade of gray. As already noted, that correlate can hardly be the intensity of light (or luminance) reflected to the eye from a surface, since luminance is in part a function of the illumination falling upon the surface, so that a given luminance value can emanate from any combination of surface color and illumination. However, the perceived shade is more or less constant despite variations in illumination. Now it has been known for some time that the color perceived is very much affected by the luminance of the region adjacent to the surface under discussion. Hering (1920) suggested an explanation which, in modern terminology, would be called lateral inhibition. The perceived color is governed not only positively by the luminance of the surface in question but negatively by the luminance of adjacent surfaces; i.e., the latter have an inhibiting effect upon the critical surface's lightness. Without any further discussion of this mechanism here, one can see that the correlate of the shade of gray perceived could thus not simply be the local stimulus (luminance of the critical region) but could be some inter-action between the neural representations of adjacent stimuli.

Constancy can then be explained by maintaining that there is a trade-off between increased excitation of the critical region and in-creased inhibition from adjacent regions as illumination increases. The net result is the maintenance of some constant value of excita-tion in the neural projection of the critical region. Stated in this way it begins to sound like a theory in which the ultimate correlate is not the interaction per se but the neural representation of the critical local stimulus. We might thus regard it as an explanation designed to preserve the essential idea behind a *simple* stimulus theory. However, one might instead assert that it is the interaction itself that is the fundamental correlate and that as long as the ratio of luminances be-tween adjacent retinal regions remains unchanged (as would be the case in daily life despite variations of illumination), the interaction will remain unchanged and therefore the percept will remain un-changed (Wallach, 1948). Stated in this way, it is a clear example of a spontaneous interaction theory. But, if one chooses to ignore in-ternal processes and focus entirely on the sensory information, one might simply say that the stimulus for lightness is the ratio between adjacent retinal luminance values, a higher-order feature of the stim-ulus. Stated thus, it is an example of a modified stimulus theory.

To continue with examples of how spontaneous interaction theory might deal with some of the features of perception given in our list, the problem of the organization of the field into figure and ground and into distinct, segregated units was emphasized by the Gestalt theorists. They dealt with such organization in terms of various descriptive laws, but governing all these were presumably spontaneous interactions. Thus, for example, units formed clusters based on prox-imity and similarity because of forces of attraction. However, it was further believed that underlying all organizational processes was a principle of functioning governed by a tendency toward simplicity (prägnanz). Here internal events were held to be self-regulating and directed toward the minimum energy level that the prevailing stimu-lus input would allow. Given several possible organizations of an am-biguous pattern, the preference of the perceptual system was for the simpler or simplest possible organization. So here we see how this theory dealt with the problem of preference in cases of stimulus ambiguity.

Others of the characteristics of perception given in our list may or may not be readily accounted for by this kind of theory. Consider the problem of enrichment on the basis of memory content. It would have to be argued that the internal representation of a memory (or trace) is spontaneously activated given a particular stimulus and that representation interacts with the representation of the stimulus, so that the percept is a joint product of the two. This is precisely the language used by Koffka (1935) and others in the Gestalt tradition in dealing with experience effects. Note that a cognitive process is not assumed here because no reference is made to a "comparison" of stimulus and trace or to a "decision" that they are similar or dissimilar. The process is thus not held to be thoughtlike. Moreover completion, defined as the presence of properties in the percept that are not strictly in the stimulus, is no problem at all. The correlate is the interactive event, not the mere representation of the stimulus. That is why, as noted above, perceived motion in the case of stroboscopic stimulus conditions follows so clearly from this kind of theory despite the absence of any stimulus motions.

However, as is true for stimulus theory, certain phenomena are not easily explained by an interaction theory and are, in fact, incompatible with it. If, for example, perceptual constancy cannot adequately be explained on the basis of higher-order features such as relationships, ratios, or the interactions to which they give rise (which I believe is the case and will take up at length in a subsequent chapter), then that leaves us with an explanation according to which the perceptual system must take account of one kind of information in assessing another kind. As I will try to show later (Chapter 9), such an explanation is best understood in terms of computation or inference from certain rules. Oddly enough, the incompatibility of rule-following or taking-into-account explanations of constancy with the interaction theory has not been noted by many, perhaps because the same theorists promulgated both sets of ideas. Historically it happened to be the case that the Gestalt psychologists almost single-handedly were responsible for pointing up most of the complexities of perception given in our list (and their incompatibility with the then extant stimulus theory), so that it has been assumed that their own theory did in fact do justice to them all. Thus, for example, Köhler (1929) and Koffka (1935) implied that the constancies must be understood in terms of an invariant relation between information such as distance, slant, or eye movement with stimulation such as visual angle, image shape, and image locus. Yet the phrase "invariant relation" points to a process quite different from a spontaneous interaction.

So much for a brief account of the spontaneous interaction theory. How might a cognitive theory deal with the basic facts of perception? To begin again with the ambiguity of the local stimulus, for example, visual angle, this would presumably be resolved by a process of taking account of other relevant information. Assuming the perceptual system has available in some form "knowledge" about the principles of geometrical optics, objective size could be inferred or computed by taking account of distance. In following the same rules and making inferences from them, various anomalies, such as the one mentioned above of perceived motion of the afterimage, become perfectly predictable. But by and large constancy would result from such a process. Enrichment is not a problem for this kind of theory because inference concerning what object in the environment is producing a particular stimulus would naturally be very much a function of relevant prior experience or of internally generated hypotheses. The description that underlies the percept would incorporate the known object. Thus the kinds of enrichment entailing recognition, identification, and effects of experience on the perception of patterns such as that in Fig. 1-4 need no further discussion at this point. As to completion of the kind in which attributes such as motion or contours are perceived that have no physical counterpart in the stimulus, the general argument would be that perception is only in part determined by the stimulus, since internal "constructions" or "descriptions" would play the fundamental role. Thus, if the "solution" to the problem posed by alternate stroboscopic flashing of spatially separate stimuli were to be "motion of a single object back and forth," that is what will be perceived. Therefore, it should be emphasized that the correlate of perception for cognitive theory is not merely the stimulus (no matter how abstractly described) or the spontaneous interactions produced by the stimulus but rather a complex interplay of stimulus and internally generated constructions culminating in a description.

To the extent that perception entails solving the problem concerning what the stimulus represents, where the stimulus lends itself to several possible solutions, it should not be surprising that perception will occasionally be delayed. In fact one might reverse the question and ask why, if perception does depend upon such a process, it is generally so immediate (i.e., takes so little time that it is experienced as immediate). There are several answers to this. First, when I say that perception is delayed, I obviously mean a particular perception, the preferred one that, once achieved, will persevere. Before that, something else is perceived. Thus, in laboratory-produced stereoscopic depth, a two-dimensional array is perceived before the depth. Second, not all perception seems to fit under the rubric of problem solving any more than all of thought fits under it. Where it does not, delay is not to be expected. Why this is so for perception will require further discussion, but for now I will only say that examples such as constancy situations seem different from others. Perhaps there is a time early in life when a perception which for the mature organism no longer seems to require solution does require it, just as tying a shoelace once was but is not later a "problem." Other kinds of perception such as that of form also generally do not seem to be such as to require solutions, i.e., do not seem to constitute a problem (although that does not mean that cognitive processes of a different kind are not occurring).

If alternate solutions or constructions of what a stimulus represents are possible, different perceptions given the same stimulus and perceptual reversal are not particularly anomalous facts. On the other hand, as concerns reversal, one might well ask why a solution that is already achieved and that accounts for the stimulus should ever be given up. Why does the perceptual system not simply maintain a percept once the stimulus has been interpreted in a particular way? So we will have to consider this problem in greater depth later.

Nor is there any difficulty for a cognitive theory with the fact that at times one perception seems to depend upon another one. It may be that only after a particular perception occurs (for whatever reason) does a general problem arise for the perceptual system that calls for a solution. In Example 2 of Chapter 1, for instance, the illusory effect of motion of part of a stereo pattern during head motion, only after depth is achieved does zero or reverse parallax pose a new problem. So this fact about perception (that has only recently been noted at all by its students) is perhaps one to which only a cognitive theory can do justice. It certainly poses great difficulties for the other two theories.

The items in our list that do pose difficulties for a cognitive theory are the facts of perceptual organization and of contextual effects. Why is a contour spontaneously assigned to one region rather than another and why are certain units spontaneously grouped with others to form a unit? As to contextual effects, to be sure, these are precisely what one would expect if intelligent processing underlies perception. Thus, for example, where context provides a conceptual frame (Minsky, 1975) or meaningful setting (Palmer, 1975), items within that setting ought to be perceived accordingly. But context defined purely in terms of the presence of other stimulus objects or structures where identification is not the issue is another matter. Why, for example, does the motion of one region induce motion in another and why does a tilted rectangle lead to the impression that a vertical line within it is tilted in the opposite direction? We have seen how the other theories would tackle problems of this kind—which is not to say that the answers were necessarily convincing—but we will have to consider whether these very fundamental facts about perception lend themselves to the kind of explanation that is the essence of cognitive theory. In short, is there anything about these phenomena that is understandable in terms of a problem-solving process or a rational inference, or are they in fact simply the result of stimulus relationships in which what is perceived may even fly in the face of rational analysis?

The outline of a cognitive theory given above and at the end of Chapter 1 probably suffices to set it apart from the other kinds of theory, but its very essence may entail certain as yet unmentioned characteristics. Thus, for example, many theorists have found it necessary to speak of decision processes, and I too will argue that certain perceptual effects can best be understood as the end result of a decision to describe the proximal input in one way rather than another. Indeed this decision may well be the functional underpinning of what we mean by attention. But if "decision" here means anything like what it means in daily life where it is a conscious choice to act in one way rather than another, it may be well to acknowledge it explicitly. In that event it would seem that a higher agency of the mind, call it the executive agency, has available to it the proximal input, which it can scan, and it then behaves in a manner very like a thinking organism in selecting this or that aspect of the stimulus as representing the outer object or event in the world. In short, cognitive theory at its essence incorporates a homunculus concept. This has always been considered so clearly objectionable that theoreticians in psychology studiously avoid it. Interestingly enough, however, workers in the field of artificial intelligence occasionally do have recourse to an executive function (Neisser, 1967).

There are, it seems to me, good reasons for subscribing to the view that an executive agency exists that performs the kind of functions alluded to above. For example, the phenomenon of recognition must be based on some kind of relating of a present perception to a memory. As noted above, the Gestaltists tried to deal with this fact in terms of a stimulus-trace interaction, thus making it spontaneous, automatic, and internally self-generated. That is, no outer or higher agency is implicated. The relevant memory or trace is presumably elicited on the basis of similarity. They spoke of "trace arousal" as the fundamental process. But besides the problem of accessing the relevant memory, recognition implies a decision that the memory adequately matches the present percept. Moreover the accessing process may be more akin to "scanning" than to automatic selection. Thus the better explanatory model here would seem to be one of a higher agency of mind comparing a percept with a specific memory on the basis of certain criteria of what constitutes an adequate match after isolating the latter by some process of internal scanning.

Another good reason for postulating an executive agency in my opinion is that the stimulus input that leads to a description of the object or event is in a certain sense introspectively available. I will argue that there are hierarchically based levels of description that occur beginning with one that is correlated with the stimulus, the proximal mode of description. This suggests that the proximal stimulus information is available rather than being swallowed up, so to speak, by the processes that lead to constancy or world-mode levels of descriptions and that it can be internally scanned or examined. If so, there must be an agency that does this scanning or pre-perceiving. These ideas about levels of description will be spelled out in subsequent chapters.

COMPARISON OF THE TWO CONSTRUCTIVE THEORIES

The difference between a stimulus theory on the one hand and a constructive theory on the other is probably clear enough, but it is important to bring out the difference between the two kinds of constructive theories. In my opinion, the essential difference is this. According to an interaction theory, stimuli or their internal representations interact, thereby affecting or modifying one another, or the interaction is thought of as a process that underlies emergent properties. Thus, for example, grouping results from the effect of the units upon one another, color phenomena, constancies in general, and contextual phenomena from the effect of one stimulus region upon another or from their interplay, enrichment from the effect of a memory trace *on* a registered stimulus.

On the other hand, for cognitive theory, or at least for the kind I am here elaborating, the stimulus input is not so much transformed by spontaneous interaction as it is interpreted by a higher cognitive agency outside the stimulus domain. In fact, the proximal state of affairs is available for such interpretation in a form not too different from its physical characteristics given in the retinal image. Thus grouping is something imposed upon the unmodified proximal array by a cognitive agency, lightness color perception results from an interpretation of the array of luminances as given retinally, and enrichment results from the imposition of a description on the organized stimulus in terms of the properties of the known object.

Other Contemporary Approaches to Perception

The purpose of this chapter was not to draw conclusions about the adequacy or fruitfulness of the different theories but rather to make clear the main ingredients of the cognitive theory advocated here by considering it in the light of what we know factually about the nature of perception and by contrasting it with other kinds of theories. However, we can already glimpse some of the strengths and weaknesses of these different approaches. This book is intended as a statement of a cognitive theory of perception rather than as a polemic against other theories. But in building a case for a cognitive theory, a critique of the other theories is everywhere implicit. Moreover it is hoped that as various problems, phenomena, and findings are considered in subsequent chapters, the exposition of the other theories given here will enable the reader to evaluate them and to consider how, if at all, they might cope with the facts. In certain chapters, though, I will explicitly compare and contrast the different theoretical approaches to the problem under consideration.

I have not included reference to several important contemporary approaches to perception. Thus I seem to have neglected the exciting new discoveries in neurophysiology of feature-detector mechanisms and the attempt by many to explain various of the facts of perception along such lines; I have not referred to the approach that goes by the name of information processing that is so dominant today in the field of perception and cognition; and I have not mentioned the approach to perception (and cognition in general) from which information processing arose, namely, the field of artificial intelligence and computer simulation of cognition.

As to the research on feature-detector mechanisms, I think it correct to say that this does not represent a unique theory. Thus far, the kind of mechanisms that have been discovered can be regarded as the neural events that represent (or encode) the local proximal stimulus. Thus, for example, the rapid discharging of a cell at some level in the visual system when a contour moves across a specific region of the retina might well be the explanation of how the perceptual system "knows" about such proximal-stimulus motion (Barlow, Hill, and Levick, 1964). If so, this would be compatible with each of the theories as outlined in this chapter. It thus does not represent a distinct theory of perception.

As to information processing, this is not so much a specific theory about perception as it is a program for analyzing the stages of processing that are assumed to occur from the moment of stimulation to the ultimate cognition, decision, or action. As such, the approach seems to be theoretically neutral. Depending upon the stage under analysis, one finds emphasis on aspects of each of the three theories of perception discussed here (for example, how the information about the proximal stimulus is extracted, how long it remains available in that form, how this information may be transformed by processes such as lateral inhibition, and how this in turn may be "recognized" or "interpreted" on the basis of rules derived from past experience). Some of the work coming out of this approach undoubtedly does have theoretical implications, and where relevant, I will therefore go into it. In general the theory I develop emphasizes a sequence of stages of processing.

Research in the field of artificial intelligence again does not represent the promulgation of a specific theory of perception. Rather it represents the attempt to construct machine models that simulate some particular cognitive process. When, for example, it succeeds in developing a description of how a machine could arrive at the correct perceptual analysis of a three-dimensional scene (i.e., "decide" what structures in what arrangements are most probably present in the scene given the particular stimulus array), this may support the belief that this is how the human mind achieves the analogous end result. At this point we would then have to consider what kind of psychological theory best fits that kind of processing. Again, therefore, where it seems relevant to theory, I will refer to research based on this approach.

3

Form Perception Based on a Process of Description

AS NOTED AT THE END OF CHAPTER 1, not all of perception seems to require a process of problem solving or reasoning, perhaps because one has neither to make an inference from a rule nor to hypothesize what the stimulus might represent in order to achieve the perception. Much of form perception seems to be in this category. Yet I will argue that cognitive events are at work here too, that one cannot simply understand form perception in terms of a picturelike internal representation of the retinal-image shape or in terms of a sum of the separate features that the object might be said to possess.

As far as I can see, little progress has been made in the area of form perception. The sensory physiologists have made exciting discoveries about how edges and contours are represented by central neural events (Hubel and Wiesel, 1962). But surely contours are only the building blocks of which forms are normally constituted so that the central problem remains of understanding why a figure as a whole appears the way it does. In fact, I will argue that the emphasis on contour detection is entirely misplaced because, as far as form is concerned, a contour simply marks or delineates a location. What matters for form perception is the set of all such locations; and if these can be delineated without contours, contours are not necessary. That is why, in addition to depth, we perceive regions of particular *shapes* in two random dot patterns viewed binocularly despite the absence of any physical contours (Julesz, 1971). Illusory contours (Fig. 2-4) also support this conclusion.

The problem of form perception is to explain why particular figures look the way they do and consequently appear to be similar to or different from other figures. How we manage to identify a form as a member of a particular category is a separate issue. If one examines the contemporary literature to find out what the prevailing view is about form perception, one finds that the most relevant topic is referred to as "pattern recognition." This topic seems to fuse two problems into one, namely, the perception of shape and the categorization of it. This emphasis on categorization arose out of interest in the computer simulation of processes such as reading in which the problem was one of building a machine that could scan a pattern and arrive at the identification of what it was. The categorization decision was what mattered. In daily life one might say that here too what matters for behavior is arriving at decisions concerning what kind of objects confront us and that the specific shape of an object is only a means toward that vital final step of identification.

While agreeing with the importance of this final step, which I will here somewhat loosely refer to as recognition and later as the interpretive mode of description, this emphasis results in bypassing the very central process and experience of shape perception per se. We perceive the individuality of an object including its specific shape. Therefore, each member of a category looks different and we are not only aware of this but it too is important in our behavior. Besides, where form is the relevant dimension, the process of categorization begins with form perception. Therefore, we first must understand more about the basis of phenomenal similarities and differences among shapes before we can understand the emergence of specific categories. Finally, not all objects are familiar, particularly to the child, so that form perception *without* the final step of recognition occurs very often. In any event, the emphasis in this chapter is on form *perception*, although the problem of recognition as a final stage in the descriptive sequence will also be discussed.

The Gestaltists pinpointed the problem of specific shape when they noted the equivalence of form following transposition of size or retinal locus. They did not say much more about it, but instead emphasized the problem of perceptual organization. In the first part of this chapter, I will presuppose that a given form has been organized by the perceptual system as one unit and go on to address the question of why, as a form, it looks the way it does. Later in the chapter, I will take up the problem of organization as such.

It may be helpful first to give an outline of the thesis to be developed in this chapter. I will maintain that the basis of form perception, i.e., of the subjective experience of specific shape or, otherwise expressed, of the phenomenal similarities and differences among shapes, is a nonconscious, nonverbal structural description of the shape. The description is given by the executive agency that is outside the sensory domain based on the inspection of the proximal input. Such a description requires as a first step an organizational decision of what units belong together and of what is figure and what is ground. The specific shape description then begins with the perceived location of points or parts or demarcations of boundaries that, via organizational decisions, constitute one figure and integrates them into larger subunits such as lines and regions. The spatial relationships that constitute the geometry of the whole and of subparts, if any, form the essential nucleus of the description, but orientation in relation to the up-down and sides of the environment is taken into account as well. Certain characteristics of a figure are considered to be salient or singular by the executive agency, and these are weighted more heavily in the description. The process is hierarchical, with descriptive properties emerging at higher levels that can have no reality at lower levels. The final step is a description of the category to which the object belongs, if it is known, and this can even affect the very description of the form under some conditions.

Evidence Suggesting a Process of Description in Form Perception

PERCEIVING THE PATH OF A MOVING TARGET

A question of central theoretical interest is whether or not perceptual experience identical to or very similar to that of normal perception can be achieved when the image of the form is not extended over the retina as it usually is. Suppose, for example, that the observer fixates a stationary point while another point moves along some path. In this case an image of the entire path *will* be spread over the retina. Assuming the rate of movement is fast enough, the first-seen part of the path may still be iconically represented when the last-seen position of the point is in view, by virtue of neural persistence. In that event one might say that as far as the nervous system is concerned, an image of an entire "figure" is present on the retina just as if an entire figure were simultaneously visible. Needless to say, one *can* achieve form perception under such conditions.

But suppose the observer were to track the moving point. In that event, only a small (foveal) region of the retina would receive stimulation. If a path of a specific shape is truly perceived under such conditions (rather than merely being inferred or judged to be present), *that* result would be of real theoretical interest. There has been a controversy over this question.

Why do some students of perception believe that an extended simultaneous image is necessary for form perception? Perhaps because, as I suggested at the outset, they consider form perception to be reducible to contour detection. But such an extended image should not be necessary if form perception is reducible to the perception of the location (or direction) of the constituent parts of a figure and the description of the spatial properties of the configuration to which these perceived locations collectively give rise. Now ordinarily, when the contours of a figure stimulate the retina, by virtue of local sign, a term used in the last century to refer to the qualitative uniqueness of each retinal location (Lotze, 1886), each stimulated retinal point signifies a distinct direction. Therefore, one can interpret the outcome even of the typical conditions of form perception in terms of the collectively perceived oculocentric directions of the parts of a figure. This would already be a departure from the current emphasis on contour detectors. But we can take a further step. In humans and other species that move their eyes, the perceived direction of a point with respect to ourselves (referred to as egocentric or radial direction) is some joint function of retinal locus and eye position.

We performed the following simple experiment (Fig. 3-1) (Rock and Halper, 1969). Condition 1: The observer fixates one luminous point while another moves around in a particular path in a dark room. Since the latter point traces an extended path over the retina, we can safely predict that its path will be discerned. However, the speed of the point is relatively slow, so that we should not expect a simultaneous iconic image of the entire path. Observers have little difficulty in perceiving the path in this condition. They are able to draw an accurate picture of it. Condition 2: The observer tracks a single luminous point as it moves along the same path as in condition 1 with no other point visible. Here no image is spread over the retina. Only a small region of the fovea is stimulated. However, by taking account of changing eye position, the perceptual system is able to detect the changing egocentric directions of the point. The result is that observers perceive the path of the moving point as well in this condition as in the first. Condition 3: The observer tracks the moving luminous point but tries to note the path of a second stationary point. The stationary point here produces an image that *is* successively spread over the retina. But the observer is unable to use this information and has no impression whatsoever of a path traversed by the stationary point. Position constancy obtains, which means that path perception is governed not by changing local sign but by changing egocentric direction. The stationary point does not change its egocentric direction. Therefore, no motion path is seen.

A simple method of performing this kind of experiment is to move a narrow slit in an opaque surface over a luminous figure seen in the dark. Then only a single point of the figure will be visible at any time. This method is essentially one that has been referred to as the "anorthoscopic" procedure (Zöllner, 1862; Helmholtz, 1867; Parks, 1965). I will take up the problem of anorthoscopic perception as an example of problem solving in Chapter 7. As will be brought

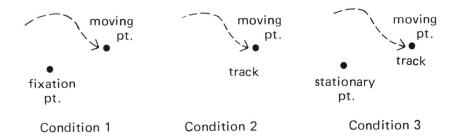

3-1. Three conditions of experiment on the perceived path of a moving point. Condition 1: Observer fixates a stationary point. Condition 2: Observer tracks the moving point. Condition 3: Observer tracks the moving point but judges the path of the stationary point.

out, there is one important difference between the kind of effect discussed here with a moving point and the anorthoscopic effect as it is usually studied; namely, the former entails only path perception rather than form perception. These are obviously related, but one can legitimately argue that an important issue left unanswered by the simple experiment with a moving point described here is whether extended contours such as characterize ordinary form perception can be perceived in the absence of extended retinal contours. To anticipate, the answer to this question is that the change from path to figure perception can be produced by the simple expedient of running the experiment with room lights on and using a dark-line figure rather than a luminous one. In any event for now the conclusion is warranted on the basis of our simple experiment with moving points that not only is the perception of the shape of a path possible without an extended image (condition 2, tracking a single point) but also that it seems not to occur when an image is spread over the retina where the object creating that image is seen not to be moving (condition 3).

The conclusion then seems inescapable that the perceptual system is integrating the set of successive directions given by the visible element over time into a unified whole. The executive agency detects that the element seen first is one end of a path and that, for example, it is downward and to the left; the element seen shortly thereafter is farther to the right and higher. Integrating these relative directions yields a path with the shape of an oblique segment sloping upward to the right. In other words, a description of a form can be achieved without the customary retinal image or iconic representation. If so, it is plausible to suppose that a similar process of directional integration and description accounts for form perception when an extended retinal image is available in the ordinary case.

ORIENTATION

Consider next the problem of orientation in form perception. Figures that are seen tilted or inverted with respect to their customary orientation in a frontal plane will look quite different and thus often not be recognized. Well-known examples include the change from square to diamond by virtue of a 45-degree rotation and the difficulty in recognizing inverted pictures of faces or handwriting. Almost any figure will undergo this change of appearance, provided the observer does not realize that the figure is disoriented. Thus, for example, if with no prior discussion, Fig. 3-2 is shown, it will rarely be perceived in such a way as to lead to recognition as a particular geographical outline. Because orientation affects perception, recognition will not occur. The reader, however, will undoubtedly easily succeed in identifying the figure because the discussion provides a set to expect novel orientation. The central question here is why this change in phenomenal shape occurs despite the fact that there is no change in the internal geometry of the figure. Other kinds of transformation, such as of size or position, that preserve the figure's geometry do *not* lead to change of perceived shape.

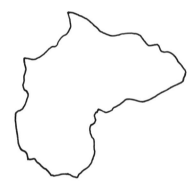

3-2. A familiar geographical outline rotated 90 degrees counterclockwise.

In my own work on this problem the major finding is that it is *not* the change in orientation of the retinal image of a figure that leads to the phenomenal change in its shape. Rather it is the change in the assignment of the directions top, bottom, and sides to the figure that is crucial. Thus, for example, *a* and *b* in Fig. 3-3 look different (assuming one tries to remain naive and does not rotate either one in imagination). Now if one looks at *a* with head upright and *b* with head tilted 45 degrees, the original difference in appearance between the two figures remains (Fig. 3-4) Yet by doing so, the orientation of the retinal image of *a* and *b* becomes identical. The evidence is very substantial on this point (see Rock, 1973). It seems clear then that what matters is that in *a* certain regions and in *b* different regions are assumed to be at the top, bottom, left, and right. It matters little which specific kinds of information are used in arriving at the location of these coordinate directions, i.e., whether as in the example here both gravitational and visual information cooperate in informing us as to which way is up and which down or whether it is only gravitational information (as in a dark field) or whether it is purely egocentric information (as in viewing a figure in a spatially horizontal plane).

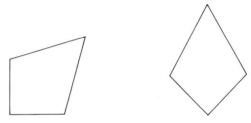

3-3. Two identical figures that look different as a function of orientation.

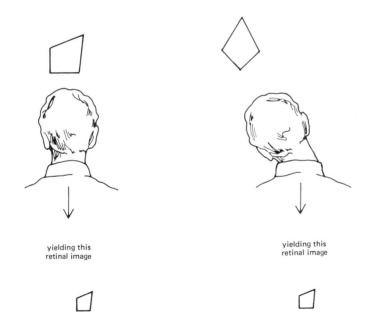

yielding this
retinal image

yielding this
retinal image

3-4. The two drawings of Figure 3-3, although viewed so as to yield identical retinal images, nevertheless look different to naive observers.

We have even been able to show that forms sensed only *tactually* are experienced as different and therefore often not recognized when their orientation is changed. Therefore, the effect of disorientation on form is not a uniquely visual phenomenon, and once again it is unlikely that the altered perception can be understood as a change in the specific pattern of receptors stimulated. In what follows, therefore, I will assume that what I have said thus far is true and conclude that what seems to matter is how directions are assigned to the figure.

This brings us to the question of why such a change in the assignment of directions to a figure should produce such a profound change in phenomenal shape. When I say "profound change," I mean that the difference between the shapes experienced can easily be as great or greater than the difference between figures of entirely different geometric composition (Fig. 3-5). The answer that suggests itself is that a figure is described very differently as a function of how directions are assigned to it. Consider the example in Fig. 3-3. Where *a* would be described as an irregular quadrilateral resting in a stable position on a side, *b* would be described as a symmetrical diamond figure in unstable equilibrium standing on a point. Therefore, these are two very different *things* in the world. In other words, it is not simply that the figure looks different in different orientations but that it looks different in certain respects. The specific appearance in each case can be characterized by a specific description.

A   B   C

3-5. (a) Outline of the African continent; (b) Figure *a* tilted 90 degrees counterclockwise; (c) a figure of different geometrical composition from *a* but which nonetheless looks more like *a* than does *b*.

There is one kind of orientation transformation in the frontal plane that does not lead to a phenomenal change of shape, namely, a mirror image or left-right reversal. It is well known that children confuse letters such as *b* and *d* and that they and animals have difficulty learning to discriminate forms that differ in this respect. Less well known is the fact that adults also confuse figures with their left-right counterparts, provided that novel rather than highly overlearned patterns (such as letters and numbers) are used (Rock, 1973).

If we assume that what matters in the process of describing a figure as far as orientation is concerned is what regions are at the top, bottom, and sides and that, moreover, the sides are taken to be equivalent, then the description of a figure and its mirror image would be essentially alike. Thus if a b is "a vertical straight line with a closed loop extending sideways at the bottom," so too is a d. The perceptual equivalence of left and right makes sense because there is no basis in the environment for the kind of polarity that exists for up and down. In fact "left" and "right" do not characterize the world as up and down do; they are ephemeral, egocentrically imposed directions that reverse when we approach an object from the opposite direction. Thus "side" can be defined as either end of the horizontal axis of a figure. In support of this view is a recent finding that 180-degree rotation of a wire figure about the Y axis, i.e., a depth reversal, also has little if any effect on perceived shape (see below, p. 87). "Front" and "back" can thus also be thought of as "sides." (How we do come to discriminate figures from their mirror images, such as b and d, is a further problem that will not be discussed here, but it surely has to do with focusing attention and high frequency of exposure.)

While the descriptions in the examples given above can be elicited from subjects, the fact is, of course, that normally we do not consciously engage in such a process of description. Therefore, it has the status of a hypothetical process which proceeds as if it conforms to the way in which we would consciously and verbally describe a figure. Whatever the units or "language" of such description, many animal species and preverbal children must be capable of employing them, since they too perceive form and no doubt in much the same way we do. To do justice to form perception, we must assume that the description entails some complex interplay of both the internal geometry of the figure and its relationship to the system of spatial reference imposed upon it.

What does it mean to say that a form is undergoing description which is neither conscious nor based upon natural language? If the notion is to be considered more than a metaphor, it must mean that the figure is analyzed in terms of its properties and spatial relations. Examples of "units" of description would be characteristics such as "parallelism, convergence, straightness, curvilinearity, sameness on both sides, verticality, horizontality or obliqueness, and pointedness." Of course, it is the concatenation of these characteristics into an overall structure that will distinguish one form from another. These units obviously must exist in the observer's repertoire, whatever may be their origin. The kind of description hypothesized is propositional, almost by definition. That is, the properties that enter into the description can be interpreted as predicates of the figure, e.g., "the figure is symmetrical."

Some critical readers may feel that the concept of description suggested here is redundant because the phenomenal percept itself can be thought of as containing description. For example, a symmetrical figure may appear to be symmetrical; i.e., the percept can be characterized as tacitly including symmetry as part of its phenomenal content. Why then add a hypothetical process of description? Or the argument may seem circular to some readers because it seeks to explain the percept by terms that already describe the percept. Or still other readers may feel that the language used here to illustrate hypothetical descriptions is phenomenological, whereas what is wanted is language that refers to the description in some other terms.

I would answer that the percept itself is analogic, picturelike, and concrete (Dretske, 1981). Description, on the other hand, is propositional and abstract. Thus, for example, a symmetrical object may yield a percept that has an appearance of sameness, duplication, or similarity of regions, but that is not the same as the hypothetical description of it, which might be "halves of the object on each side of a dividing axis are mirror images of each other." Therefore, the percept as such does not include description. The confusion is that we can easily access the percept and describe it consciously if asked or if there is reason for doing so. The conscious description may then mirror the determining unconscious one—although not always or not in every particular—but that should occasion no surprise. The hypothetical description after all is the correlate of the percept, so that one should expect aspects of the object's phenomenal appearance to be correlated with aspects of the description. That being so, it is understandable why the conscious description, if elicited, would in large measure mirror the unconscious one. However, the conscious description is not the percept either but an abstract propositional analysis of it.

Admittedly, it is unfortunate that at this stage of our knowledge we can do no better in describing the hypothetical description than to use natural language. The reader should bear in mind, however, that wherever this occurs in this chapter it is intended to characterize the description on a functional, hypothetical level and not to characterize the perception per se. Thus the description is to be thought of as an encoding process. What enters into the encoding will account for an object's phenomenal appearance and for similarities and differences among objects of different shapes. What is important for phenomenal differences will be paramount in the description.

A theory of form perception based on a process of cognitive

description may strike many as radical, farfetched, and unwarranted, certainly on the basis of the meager evidence thus far presented. It is true that virtually the same idea has been promulgated by those working in the field of artificial intelligence (Clowes, 1967; Narasimhan, 1969; Winston, 1975). Their approach, however, has been directed at the goal of finding principles for the operation of a "machine" that *could* successfully identify forms, whether or not the human mind does in fact follow such principles. My position is that we *do* in fact operate in this way. A few psychologists have advanced the idea but have not yet produced much evidence in support of it (Anderson and Bower, 1973; Reed, 1974; Sutherland, 1968, 1973; Palmer, 1975). We have every reason to require a good deal of solid evidence before we agree that such hypothetical cognitive events are necessary for the explanation of perceptual experiences which have been thought to be explicable solely in terms of sensory-physiological mechanisms. In the remainder of this chapter I will attempt to summarize this evidence.

COMPLEXITY

Consider the matter of the simplicity or complexity of a figure. Some years ago I collaborated on an experiment in which subjects viewed a single novel figure under incidental conditions for some seconds (Rock and Engelstein, 1959). Figure 3-6 shows one of the figures. Although the subjects were not trying to learn or remember the figure, they undoubtedly were attending to it. Then, some time later, even weeks later for some subjects, an unexpected recognition test was given. Despite the great similarity of many of the test choices to the original figure, all subjects were able to select the correct one. Since the observer viewed the original figure incidentally, one might think that the perception and perfect storage in memory of the figure entailed little more than the passive registration and storage of an iconic pictorial representation.

But suppose the figure had been much more complex? If the perception and memory formation were simply iconic, the outcome should be the same. It does not matter whether a camera takes a picture of a simple or a complex scene as far as the outcome is concerned. On the other hand, if processing of a kind analogous to description occurs during perception, it is questionable if a sufficiently detailed description of a very complicated figure would be achieved without deliberate effort. We investigated this question with figures such as the one in Fig. 3-7 (Rock, Halper, and Clayton, 1972). Here again the subjects attended to the figure but were not trying to learn it. While the overall shape taken globally might be said to be simple enough—as simple as the one used in the previous study—the subtle-

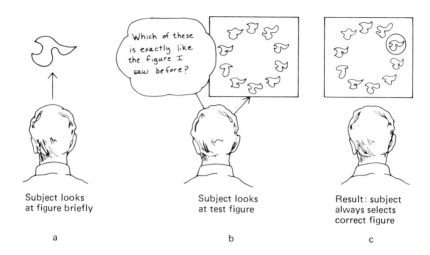

3-6. (a) A relatively simple figure used in the experiment on recognition; (b) recognition test; (c) result. After Rock and Engelstein, 1959.

3-7. A relatively complex figure used in the experiment on recognition. After Rock, Halper, and Clayton, 1972.

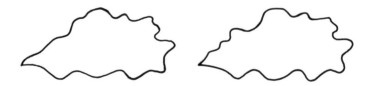

3-8. Test figure for the experiment using Figure 3-7.

ties and nuances of the edges of the figure are quite complex. After the subjects viewed this figure for a few seconds, a two-choice recognition test was used as shown in Fig. 3-8. One of these is correct and one differs in that in one region the specific shape of the contour has been changed (the upper left region in the figure). However, as is evident, the global shape is the same in the two alternatives. Readers can see if they can tell which of these is correct. Our subjects did no better than chance here even when the test came directly after the figure. On the other hand, as a control, if the figure used is just the portion of the contour that was critical in the larger figure as in Fig. 3-9, then, in the same kind of test (Fig. 3-10), subjects have no difficulty in discriminating (see Table 3-1). Presumably the reader does not either. Taken together, these results imply that when a given region of a figure is a nonconsequential part of the whole, something is lacking in the perception of it, with the result that no adequate memory of it seems to be established. But when that same physical region of the contour *constitutes* the form, there is no difficulty in perceiving and storing all its nuances.

3-9. Control experiment using only portion of the contour of Figure 3-7.

3-10. Test figure for the control experiment using Figure 3-9.

What determines whether a region will constitute part of the over-all shape or be inconsequential with respect to it? It would seem to be a matter of part-whole relationships and relative size. With respect to the large unit that is the figure in Fig. 3-7, the convolutions of the contour are small and are seen simply as perturbations that have little effect on the global shape. That is why the two versions in Fig. 3-8 look alike. But when a subpart of Fig. 3-7 becomes the unit or figure, as in Fig. 3-9, the same convolutions *become* the shape. The size of the perturbations relative to the whole of Fig. 3-9 is now such that they enter into the shape description. By the same token, the components of the contour of Fig. 3-6 are sufficiently large in relation to the whole as to enter into or characterize the shape of the whole. Therefore, the description of the shape does not exclude any components here, and memory for this figure is qualitatively very good indeed.

Another way of putting this is to say that in Fig. 3-7 the perturba-

Table 3-1: Recognition of Complex Figures

	Number Correct	Percentage	Number Incorrect	Percentage
Experimental Condition (Fig. 3-7)	8	50	8	50
Control Condition (Fig. 3-9)	15	96.7	1	6.3

tions characterize the mode of the contour but not the shape of the figure; whereas in Fig. 3-9 the same perturbations now characterize the shape of the figure. Compare the analogous effects shown in Figs. 3-15 and 3-16 (Goldmeier, 1972). It suffices to describe mode perturbations as just that, and hence one might say that two descriptive components are encoded for Fig. 3-7: a certain global shape and a convoluting contour.

One can argue that these experiments bear on memory and not on perception, that as far as perception is concerned nothing is lacking for the complex figure. This is a difficult issue to resolve. We were able to obtain the same kind of results when the entire sequence was run by tachistoscope and a single test figure that called for a "same" or "different" response followed after only 200 milliseconds. Similarly, the reader may agree that when Fig. 3-8 was first viewed the difference between the two versions was not noted despite their simultaneous presence. To do so seems to require deliberate, careful part-by-part comparison. Figure 3-11 illustrates the same point; without such a deliberate comparison *a* and *b* appear to be identical although half of the homologous parts are in fact different (Palmer, 1981). Surely if a figure is sufficiently complex—e.g., a random dot pattern—there can be no dispute that perception will fail to encompass all its nuances. Perhaps the confusion about this issue is that we as observers are aware of the presence of the entire figure and thus aware of the *potential* that provides for perceiving everything about it if one had enough time to study it. But the potential for such perception is not the same as the realization of it. In any event, logically, it seems to me to be difficult to explain why, if everything is adequately perceived, some features do not establish memories. Therefore, I would explain these results by maintaining that form perception entails description but that given great complexity, and no *focusing* of attention on specific details, what will be described is the global character of the shape, and not the details.

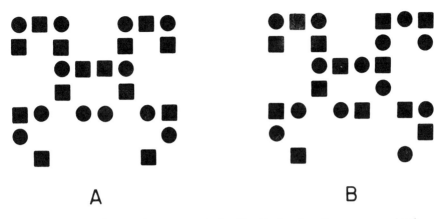

3-11. Two figures that appear to be identical unless they are examined carefully. After Palmer, 1982.

ATTENTION

All this leads to the next line of evidence. If such a descriptive process is indeed a necessary aspect of normal form perception, what would be the consequence of eliminating it? What might be the consequence of exposure to a figure under conditions where one is not attending to the *entire figure*? We studied this question using methods that would guarantee that the observer on the one hand received adequate central stimulation by a figure but on the other hand would not be attending to it. Figure 3-12 illustrates one of the methods we used (Rock and Gutman, 1981).

Two overlapping novel outline figures, one red and one green, are shown simultaneously for a brief period, e.g., 1 second (Fig. 3-12a). Following a short interval another pair of such figures is shown and so forth. Subjects fixate on a small dot in the center of each pair. They are instructed to rate all figures of a given color on the basis of how much they like it (an aesthetic scale). This task is difficult because each pair is shown so briefly and thus it can be presupposed that subjects will be forced to attend to only the figures of the appropriate color. The other figure in each pair therefore stimulates the eye in the same way as the attended one, but it is not attended to. Following this presentation the subjects were given a test in which there were an equal number of figures from the attended series, from the unattended ones, and new ones. They were to encircle those they recognized from the presentation regardless of color (Fig. 3-12b).

Without going into details, what we found was a fairly good level of recognition of the attended series, as might be expected, and essentially no evidence of recognition of the unattended series (see

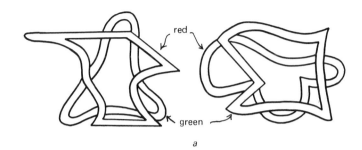

a

Subjects circle many
figures to which they
had attended (in this
example those that had
been red) but no more
that had been green
than those that are new.

Exposure   *Test*   *Result*

Subject fixates center   Mixture of figures that
dot and rates the red   had been red, that had
figure. Ten overlapping   been green, and new
pairs like this were   ones. All figures in test
shown.   are black. Subject circles
                              all figures recognized.

b

3-12. (a) Overlapping figures used in experiment on attention; (b) details
of exposure of figure, recognition test, and result. After Rock and Gutman, 1981.

Table 3-2). In a follow-up experiment we wanted to show that what
we are studying here is failure of perception, not merely selective
memory for that which has been perceived with and without attention. We therefore presented a series that contained one *familiar*
figure paired with an unfamiliar one, where the familiar one was in
the color attended to and another familiar figure paired with an unfamiliar one, where the familiar one was in the color *not* attended to.
One familiar figure was an outline of a house, the other the outline
of a Christmas tree. Otherwise the procedure was the same (Fig. 3-13).
The result was that virtually all subjects recognized in the test the one

Table 3-2: Recognition of Figures

	Mean Number of Attended, Unattended, or New Figures Encircled		
	Attended	Unattended	New
(N = 40)	3.2*	0.95*	0.75*

*The total number in each category presented in the test was 5.

familiar figure that was in the attended color but did not recognize the one that was in the nonattended color. We assumed that if a figure such as a house was adequately perceived, it would *immediately* lead to recognition and, if it did, it would hardly be forgotten a few moments later. In other words, the familiar figure, if perceived and recognized, would stand out and more or less surprise the subject. Therefore, failure of recognition here seems to support our belief that the fundamental deficit is of form perception.

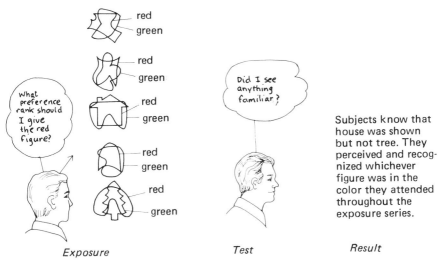

Same procedure and task as in previous experiment.

3-13. Variation of experiment with overlapping figures in which two in the series contain familiar objects.

But why should form perception depend upon attention? It is not surprising that it is impossible to understand what one person is saying while attending to what another person is saying, because that obviously entails cognitive processing of a kind requiring contact with relevant memories that can yield meaning, i.e., processing on a semantic level. If, however, form perception entails a process of description that is also cognitive in nature, the necessary role of attention is also not surprising. What attention involves is precisely the kind of processing that leads to such perception. Hochberg (1970) and Neisser (1967) have expressed similar views.

Returning to the earlier finding concerning failure of perception of nuances of complex figures, we must deal with the fact that we do obviously discriminate such nuances in complex figures encountered in daily life. Thus we perceive all faces differently, even those of identical twins, and countless other examples of our tendency to make fine discriminations among similar configurations will readily come to the reader's mind. True, but it is also the case that we make such perceptual discriminations only after much experience with that category of object. At the outset, when we first meet the twins, we are in precisely the same situation as are the subjects who were shown Fig. 3-7. There is experimental evidence for this assertion (Gibson and Gibson, 1955; Pick, 1965).

It would seem, therefore, that these examples from daily life confirm that at the outset of encountering a new category of complex object, we describe only the global properties. Eventually, however, no doubt because we must notice more if we are to be able to make the necessary discriminations, we begin to do so. Thus eventually the description becomes more articulated and detailed. That in turn allows for more articulated memories.

SALIENT AND SINGULAR FIGURAL CHARACTERISTICS

If the specific shape perceived is a function not directly of the stimulus shape but of how this is described, one might ask what factors other than those already mentioned—i.e., the geometrical relations, assigned directions, figural complexity, and attention— might affect the description? For example, one might ask whether certain geometrical relations are more important than others. Consider Fig. 3-14a, consisting of two parallel angles (Goldmeier, 1972). There are various relations here one can specify, such as the specific angle formed by the legs of each and the parallelism of the two angles with respect to one another. Are these of equal importance? To answer this, the reader can decide whether Fig. 3-14b or c appears to be more similar to a. It seems clear that c does. Now both b and c entail geometrical changes of a, b by changing only the lower angle, thereby destroying the parallelism, c by changing both angles by the same amount. Thus in an absolute sense, c represents more of a change than b. So in this case, parallelism is a more salient geometrical feature than specific angle. The hypothetical description of a therefore might be "two parallel obtuse angles" without any precise specification of the exact angle. Given that description, it is clear why c appears to be more similar.

Undoubtedly the reason for the saliency of parallel lines is that this relation is a unique or singular one among the various possible orientational relations that two or more lines can have to one another. Singularity is a concept first noted by Wertheimer (1923), who referred to prägnanzstufen (pregnant steps). It was later emphasized by Goldmeier (1972) in discussing the problem of similarity. More recently Rosch (1975) has referred to prototypes or good internal examples of natural categories that can serve as reference points in relation to which other category members are judged.

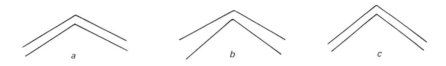

3-14. (a) A figure with parallel angles. (b) Variation in which the angles are no longer parallel because the lower angle is changed. (c) Variation in which the angles remain parallel because both angles are changed to the same degree. After Goldmeier, 1972.

Consider next Fig. 3-15a, also studied by Goldmeier (1972). Of the various features one can specify, there is the overall circular configuration, the overall size, the size of the small circular dots, and the spacing between them. Obviously the overall shape is most important, but what about the relative importance of the other features? Again the reader can decide whether Fig. 3-15b or c looks more like a. It seems clear that b does. Observers in an experiment were unanimous about this. Yet Fig. 3-15c is an exact enlargement of a, which means that no figural relations are changed. What seems to be happening here is this: One can think of the form of a configuration and one can think of the material that makes it up. In this case, the form of a is a circle and the material consists of dots. In many figures the material consists of thin lines. Apparently in a pattern such as Fig. 3-15, we do not apprehend the material per se as entering into the form relations. The shape is described independently of the material, although the material is also described. Therefore, if we enlarge the figure, as in b, it is best to keep the material unchanged. Then both the shape and material descriptions are unchanged. If we change the material, the observer is struck by this change, and this leads to an overall impression of difference. However, if the figure is small, as

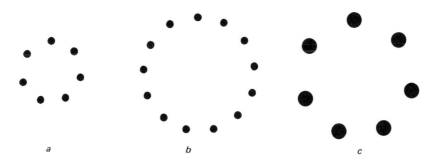

3-15. (a) Standard figure. (b) Enlarged comparison figure in which dots and spacing between them is the same as in *a*. (c) Comparison figure which is an enlargement of *a* in all respects. After Goldmeier, 1972.

in Fig. 3-16*a*, so that the size of the material is appreciable in relation to the size of the figure, the material ceases to be mere material. It becomes part of the form. Thus Fig. 3-16*c* is more similar to *a* than to *b* for most observers.

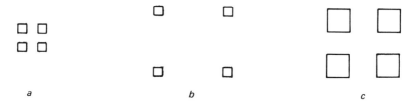

3-16. (a) Standard figure. (b) Enlarged comparison figure in which the small squares are the same as in *a*. (c) Comparison figure that is an enlargement of *a* in all respects. After Goldmeier, 1972.

Symmetry is a particularly important feature of form. If one fig-ure is symmetrical and another is constructed in such a way as to be objectively similar to the first but lacking in symmetry, the two will probably look quite different. Symmetry can be regarded as a singular value. But it turns out that for symmetry to emerge psychologically, it must be symmetry about a vertical axis. This was demonstrated in an experiment illustrated in Fig. 3-17 (Rock and Leaman, 1963). Figure 3-17*a* is symmetrical about both vertical and horizontal axes; Fig. 3-17*b* is symmetrical only about the vertical axis; and Fig. 3-17*c* is symmetrical only about the horizontal axis. The overwhelming majority of observers chose *b* as more similar to *a* than *c* was to *a*. The experiment can be repeated by turning the page 90 degrees. Now—as the reader will appreciate—*c* appears more similar to *a* (see

Table 3-3). Observers give these responses immediately, without knowing the basis of them. Since b and c entail the same degree of change, the outcome cannot be understood in terms of either degree of change quantitatively considered or degree of change of figural relations.

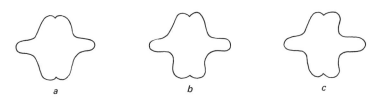

3-17. (a) Standard figure that is symmetrical about its vertical and horizontal axes. (b) Comparison figure symmetrical about its vertical axis. (c) Comparison figure symmetrical about its horizontal axis. After Rock and Leaman, 1963.

That the powerful effect of vertical symmetry on the appearance of a figure is of a psychological nature is brought out by a subsequent study in which it was shown that b in Fig. 3-17 will look more like a than c does even if the observer's head is tilted 45 degrees in viewing the three figures (see Table 3-3). Therefore, it is symmetry about the perceived vertical direction in the environment that matters, rather than symmetry about the vertical retinal-cortical axis. The executive agency apparently describes a figure with symmetry about a phenomenally vertical axis as "the same on both sides" but does not tend to do so if the perceived axis is in some other orientation. The readily notable equality or inequality of the sides of a figure that underlies perceiving symmetry about a vertical axis or the lack of it must be a ramification of the same fundamental equivalence of the sides of phenomenal space that leads to confusion of figures with their left-right reversals, as discussed earlier. In other words, unlike the top-bottom spatial polarity in which opposite directions differ phenomenally (anisotropic), in the left-right polarity, opposite directions do not differ phenomenally (isotropic). This lack of difference has two consequences: We confuse figures with their left-right reversals (mirror images); for a single figure we are sensitive to whether its two sides are the same or different precisely because they are not affected by any spatial anisotropy.

One final example. In Fig. 3-18, b looks quite different from a; however, d looks fairly similar to c. Yet c is a turned 45 degrees and d is b turned 45 degrees. Therefore, physically speaking, c and d are as similar to (or different from) one another as are a and b. The reason b looks different from a is that we immediately detect that its

Table 3-3: Similarity Based on Vertical Symmetry

| | Number of Selections | | | |
Condition	Vertically Symmetrical Test Choice	Horizontally Symmetrical Test Choice	Unable to Choose	Total
Subject Upright	159	37	4	200*
Subject's Head Tilted 45°	146	51	3	200*

*In each experiment, the results are based on 20 subjects each of whom viewed 5 different figures. The figures were first shown in one orientation and then rotated by 90° (see text).

angles are not right angles, because the sides in *a* and *b* are at or close to the horizontal and vertical directions. These directions are singular. Since this is not true for *c* and *d*, we fail to be struck by the difference in angles and, therefore, the two figures do not look particularly different. Otherwise expressed, *a* is described as a figure with right angles and vertical and horizontal sides, but *b* is not described that way at all—hence their different appearance. *C* is described as a figure with oblique sides symmetrical about a vertical axis and containing four angles whose precise magnitude is unspecified and *d* is described in about the same way—hence their equivalent appearance.

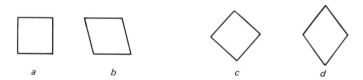

    a   *b*   *c*   *d*

3-18. *a* and *c* are identical except for orientation, and *b* and *d* are identical except for orientation. However, *b* looks quite different from *a*, whereas *d* looks fairly similar to *c*. After Goldmeier, 1972.

Thus, in summary, there are various factors that govern the description of a figure, or perhaps one should say there is an ordering in the saliency of the characteristics that govern the description. This has much to do with the specific phenomenal shape achieved and therefore—I would add—much to do with how the figure is encoded in memory.

AMBIGUOUS FIGURES

That the same proximal stimulus can lead to qualitatively different percepts is a fact with which any theory of perception must deal. I will postpone discussion for the moment of the further fact that the percept can *change* over time and focus instead on the differing percepts than can occur for either the same or different observers. Clearly come central mechanism or process must be invoked as explanation. I am not referring to ambiguity regarding identification, where a certain configuration might be said to be a representation of one thing or another, as in an ink blot. For in that case one might say that understandably enough an insufficiently elaborated figure could represent this or that and there is no reason to maintain that the form perception differs with one interpretation or the other.

But when perception differs, as, for example, in Rubin's famous figure (Fig. 2-2), clearly form perception must entail some processing that can explain that difference. Rubin and the Gestalt psychologists invoked the concept of figure-ground organization. The essence of this concept is not, contrary to popular opinion, that one or another region stands out from the background (although that is true) but that the contour dividing two regions ends up *belonging to* the region that becomes figure. It therefore gives that region rather than the other a specific shape. But this is more a matter of describing what figure-ground organization is like than it is of explaining it. There have been some attempts to explain the phenomenon physiologically, but they are no longer taken very seriously (Köhler, 1940; Hebb, 1966). Besides it is doubtful if such theories could do justice to other kinds of ambiguous figures.

On the other hand, some further penetration into this problem does seem to be achieved by viewing the process in terms of differing descriptions. Given the ambiguity of the stimulus, it is of course no problem that it could be described differently. Therefore, for whatever reason, the perceptual system may proceed by describing one way rather than the other. Thus, e.g., in Fig. 3-19, if the black region is described, the central contour is taken as belonging to it as an edge, and that entire region becomes one with a particular shape.

The point I would like to emphasize is that the two possible percepts, black or white figures, not only look different but the way in which they look different is based precisely on the way each would be described. In this simple example, the black region is concave, the white one convex. If no such figure-ground organization occurs, the central line would be described as curved to the left, but it would not

3-19. Figure-ground pattern in which the central contour becomes an edge of either a black concave figure or a white convex figure.

be either convex or concave (Fig. 3-20). Only a two-dimensional surface can have that characteristic, and it requires that its boundary be taken as an edge.

3-20. Figure in which the central contour is not an edge of the region on either side.

A less well-known example of ambiguity is shown in Fig. 3.21 (Attneave, 1968; Palmer, 1980). It seems that we tend to perceive an equilateral triangle as pointing in a particular direction at any one time. Except for the case when the triangle is not given in an upright position, where strong preferences would make it difficult to perceive it in any way other than pointing upward, it is quite ambiguous as to which way it is pointing. Again, the point I want to emphasize is that a given description seems to underlie a given percept. If Fig. 3-21 is seen pointing one way, it would be described as having an axis of symmetry along that direction.

But perhaps the best example of the dependence of perception on description in ambiguous figures is given by cases where the ambiguity is not one of figure-ground or of depth (as in reversible perspective patterns) or of orientation, but rather one of interpretation. Jastrow's (1900) example of the duck or the rabbit is of this kind, as is one I have used of a chef or a dog, as is Bugelski and Alampay's (1961) example of the rat or the man and Boring's (1930) well-known example of the old and young woman (Fig. 3-22). The designation "of interpretation" may seem to suggest the kind of example I rejected earlier in referring to an ink blot as not being a good example of perceptual ambiguity. But in the present cases, it is not merely that we interpret the

3-21. A triangle that can be seen as pointing in different directions with an axis of symmetry appropriate to the direction in which it is seen as pointing.

stimulus differently. We perceive it differently. I discuss this issue below but for now simply wish to point out that it is only possible to do justice to the manner in which the duck percept looks different from the rabbit percept by saying that we perceive the one in the way we would describe a duck and the other in the way we would describe a rabbit.

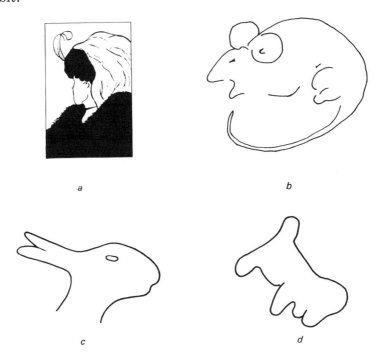

a   b

c   d

3-22. Four reversible figures.

The Applicability of the Description Theory to Other Facts

In the preceding section I have presented the kind of evidence that seems to require postulating a process such as description. In this section I will try to suggest how this theory can be applied to certain other well-known facts of perception and cognition.

TRANSPOSITION

Consider the phenomenon of transposition of form, namely, that a form remains phenomenally unchanged qua form despite changes in its size, retinal locus, or in many cases, *retinal* orientation. Some may consider this a fact that needs no explanation, since form is clearly a function of the geometry of the image and in transposition there is no change of such geometry. One might say that the higher-order character of the stimulus is unchanged. But clearly the stimulus input is variable in absolute terms, which means that the ensuing neural events must be variable, at least until some later neural event. Certainly it has been recognized that some mechanism is required if a machine is to identify patterns that are transposed.

If, however, description underlies form perception, transposition is the very kind of fact one would predict, with one important proviso. The description must be one that separates form from other properties, so that one distinctive part of the description is concerned only with form. I say this because we are not unaware of other properties, as, for example, size, so that when the same form is seen again in a different size we may be perfectly aware that while the form is unchanged the size is different. (This may not always be the case, however, as, for example, in the transposition of melodies. Here even trained musicians may not be aware of the change unless they attended to the key or octave in the first place.) The fact, however, that we often are aware of change of other properties is one more reason why we cannot regard transposition as simply a pseudo-problem. (The reader is reminded that there are occasions of transposition when changes of other properties, such as the "material" of a figure (Fig. 3-15), are important enough to influence the overall shape impression.) Apparently then, we must assume that a full description of a figure entails not only its shape but other properties such as size, location, color, and type of contour.

ABSTRACTION AND CONCEPT FORMATION

If the full description consists of a set of relatively *independent* (albeit associated) descriptions, one for each property of an object, that is a process compatible with abstraction. If moreover the description process does separate form from other properties, one might say that the description of relatively invariant shape characteristics provides the basis of concepts, from even a single encounter. In other words, in the world in which we live, categories of things are generally based on form rather than on other properties such as color. Therefore, if the first or primary description we make of an object concerns its form, that becomes a mental representation capable of accounting for the category in question, not merely of the specific instance encountered.

Thus if the child on first seeing a dog describes its global shape (bearing in mind the discussion above of how subtle nuances are often left out of descriptions of novel figures), it is not surprising that the commonality between that dog and a subsequently encountered different dog is perceived, this despite the fact that the differences are undoubtedly also perceived if they are sufficiently salient (size, color, hair texture, barking, etc.).

INTERSENSORY EQUIVALENCE

Another fact that may find its explanation with the concept of description is the phenomenal equivalence of form across various sense modalities, *intersensory equivalence.* A wooden triangular block will look triangular if seen and feels triangular if grasped in the hand. Again, some may want to argue that this is not a special problem requiring explanation because we can pick up the higher-order information concerning geometrical relations in many ways and it matters little through which modality we do it. In fact, one might want to regard this fact as a special case of transposition, modality transposition. But the argument I made above against this view applies all the more here. It is by no means obvious—certainly not on the basis of neurophysiological processes—why such different sensory input should lead to a phenomenal property, shape, that is more or less the same. But if the stimulus in any modality leads to a description of the kind suggested here, that description qua shape may well be identical. Of course, shape perceived haptically, i.e., via touch, grasping, or pressure or vibrations against the skin, is not as easily achieved or as good (i.e., either as veridical or as articulated) as it is via vision. But that is a matter that need not concern us here. What is important is the idea that regardless of modality of input, the final mental product may no longer be in a sensory "language" but is rather in a transmodal "language," and that is why intersensory equivalence, recognition, and transfer are possible. The same executive agency describes the input to the different modalities.

There is another interesting parallel between visual and tactual perception of form. I have argued that visual form can be thought of as resulting from the formulation of a description based on the information from a set of directions of the constitutent points of a figure relative to one another. The best evidence for this view derived from the perception of the path of a moving point while tracking it, where this was the only kind of information available. In active tactual or haptic perception, the information would seem to derive from the position of the fingers relative to one another, taking into account how each finger is bent with respect to its joints and so forth. Moreover manipulating the object over time enters in as well. Therefore, this is a very different kind of information from that which might be provided in passive tactile perception where a form is impressed against the skin. In the latter case the situation is analogous to the extended retinal image in vision, but tactile form perception of this kind is poor compared with haptic form perception.

Clearly what matters in haptic perception is the acquisition of information about spatial relationships which can be conveyed in an infinite number of combinations of specific sensory inputs. Thus in both modalities it is the spatial information that counts, not the specific sensory pattern of stimulation (Gibson, 1962). But the point can be made even more emphatically by considering tactual perception when, let us say, only the pad of a finger is used to explore a shape such as one in bas-relief that is large enough to require moving the finger along it. An extended contour of a given shape is perceived. Since only a circumscribed sensory region is stimulated at any given moment, the form can obviously only be apprehended by integrating the successive spatial locations with one another as given by the changing position of the finger. Therefore, this procedure is precisely analogous to the perception of the path of a moving point in vision when one tracks that point. I would argue that both procedures allow the description of a form.

Then there is the interesting phenomenon of visual capture. Given a conflict between vision and touch, as in simultaneously viewing an optically distorted object while grasping it, vision is not only dominant but it leads to the misperception of the "feel" of the object (Gibson, 1933; Rock and Victor, 1964; Rock and Harris, 1967; Hay, Pick, and Ikeda, 1965). For example, if a square looks like a rectangle because it is viewed through a cylindrical lens, then even when it is simultaneously grasped by the fingers it both looks and feels like a rectangle (see Fig. 3-23). If the percept via any modality results from a cognitive description that is essentially transmodal, we can at least understand why the potentially different descriptions from each modality are expressed in a common "language." Of course, in the case of conflicting information, the descriptions should differ in their specifics. But given the tendency of the perceptual system to give more weight to visual information, at least as regards spatial properties such as shape or size, we can understand how a *single* visually dominated description might result. Given that outcome, we can then understand why the observer would say that the object feels like the way it looks. What is meant is that the unified description applies to either vision or touch.

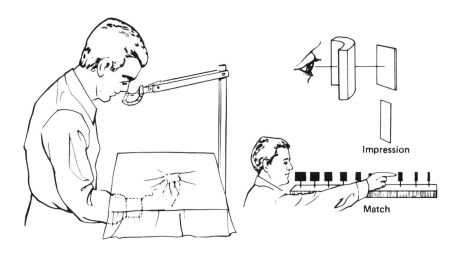

3-23. Illustration of an experiment on conflicting information from vision and touch. After Rock and Victor, 1964.

The Problem of Perceptual Organization

It is understandable why many students of perception would overlook the problem of perceptual organization. On the one hand, our perceptual experience is characterized by a world of distinct and segregated objects; on the other hand, on a conceptual level, we believe the world is constituted in this same way. Typically we organize the world perceptually more or less along the same lines in which we believe it to be organized in reality. Therefore, by either an implicit naive realism or an assumption that the proximal stimulus directly conveys to us the units that are isomorphic with phenomenal experience, we may fail to appreciate that perceptual organization represents an achievement based on some kind of internal processing.

The fact is that the light rays from two separate points within an object have no more connection with one another than the rays from one such point with those from a point outside the object. Therefore, it is a problem why we usually group together into one phenomenal thing all the proximal stimuli related to one object rather than group some stimuli from the object with others from the surfaces between objects, or for that matter, it is a problem why such organization occurs at all. The problem is easier to grasp when the pattern of stimulation is ambiguous in the sense that it can be organized in different ways (as shown in Fig. 3.24). But it is worth emphasizing that, logically, the problem is no different when the pattern of stimulation is more typically not of this kind, as in daily life.

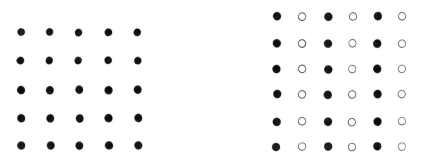

3-24. Patterns that are ambiguous and can be grouped in different ways.

The one case of organization that most investigators do acknowledge concerns figure and ground. As noted above, that the contour "belongs" to one region at a time and gives it a particular shape has been known ever since Edgar Rubin called this fundamental fact to our attention. Yet, as far as I can see, we have learned nothing of importance about it in the years since and have no explanation of it. The Gestalt psychologists incorporated it into their principles of organization and hinted that its explanation was to be sought along the lines of neural events directed at prägnanz. Setting aside the physiological aspect of this theory, there is something of interest in the idea that the perception of *one* region as figure achieves a greater simplicity than would the perception of two meshing figures, and there is some experimental support for this hypothesis (Dinnerstein and Wertheimer, 1957). The problem of preference based on simplicity will be further explored in a subsequent chapter.

It seems to me, however, that the concept of description proposed in this chapter offers a fresh approach to the problem. To review what was said earlier, if the perception of a specific shape is a function of a process of description, that region so described is figure. Ground does not undergo description of shape but only, say, of color, texture, and so forth. Consider an ambiguous pattern such as that shown in Fig. 3-25a. If, for whatever reason, the white region is at a given moment taken as the region the shape of which is described (shown unambiguously in Fig. 3-25c), then what is described are the spatial relations of that region. The central contour "belongs" to that region in the sense that the geometrical relations contained within the boundaries on all its sides delineate its shape. In this case the shape becomes one with soft rounded protrusions toward the left. But when the black region is the one described (see Fig. 3-25b), the central contour belongs to that side and contributes to the geometrical relations on that side. In this case, the shape becomes a claw-like structure with sharp angles protruding toward the right.

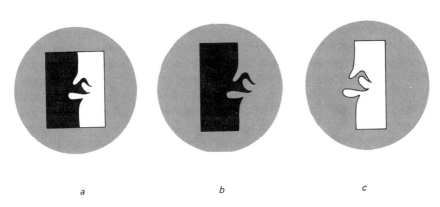

a   b   c

3-25. (a) An ambiguous figure-ground pattern that can be perceived as a black region, as in (b), or a white one, as in (c). The two figure percepts have entirely different shapes based on entirely different descriptions.

Now, while we are capable of perceiving more than one figure at a time—for example, we seem to be able to perceive both figures in Fig. 3-26 simultaneously—the stimulus is different in the ambiguous pattern. Here we would have to assign the same central contour simultaneously to define two distinctly shaped regions. There is only one central contour, while two phenomenal edges are required for the perception of two shapes simultaneously. Therefore, the preempting of the single contour for one or the other shape description in which that contour becomes an edge accounts for the fact that only one region is figural at any given moment (although oscillation from one to the other can be very rapid). The stimulus does not support two simultaneous shape percepts.

3-26. Two figures can be perceived simultaneously here because there are
two central contours, not one as in Figure 3-25*a*.

This analysis explains why the two phenomenal shapes on either
side of the central contour are completely different despite the physical identity of the contour. As is well known, they are so different
that, if one has been seen at one time, the other will not be recognized if seen at a later time (Rubin, 1921). It is not contour per se
that constitutes shape (or even any other marker of a boundary one
might substitute for a contour) unless the figure itself is an open line
as in Fig. 3-20. In this case, it *is* the line that constitutes the shape
and its geometrical properties are what is described. Normally it is
the region bounded by the contours that has shape. These *regions*, as
in Fig. 3-25, are geometrically speaking quite different, and it is these
regions that undergo description.

Assuming this analysis is correct, two further problems remain.
One is the basis for selecting one region over the other as figure;
the other problem is the basis for reversal or alternation from one to
the other over time. As to the first, certain principles given to us
primarily by the Gestalt psychologists seem valid. Factors such as
surroundedness and symmetry have been shown to play a determining
role. Since an analysis of the selection of one organization over another
based on such factors seems more relevant to the problem of preference for one solution over another than to the topic of description, I
will postpone discussion of it until a subsequent chapter devoted to
preference in perceptual problem solving. But the other problem, of
reversal, is relevant to our present topic; so I will come to that
shortly.

As far as other principles of organization are concerned, e.g., those
subsumed under the Gestalt laws of grouping, little progress has been
made in the last half century. These principles continue to be illustrated in textbooks, and except for some work on grouping by
similarity in texture patterns (Julesz, 1975; Beck, 1966), and the
uncovering of a principle of preference for convexity in figure-ground
organization (Kanizsa, 1975; Kanizsa and Gerbino, 1976), no new
"law" has been added, nor have any of the original "laws" been shown
to be incorrect. The Gestaltists believed that the explanation under-

lying these laws was based on various interactive forces generated by the stimuli as projected into the brain. Thus, for example, grouping occurred on the basis of proximity because, other things being equal, the closer together the neural representation of the stimulus units in the brain, the stronger the force of attraction between them. Such forces were presumably manifestations of the more general principle of prägnanz (or tendency toward simplicity).

This kind of explanation is no longer taken seriously even by many of those who remain sympathetic to the Gestalt approach to psychology. Moreover it has been shown that a factor such as proximity must be understood in terms of the *perceived* separation between units rather than the physical retinal-cortical separation between them. Thus first the observer must perceive what units are nearest to what other units and only then do the units form clusters on the basis of proximity, another example where one perception (a particular grouping) is based on a prior one (proximity). See Fig. 3.27. Given this kind of finding, it is difficult to argue that forces of attraction can explain the grouping, since that kind of mechanism requires that proximity be defined in terms of the physical nearness of the cortical representation of the units (Corbin, 1942; Rock and Brosgole, 1964; see also Olson and Attneave, 1970, for a related analysis of grouping on the basis of similarity). Attempts have been made to reduce some of the Gestalt principles to quantitative information-theoretical statements that would permit more precise predictions, and I discuss this approach in a later chapter, pp. 146–152).

Consistent with my suggestion about figure-ground organization, I would like to suggest that grouping on the basis of factors such as proximity, similarity, common fate, and good continuation is the result of a decision to describe the stimulus array in one way rather than other possible ways. Since the array is logically ambiguous concerning what belongs with what, the organizing principles imply solutions to problems based on preferences. Therefore, I will postpone a full discussion of this problem. At this point I merely want to suggest that a particular grouping is linked to a particular description and therefore is of the nature of a decision rather than of a spontaneous interaction. To illustrate, consider Fig. 3-28, which is surely perceived by everyone as two curved lines *ab* and *cd* crossing one another. It must be understood that this organization is not "given" by the stimulus and that logically one *could* perceive this array as two curved "angles" touching, such as *ac* and *bd* (or *ad* and *bc*). Clearly the preference is for units that are good continuations of one another. All I wish to suggest here is that the executive agency first detects this good continuation, and the decision is then made that those parts that constitute it (e.g., *a* and *b*) belong together as one entity (*ab*).

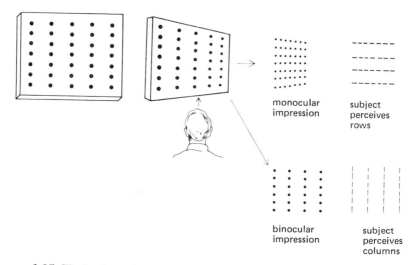

monocular   subject
impression   perceives
                   rows

binocular   subject
impression   perceives
                   columns

3-27. Illustration of the experiment on grouping based on proximity. After Rock and Brosgole, 1964.

This therefore implies that the system describes what is present as "two curved lines crossing at their respective points of inflection" or the like. I will tackle the question of why there is this preference in a later chapter.

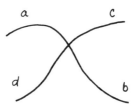

3-28. Illustration of perceptual organization based on good continuation.

THE PROBLEM OF REVERSAL

While, logically, many patterns are potentially reversible and generally with some special effort can in fact be reversed, some seem to reverse spontaneously. These are characterized by the absence of any overpowering determining principle favoring one alternative over the other or by an even balance between such determining principles. For example, in Fig. 3-25 neither region is more surrounded than the other nor contrasts more with the gray around it; in Fig. 2.2, the central region representing a vase is favored by surroundedness, but the outer regions representing faces are probably favored by virtue of their great familiarity, thus resulting in a balance of determining factors. Although this chapter is concerned with form perception, I will also deal here with the family of perspective-reversing figures of which the Necker cube is one case (Fig. 1-3), since the issue of reversal transcends any particular type of pattern. The easy reversibility of the Necker cube is, again, no doubt based on the absence of any strong principle favoring either depth organization. (There is some preference for perceiving the upright rather than the tipped version, but it is not so great as to interfere with reversal.)

The question I would like to pose about reversible figures is this. Is reversal a fact that makes perfect sense given the kind of ambiguity involved and, therefore, a fact not requiring special explanation? If a stimulus can lead equally well to either of two percepts, we should expect instability and change, there being no reason for predicting preference and, therefore, stability. Perhaps so, but the problem would still remain of explaining the critical choice and, more important, of explaining why the reversal occurs when it does. To put the matter differently, one might argue that despite the ambiguity, the executive agency initially "decides" on some basis (perhaps chance) what the stimulus represents. Why then does it not stick to that decision? Something like psychological inertia could equally well be assumed. This issue seems important in the light of the thesis of this chapter, that perception is based on a process of description. If, as I suggested above, when one describes the shape of the black region of Fig. 3-25a, one perceives that region as figure, then psychologically the end product would seem to be the same as when one views Fig. 3-25b and describes its shape. Therefore, once that occurs, why should there be any change? This leads me to believe that reversal is indeed a puzzling problem that does require explanation.

The prevailing theory about reversal is that the neural events that underlie or cause a particular percept undergo satiation (Köhler, 1940; Köhler and Wallach, 1944) or fatigue (Attneave, 1971) with continuing inspection of a pattern. Consequently there is a tendency for that neural event to self-terminate and, in the case of ambiguous patterns where an alternative is available, to be replaced by the neural event that determines the alternative percept. According to this view, reversal is automatic or spontaneous and inexorable.

But does reversal really occur spontaneously? All laboratory studies of this problem employ a method that one might reasonably feel is the only possible one, namely, informing observers of the two alternative percepts and then requesting them to signal every time a reversal occurs. In this way data have been collected indicating the amount and rate of reversal over time. It does not seem to have occurred to anyone that this method not only points out the alternative perceptions to the observer but implicitly suggests that the figure will reverse. Therefore, the findings may be a function of the method. Yet there would seem to be little choice, since if we do not instruct observers about reversibility, how can we expect them to report it so that we can ascertain when and how often it occurs?

We have evolved techniques in our laboratory for circumventing this problem. One such method consists of first creating a set in observers to report any change that might occur while they view figures. In a preparatory series, some figures are not at all ambiguous and some are (but are nothing like the well-known reversible figures or those to be shown to these observers). At the tap of a pencil that comes every 5 seconds, observers are to describe what they are perceiving at that moment, a sampling method first used by Hochberg and McAlister (1953). With those preparatory figures that are essentially nonreversible, therefore, the observers understand that they should go on reporting the same percept throughout. What all this achieves is a state of mind of observers which would lead them to report a change if it occurred but would not necessarily lead them to expect a change to occur. Moreover they are not informed about the alternatives or reversibility of the critical figures. Another method consists simply of presenting the reversible figure with no instructions other than to view it (or fixate a point in some conditions) and describe what is seen. Then directly afterward the observer is carefully questioned about reversal during the exposure period. In this postexposure interview (also used with the previously described method) the alternative percepts are shown unambiguously and the observer is specifically asked whether both had been perceived at any point. It is not difficult to arrive at reliable facts with these methods (Girgus, Rock, and Egatz, 1977).

As can be seen in Table 3-4, a high proportion of observers do not reverse at all even over a 1- or 3-minute inspection period. We used the Rubin vase-face pattern (Fig. 2-2) and a perspective-reversal pattern (that could be seen as a hallway or a truncated pyramid) as critical figures. We also tested certain moving configurations known to lead to frequent reversal of direction in laboratory studies with similar results (Wallach, 1935). By way of control data either the same observers were subsequently shown these very figures with the more traditional instructions or new groups of observers were so tested and the traditional results were obtained: frequent reversal occurred.

Why then did some observers reverse even using our new method? A possible answer is that our observers have, from experience in daily life, some knowledge of and familiarity with reversible figures of the kind tested. Therefore, they are not really fully naive. Another possible answer is that our method does not fully achieve its intended

Table 3-4: Mean First Reversal and Mean Number of Reversals

Experiment	Duration (Seconds)	Figure	Mean Tap at Which First Reversal Was Reported		Mean Number of Reversals Reported			Percentage of Subjects Who Never Reversed	
			Sampling Condition		Sampling Condition		Informed Free		
			Uninformed	Informed	Uninformed	Informed	Responding	Uninformed	Informed
1	30	Vase-Face Figure-Ground Pattern	5.0	1.25	.55	4.25		55	0
2	30	Vase-Face	4.2	1.1	1.2	3.85	6.9	50	0
		Pyramid-Hallway Reversible Perspective Pattern	3.9	1.55	1.5	3.40	7.4	35	0
3	60	Vace-Face	8.5		2.4		9.1	55	
		Pyramid-Hallway	7.4		2.35		9.1	50	
4	180	Vace-Face	17.6	2.65	8.35	15.6		35	0
		Pyramid-Hallway	14.9	3.3	9.75	17.0		35	0

Note: Subjects who did not reverse at all were arbitrarily assigned a score equivalent to the last tap of the pencil, i.e., 6 in Experiment 1, 12 in Experiment 3, and 36 in Experiment 4. After Girgus, Rock, and Egatz (1977).

purpose either because the preparatory series and accompanying instructions do suggest the possibility of perceptual change or because, even with no instructions, the prolonged exposure leads the observers to consider whether some change is not supposed to occur. If so, they begin to search for alternatives, and that changes the equation.

Assuming these reasons are correct, the conclusion seems warranted that potentially reversible figures do *not* spontaneously reverse if the observer is naive with respect to the alternative interpretation. Rather the perceptual system tends to retain the initial description. Precisely why sophisticated observers who are aware of the alternative organization reverse is not entirely clear because such reversals are not simply correlated with voluntary intention to reverse. The deliberate attempt to reverse does not always succeed nor does the deliberate attempt not to reverse necessarily prevent it. The most one can say at this time, therefore, is that the awareness of a highly available alternative leads the system to switch from one description to another.

I am not implying that spontaneous reversal necessarily poses an insurmountable difficulty for a cognitive theory of perception. If it were to occur, one can speculate that it is determined by an altered description rather than by some spontaneous neural switching governed by satiation. But then we would want to know the motive for the change of description. *Psychological* satiation or boredom with the consequent search for novelty could well be that motive. Prolonged exposure to a figure such as we employ in the laboratory in studying reversal is a very unnatural state of affairs. It may thus ultimately lead to a search for something different, particularly if the observers begin to wonder why they are supposed to continue viewing the figure. However, this argument is still compatible with the claim that there is a tendency for a naive observer *to maintain* a particular description, at least up to a point.

ORGANIZATION AND SPECIFIC SHAPE

To avoid the confusing of issues, I have somewhat arbitrarily separated the problem of organization from that of the phenomenal shape that is achieved. To some extent this is justified. For example, we cannot explain the differing appearances of the configurations in Fig. 3-29 by invoking organization. Within each item organization plays a role in yielding one unified whole, and figure-ground organization enters in as well. But such processes do not explain why these figures look the way they do, i.e., have the phenomenal shape they have. That is why I tried to keep the two problems separate. Part of the confusion here may derive from the fact that the Gestalt psychologists used the term "organization" in two ways: one, to refer to the problem of unit formation and two, to refer to the relationship of parts to one another in the formation of wholes. I have restricted my use of the term to the first of these meanings. The second meaning does, of course, directly pertain to the problem of specific shape, but the issue I am now discussing concerns the role of organization qua unit formation and segregation in shape perception.

3-29. Figures whose different phenomenal shapes cannot be explained on the basis of organization defined as unit formation.

Obviously organization often does have much to do with perceived shape. Thus in Fig. 3-28, *ab* is a very different shape from *ac*, and the same can be said about the potential alternatives in all illustrations of grouping and figure-ground organization. The principle here would seem to be this: organization determines what parts in the field are taken collectively as belonging together as a whole, and that whole is then described in terms of its geometry, orientation, and other factors such as those discussed in this chapter. In Fig. 3-29 there is little ambiguity about what the wholes are, but in other cases there is. (One might legitimately argue that the opposite is also true, namely, that the geometrical description determines organization. This argument is based on the theory that perceptual organization is a function of economy or simplicity of description and that such economy is governed by geometrical regularities. This problem will be discussed in Chapter 6.)

PARTS AND WHOLE

However, wholes can have subparts that often maintain some degree of integrity, i.e., natural parts. Therefore, here again organization becomes relevant. Thus in Fig. 3-30 we can see that the two parallel lines tend to be grouped together and apart from the rest of the pattern. That explains why the maintenance of their spatial relationship to one another is more important in characterizing the appearance of the entire figure than the relationship of each of these lines to other parts of the figure. (Figure 3-30*c* appears to be more similar to *a* than does *b*, Goldmeier, 1972.) Therefore, we must amend the above principle to deal with organization and description hierarchically. Consider Fig. 3-31*a*, created by Palmer (1977). There is first of all an overall impression of shape, but in addition, the figure appears to have two subparts, a triangle at the top and an open box at the bottom. Since, logically speaking, no line component physically belongs more with one than with another of the remaining lines, selective organization must be at work here. No doubt factors such as proximity and closure and perhaps even recognition of familiar units are responsible for the perceptual outcome. Needless to say, what is a good part in one configuration is not necessarily a good one in another configuration. In Fig. 3-31*b* it is no longer the case that an open box is a natural part of the whole, although that combination of lines in the same location is still physically present. In any event, we must assume that the description includes the overall pattern and also the subparts.

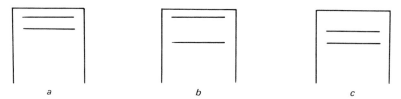

3-30. (a) A standard figure in which organization emphasizes a pair of parallel lines. (b) A comparison figure that alters the spatial relationship between the lines. (c) A comparison figure that preserves the spatial relationship between the lines but alters their overall position. After Goldmeier, 1972.

3-31. The effect of organization on the emergence of certain subparts of whole patterns. After Palmer, 1977.

The point here is not simply that organization can lead to either the phenomenal presence or absence of certain parts in larger configurations, as was shown long ago by Gottschaldt (1929). Rather the point is that organization leads to certain parts and that the overall appearance of the figure is governed by which parts emerge because the description hierarchically includes such parts. It follows that two figures will appear similar if their organization is such as to preserve the same parts and will appear different if that is not the case. Figure 3-32 illustrates the point (Palmer, 1978). The standard figures in the central column look similar to the variants in the left column (which preserve the organization into parts) and different from the variants in the right column (which do not preserve the organization into parts), although the degree of change defined objectively is the same for the two kinds of transformations.

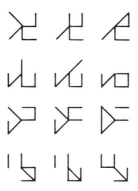

3-32. The standard figures in the center column look similar to those in the left column, which preserve the organization into subparts, and look different from those in the right column, which do not. After Palmer, 1978.

A more general comment about the relationship between parts and wholes is in order here. There has been a great deal of discussion and controversy about the issue ever since the Gestalt psychologists enunciated their famous dictum to the effect that the whole is different from the sum of its parts. If, as was intended, the "whole" referred to here is defined phenomenologically, there can be little argument about the facts, which contemporary theorists no longer question. There simply are no such properties as characterize whole figures or auditory structures such as melodies which are given by the parts or the sum of the parts. One cannot predict the whole from the parts. Thus whole qualities are emergent. There is no reason for materialistically inclined thinkers to recoil from such facts, at least from the standpoint of the approach taken here. The process of description is based on figural relations that are provided by the stimulus but the relations must be noted and described before they acquire psychological realization. The Gestaltists dealt with emergent whole properties in terms of the interaction of parts, which is the second meaning of organization referred to above. As to the relation between parts and wholes, there are two separate issues: is the whole constructed from parts, and does the whole, however constructed, have phenomenally distinct parts? My answer would be that wholes are constructed from the parts and their interrelation, where parts are defined in terms of components of the proximal stimulus, but not all wholes, once constructed, are perceived as containing natural subparts. Consider, for example, a simple figure such as an outline of a circle. It seems plausible to think that in this case we arrive at the perception by integrating the information concerning the relative locations of its constituent parts, namely, the points that make up the retinal image of the circle. But the points do not have the status of parts when the circle is perceived. The same can be said about the perception of the path of a moving point where the information that is integrated is essentially nothing more than a set of locations. Here too the point can describe a path that has no natural parts.

When, however, the figure consists of two lines, as, for example, an angle, not only is it plausible to believe that the whole is built up of two parts, the lines, *and* their interrelationship, but the lines here do seem like natural parts. In this case, then, there is some correlation between what parts constitute the building blocks of the whole and what regions are perceived as parts along with the whole. In any event, the constructive process can be said to be hierarchical; namely, points lead to lines and lines to an angle, and the relationship of angles to a figure such as a triangle. There is then the further step in which the whole affects how the parts appear, but logically that does not imply that the parts were not first processed independently. They simply undergo phenomenal change as part of the processing of the whole. Contrary to widespread opinion, I do not believe that the Gestaltists meant to imply that the whole is not constructed from the parts, only that once the whole emerged, the parts take on contextually based characteristics. The confusion arises partly for this reason and partly because they did argue that certain parts had no psychological reality, as when organization leads to their effective camouflage. But it is not always the case that parts are engulfed in the whole structure.

Some recent research points up the importance and reality of figural parts. Thus, for example, in the so-called impossible figures (Fig. 12-1), it is clearly the information localized at corners that indicates a particular depth organization. The "impossibility" arises out of the incompatibility of the particular depth arrangement cued by all the corners. Similarly investigators building models for computer vision have shown how line junctions and intersections, which after all are localized parts of the whole pattern, can be integrated to arrive at correct three-dimensional interpretations of the entire array (Guzman, 1965; Waltz, 1975). More generally, for figures whose visual angle is sufficiently great, regions in the periphery are too blurred for adequate description so that processing part by part via change of fixation is required (Hochberg, 1970). The description of the whole figure or schema must thus be constructed over time.

A clear example of the reality of both whole and part description and their interaction *in recognition* is illustrated in Fig. 3-33 (Palmer,

1975). When subparts representing features such as the eyes and nose of a face are poorly or inadequately drawn, there is nonetheless no difficulty in identifying them provided that they are seen within the global outline of a face (Fig. 3-33a). Isolated, however, they would not be identifiable (Fig. 3-33b). Drawn in a more careful detail, they are identifiable even without benefit of context (Fig. 3-33c). Conversely, the head outline, which is only poorly represented by a cartoon outline here, undoubtedly benefits by the presence of the parts in their correct locations. In turn, the recognition of the head would benefit by the presence of some representation of a body beneath it.

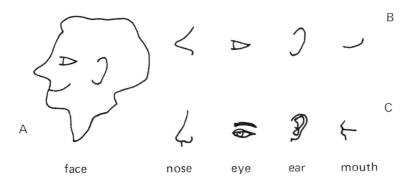

3-33. (a) Poorly drawn features of a face are recognizable in the context of the outline of the head but not (b) out of that context. Well drawn features (c) are recognizable even out of context. After Palmer, 1975.

But we must not lose sight of the fact discussed earlier (pp. 53–56) that the global features are described but fine details and nuances, at least in initial encounters, are not described. Thus the specific shape of one region of the contour of Fig. 3-7 is not adequately perceived. The same is probably true for parts of familiar objects as, for example, the features in faces of animals or members of races with which we do not have a great deal of experience. There is a difficulty about this fact that should be brought out. If, as I have maintained, descriptions of the whole are based hierarchically on prior descriptions of the constitutent parts, then it would seem to follow that all details must in fact be described. Yet the evidence suggests that they are not. One possible resolution of this contradiction would be that the description of the location of all constituent parts relative to one another that occurs at an early stage, preattentively, is superseded by the later description linked to attention that emphasizes global characteristics. Thus the early-stage description drops out and forms no part of the internal representation. Another possibility is that to begin with what is described is first determined by the whole array as scanned by the executive agency. That being the case, detailed spatial relations can be ignored while more global ones are emphasized.

Many of the geometrical illusions suggest a powerful effect of the whole on the description of parts. Admittedly, this kind of general statement does not specifically explain any of the illusions, but it may nonetheless represent a direction worth pursuing. If one thinks of form perception in terms of direct iconic representation, of course it is surprising that two lines in an illusion pattern whose retinal images are of equal size should appear unequal. But if form perception depends upon description, and if context affects description as it evidently does, these illusions are not necessarily anomalous. What is suggested from this approach is that the description as an unconscious process is so intractable that even the instruction to compare two specific lines, which should lead to the isolation and conscious description of their lengths *without* regard to context, cannot overcome it. It is not so surprising that a line that is part of a longer configuration, as in one half of the Müller-Lyer illusion, will assimilate to that whole configuration and lead to a description of size that is some function of the whole.

To sum up, what I have tried to say here about parts and wholes is the following: (1) Wholes are constructed from the parts in the proximal stimulus by a process of description of how the parts relate to one another. (2) Wholes have emergent properties based on these relationships that, by definition, do not inhere in the parts. (3) Wholes may have natural, phenomenal subparts that constitute an important aspect of their appearance, but not all wholes have such phenomenal parts. (4) Natural parts, where they exist, need not necessarily be the same as the parts from which the whole is constructed (for example, in drawings of three-dimensional figures, corners are important building blocks of the whole but are not necessarily perceived as subparts). (5) Wholes modify or even camouflage how parts appear, and this fact bears on 3 and 4. (6) Related to 5 is the fact that the description of wholes may be global, in which details and nuances drop out. (7) The final description has attributes or features that characterize the whole, and thus these features do not inhere in the parts from which the whole is constructed. Therefore, a listing of such attributes should not be confused with a list of features that do inhere in the parts. However, there can be certain features that characterize parts and that do maintain their identity within the whole.

THE PERCEPTION OF THREE-DIMENSIONAL OBJECTS AND
THE PROBLEM OF ORIENTATION RECONSIDERED

The entire focus in this chapter has been on the perception of two-dimensional form despite the fact that the world contains primarily three-dimensional objects. By and large, though, what has been said about two dimensions can easily be extended to the third. Thus it seems probable that few if any entirely new principles need be invoked to deal with object-form perception in daily life. Presumably the shape of each face of an object is described as a two-dimensional structure and depth relations are incorporated into the overall description insofar as they yield spatial relationships about the structure of the object.

When a two-dimensional figure is not in the frontal plane, the description of its shape must incorporate information about how it is oriented. Thus the elliptical retinal representation of a circle at a slant can lead to the perception of a circle if the description is such that all its diameters are equal (shape constancy).

There are, however, one or two points of interest about the orientation of a three-dimensional structure that have emerged in recent research (Rock, DiVita, and Barbeito, 1981). For example, it has been demonstrated that the reversal of a three-dimensional wire figure front to back has no effect on its appearance qua shape and thus no adverse effect on recognition. See Table 3-5, Y-180° and Fig. 3-34, 3-35. The table gives the results of a recognition test in which the orientation of a figure was changed by rotation of 90 or 180 degrees about its X, Y, or Z axis or remained unchanged in orientation (0 degrees). This fact suggests that the front and back of a figure can be thought of as its sides just as can its left and right regions. Accordingly, since left-right reversal has essentially no effect on perceived shape, it would follow that front-back reversal would not either. By contrast, other kinds of change of orientation of these wire figures, such as 90- or 180-degree rotations about a horizontal (X or Z) axis yield the same kinds of phenomenal changes for naive observers as do such transformations in a frontal plane (see Table 3-5).

However, one unexpected finding was the substantial phenomenal change (and thus drop in recognition) produced by 90-degree rotations about a vertical (Y) axis (Fig. 3-34). It had been expected that, since this transformation entailed only shifting around of front, back, left, and right sides with no change in top or bottom, there would be little change in the appearance of the three-dimensional wire objects. With hindsight it is now clear that this effect is based on the major qualitative change in the retinal projection of these figures that occurs with such a rotation. This kind of change does not occur

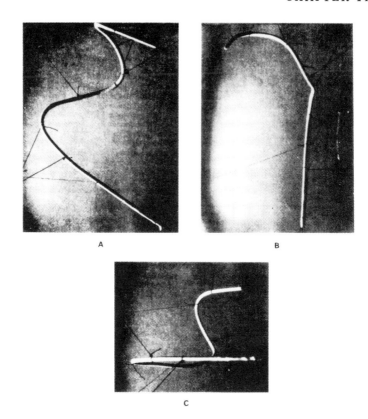

3-34. Separate views of a three-dimensional wire figure used in an experiment by Rock, Di Vita, and Barbeito, 1981. (a) Front view; (b) side view (90 degree Y axis transformation); (c) bottom view (90 degree X axis transformation).

in typical experiments on shape constancy where only a quantitative transformation—i.e., compression of the image along one axis—occurs, nor is it likely that it would have been noted with the solid figures we typically encounter in daily life or in the few laboratory experiments done with solid figures where most of the object is occluded by the front surface.

The fact that the qualitatively different retinal projection affects the perceived shape of the wire object is theoretically important. Since the figures are seen under conditions of adequate depth information, there is no difficulty in recovering the internal spatial relations that characterize the object's shape. Bearing in mind that no part of the figure is hidden, the shape should be described in the same way regardless of the observer's vantage point. Thus it seems necessary to conclude that a dual description occurs, an egocentric

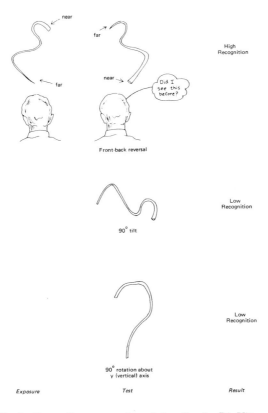

3-35. Illustration of an experiment by Rock, Di Vita, and Barbeito, 1981, showing the appearance of the figure and the results for a front-back reversal (180 degree rotation about the Y axis), a 90-degree rotation about the Z axis, and a 90-degree rotation about the Y axis.

one based very much on the retinal projection of the figure and an objective one that transcends the momentary retinal projection and refers only to the object.

This last conjecture relates to a fact about orientation not taken up in the brief discussion of this problem earlier in the chapter. Contrary to what was implied there, it is not always true that change of a figure's retinal orientation has no effect on its appearance, as when the observer views an upright object from a tilted position. For material such as printed or written words and pictures of faces, there is great difficulty in recognition under such conditions even though there is no change in the assignment of direction.

To explain this kind of effect, I have speculated that the perceptual system (or rather the executive agency) strives to achieve a description of a figure on the basis of the figure's true top, bottom, and sides and

Table 3-5: Recognition of Three-Dimensional Wire Figures

		X		Y		Z		
	$0°$	$90°$	$180°$	$90°$	$180°$	$90°$	$180°$	New
No. of Yes Responses ($N = 28$)	23	6	17	12	24	13	16	86*
% of Yes Responses	82	21	61	43	86	46	57	22

Test Orientation spans the X, Y, Z columns.

Note: $X = X$ axis; $Y = Y$ axis; $Z = Z$ axis.
*$N = 392$ for new figures (14 figures/subject $\times$ 28 subjects).

that this occurs in all kinds of figures. The reason I say "strives" is that there seems to be a primitive tendency to describe shape on the basis of the directions directly given by the retinal (or egocentric) coordinates. Since the true directions of a figure are generally provided by other information concerning what is up and down in the environment, these directions will not coincide with the retinal-egocentric ones unless the observer is upright. Therefore, the description based on the retinal-egocentric coordinates must be replaced and superseded by a description based on the environmental coordinates. Ordinarily, for a single relatively simple figure, this process is effortlessly and easily achieved. But for certain material, it is not. Thus the observer is left with the inappropriate retinally based description (Rock, 1973).

Therefore, we have here another example of description based on the retinal (and thus egocentric) state of affairs similar to the one that occurs with three-dimensional wire figures rotated about a vertical axis. In both cases, there is a difficulty in recovering or achieving a description of a structure in terms of its objective properties because another description intervenes that is governed by the egocentric relation of the object to the observer. In both cases it would seem necessary to say that a dual description occurs.

Perception and Recognition

At the beginning of this chapter I distinguished the problem of form perception from that of categorization or recognition. Typically, however, the objects we see are familiar, so that along with the perception of an object's form there also is recognition and identification or categorization of what kind of object it is. Granted that perception and recognition can be and should be distinguished—one can have perception without recognition, and even when an object is identified, the perception as such can be said to remain unchanged—it seems to me that the theory of description advocated here brings them closer together. The description that underlies form perception predicates certain properties about the object; e.g., it is "round" or "elongated" or the like. If so, that is a kind of categorization.

The descriptive categorizing that occurs in form perception often will pertain only to aspects of the whole object, whereas the categorization that occurs in recognition will always refer either to the whole object or to identifiable parts of it. Moreover the perceptual categorization is presumably not dependent on past experience, whereas recognition categorizing is by definition a function of past experience. So there are clear differences. Nonetheless we can view form perception and recognition as very similar processes. Both have the status of propositional descriptions and both entail categorization. When a familiar object is perceived, it is plausible to suppose that the following sequence occurs: (1) The object qua form is described. (2) Via similarity of the description, previously encountered objects stored in memory are accessed, if such exist. If not, the process ends there. (3) The accessed memories lead to a further description of the object in terms of the properties of the known category, e.g., "it is a dog." In other words, there is a double description. But the second description does not displace the first, as some theorists seem to imply (although it might have a differential weighting in retention). The two together are important, with the first very much a function of the stimulus. Thus the dog that is perceived and recognized is specific in shape, perspective, and the like.

In certain cases, however, the form description itself depends upon recognition, as was brought out in Example 3 in Chapter 1 (the fragmented figure) and in the discussion of ambiguous figures earlier in this chapter. Initially, a hard-to-recognize configuration will therefore be described directly on the basis of its geometry, principles of organization, and orientation. Once identified, however, the form description is different and corresponds to the characteristics of the identified object as seen from a certain perspective. This kind of effect, for which I have suggested the term recognition-perception, may be far more general than I have implied thus far. In examples such as fragmented figures or reversals of certain ambiguous figures the process is drawn out in time so that we can directly experience the change from one perception to another. Another example of this kind is the initial difficulty we sometimes have in deciphering a cursively written word. Then suddenly we do identify it. All the letters are now perceived, whereas at the outset they were not. But logically it seems to me that any time we cannot expect an object or picture to look the way it does without recognition we have a case of recognition-perception. Thus, the drawings in Fig. 3-36 are deliberately made without any of the known pictorial cues such as perspective, interposition, and attached shadow. Therefore, it is plausible to suppose that observers not familiar with the objects represented would not perceive these figures the way we do. We perceive them as appropriately three-dimensional. The same kind of effect may occur even with the objects themselves and not merely with pictures of them. If true, there are many cases in daily life where the perception of three-dimensional form depends upon a description that derives from recognition. It follows that there are stages of processing of which we are unaware and which must include a stage where the object is first described in terms of stimulus properties and the like and only then, on the basis of similarity, is the memory accessed that accounts for the further description.

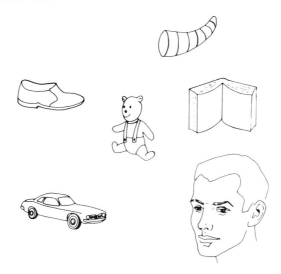

3-36. Drawings made to eliminate or minimize the known pictorial cues to depth, such as perspective, interposition, and shadow. After Rock, 1975.

Modes of Description

Perception has the character of reference to external things and events, of intentionality in the language of philosophy. Therefore, the description that underlies typical perception in daily life is couched in "language" that is appropriate to the external state of affairs. This fact is perhaps most clearly evident in cases that we refer to as entailing constancy because, while stimulation is variable (and thus earlier investigators said that sensation was variable) the percept is not. We thus continue to describe the object in terms that refer to *it* as an unchanging entity, at least when constancy is fully achieved.

But when we discuss the problem of constancy in greater detail in Chapter 9, I will argue that there is another mode of description that closely parallels the varying stimulus. To anticipate, I will argue, as some others have in the past, that there is a description that gives a relatively faithful account of the proximal stimulus even at the same time as there is a dominant description that is faithful to the outer object. If the latter were to be called the constancy mode, the former might be called the proximal mode. Since, however, "constancy mode" is somewhat restrictive, referring as it does only to situations where constancy is achieved, I will use the more general term "world mode" to include all description that aims at the outer state of affairs and does not in any way refer to the characteristics of the stimulus as such.

Form perception is primarily based on world mode description, but then one might want to distinguish two- and three-dimensional world mode description. If so, most of this chapter has been concerned with the two-dimensional world mode, although three-dimensional object perception was discussed as well. However, a few examples were considered where a dual description seems to occur, namely, in viewing certain kinds of upright figures from a tilted or inverted position of one's body or in viewing three-dimensional wire figures. In these cases, I argued that in addition to the effort at recovery of the objective structure in the environment by the appropriate world mode description there is another description that is based on the specific character of the retinal projection. It might be appropriate, therefore, to refer to the latter description as in the proximal mode. There is reason for believing that the proximal mode description comes first and the world mode description is based upon it (see Chapter 9).

While I have not discussed the special case of picture perception, it seems to me that still another mode of description is relevant here, namely, the pictorial mode. It is not necessary to introduce this further complication for those cases of drawings or pictures in which the thing represented is essentially two-dimensional, as with many of the illustrations in this chapter. In such cases we can consider the drawing itself to be the object under consideration. But where the drawing is meant to represent something else, for example, a three-dimensional object or scene, the distinction is necessary. For then we do have a dual awareness of the picture, namely, *as* a two-dimensional entity on paper or canvas and *as* the three-dimensional entity or entities it represents. Thus I would refer to the pictorial mode and the world mode of description as occurring simultaneously in viewing such pictures.

Whenever in world or pictorial mode perception the object, array, or event is known, there is a final description that refers to category. Therefore, we can speak of a final, interpretive mode of description that is appended to and integrated with the other modes of description.

The Process of Description Summarized

It may be helpful at this point to summarize all that has been said about the process of form description and to try to suggest what the sequence of events might be like. It seems to me to be premature to aim for a precise algorithm or mathematical formulation of the process. Instead I will rough in the stages or aspects of the process that might be assumed to be necessary. The sequence suggests a hierarchical ordering in which later stages presuppose and, in some cases, supersede earlier ones.

1. The locations of the points that constitute the figure or its boundaries are detected. Any form of demarcation is suitable, whether it be actual stimulation by a contour or binocular disparity among otherwise undetectable contours or the like. The information for location may derive from local sign on the retina or the egocentric localization of each figural point taking account of eye position.

2. From this information, the location of these constituent points relative to one another is derived.

3. Decisions are made by the cognitive apparatus as to which such points belong to one another as parts of larger units (organization).

4. The spatial or geometrical relationships of these larger units is then described, more likely by parallel rather than serial processing. This description entails emergent properties that come into existence by virtue of spatial relationships as, for example, parallel or converging sides and symmetry. Where a region is organized as "closed," the description encompasses solid surfaces rather than simply perimeter contours, and shapes emerge that characterize such surfaces. For example, a region can become convex or concave where the contour of it, in and of itself, cannot. The contour becomes an edge. Such descriptive processes entail attention or perhaps are synonymous with attention.

5. Natural parts, if any, that emerge via selective organizational processes are described as parts but also in terms of how they fit into the whole. Not all figures have such natural parts.

6. The process of description includes reference to the orientation of the figure in relation to the directional coordinates of space. Whether this process occurs simultaneously with those in 4 and 5 or only after is not clear. The description achieved has the character of a two- or three-dimensional world mode, which in some cases is based on a prior, proximal mode.

7. Certain aspects of description can be salient, and description is often in terms of closeness to or distance from certain singular values such as "verticality," "symmetry," and "straightness," Conversely, at least in initial exposure to figures, subtle nuances of complex shapes or nonsalient dimensions such as left vs. right sides will not be included in the description. With repeated exposure and attention to such features, they ultimately are described.

8. Where the phenomenal shape thus achieved is one that is known, the further description of it as belonging to a category occurs (the interpretive mode).

9. In certain cases, where identification occurs, a perceptual rede-

scription of the figure may occur as well. The figure is then described as the identified object would be described (recognition-perception).

Final Comments on the Nature of Description

A theory of form perception must do justice both to the fact of the infinite variability of shape and to the similarities and differences among shapes. The spatial relationships that are so fundamental in characterizing form simply cannot be accounted for by a sum of parts or features, although such features may be present, because it is their spatial juxtaposition that is crucial. While such features may exist as natural parts of figures, that hardly means that the figure is nothing more than the sum of them. Besides, in the most general case of an irregular novel figure there may not even be such easily identifiable features.

One confusion here may be with the meaning of "feature." A feature could refer to an identifiable part or unit that must first be extracted or detected and then along with other features assembled into an overall pattern. Or "feature" could refer to an identifiable emergent characteristic of the form once it is achieved rather than as one of the parts that produces it. Here is where the experiment on tracking a point moving along a simple path becomes crucial because, in this situation, there are no proximal-stimulus features such as contours or corners or other parts that could be said to be "givens." There is only a set of directions. Therefore, in this case and, to some extent, in general, some features of a figure achieve psychological reality only at the same time that the figure as a whole emerges in experience. In other cases it does seem necessary and correct to say that a figure is constructed from subparts or features that therefore have an independent reality.

Therefore, we can talk about certain characteristics of the description that can be isolated and thought of as potential "units" in the description of any figure, for example, whether the edges are curved or straight, whether the figure is open such as a line per se or closed and thereby described as a solid thing, whether it is elongated or compact, what the orientation is of its main axis, and whether it has many sides or few. The geometrical relationships among parts can perhaps be thought of as units of description, such as parallelism or convergence of sides. Certain relationships *between* figural relationships must enter into the description. But to repeat, these are features that characterize the figure and should not be thought of as parts that can be put together to yield the whole. It is also likely that the perceptual system makes use of "ideal forms" and describes in terms of the presence of these with or without transformation (Bregman, 1977). Thus, for example, a parallelogram could conceivably be described by a child unfamiliar with it as a rectangle with slanted sides on opposite ends. To some extent, therefore, description may make use of contents provided by prior experience.

In any event the problem is to account for our immediate perception of the shape of a completely novel figure, our ability to discriminate it from virtually all other shapes and to store it in memory with an impressive degree of faithfulness. If such perception cannot be based on a list of features and if, as I have implied in this chapter, it cannot be done justice by assuming that the correlate is simply an internal analog "picture" based on the retinal "picture," then there would seem to be no viable alternative to a theory of structural description. One advantage of such a theory is that an infinite number of descriptions can be generated. Moreover the problem of similarity and dissimilarity can be dealt with in terms of the similarity and dissimilarity of descriptions, as has been discussed here in connection with various examples.

On the other hand, there are certainly many difficulties with the theory. Can a description do justice to our perception of a shape as, for example, that shown in Fig. 3-6 such that a memory is established accurately enough to enable us later to discriminate it from various similar shapes? It would have to be a very complex description with a good deal of geometrical "precision" incorporated into it. However, if the percept and memory of it were based on a pictorial analog, this particular problem would not arise, one "picture" truly being worth a thousand "words." So, for example, in the case of Fig. 3-6, the description would be something like the following: "a closed, curvilinear shape with an elongated, pointed, horizontally oriented protrusion at the top and a rounded, compact region to one side at the bottom, etc." Notice that the description as far as it goes is not precise enough to specify the shape of the figure.

THE ROLE OF THE STIMULUS

If the determinant of perceived shape is the description based on the stimulus and not the stimulus per se, it would seem to follow that we can dispense with the stimulus once it leads to the description or if we can achieve an appropriate description without it. Something of this sort may happen in dreaming. We perceive things in dreams, but the experience is certainly not exactly like that of waking object perception. The shape of a path achieved in tracking a moving point and the related anorthoscopic paradigm (to be discussed in Chapter 7) approaches this state of affairs in that the stimulus is little more than a moment-to-moment indicator of how to proceed with the description of the figure being revealed. Still one may wonder whether a stimulus-free description, i.e., one achieved without the customary iconic representation, could yield a percept that would be the phenomenological equivalent in every respect of a description under the typical conditions. Of course, one reason why it might differ is that the stimulus allows the description to achieve a high degree of specificity and precision that would be difficult to achieve in its absence.

One might conclude, therefore, that the only role of the proximal stimulus of the object is to make possible the complex structural description, since without the stimulus, that would hardly be possible. This is indeed a legitimate argument that follows from the description theory as thus far elaborated.

While this function of the stimulus is a necessary one, I would argue that it is not sufficient to fully account for perception. What characterizes perception and distinguishes it from other cognitive processes such as imagining is its rootedness in the stimulus. This point will be developed further in subsequent chapters where the focus is on examples of perceptual problem solving. To anticipate, however, the claim is made that perception must be supported by the stimulus. For a particular solution to the problem posed by a stimulus to be viable, certain components must be present in the stimulus (see Chapter 5, pp. 120-125, for a discussion of the concept of *stimulus support*).

I will argue, therefore, that in form perception the stimulus plays the further role of supporting the description to which it gives rise. Without it, the phenomenological quality of form *perception* would be lacking and the description, assuming it could be accurately maintained, would only be capable of yielding imagery or dreams or memory manifestations, i.e., recognition, visualization, and the like. This necessary role of the stimulus may explain why form perception has a sensory or pictorial quale which would be lacking were the propositional description the only cause of such perception.

This last point leads to an interesting implication of the description theory for certain facts about memory. If, in recognition, access to a memory depends upon similarity of the perceived percept to a previous one and if perception is based on description, it follows that memory access depends upon similarity of description. Consider then the problem of accessing a memory of a visual form or an auditory pattern such as a melody. If presented with a familiar face or several bars of music, we can assume that one achieves an adequate description because the stimulus is present just as it was on the prior occasion. Thus the description can be as detailed as is necessary and it will match that stored in memory. But no such possibility exists when we must recall or reproduce the face or the melody. In that case only associative redintegration can lead to access to the qualitative characteristics of the memory structure. Recall by association may be adequate where all that is required is to evoke a single unit from memory, for example, a name. But when a complex structure must be evoked, perhaps only the perception of that structure can lead to the nuances of description that can access it via similarity.

Another difficulty with the theory concerns the units or language or concepts used in the description. These would have to be analogous to those we would employ were we to give the description in natural language. In the example above, concepts such as "elongated" and "horizontal" are employed. We must then assume that such concepts are therefore available in some internal lexicon. Whatever may be their origin and their nature, it seems plausible to me that they are the same as those that constitute the language of thought in general. That is, whatever the concepts are that underlie thinking, whether in animals, children, or adults—and which must preexist if a natural language is to be learnable at all—these same concepts may be those that are used in the process of describing forms. But since we know next to nothing about the language of thought, we can say little more at this time about the units of perceptual description.

4

Perception as Problem Solving:
i. Solution Finding

SOME BUT NOT ALL EXAMPLES of perception appear to be the end result of a process very like problem solving. In the case of form perception, as we have seen, "description" would seem to be an appropriate designation of the hypothetical cognitive event underlying the phenomenal outcome. It would seem to be inappropriate to invoke the designation of "problem solving" because, by and large, there is no problem to be solved. The processes of description can run their course in a relatively straightforward fashion guided by the proximal stimulus and internalized principles of organization. There are other kinds of perception where it would also be inappropriate to speak of "problem solving."

What characterizes examples where it *does* seem appropriate to do so is first of all their qualitative ambiguity. The stimulus in these cases can be perceived in different ways. Often too, there is some delay before arriving at the perception. That in turn means that one percept occurs at the outset and only later gives way to another. For example, for observers who have never seen a drawing of the kind shown in Fig. 4-1, it is probable that it will look like an abstract design containing rectangles of varying shades of gray. However, with continued viewing or with the suggestion that it can be seen as a partially transparent inner rectangle in front of a black and white background, most observers will perceive it in that way. The smaller rectangle then appears to be of uniform color through which one sees the colors of the background rectangle.

The difference between such cases and those entailing only form perception would seem to be this. Once the form is perceived, in the most typical case of a novel figure, there is no possibility for further perceptual change. The proximal stimulus does not represent anything else other than what is described at the outset. Therefore, while the literal percept is achieved, the processing stops there. Even if the executive agency were to search for a different solution, none would occur.

4-1. Transparency display. After Metelli, 1974.

The Literal Percept and the Preferred Percept

The initial percept, which I will call the *literal percept*, is generally one that is in close correspondence with the proximal stimulus; the final percept is not directly correlated with the proximal stimulus but often is correlated with the distal state of affairs. The final percept is preferred, and once it occurs it usually persists. The initial, literal percept is generally of the kind I have described as in the two-dimensional world mode. It is a perception of something in the world but typically is two-dimensional. The final or preferred percept is generally of the kind I have described as the three-dimensional world mode. It is of a three-dimensional object, array, or scene in the world.

Achieving the literal percept requires perceptual organization and description of the resulting units in the manner discussed in the preceding chapter. However, given the tendency of the perceptual system to apply certain principles of organization—whatever may be the basis of this tendency—the literal percept is achieved quickly and more or less universally. Thus, for example, a dark compact region on a light background will initially be perceived as "figure." I will argue that whether or not this literal percept is consciously experienced prior to the final one, there is a stage in the sequence of processing in which it occurs.

It is surprising that the existence of a stage of perception of the kind I here call literal has not been noted before, at least as a theoretically important fact. It is a pervasive phenomenon, and the evidence on which it is based has been known in most laboratories around the world for some time, but for some reason it has been overlooked. For example, investigators know that the transparency effect is not necessarily immediate or that the kinetic depth effect takes some time to develop, and certainly everyone knows that fragmented figures are not recognized right away, to give a few examples. Therefore, before these perceptions develop, the observer is perceiving something else, and that something else is in closer correspondence with the proximal stimulus. To be sure, theorists have speculated about what might occur in the development of a percept, whether it be a stage of analysis of features or of accessing of relevant memories, but the presence of a different perception on the way to the achievement of the final perception has been ignored.

What this analysis suggests is that the final or preferred percept is of the nature of a preferred *solution*, but first that solution must be "found" by the perceptual system. Something must suggest or lead to it as a hypothesis. In this chapter I will emphasize this aspect of perceptual problem solving, i.e., the aspect of finding or arriving at the preferred solution. It will try to give evidence in support of such a hypothetical process. In the next chapter I will discuss what must then happen if that solution, once "suggested," is to be accepted, i.e., is to lead to an enduring, viable percept. In a subsequent chapter I will take up the problem of preference.

Solution From Below

In some cases it would seem that there is a "clue" or independent source of information within the literal percept that suggests the final, preferred solution. I will refer to such cases as evidencing "solution from below." Alternatively, in more current terminology, one might describe these cases as "data driven" (Lindsay and Norman, 1972). On the other hand, in some cases there does not seem to be any such isolable factor within the literal percept. Therefore, I will refer to these cases as illustrating "solution from above." Again, in more current terminology, one might describe such cases as "hypothesis driven."

"Solution from below" and "solution from above" are terms that were introduced to describe a distinction Karl Duncker made in analyzing problem solving in the domain of thought (Duncker, 1945). In some cases the presence of an object or attention to an object suggests a solution. For example, there is the well-known problem of how to deal with an inoperable stomach tumor by radiation without damaging the healthy tissue surrounding it. One solution is to use converging rays no one of which is itself too strong but the combined impact of which on the tumor is substantial. Duncker found that when the problem is presented with a sketch in which a lens is shown (Fig. 4-2), significantly more subjects solve the problem. Of course, the lens in the sketch is strictly speaking irrelevant and is not serving the purpose of converging rays onto the tumor. Nonetheless its presence must play the role of suggesting the possibility of using converging rays in the solution, although the subject may remain unaware of this fact. Duncker called this "problem solving from below."

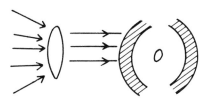

4-2. Sketch of the tumor problem. After Duncker, 1945.

Another example of this effect in the literature is a finding concerning the well-known two-cord problem (Maier, 1931). The problem is to tie together two suspended strings that are too far apart to be grasped simultaneously (Fig. 4-3). The solution is to make one string into a pendulum by attaching a weight at the bottom, setting it into motion, and grasping it as it swings inward while holding the other string. It was found that the solution can be facilitated if the experimenter "accidentally" brushes against one string, setting it into slight motion. Apparently, seeing a string in motion suggests the solution, although the subject is generally not conscious at all of the role of this "clue."

4-3. Sketch of the two-cord problem. After Maier, 1931.

In solution "from above," no externally present object or event triggers the solution. Rather, the problem is analyzed in terms of its requirements and subjects then search their memory for the appropriate object to achieve that requirement. Thus, in the tumor problem the subject might entertain various "functional solutions" and finally arrive at the formulation "find a way to concentrate heavy radiation at the tumor only." Given that requirement, the subject might or might not think of using a lens.

Perhaps then, in perceptual problem solving, a clue (such as a recognizable part in a fragmented figure) leads to solution "from below." Without such clues, the system analyzes the problem "from above" and formulates the requirements to be met. For example, "What event in the world could produce a line segment simultaneously changing its length and orientation?" There are two possible solutions here, a two-dimensional line changing in these ways or a line rotating in the third dimension, but there is a clear preference for the nonliteral one, at least once its possibility is realized.

4-4. Illusory contour figure. After Kanizsa, 1955.
4-5. Weak illusory contour figure.

A good illustration of solution from below is that of the perception of a figure with illusory contours (Fig. 4-4.). Ordinarily, one seems immediately to perceive these figures, but by making conditions somewhat less "good" (Fig. 4-5), the delay can easily be shown to occur. Methods of revealing the delay are easily achieved as, for example, separating the corner fragments more than is usually done, using naive observers who have never seen this kind of effect, and not hinting that the pattern can be seen differently than it is at the outset. Moreover, as the following analysis will show, even when the effect seems immediate, there is good reason for believing it is the end result of a prior stage in which a different perception occurs first.

The fact is that in a pattern such as that of Fig. 4-5 we have every reason for predicting that the initial percept will be of three incomplete circles, each figure on the common ground (the literal percept). The figure-ground principle of surroundedness leads to this prediction: each of the three figures is surrounded by white regions. The perception of the inner region as a white triangle overlapping the three corner fragments of circles, which then become amodally complete circles, therefore requires a figure-ground reversal that ordinarily would not be expected to occur. The question of interest, therefore, is what leads to this change.

There are probably several factors that can play this role. One is undoubtedly the fact that the circular fragments are incomplete circles and therefore suggest to the perceptual system the possibility that something is covering them in each corner (Fig. 4-5). Another is the alignment of the edges of the missing corners of the circles, i.e., the edges across any two corners. We have shown in our laboratory that when unfamiliar irregular fragments are used (Fig. 4-6), so that incompletion can hardly be a factor, significantly more naive observers perceive the inner triangle figure when these edges are aligned then when they are not (Figure 4-6a vs. 4-6b and Table 4-1). However, when these edges are not aligned, most observers do perceive the triangle when incomplete circles are used (Fig.4-6c). Therefore, *both* incompletion and alignment are factors that can elicit the hypothesis of a figure present in what at first is the central "ground" space (Rock and Anson, 1979).

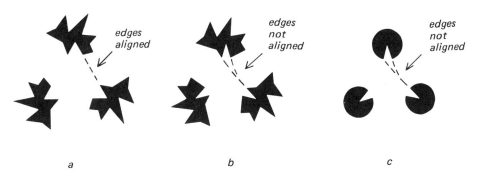

4-6. (a) Illusory contour figure with corner edges aligned. (b) Same illusory contour figure with corner edges not aligned. (c) Illusory contour figure with corner edges in incomplete circles not aligned. After Rock and Anson, 1979.

It is interesting to note that the edges across corner fragments need not be aligned even with unfamiliar shapes as fragments (see Fig. 4-6b) *once the observer is aware of the possibility of perceiving the center triangle, as the reader now is.* So "set" or "knowledge" is still a third relevant factor in eliciting a hypothesis. The triangle then appropriately appears to have curved edges. But without such a set, few observers achieve the triangle percept in this case, i.e., a display without either incompletion or alignment. Without any

Table 4-1: Perception of Illusory Figures

Condition	N	No. Perceiving Figure	%
Irregular Fragments Aligned	20	15	75%
Irregular Fragments Not Aligned	20	6	30%
Incomplete Circle Not aligned	20	18	90%

of these factors, there would seem to be no information that can elicit the necessary hypothesis. There is a parallel here with what can happen in actual problem solving. One may not think of the solution oneself—since this requires "finding it" so to speak—but one can easily understand the solution once it is given. The fact that neither alignment nor incompletion is necessary to perceive a figure with illusory contours serves to substantiate the claim made here that their role in the problem-solving process is one of cluing the solution.

At any rate, we see in this example that a literal percept does occur first. We also see how certain features of that percept can suggest a different percept. Finally we see that once the second percept is entertained, it is preferred and moreover it is difficult to revert to the initial one.

As a second example, consider the perception of fragmented figures such as was discussed in previous chapters (Figs. 1-4 and 4-7a). I need hardly prove that many of these figures are difficult to recognize for an observer who has not seen them before. Perhaps this will now be the case for at least some readers. Typically, there is a long delay even when one finally succeeds. On the other hand, it was demonstrated many years ago that the *re*-recognition of these figures is easily and rapidly achieved (Leeper, 1935). That is, once having recognized one of these figures, when it is seen again it is now recognized immediately. Although I am using the term "recognition," that is only the end result of the appropriate *perception*. In the first encounter, then, some factor or factors must lead *from* an initial perception, a "nonsense organization," *to* an altered perception which is then recognized, the "recognition-perception organization." Once that has occurred, however, the transition is virtually immediate, as is evidenced in the instant recognition that occurs when the figure is seen again. Yet, logically, it must be the case that even here there is a transition from the nonsense to the recognition percept. At the outset of the second encounter, memory cannot be brought to bear on what is perceived until something is perceived to access a particular memory.

But what I want to focus on now is the question of what leads to the transition during the first encounter. One possible answer is that in the process of examining the figure in an effort to identify it, the observer perceives and identifies a part. That in turn can serve as a clue to the whole. Thus, for example, in Fig. 4-7 there is a part that looks like part of a wheel. To test this, we performed the following experiment. The figures were modified so as to eliminate as a distinct part that fragment which we guessed might be critical. For example, we eliminated that wheel as shown in Fig. 4-7b, or the figure was also modified but in this case so as to facilitate the role of the same part, by improving it. For example, we made the part even more like a wheel (see Fig. 4-7c). Thus these modified figures should either hamper the perceptual transition to recognition or facilitate it. Needless to say, a given observer was shown only one or the other of these modified drawings for any given figure. The task for the observer was simply to identify each figure in the series.

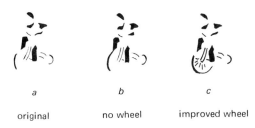

a

b

c

original   no wheel   improved wheel

4-7. (a) Original fragmented figure of child on tricycle. (b) Figure modified to eliminate part of the wheel. (c) Figure modified to improve wheel.

The result was that there were far fewer successes for modified figures of the first kind and more success than for the original for modified figures of the second kind. For the figures that were recognized in the 60 seconds allowed, reaction time was fastest for the improved figures and slowest for the impoverished figures (see Table 4-2). Note again that, as was true for the illusory contour figure, there is no difficulty in recognizing Fig. 4-7b given the knowledge that the reader has of what it represents even though there is no recognizable part here. This fact underscores once again the point that the first stage is the elicitation of the correct hypothesis and that, for this to occur in the case of fragmented figures, the perception and recognition of a part seems to be an important de-

Table 4-2: Recognition of Fragmented Figures

Type of Figure	N	Number of Recognitions	In %	Mean Reaction Time† In Seconds
Original Figure	72*	52	72%	12
Modified with Part Obliterated	72*	39	54%	19.2
Modified with Part Enhanced	144*	122	85%	8.5

*Based on 12 subjects, 6 figures per subject or 24 subjects in the case of the enhancement condition.

†Based only on figures recognized within the 60 seconds allowed.

terminant. Another determinant is obviously "knowledge," "set," or the like. Given the latter, the part is no longer necessary.

Precisely how recognition of a part can lead to reorganization and recognition of the whole we do not know. After all, it is not enough to say that "wheel" leads to the idea of "tricycle." The final percept is not merely one of identifying what category of object the figure represents, the interpretive mode. It is also one of perceiving a particular drawing of a tricycle (in fact a child on a tricycle) from a particular perspective (the three-dimensional world mode) in which each part plays its appropriate role. But this kind of question is not the one I wish to investigate in this chapter. Before concluding with this example, I might point out that in one respect it is different from many other situations in perception in that observers are *consciously* searching for a solution. Perhaps that is because they are told to try to identify the figure. Without this set, given the difficulty of these figures, there would be few cases of successful recognition of most of them. A recent experiment has established precisely this fact (Reynolds, 1983). But, more generally, I would argue that there is an active search for a solution other than the literal one, conscious or unconscious, even in the case of solution from below where clues may serve to elicit it.

In any event, we again see the stages in the process outlined earlier. At first the literal percept occurs which is region for region in close correspondence with the fragmented stimulus. Then a clue leads to a second, preferred solution from which time on the sequence is no longer reversible.

The next example is that of anorthoscopic perception discussed briefly in the preceding chapter. In the case where a figure moves behind a stationary slit in an opaque surface, with the kind of simple unfamiliar curvilinear figure we use in our laboratory (Fig. 4-8), the subject often begins by perceiving a small dark element moving vertically up and down the slit, the literal percept. This is essentially what is taking place on the retina. There is good reason for predicting that this is what will be perceived under these conditions, namely, the fact that lines moving behind a large aperture tend to be seen as moving in the direction of the longer axis of such an aperture (Wallach, 1935). Nonetheless, after a while, some observers will suddenly perceive a line figure moving at right angles to and behind the aperture, the anorthoscopic effect. Let us assume that the eyes remain stationary in viewing the slit, so that the change in perception cannot be explained in terms of a spreading of the figure's image over the retina. In point of fact, this assumption is justified (see Chapter 7, pp. 176-191).

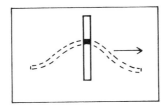

4-8. Anorthoscopic display. The curved-line figure is seen part at a time through a narrow slit in the opaque surface.

What might lead to this transformation from the literal to the veridical perception? We have isolated certain factors in our laboratory. One such factor is the visibility of the ends of the figure. When neither end of the figure is visible, the stimulus is logically ambiguous: it could represent, literally, a small element moving vertically and simultaneously changing slope, or it could represent a small part of an extended figure moving horizontally. When, however, an end is in view, and provided that the slit width is great enough for both the element and gap to be detected, at that moment the information is not ambiguous (Fig. 4-9). The end of the figure is a distinct region that can then be seen to be moving horizontally. The perception of horizontal motion of the figure is of course the condition sine qua non for the perception of an extended line figure. We have found that when the ends of the figure are not visible, as when the figure is made to reverse its direction before its end comes into view, few observers see a line figure unless certain other kinds of information are provided that require a wider slit.

This factor, visibility of the ends of the figure, is a clear example of independent information that can elicit the necessary hypothesis for perceptual change. As noted above, the basis of it is fairly obvious. Yet it is interesting to realize that this information is present

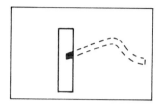

4-9. Anorthoscopic display using a wider slit to ensure perception of ends of the figure.

only for brief moments during the total period of observation. This means that it is information that suggests a certain perception which must then be able to sustain itself over time. One does have the impression that each successive view of the end of the figure revives or supports the percept just at the moment when it might otherwise be about to change back to the initial literal percept.

While I am claiming that seeing the ends of a figure is a hypothesis-eliciting clue, it does not suffice for the anorthoscopic effect. Other factors—to be considered in a subsequent chapter—are important. But without sight of the ends of the figure, some of these other determinants will not suffice to suggest to naive subjects the anorthoscopic-figure hypothesis. Once again, however, subjects who are aware of the possibility of the figure solution do not need to see the ends of it to achieve that percept.

These are the clearest examples I can think of and for which we have evidence of stimulus factors that, via the literal solution, can play the role of cluing a particular solution. There are undoubtedly others. For example, in viewing pictures that can be perceived as three-dimensional, there may well be certain components that suggest three-dimensionality without which a literal, two-dimensional perception would occur. For example, the contour indicating a horizon separating ground from sky may be such a clue in an otherwise poor drawing of a landscape. Or components such as the vertices of three-dimensional figures isolated by investigators working in the field of artificial intelligence may play this role (Gúzman, 1969; Clowes, 1971). Figure 4-10 is an interesting example. It may appear two-dimensional at first but often reverses to a three-dimensional structure. This is theoretically interesting because there are reasons for predicting preference for the two-dimensional solution, namely, the symmetry and regularity of this form as a two-dimensional structure (see Chapter 6, p. 146). But there are components here that are often part of three-dimensional figures, such as the vertices and larger subparts isolated in Fig. 4-11 a and b, respectively. These parts could serve as such clues.

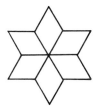

4-10. Ambiguous figure that can be seen two- or three-dimensionally. After Woodworth, 1938.

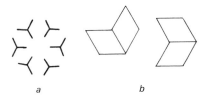

a   *b*

4-11. Components of Figure 4-10 that could serve as clues to three-dimensional perception.

Solution from Above

What all these examples have in common is the presence in the literal initial percept of a clue, i.e., a component or transformation that can play the role of "suggesting" the perceptual solution that then occurs. The criterion that establishes a clue as one that can lead to solution from below would seem to be independent information isolable from those aspects of the stimulus that are absolutely crucial for the preferred solution. By and large that clue will be unambiguous. The clue emerges as part of the literal solution. The test that a factor is such a clue is its dispensability. In other words, given knowledge of some other kind and thus given a sophisticated observer, the clue is not necessary for the preferred solution. As will be made clear in the next chapter, certain stimulus information is absolutely indispensable for particular perceptions, so that the information in clues of the kind under discussion here is clearly of a different kind.

There are, however, examples that have the earmarks of problem solving but where there is no such obvious clue in the stimulus. An example of this kind is the perception of a rotating structure as three-dimensional, referred to as the kinetic depth effect (Wallach and O'Connell, 1953). To simplify matters, consider an oblique rod that rotates about a vertical axis. Then the successive transformations will look like those in Fig. 4–12. To eliminate all depth information other than the transformation itself, a shadow pattern of the rotating figure is viewed. Observers generally perceive a rigid rod of constant length rotating rather than the logically possible alternative of a rod changing length as it oscillates in a frontal plane. The latter would be the literal solution, although in this example it may not *always* be consciously experienced since the depth solution occurs fairly quickly.

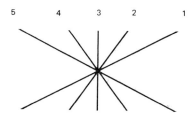

4-12. Kinetic depth effect. Successive views, 1 to 5, of an oblique rod rotating about a vertical axis.

It is the conjoint change of contour length and orientation that is important. Neither of these factors nor both together seem to be the kind described in our earlier examples, namely, unambiguous, independent, dispensable clues that strongly suggest one solution. These changes are perfectly compatible with the literal solution of a contour simultaneously changing length and orientation. But in the search for a solution, these concurrent transformations very much influence the solution that is selected. It is interesting that one *can* perceive a transformation entailing only length change (Fig. 4-13) as a contour of unchanging length rotating in depth, but naive observers will arrive at this solution far less frequently than when both length and orientation change together. In any event, it would seem

4-13. Successive views of a horizontal rod rotating about a vertical axis. The vertical stem remains in the same place.

that the depth solution is best understood as one arrived at by analysing the stimulus transformation and inferring the probable outer event, without benefit of an independent cluing factor.

Another example of this kind is phenomenal transparency as illustrated in Fig. 4-1. Here too there is no unambiguous information or separate clue that can elicit the transparency solution. Yet it does seem appropriate to view this stimulus array as posing a problem for the perceptual system. The literal percept of four different lightness values is apparently not satisfactory so that the executive agency searches for an alternative solution. There is a clear preference for the transparency solution once it is found.

Concluding Remarks

The critical reader may ask whether there is anything to be gained by viewing perception as the end result of a process of problem solving. My argument is that at least in the kinds of examples given here the parallel with problem solving as it occurs in thought seems reasonably close. In the next chapter evidence will be given of a different kind, supporting the proposition that what is perceived has to be thought of as a solution because it must rationally account for the facts of stimulation. Therefore, it is best to postpone a critique of the problem-solving view.

Apart from this general question, the reader may remain skeptical about the claim that there is a stage of the overall process corresponding to what I have called "solution finding." Since we cannot directly observe the alleged process of hypothesis elicitation or selection, evidence for it must necessarily by indirect. What I have tried to show for one kind of perceptual problem solving, the kind "from below," is this: one can demonstrate that certain features or components of the stimulus play a role via their presence in an initial perception in leading naive observers to achieve a particular final perception (e.g., incomplete or aligned fragments in illusory-contour displays; recognizable parts in fragmented figures; visibility of the ends of a contour in anorthoscopic displays; etc.). Yet these features are not necessary for the perception in question because once the observer is no longer naive or is given the appropriate set or instructions, that perception is easily achieved without these features. Therefore, the distinction between what one *spontaneously* perceives and what one *can* perceive seems legitimate. But this is precisely the reason for distinguishing between a stage of solution finding and one of solution understanding or acceptance. That is, the difference between someone who understands or accepts a solution and those who do but also have arrived at it themselves is that only in the latter case was there the initial step of finding the solution.

The story is not altogether clear regarding the other kind of solution finding, "from above," where there is no independent clue that can be dispensed with once the solution is elicited. However, it is plausible to assume that even in these cases the solution must first arise in the form of a hypothesis and is then maintained because it is "better" than or preferred over the initial or literal solution. Another way of putting this is to say that the perceptual system is not satisfied with the literal solution and is thus driven to seek an alternative. The possible reasons for this dissatisfaction will be discussed in a subsequent chapter, but by way of anticipating, I will argue that the literal solution is unsatisfactory because it entails acceptance of unexplained coincidental covariation of certain stimulus changes, or unexplained coincidental regularities within the stimulus.

In other words, even though a perception is achieved, the literal one, and even though there may be no separate clue that tends to lead to another perception, it would seem that the executive agency is dissatisfied with the perception achieved and is actively searching for an alternative. The reason for this that I will propose (Chapter 6) is that the literal percept fails to account for certain covariations or proximal stimulus regularities that therefore must be accepted as mere coincidence. For example, in the kinetic depth effect display, the literal percept is of an object changing its length but also simultaneously changing its orientation. That covariation is unexplained. But the preferred percept, of an object rotating in depth, fully and elegantly accounts for this seeming coincidence. This example should suffice to illustrate why there is a search for a different solution other than the literal one and why, when "found," it is preferred.

More convincing evidence that there is a stage in the overall process during which a potential solution arises, prior to the stage of accepting or rejecting it, derives from a recent experiment in our laboratory (Reynolds, 1981). The rationale behind the experiment was as follows. Suppose a stimulus array is presented that contains elements that are believed to suggest a particular solution but suppose further that the array also contains elements that contradict that solution. (What is meant by contradiction is developed further in the next chapter.) What we should predict is that the solution would be momentarily entertained but then rejected, and assuming the process is not conscious, we would ordinarily have no way of knowing it had been entertained. But what if processing could be arrested before the contradiction became evident?

The stimulus pattern is illustrated in Fig. 4-14. Ordinarily observers do not perceive a white triangle with illusory contours in the central region of this display because the background lines are visible in the region where such a figure, being phenomenally opaque, would occlude these lines. But if the pattern disappears after a brief exposure (50 milliseconds) and is followed almost immediately by a disrupting pattern consisting of three complete circles in the regions where the incomplete cirlces had been, most observers *do* perceive the illusory triangle. It is as if there was no time to check the triangle solution against the contradictory information given by the background lines because the disrupting pattern eliminates the entire percept by a process analogous to what is called backward masking. If, however, the interval between original and disrupting figure is increased, now observers no longer perceive the triangle figure. This occurred with an interval of around 200 milliseconds. See the illustration of the experiment in Fig. 4-14.

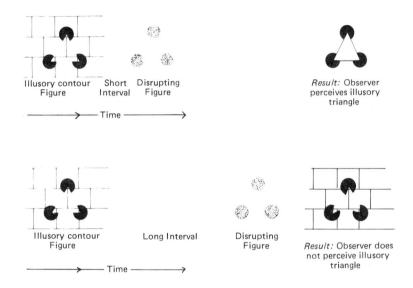

4-14. Illustration of an experiment on the perception of an illusory contour figure. After Reynolds, 1977.

Sometimes, however, the process of entertaining the hypothesis that is clued may actually be revealed in consciousness. For example, if a straight oblique line is moved anorthoscopically behind a narrow slit and its ends are visible, there will be a brief moment when a figure is seen. However, with such a figure (see pp. 182–184), that perception is not sustained during the time the ends are not visible, so that a moment later the perception changes to an element moving vertically along the slit. Another example is illustrated in Fig. 4-15*a*, where there may well be brief moments when the figure looks three-dimensional. But that solution lacks stimulus support and therefore by and large is not the prevailing one. By the same token, Fig. 4-15*b* might momentarily be seen as a complete circle with a triangular figure covering it at the bottom. But that percept can at best be fleeting in this case. What is lacking is the support for a triangle per-

a   *b*

4-15. (a) A figure that may suggest three-dimensionality without
leading to a sustained perception of a three-dimensional object. (b) A
figure that may momentarily suggest a complete circle covered by a triangular object.

cept made possible by other circular fragments as in an illusory
contour pattern (Fig. 4-5).

Assuming then that possible solutions arise, whether from "below" or "above," the further question to be faced is their ultimate
fate. Are they accepted and sustained by the perceptual system, or
are they rejected? What are the principles that govern such possible
acceptance or rejection? These questions are pursued in the next two
chapters.

5 ⬜

Perception as Problem Solving:
II. Solution Acceptance

LET US ASSUME that a potential solution to the problem of what the stimulus represents has been elicited, whether suggested by some stimulus clue or otherwise. I will argue in this chapter that this potential solution must meet certain requirements before it is accepted. If it fails to do so, it will be rejected.

The general requirement is a "fit" or "match" between the solution as constructed internally and the proximal stimulus or between the solution and certain other perceived properties of the objects represented by the stimulus that constitutes the literal solution. In other words, in perceiving, unlike dreaming or imagining, constructions are constrained by what is given or not given in the stimulus. First the solution must conform to, do justice to, or explain, so to speak, everything about the stimulus that has been detected or everything that has been perceived up to that moment. This refers to what is present in the stimulus. But second, to reverse the formulation of the first requirement, the stimulus (or the initial, literal perception to which it gives rise) must support the internal construction. This can mean that either the absence of a certain feature or component in the stimulus (or in the initial percept) or the presence in the stimulus (or in the initial percept) of a feature contradicting the solution can lead to its rejection.[1]

In what follows, I will give many examples of these requirements.

1. The meaning of the qualifying phrase inserted in several sentences in this paragraph, namely, "or the initial perception to which the stimulus gives rise" will be explained more fully below (pp. 128–132). To anticipate briefly, however, the qualification is needed for the following reason. Given a sequence of stages such as proximal stimulation → initial (or literal) perception → final or preferred perception, the fit that matters is often between the second and third stage

The Solution Must Account for the Proximal Stimulus: Stimulus
Conformity

Some of the examples given in the preceding chapter illustrate this principle. If one perceives the central region of Fig. 4-6*c* as a figure (with illusory contours), it must be a figure with curved sides. Or perhaps, more conservatively stated, the figure perceived cannot be one with straight sides because that would fail to account for the misalignment of the edges in the corner fragments. The fact is, as already noted, that those perceiving this figure do perceive it as curvilinear. I should add the obvious point that for those who fail to perceive the illusory figure, the perception of the corner fragments as figures also fully accounts for the proximal stimulus. Generally speaking, the literal solution will satisfy this first requirement of accounting for the stimulus data as well as will the preferred solution.

In the example of fragmented figures (Fig. 4-7), when one does succeed in reorganizing (and therefore recognizing) them, all the fragments and their interrelationships are accounted for by the role they play in the percept as a whole. At least this is true for the most part. When it is not, the observer feels dissatisfied and reports that some parts do not fit or that while the figure seems to be a "such-and-such object" there is something wrong with the perception of it. Of course, not all figures of this kind are equally well drawn, but the better ones do lend themselves to adequate perception of the whole once the solution is triggered.

In the kinetic depth effect, the perception of a rotating rigid figure of constant length does account for the transforming retinal image. To say this, however, presupposes that the perceptual system "knows" certain principles of optical projection, namely, that objects rotating in the third dimension produce retinal images that change in length and generally speaking in orientation as well. Given such knowledge, the percept accounts for the stimulus change. Needless to add, the literal perception of a figure changing length and orientation also accounts for the stimulus change. In fact, the literal percept accounts for the stimulus change more directly because of the correlation between them. Perhaps this is why the literal percept generally precedes the veridical percept, in this case if only momentarily.

As another example, consider again the case of apparent movement when the stimulus object is of the kind illustrated in Fig. 5-1. If motion is to be perceived between *a* and *b* and if the requirement

---

(i.e., between the initial and the final perception) rather than directly between the first and third stage (the proximal stimulation and the final perception).

5-1. Apparent movement from *a* to *b* requires a solution to the problem posed by their different orientations.

is to be met that the perceptual solution account for all features of the stimulus input, the solution must embody an explanation of the different arrangement of *a* and *b*. There are several such possible solutions (for example a figure bending as it moves, a figure rotating within the plane, and a figure flipping over into the third dimension), and all of them meet the requirement. Of course, another possibility is not to perceive motion at all. However, the preference to perceive motion under the appropriate spatial and temporal conditions of stimulus alternation is apparently very great. Therefore, the perceptual system will construct an acceptable solution, typically of rotation in the third dimension, so that *a* can be seen moving to *b* without violating the requirement under discussion. Even when *a* is one shape (e.g., a circle) and *b* another (e.g., a triangle) motion will be perceived, but then the observer typically reports an impression of continuous deformation of shape while the object is in motion, the circle becoming or changing into a triangle as it moves (Kolers and Pomerantz, 1971). Why the system so strongly prefers motion under stroboscopic conditions is a further problem.

Another interesting example is illustrated in Fig. 5-2*a* and *b*. Regardless of the actual direction of motion, the perceived direction of the oblique stripes in *a* is ambiguous (i.e., oblique, horizontal, or vertical), and observers typically reverse from one to the other (see pp. 182–183 and Wallach, 1935). But with spots added as in *b* the tendency to perceive motion veridically is naturally quite strengthened. Therefore, with objective vertical motion most observers will start out perceiving the stripes moving vertically. However, despite the bias introduced by the spots, observers in time will experience a reversal in the direction of the stripes and perceive them moving horizontally. How can this be reconciled with the fact that the images of the spots between the black stripes move vertically over the retina and never move across any stripe? The answer is that the spots are seen as gliding obliquely downward within the white stripes as these stripes move horizontally. Thus the vectorial sum of the two perceived motions fully accounts for the retinal displacement of its spots (c). More generally, all cases of vectorial scission (where one retinal motion direction is broken up into two perceived directions) such as has been studied and analyzed by Johansson (1950) (see pp. 219–224) attest to the principle here enunciated: the perceptual solution must conform to or do justice to or account for the proximal stimulus.

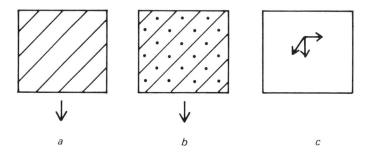

5-2. (a) Vertically displacing stripes can be perceived to be moving horizontally, vertically, or obliquely; (b) with the addition of spots, observers are more likely to perceive the display moving vertically. When observers do perceive the stripes moving horizontally, the spots are perceived to glide obliquely downward to the left as shown in (c) while being carried along to the right.

A final example is the phenomenon of perceptual transparency illustrated in Fig. 4-1. As noted in the preceding chapter, one can perceive this display either literally as four regions of differing achromatic color *or* as an inner transparent rectangle in front of the larger rectangle. Either percept accounts for the four differing luminance values that constitute the proximal stimulus, the former in terms of four differing reflectance surfaces, the latter in terms of one region of uniform density through which most of the light from the black and white surface regions behind is transmitted.

So much for illustrations of the first requirement. I turn now to examples illustrating the second requirement.

The Proximal Stimulus Must Contain What Is Implied by the Solution: Stimulus Support

To begin with a very simple example, if the solution suggested entails a three-dimensional structure, with surfaces meeting at an edge, the absence of a stimulus representing that edge will probably lead to the inability to sustain that perceptual solution. Thus in Fig. 5-3, while the outline might suggest a three-dimensional cube, that

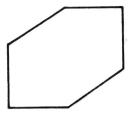

5-3. Outline of a three-dimensional cube that is not perceived as three-dimensional because of the absence of internal stimulus support.

rationale is provided by the inner logic of good illusory contour percept cannot be achieved. One can image the cube, but it seems correct to say that the cube is not perceived.

The next example concerns illusory contours. For figures of the kind illustrated in Fig. 5-4a the essence of the solution, or otherwise expressed, the description that embodies the solution, is that there is an opaque triangular figure present that is covering and therefore

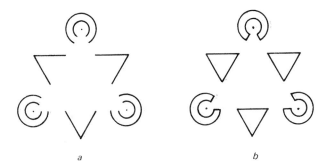

5-4. (a) Illusory contour figure of a triangle; (b) a similar pattern that does not consistently support the illusory percept. After Kanizsa, 1974.

occluding parts of the figures that are physically given in the proximal display. Moreover this figure is of a surface color very close to that of the general background. Its borders are indicated only by the regions where it occludes contours of other figures. That is why the edges terminate where they do. The construction not only accounts for what is in the proximal stimulus, but the latter contains that which is implied by the construction. There is, however, one further problem. If the contours of the triangle suggested at the corner circular fragments are present between these fragments, they should be visible no matter how weakly. Thus, I believe, the perceptual system constructs or invents a subtle difference in color to support the overall solution. According to this way of thinking, the lightness effect of illusory contour figures comes after the elicitation of the hypothesis, rather than being, via contrast, the cause of the illusory percept.[2]

Consider now Fig. 5-4*b*, where one does *not* perceive an illusory triangular figure in the center (and compare it with Fig. 5-4*a*, where one does). The difficulty here is not with the first requirement (because the solution of a central opaque figure does conform to what is present) but with the second requirement. The potential contours of a central triangular figure are present in the display (in fact much more contour than is present in Fig. 5-4*a*), but these are not such as to support or fit the interpretation that they belong to a central occluding figure. These extra contours should not be there if they are not present elsewhere along the straight edges of the triangle. A subtle but I believe important point here is that it is difficult in this case to sustain a consistent interpretation of why the edges of a central triangle are sometimes highly visible and sometimes not, whereas in Fig. 5.4*a* such a consistent interpretation is easily supportable by what is given. A similar argument explains why no subjectively contoured figure is perceived in Fig. 5-5. Since the perception of the physically present contours here is not interpretable in terms of occlusion, there being no fragments that could be undergoing occlusion, there is no basis for perceiving the central region as opaque. If it is then only an outline figure, there is no explanation for why the outline is visible in the corners but not in between.

5-5. Outline of a triangle that does not support an illusory contour percept. After Gregory, 1972.

The rules about stimulus support have yet to be worked out but, for object perception, would be somewhat as follows: Those contours (or other markers of boundaries) of the object or array under-

2. This hypothesis about the illusory lightness of the figure as a cognitive invention does not explain the *direction* of the lightness effect, i.e., why in Fig. 5-4 the inner triangle appears lighter rather than darker in color than the surrounding white of the page (and appears darker if the pattern is the negative of the one in Fig. 5-4). It is possible, however, that contrast between the emerging illusory figure and the fragments it is seen to overlap explains the direction of the effect.

going mental construction that serve to define its shape, in two or three dimensions, must be represented in the proximal stimulus. If the construction is three-dimensional, the presence of contours that uniquely would project to the eye representing the object's or display's third dimension are important, since otherwise the stimulus will tend to lead to a two-dimensional construction. Figure 5.6 is an illustration of this point. It is a drawing of a hornlike structure. In *a*, one tends to perceive a two-dimensional object, since the outer boundary is all that is given and this alone does not unequivocally support a three-dimensional construction. But in *b*, the presence of the curved contours does support a good three-dimensional construction. Boundary and edge representations are particularly important and, in this writer's view, more so than texture or other kinds of surface representation. Similar rules would hold for the perception of surface lightness, events such as motion, and other phenomenal properties.

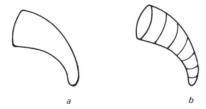

a   *b*

5-6. (a) Outline of a horn (Perkins, 1982) that does not support a three-dimensional percept. (b) With internal contours added, the figure does support a three-dimensional percept.

However, an important further principle that emerges from some of the examples given in this chapter is this: parts or features that should be present in the stimulus for a particular construction can be missing without necessarily violating the requirement of stimulus support *provided that a rationale is given for their absence.* Such a rationale is provided by the inner logic of good illusory contour patterns, but it can be provided in other cases as well. The phenomenon of interposition is one such other case. The missing parts of one structure are accounted for by the perception that they are occluded by other structures. Another example is the absence of stimulus representation of continuous motion when such motion is nonetheless perceived under stroboscopic conditions. Here the absence of such supporting stimulation is rationalized by the rapid perceived speed of the moving object. At slower rates of alternation, implying a more slowly moving object, the absence of stimulation between the end points is powerful negative evidence (nonsupporting evidence) against the apparent-motion solution, and thus it does not occur (see Chapter 7, pp. 165–176).

Consider next, the perception of a figure under anorthoscopic presentation. The solution implies that moving behind an aperture is an extended figure only part of which is visible at a given moment, the remainder being occluded by an opaque surface. That being the case, the stimulus must include components that can produce an impression of an opening in an otherwise opaque surface. We have found that when the figure is made luminous and revealed through the slit in an otherwise dark room so that the surface containing the slit is no longer visible, a figure is never perceived. Rather a small luminous element is seen moving up and down. Under such conditions, there is no support in the stimulus for the figure solution that entails as part of it that there is occlusion of all but a small part of the figure at any moment. Even when the conditions are changed, so that an invisible slit now *moves over a stationary* luminous figure, no figure is perceived. In this case, a small moving element of light is seen traversing a path, which path conforms to the shape of the figure, but an extended figure is never perceived. One may know that an extended figure is there and how it is being revealed, but such knowledge has no effect.

5-7. Simulation of anorthoscopic display with narrow opaque borders around the slit. Anorthoscopic effect does not occur. After Rock and Sigman, 1973.

The solution also refers to an occluding surface except for the region of the slit. If, therefore, the surface is removed except for a small region surrounding the slit (Fig. 5-7), there is inadequate support for the solution. The regions of the figure other than those inside the slit or behind the very narrow occluding borders of it should now be visible. Since they are not, the solution is not acceptable. In fact few if any observers report the perception of an extended figure under these conditions. The literal percept of a vertically moving element is now completely dominant throughout the exposure period. In these last two examples, no rationale is provided that explains the absence of stimulus representation of the unseen parts of the figure.

For the figure solution to be viable, other features must also have stimulus representation. If the slit is wide enough for the slope of the element to be detected, that slope must change from moment to moment consistent with the rise and fall of the element. To state this differently, if the visible element represents part of a curvilinear figure such as we typically employ, the solution that such a curved figure is present requires that the visible slope at any moment correspond to the shape of the figure in that region. If, therefore, the slope is held constant, observers generally do not perceive an extended figure.

The Solution Must Not Entail Contradiction: Negative Evidence

The last examples could be stated somewhat differently. Instead of saying that the absence of a stimulus representing an opaque surface covering most of the figure fails to support the solution, one might say that there is a contradiction between the solution and certain other perceived properties. The solution embodies an opaque surface covering everything but what is visible through the slit at a given moment, whereas no such opaque surface is perceived in front of all the regions where the figure must be assumed to be. As to the matter of the visible slope, instead of saying that the absence of a stimulus that changes its slope fails to support the solution of a curved-line figure, one might say that there is a contradiction between the solution of an extended *curved* figure and the visible parts of it that do not change their orientations.

If a solution is in the form of a description and if a description is in some sense propositional, it is understandable why such contradiction is not possible. Thus, for example, if the solution contains as one ingredient the description "region *a* is an opaque figure in front of and occluding whatever is directly behind it," part of the overall description cannot at the same time be "objects seen through and therefore behind region *a*."

A clear illustration of what is implied here is an experiment performed in our laboratory on illusory contour (Rock and Anson, 1979). A pattern containing incomplete circles such as the one shown in Fig. 4-5 was drawn on transparent material. When this is viewed from a distance with a homogeneous white background placed at some distance behind it (Fig. 5-8a), observers typically perceive the inner region as a triangular figure. Under these conditions it is not evident that the white background is actually in a plane different from that of the corner fragments. But if oblique stripes are placed in front of the white background surface (b) and depth perception is adequate—either because both eyes are used or because observers are encouraged to move their heads around—no observer

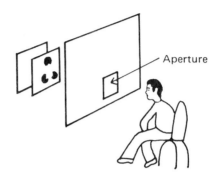

Result: observer perceives
white triangle

a

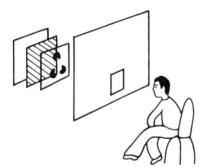

Result: observer perceives
three circular segments
in front of stripes

b

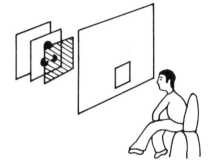

Result: observer perceives
white triangle behind
stripes

c

5-8. (a) When a homogeneous background is behind an illusory-contour figure on a transparent sheet, the figure is perceived as it is in (c), when an array of stripes is perceived in front of the figure. In (b), with the stripes perceived as behind the figure, the illusory percept does not occur. After Rock and Anson, 1979.

ever perceives the central region as a triangular figure (see Table 5-1). To do so would entail a contradiction between the solution "opaque triangle covering circles at its corners" and the perception of that same central region as transparent through which striped contours behind are visible. That this result is not simply based on the interfering effect of the oblique stripes, the retinal images of which fall across the regions where the illusory contour must arise, is

Table 5-1: The Perception of Illusory Contour

Condition	N	Number of Subjects Perceiving Triangle		
		No Stripes	Stripes Behind	Stripes in Front
Binocular stationary viewing	60	41	0	20
Head-movement viewing	60	44	0	39

indicated by a further variation. Here (Fig. 5-8c) the oblique-line array is placed in front of the illusory-contour display, between that and the observer. While this produces the same potentially interfering retinal state of affairs as in *b*, many observers had no difficulty in perceiving the central region as a triangular figure, and virtually all observers perceived it when they moved their heads and thereby achieved an unequivocally adequate perception of the two planes. Now there is no contradiction. The overall discription is: "oblique stripes, behind which is an opaque triangle covering circles at its corners."

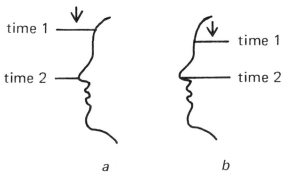

a   b

5-9. A horizontal line moves vertically, the end of which remains contiguous with the outline of the face. When the line is on the ground side of the face contour (a), it appears to be of constant length undergoing partial covering and uncovering. When it is on the figure side (b), it appears to get longer and shorter as it moves vertically. After Rock and Gilchrist, 1975*b*.

Still another example of this kind is the following (see Fig. 5-9). A horizontal line moves up and down and one end remains in contact with one side of an outline figure of a face. Consequently, the line in the display changes in length. When the line is on the left, as in *a*, it is seen by virtually all observers, 13 of 15, as going behind parts of the face and thus as remaining of constant length. When, however, it is on the right, as in *b*, it is seen by a majority of observers, 9 of 14, as changing in length (Rock and Gilchrist, 1975*b*). The point of this experiment is obvious. When the line is on the "ground" region, as in *a*, its length change can be accounted for by its moment-to-moment occlusion and disocclusion by the opaque parts of the face as "figure." When, however, the line is on the "figure" region, as in *b*, its length change cannot be accounted for in this way. "Ground" cannot occlude things. This experiment is relevant to the claim by certain investigators that the accretion and deletion of the elements (or texture) of one surface as a result of their successive appearance and disappearance as they are alternately covered and uncovered by another surface is the stimulus information necessary and sufficient to account directly for the perception of one surface behind another (Gibson, 1979; Kaplan, 1969). Our experiment suggests that appropriate figure-ground organization may be a hidden factor in accounting for the phenomenal outcome.

One might ask how *any* subjects given the condition illustrated in *b* can perceive a line of constant length. The answer I believe is that in such cases a figure-ground reversal occurs. Several of the observers who perceived the line in this way reported such reversals, and the experimenters noticed it as well. The line-length change is a transformation that seems to suggest a covering-uncovering solution, particularly in the light of the continued contact of line end with figure contour, and indeed there are reasons for thinking that such a nonliteral solution would be preferred (see Chapter 6 p. 163). The perception of the region to the left of the face contour as ground in *b* fails to support that solution, but given the "pressure" for the covering-uncovering solution, the figure-ground organization changes. The change rationalizes the covering-uncovering solution.

Further Analysis of the Concept of Support

This example brings out another principle not yet explicitly discussed. The requirement of support for a solution pertains in some cases not to the stimulus but to how the stimulus is perceived in respects other than the one under consideration. In fact this seems to be true about several of the examples already given. Thus it is because the slit is perceived as an opening or ground rather than as figure that the necessary support for achieving the anorthoscopic figure percept is present. We have done an experiment in which the slit appeared as a figural region, a vase, rather than as an opening between faces (see Fig. 5-10*a*), with the consequence that the anorthoscopic effect was seriously undermined (Rock and Sigman, 1973). When the slit appears as ground (Fig. 5-10*b*), the anorthoscopic effect occurs as usual. Of course, these perceptions, i.e., of figure-ground in the example given, in turn are supported by the stimulus, so that the term stimulus support is not inappropriate in the final analysis. Still it might be more appropriate to refer to the requirement in such cases as perceptual support rather than as stimulus support.

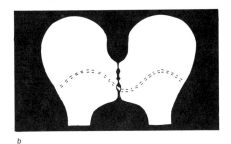

a   b

5-10. (a) When the slit or opening in a moving-line-figure display appears as the figure, the anorthoscopic effect is generally not achieved; (b) when the opening appears as ground, the effect generally is achieved. After Rock and Sigman, 1973.

There are, however, cases where it might seem that the necessary stimulus or perceptual support is entirely lacking. One such example is the progressive disappearance of a disk where nothing but the disk is visible (Michotte, Thinès, and Crabbé, 1964). See Fig. 5-11. This can be achieved by moving a disk alternately out from and behind an invisible edge in a surface. The disk is perceived as an object undergoing occlusion and disocclusion rather than an object changing its size. Where then is the stimulus support for this perception? However, the fact is that the observers typically also perceive an edge behind which the disk disappears and reappears. The two-dimensional disk enables observers to perceive the flat contour on the bottom as belonging not to the disk but to an edge in another surface. The stimulus for that edge is given. What is not given is a stimulus for that edge beyond the region of the disk. Thus there is a figure-ground reversal in the region below the bottom edge, which amounts to the appropriate perceptual support for the occlusion solution. That region becomes figural.

A similar effect has been demonstrated in the anorthoscopic paradigm when an outline figure of a circle is moved back and forth behind a nonvisible slit (Fendrich and Mack, 1980). At first one sees two spots of light (from the two simultaneously visible regions of the circle) coming together and moving apart along a vertical direction. But if the suggestion is made by the experimenter that a figure is moving back and forth horizontally, one then can see the circle. However, one also then sees a *slit with illusory contours!* Thus these examples do not contradict the principle of support, although they show once again how the perceptual system will attempt to rationalize a given percept when there is a strong force at work to favor it. "Rationalize" in this context means creating the necessary perceptual support for the final, preferred percept.

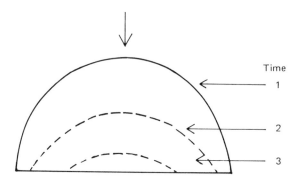

5-11. When a disk progressively disappears behind an invisible edge in an opaque surface or progressively appears from behind it, it is perceived veridically, rather than as a disk changing in size. After Michotte, Thinès, and Crabbé, 1964.

A survey of the examples given suggests that there are gradations in degree of stimulus (or perceptual) support that may be provided for a particular solution. On one end of the continuum are cases where all those features implied by a solution are represented in the stimulus. An example would be a drawing of a cube in perspective with all edges visible and differences in achromatic value among the three visible surfaces simulating attached shadow. On the other end are cases of the kind just considered (i.e., nonvisible edges of opaque surfaces), where the support is not represented at all in the stimulus but emerges only simultaneous with and as part of the solution. Most of the examples considered in this chapter fall somewhere between these two extremes.

Examples that fall near the low-support end of the continuum are of the kind called droodles (Fig. 5-12). As with fragmented figures, these figures also tend to lead first to a literal description that does not entail anything familiar. But they can be seen differently, e.g., *a* as a woman scrubbing, *b* as a giraffe's neck, and *c* as a pig seen from behind. There certainly is an insightful sudden shift in perception here as one moves from nonrecognition to recognition. On the other hand, the percepts achieved are somewhat sketchy; e.g., the objects lack true depth. Of course, all that is required in this case is that the figure look like *a picture* of the object represented, not that it look like the object itself.

One might formulate the principle that the poorer the support for a solution, the greater the burden on the perceptual system to im-

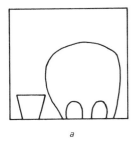 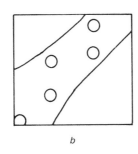 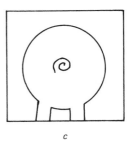

5-12. Three droodles: (a) woman scrubbing the floor; (b) giraffe's neck;
(c) pig seen from behind.

pose its internal solution on the stimulus. Perhaps one can look at
the imposition of a solution in terms of imagining in which the extreme case is one where no stimulus is present at all.

As already noted, there is a problem concerning the level from
which the support for a preferred solution derives. Earlier in the
chapter I emphasized the proximal stimulus and stimulus support. Yet
we have seen many examples where it is not *directly* the presence
or absence of a feature in the proximal stimulus that matters but the
presence or absence of a feature in what is perceived. This fact suggests the following stages or sequence of events. First, the proximal
stimulus is detected, analyzed, and organized into units and groupings including figure-ground differentiation. This stage itself entails
decisions or problem-solving operations on a lower level, culminating
in a particular description. For static displays this stage is essentially
equivalent to the literal solution, as in form perception. For event displays, the retinal motion or transformation also enters into the description that constitutes the literal solution. The description at the
level of the literal solution is in the two-dimensional world mode if
we assume that the depth associated with figure-ground organization
is minimal.

The literal solution is therefore grounded in the proximal stimulus.
It accounts for and is supported by the stimulus. In the next stage,
the preferred solution is achieved. The description that determines it
is generally in the three-dimensional world mode. If we assume that
the preferred solution is grounded in the literal solution, the "match"
that is important at this final stage is between literal solution and
preferred solution. Thus, the preferred solution, e.g., a line of constant length undergoing occlusion, depends directly upon the figure-

ground organization achieved in the literal solution and indirectly on the stimulus that leads to the figure-ground organization.[3]

Although the relationship between proximal stimulus and final preferred perception is somewhat less direct than was implied earlier, the fact is that the final percept is still grounded in the proximal stimulus. Indirectly the final percept must conform to and be supported by the stimulus.

The examples given in this chapter will suffice to illustrate the requirements that must be met if a potential solution that has been elicited is to be accepted and sustained. The analysis indicates, on the one hand, the importance of the proximal stimulus for what is perceived and, on the other hand, the insufficiency of the proximal stimulus alone as explanation of what is perceived. The stimulus has the dual role of suggesting or directing the search for a solution of what it represents *and* of serving as support for or evidence against that potential solution. But the solution is a construction imposed upon the stimulus, and it is internally generated. As was noted in discussing form in Chapter 3, the presence of the proximal stimulus as one of the overall necessary conditions for perception may explain the phenomenal quality of perception as *sensory* in contradistinction to the phenomenal quality of cognition that would be based on description or construction but without the presence of a stimulus.

The next problem to be faced, the basis of preference for one perception over another, is taken up in Chapter 6.

3. In certain cases, the picture becomes more complicated because the preferred solution may depend upon a prior preferred solution. This may happen only in the case of event perception. For example, the perceived configuration of units (literal solution) can lead to a solution of illusory contour (a preferred, static solution) which then plays an important role in the perception or nonperception of apparent movement (preferred event solution). This example is discussed on pp. 170–171. In such cases, the match that is important is between the static preferred solution and the event preferred solution.

6 ⬡

Perception as Problem Solving:
III. The Preference for Certain Solutions

IN THIS CHAPTER I take up the problem of the basis of a preference for one solution over another where both fulfill the requirements
specified in the preceding chapter. Several known theories about
preference are considered: the Gestalt view that the simplest possible
percept is preferred or the modern version of it that the percept that
can be most economically encoded is favored; the empiricist view
that the perception to which the stimulus most frequently has led in
the past is the one preferred; and the constancy view that the preferred perception is one in which the object remains constant or rigid
as a thing while changing its orientation, location, or the like. Another
theory about preference is advanced, namely, that in the case of
events, the executive agency seeks to explain seemingly unrelated
co-occurring stimulus variations on the basis of a common cause and
that, in the case of stationary configurations, it seeks solutions that
explain seeming coincidences and unexplained regularities that otherwise are implicit in the nonpreferred solution.

Various examples in support of the coincidence-explanation
principle are given as well as some in support of the theory that
emphasizes the role of past experience. As to the latter, an attempt is
made to explain precisely how past experience can affect perceptual
preference. It is thus argued that the various theories are not mutually
exclusive, and that a search for a solution that explains coincidence is
apt to be facilitated by a highly available schema in memory.

However, logical considerations and the weight of the evidence
militate against the simplicity theory. While there is evidence in support of the view that, given ambiguity of the stimulus concerning an
object property along some dimension, the precise value perceived
tends to be unique or singular, this fact does not necessarily imply a

preference for simplicity. Other interpretations are suggested.

The question is raised as to whether the manifestation of a perceptual preference implies selection from among the alternatives and, if so, how different theories would deal with such a process. It is suggested that the nonpreferred alternative is indeed realized psychologically because it is embodied in the literal solution and that it is the dissatisfaction with this solution that drives the perceptual system to search for a better one.

The Common-Cause Principle: Events

It is time to come to grips with the problem of preference for one solution over another possible solution. By "possible" I mean that different solutions can fulfill the conditions discussed in the preceding chapter concerning the fit between stimulus and percept. Yet one solution is generally preferred. Another way of putting this is to say that logically the proximal stimulus is often ambiguous but the resulting perception favors one alternative.

Consider again the conditions leading to the kinetic depth effect. To reduce these to the simplest case, we will continue with the example of a single tilted rod rotating in depth about a vertical axis at its center. The rod will produce a sequence of images of varying length and orientation (Fig. 4-12). After a brief period of observation, this sequence will give rise to the veridical impression of a rigid rod of unchanging length rotating in depth. Since this outcome occurs either without any depth cues (i.e., monocular viewing with head stationary and rod distant enough to rule out useful accommodation information) or by means of a shadow pattern cast by the rod (where depth cues if anything must call for perception of a two-dimensional object), it is clear that the perception of an object rotating in depth represents a preference of some kind over the alternative of an object that, literally, corresponds with the transforming image, namely, a thin rod simultaneously changing its length and orientation.

One can try to explain this preference in several different ways. The empiricist would say that daily life has often presented us with transforming stimulation produced by a rigid object rotating in depth and only rarely with such stimulation produced by an object changing its length and orientation. Of course, to give this explanation force it must be maintained that during these prior experiences we achieved the veridical percept and to do so we must in those cases have other information, other depth cues.

Others would say that this is simply an example of the more general principle that the perceptual system prefers object constancy or rigidity and wherever possible will interpret the transforming proximal input as representing change in the three-dimensional orientation or location of the object rather than as change of the object's shape or size. This is certainly a descriptively true statement, but the question that arises is whether it can be explanatory. What mechanism or rule enables the perceptual system always to achieve that preferred end result, or are we to suppose that the system "tries out" the alternatives and then simply selects the one that does? Another question here is whether this principle covers all the cases where preference occurs. I will show that it does not.

The Gestaltists would say that the preferred perception is the simpler one and that perception always tends toward the simplest outcome possible under the prevailing conditions. But then they would have to justify the claim that a percept that entails changes of depth only is simpler than one that entails changes of length and orientation only. After all there is something "simpler" about an object that remains in one plane. Whether later accounts of simplicity cast in the language of information theory and economy of encoding can adequately explain this preference in terms of the lesser information required to specify it over the alternative, remains to be seen.

I will take up these alternative theories later, but for now I would like to propose a different way of accounting for the preference in this example. If one perceives a thin rod changing its length and simultaneously its orientation, there are two unrelated events. But if one perceives the rod as rotating in depth, the two image transformations become explicable in terms of a *common cause*.[1] The perceptual system prefers wherever possible to account for all co-occurring changes on the basis of such a common cause. The alternative generally entails acceptance of *coincidence*.

When the projection of the rod changes *only* its length or *only* its orientation rather than both simultaneously, the depth effect either does not occur at all (orientation change only) or is very weak and requires a set or suggestion to become manifest (length change only). However, if a one-dimensional extent changes concurrently with change in direction along a second dimension, the depth effect is immediate and compelling. For example, if two points alternately approach and recede from one another (relative motion), the observer

---

1. This analysis presupposes that the changes or transformations that are con-concomitant are not only logically separable but are indeed separable for the perceptual system. Otherwise it would not be correct to say that *unrelated* events are detected whose covariation must be explained. A test might be whether observers can discriminate easily along one dimension, e.g., orientation, despite irrelevant changes of the stimulus along another dimension, e.g., length.

will perceive literally just that. But if simultaneous with that transformation the points as a pair have a common motion in a direction
different from the path of their relative motion, they will appear to
have a fixed separation and to be moving back and forth in the third
dimension (Börjesson and von Hofsten, 1972). Thus it would seem
that this is another example where "common cause" can be invoked.
The two proximal stimulus transformations would be unaccountably
coincidental without the depth-change solution.

The same principle can account for the preference in examples
discussed in other chapters. In the anorthoscopic paradigm, where
one views a figure successively through a narrow slit (see pp. 176–
191), there is a preference to perceive an extended figure through the
slit rather than an element displacing along the axis of the slit, provided that the slit is wide enough for change of slope and curvature
to be detected. The stimulus transformation then consists of vertical
displacement of an element along the slit simultaneous with changing
slope and curvature of the element (see Fig. 7-14). Therefore, one
can perceive the element, literally, doing just that, but this perception leaves the simultaneous changes as simply unexplained co-occurrence, whereas the perception of an extended figure successively
revealed elegantly accounts for these co-occuring changes by a common cause. We have found that if slope change is eliminated either
by displaying an oblique straight line or by displaying a curved line
but narrowing the slit until change of slope cannot be detected, the
preference for the perception of an extended figure is eliminated.
There are now no longer co-occurring changes to be explained.

There is actually a correlation between the specific slope of the
element visible at any moment and the rate of its displacement along
the slit. If, for example, the portion of the figure behind the slit is
steeply sloped, the rate of displacement of the visible element is
fast; if that part of the figure is almost horizontal, its rate of displacement is slow. Moreover change of slope is correlated with the
visible curvature of the element. These correlations are accounted
for by perceiving an extended figure. Conversely, these correlations
must remain purely coincidental when a vertically displacing element
is perceived. There is one other fact that might be explicable in terms
of the common-cause principle. If we compare the case where the
figure moves behind a stationary slit with the case where the slit
moves over a stationary figure, we find that figure perception occurs
more readily, more frequently, and is more stable in the latter than
in the former case. While there may be other explanations of this
fact, one possibility is that when the slit is moving, to perceive an
element displacing within it entails one additional coincidental

change. The element is unaccountable and independently going along with the slit. This particular change does not arise in the case where the slit is stationary. Therefore, *more* independent transformations are accounted for by one "cause" in the case of the moving-slit paradigm than in the case of the moving-figure paradigm.

A critical test of the common-cause hypothesis is to create stimulus conditions that would be produced by an object that *did* change in one dimension rather than by an object that remained rigid or constant as in all the above examples. Suppose in a kinetic depth display the object *did* change its length as it rotated. Two outcomes are possible: (1) the object is perceived to rotate in a *two-dimensional* plane while changing its length; (2) the object is perceived to rotate in *depth* while changing its length. If outcome 2 occurred, i.e., the object was perceived to change its length as it rotated in depth, it would suggest that the crucial factor was a preference for a "depth" solution per se, not for a solution based on a common cause. That is because this solution does not account for the covariation of length and orientation as resulting from one cause. If outcome 1 occurred, i.e., the object was perceived to rotate in a two-dimensional plane while changing its length, it would suggest that common cause rather than a preference for depth per se was the explanation of the typical kinetic depth effect.[2]

Certain well-known phenomena can be interpreted in terms of the rejection-of-coincidence principle. Consider the example of the launching effect described by Michotte: one visual object, A, moves until it reaches a second stationary object, B, whereupon A stops and B moves away in the appropriate direction and speed. The impression that A has caused B to move is irresistible. Not to perceive causation here is to accept the relationship between the behavior of the two objects as purely coincidental; the spatial and temporal contiguity, the shared direction of motion, and the equivalent velocity. As Michotte (1963) has shown, varying any of the relationships will disrupt or destroy the impression of causality. Temporal contiguity alone is a powerful determinant of perceived causation even in cases that do not fall under the launching effect. Thus, for example, if a loud noise occurs just as a light goes out, there is a feeling that one has caused the other. This is a clear example of rejecting coincidence even though we "know" better.

---

2. Another possibility, however, is that an object of constant length will be seen rotating in depth in some complex way, e.g., tumbling while rotating, and that outcome is also compatible with the common-cause hypothesis. However, this solution may not be spontaneously elicited because of its complexity.

Still another example that seems related to the common-cause principle is the principle of grouping referred to by Wertheimer as that of "common fate." A set of elements that otherwise would appear as an aggregate of unrelated objects will be grouped together if they move in the same direction at the same speed. This principle has assumed great importance in Johansson's (1950) explanation of various motion effects in terms of vector analysis. The component of motion of several objects that is common to all is held to be extracted and results in a grouping or organization of those objects. But perhaps what underlies this powerful principle of grouping is the assumption that objects sharing these motion relations must do so on the basis of a common cause: they move together in the same direction because they constitute, in effect, one entity. Otherwise we again would have to accept this relation as one of coincidence.

The Principle Modified to Include Preferences in Stationary Configurations: Coincidence Explanation

So much for examples of *events* that illustrate the common-cause principle as the basis of preference. Does the principle apply to stationary configurations as well? I believe it does. Some cases illustrate it quite clearly, other cases call for some revision of the principle, and in still other cases the principle can be justifiably invoked but other hypotheses concerning preference also seem applicable.

Consider first an example of transparency such as is illustrated again in Fig. 6-1c. The reader may perceive this configuration as a small transparent rectangle in front of a larger one. The smaller rectangle then appears to be uniformly colored somewhat like a neutral density filter through which one sees the white and black background colors of the larger rectangle. The alternative to this percept is one in which there are four distinct regions each of a different color on the achromatic scale; and this of course would be the literal percept referred to in the preceding chapters. The perception of transparency is preferred, at least once it is achieved. No transparency effect occurs if we divide up this configuration into halves as in Fig. 6-1a and b (Metelli, 19).

The feature of this configuration that enables the transparency solution and leads to the preference is obviously the central vertical contour. This contour is the dividing edge between the colors of the larger rectangle but also between those of the smaller rectangle. To perceive the figure as nothing more than four different colors is to accept as unexplained coincidence these changes in color along this single contour; whereas to perceive a uniformly colored transparent rectangle in front of a larger rectangle is to account elegantly for this feature by a single explanation. "Single explanation" would seem to

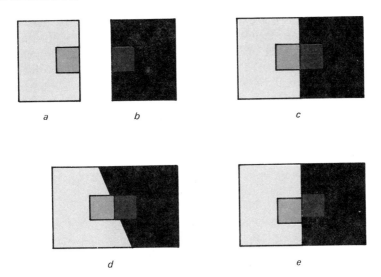

6-1. (a) and (b): The two halves of the transparency display in (c) do not yield a transparency effect. After Metelli, 1974. (d) and (e) also eliminate the effect.

be a better term than "common cause" in dealing with stationary configurations, because "cause" generally refers to an event. That the collinearity of inner rectangle dividing edge with outer rectangle dividing edge is crucial is evident from Fig. 6-1*d*, where the transparency solution is very difficult to achieve and certainly not preferred.

Another feature of Fig. 6-1*c* is important; namely, the two inner gray regions tend to be spontaneously organized as the two halves of one rectangle. Therefore, the transparency solution nicely accounts for the dual colors of what is clearly one "thing." A transparency effect is not easily achieved in Fig. 6-1*e*, although the collinearity of the dividing edges is nonetheless present.

It is important to make clear that all variations of Fig. 6-1 could lead to the transparency effect in that they satisfy the other conditions discussed in the preceding chapter as necessary for a solution. Were the two inner gray regions part of one uniform transparent surface, this would account for the proximal stimulus. Nor is there anything absent from the stimulus configuration that would have to be there were this a transparency display. Nor is there any contradiction. Of course, in this regard, the particular lightness or achromatic values used is important. The inner gray on the right could not be lighter than the one on the left given the outer black on the right. This aspect of the problem has been investigated by others, but it is interesting to think of these requirements in terms of the concept of stimulus support as discussed earlier (see Metelli, 1974). The achromatic values must fit in with the logical requirement of a transparency solution. But the main point I want to make is that despite the adequacy of all variations of Fig. 6-1 for the transparency solution, it is preferred only in *c*, because only in this case are there coincidental stimulus features that a common explanation elegantly explains. One further point of interest is that the preference for the common-explanation solution becomes greater as a function of the number of coincidental features. Compare Fig. 6-1 with Fig. 6-2.

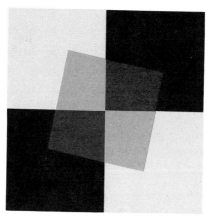

6-2. An improved transparency effect based on an increase in the number of coincidental features. After Metelli, 1974.

Another phenomenon that suggests a preference based on this principle is that of illusory contour (see pp. 104–106). With patterns of the kind shown in Fig. 4-5 naive observers do not necessarily achieve the effect immediately, but once they do, the perception of the inner figure with illusory contours is irreversible. I stress this fact again because it is important to be clear that an alternative is available that more literally accords with the proximal stimulus, namely, several unrelated figural fragments. To achieve the illusory-contour percept entails reversing figure and ground in which a region that otherwise would not become the figure now does so. Moreover this percept is without benefit of complete stimulus support given the absence of physical contours corresponding to all its phenomenal contours. Therefore, there must be a strong reason for this preference.

For a pattern such as that in Fig. 4-5, the illusory-contour percept provides a single explanation for what would otherwise be unexplained coincidence: incomplete circles whose missing parts have edges aligned or collinear with those of other incomplete circles and the potential presence of a triangular figure in the white central region. To be sure, not all these features are essential. As we have seen (pp. 105–106), incompletion is not a necessary factor, since the effect can be achieved with a pattern such as that in Fig. 2-5a. However, the effect seems to be stronger with incomplete circles and for the pattern in Fig. 4-4. Alignment and the appropriate juxtaposition of the three fragments with the critical "gaps" remains. The illusory-contour solution provides a common or single explanation for these factors. Conversely, the more coincidence or otherwise unexplained regularity there is, the stronger the preference for the illusory-contour percept. Thus, in Fig. 4-4, the effect seems to be more immediate, "better," stable, and irreversible than in Figs. 4-5 or 4-6a. Here, of course, more elements have been added that are aligned.

In the type of pattern that is referred to in the literature as interposition or overlapping (Fig. 6-3) there is a clear preference to perceive one figure (in this case, one rectangle) in front of and partially covering another figure (in this case, another rectangle). It is possible, however, to perceive this pattern differently, either as two figures in one plane sharing a contour partially common to both (which in this case would be an L-shaped figure and a rectangle) or as one figure overlapping another but the reverse of what is usually perceived, in this case as an L-shaped figure in front of and partially covering a figure that has a straight bottom and left side and an ill-defined top and right side where its upper right corner is behind the other region. Admittedly this last possibility is purely a logical one and is difficult to achieve even with effort. Since interposition is considered a pictorial clue to depth, it is well known, and various explanations of the preference have been proposed including attribution to past experience and the tendency toward simplicity or economy of encoding (Buffart, Leeuwenberg, and Restle, 1981). Once again, however, it is possible to invoke the principle that the perceptual system seeks and prefers an explanation that accounts for the stimulus without accepting coincidence. The critical region is the contour shared by both figures. To perceive both figures as in one plane is to accept the coinciding or meshing of part of the boundaries of both figures along this common contour, whereas to perceive one figure overlapping the other is to account for this region of the stimulus without entertaining any such coincidental arrangement in space.

In fact we can widen the discussion to include the phenomenon of figure-ground organization, since the same fact of a single contour separating two regions is at issue (Dinnerstein and Wertheimer, 1957). The really central aspect of figure-ground organization, as noted earlier, is the biased belonging of the dividing contour to one side or

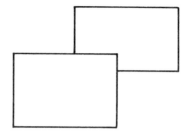

6-3. Interposition pattern.

the other as in Fig. 3-25. The contour gives one side a shape but not the other, at least at any moment. Figure-ground reversal then means that the contour now gives shape, a very different shape, to the other side. But why do we never perceive simultaneously two figures, i.e., two shaped regions sharing a contour?

In discussing this problem earlier, I suggested that one reason for the tendency to describe at any one time only the shape yielded by the belongingness of the contour to one region is that a single-contour stimulus does not adequately support a percept entailing two figures. This explanation can then also be applied to the case of interposition. But what I am suggesting now is another reason for the perceptual outcome in the more general case of figure-ground organization as well as in the specific case of interposition. The point is that figure-ground organization can be thought of as another case of preference, a preference to perceive one figure overlapping or in front of a ground. What I am suggesting is that this preference is based on the possibility of explaining the stimulus array without the necessity of accepting the coincidental meshing of the borders of two figures.

From this point of view interposition is just a special case of the figure-ground organizational preference but where the ground happens also to be another figure. In other words, at the dividing contour the figure perceived as "behind" is ground for the figure seen as "in front." However, there is more to the interposition effect than this. The analysis thus far would explain the preference for perceiving one region as figure overlapping another region as ground, but it does not explain why one of these regions rather than the other becomes figure. Perceiving either as figure (with the other serving as ground for it) eliminates the coincidence of two figures sharing the same contour. If, however, in the example of Fig. 6-3 the L-shaped region were to be seen as figure, there would be another coincidence; namely, the inner contours of the L would be perfectly aligned with two of the contours of the rectangle—in fact, in this example these alignments form two straight lines—and yet these aligned stimuli are purely coincidental from the standpoint of that solution. For if the rectangular region is ground for the L region, it is not a rectangle at all but some other ill-defined figure, parts of which go under the L. I am here referring to continuity of direction at the junction points of interposition patterns and suggesting that it accounts for which region is seen in front and which behind. When, however, the lower rectangular region is seen as figure, the continuity of direction along its upper and right contours is explained by perceiving each of these line segments as one entity. There would seem to be little doubt that such continuity of direction is one determinant—although not the only one—of the particular depth organization achieved in interposition patterns. What I am suggesting is that the basis of the operation of this factor is the preference for an outcome that explains what would otherwise be a coincidental alignment. This principle is similar to the concept of general viewpoint that has been advanced by investigators in the field of artificial intelligence (Huffman, 1971). It is proposed that observers tacitly assume that the appearance of some picture feature will not change *qualitatively* if they change their viewpoint slightly. Thus, the nature of the momentary percept is held not to be simply an accident of viewpoint.

The last example I would like to consider is the preference to perceive symmetrical regions as figures rather than as ground in ambiguous patterns (Fig. 6-4). There seems also to be a preference to perceive the black regions as figure here despite the use of a middle gray background—intended to equate the contrast of the white and black regions with the background—but by using the two patterns of Fig. 6-4 this factor can be controlled. The dominance of the symmetrical regions is then simply greater in *a* than in *b* where the two factors, blackness and symmetry, summate. It has recently been shown that another factor may be operating in patterns of this kind, namely, the preference for convex regions over concave ones, as can be seen in Fig. 6-5 (Arnheim, 1954; Kanizsa and Gerbino, 1976). Here convexity seems to be even more powerful than symmetry. But in Fig. 6-4 this factor is roughly equal for all regions so that it would seem correct to believe that symmetry is a determinant of figure-ground organization.

Again various explanations have been advanced, but here too I would like to suggest that the preference has to do with a solution that accounts for or provides an explanation for what would otherwise be coincidence. Some of the contours in the proximal stimulus are symmetrical with respect to one another. This regularity is "explained" if one perceives these contours as belonging to one region as figure, in other words if one perceives symmetrical figures, but remains purely coincidental if one perceives these regions as ground. In the latter case the fact that one contour of one figure is sym-

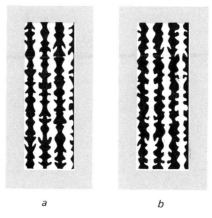

a   b

6-4. Figure preference based on symmetry; the preference to perceive black rather than white as the figure creates a stronger symmetry effect in *a* than in *b*. After Bahnsen, 1928.

6-5. Figure preference based on convexity despite the presence of vertically symmetrical regions. After Kanizsa and Gerbino, 1976.

metrical with one contour of a different figure, i.e., is a perfect copy of it except for left-right orientation, is an accidental occurrence. That is because only figures are "things," so that the symmetry within the retinal image would not be "caused" by symmetrical things in the environment with this organization.

If this way of looking at the symmetry effect is correct, one might predict other similar effects. For example, suppose some contours are parallel to one another but others are not. Then to perceive regions as figures whose sides are not parallel is to accept that parallelism as coincidental. There does appear to be a preference to perceive the regions whose sides are parallel as figure (Metzger, 1953) (Fig. 6-6).

In these last several examples the reader may have noted that I have departed from the principle of common cause in two respects. First, as already noted, I have substituted the term "single explana-

A   B

6-6. Figure preference based on parallelism. After Metzger, 1953.

tion" in order to deal with the examples of stationary configurations. Second, and more important, in these phenomena the "explanation" is not one that accounts for covariation, i.e., two or more simultaneously transforming stimulus features, but rather one that accounts for a relationship between or among stimulus features that can be thought of as coincidental. The common thread between the dynamic and configurational cases is, I believe, the preference for solutions that account for seeming coincidence. In the dynamic cases, the potential coincidence is temporal, where either two stimulus dimensions are transforming simultaneously—e.g., contour length and orientation in the kinetic depth effect—or two events are temporally contiguous—e.g., A's motion and B's motion in phenomenal causality. In stationary cases, the potential coincidence is spatial, where there are certain detected regularities such as alignment of contours or symmetries and these become coincidental if they are not produced by certain structures in the environment.

Among the examples already considered as illustrating the coincidence principle of preference several pertain to organization and grouping. Earlier I suggested that one can think about all grouping effects in terms of a cognitive process of decision (p. 71). The question now before us is why there would be a preference to "decide" to group in accord with the principles suggested by the Gestalt psychologists. I have already tried to answer that question for continuity of direction, common fate, figure-ground organization in general, and symmetry as a determinant of such organization in particular. The factors not yet considered are proximity, similarity, and closure.

As far as similarity is concerned, it clearly would be a matter of unexplained accidental placement if units that were similar to or identical with one another, with all other factors equal, were not in fact part of one larger whole. In other words, the similarity among units in the vertical direction in Fig. 6-7 remains unexplained and coincidental if the grouping were to yield horizontal rows. The same reasoning can be applied to grouping on the basis of proximity. Closure is a factor not easily demonstrated without confounding it with other factors. The Gestaltists referred to closure in another sense, namely, as a tendency operating on configurations that were incomplete, such as a circle with a gap. But this meaning is not the same as the one implied when closure is regarded as a principle that governs what is grouped with what. When a closed unit is created, figure-ground organization becomes the relevant principle of organization and the term "closure" seems redundant.

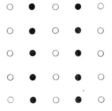

6-7. Grouping based on similarity.

Alternatives: The Simplicity Principle

It is time to consider whether this principle is different from the closely related and well-known principle of preference for simplicity and, if it is, whether it does a better job of accounting for the facts. Certainly many of our examples could be—and in fact have been—regarded as cases where the simplicity principle governs the outcome.

Perhaps the first point to make is that the coincidence-explanation principle does not necessarily predict that the outcome is "simple." That is, the search for a simple, single, or common *explanation* is not the same as the achievement of a *percept* that is simple. Thus, for example, in the case of the illusory-contour figures, the percept in which such contours do not arise is, let us say, of three separate units (Fig. 4-5). The percept in which such contours do arise is of these three units *plus* another figure in front of them. Therefore, not only does an additional figure emerge, but two phenomenal planes emerge instead of one. If we rule out completion as a factor by considering the example in Fig. 2-5, it is not possible in this case to invoke simplicity of the percept as a principle explaining the preference. However, the illusory-contoured triangle does account satisfactorily for the contour alignments and arrangement of "gaps" among the three units.

In the case of interposition, it is certainly true with the typical example of Fig. 6-3 that the percept is simpler in two respects when the effect occurs: the less regular L-shaped region becomes more regular, a rectangle, and the shape of both figures is now the same. But I would argue that this is a special case. The more general case is, of course, where the retinal image represents two figures of any shape, as in Fig. 6-8. Now when the interposition effect occurs, simplicity is not achieved in either respect: the figure seen as behind is not simpler than when it is seen as coplanar and, in fact, is less simple because I have deliberately drawn this region to be more or less symmetrical when it is *not* seen as behind; moreover that figure does not become similar to the other. But again, the interposition solution does account for the coincidental features discussed earlier that still prevail in this more general case.

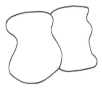

6-8. The more general case of interposition in which the two regions are irregular, unfamiliar shapes.

Thus the two principles are not the same, and moreover, in at least these examples, the simplicity principle cannot account for the outcome. The examples of events are particularly useful for comparing these principles. On logical ground it is not clear if simplicity is relevant at all to examples such as phenomenal causality. It seem to me not to be. Whether the motion of *b* is caused by the motion of *a* or simply occurs after the motion of *a* ceases is irrelevant as far as simplicity of perception is concerned. The percept of the event must still include the two motion sequences.

In the Gestalt approach to the preference for simplicity, the emphasis is on the tendency of self-regulating brain events to be directed toward the minimum energy level consistent with the prevailing stimulation. Regular perceptions reflect this underlying tendency toward minimum energy distribution. In the more modern version of this kind of theory, the emphasis is on the description or encoding of the possible perceptions of the ambiguous input. The preferred percept is the one for which such description is most economical. (Hochberg and McAlister, 1953; Attneave, 1954; Garner, 1974; Restle, 1979; Buffart, Leeuwenberg, and Restle, 1981.) However, the percept that can be encoded more economically or briefly, i.e., with fewer parameters, or otherwise expressed, with the minimum information load, will tend to be the most regular or "good" figure. That is because regular, symmetrical configurations or events are, from the standpoint of information, redundant and can thus be described economically. Therefore the evidence supporting this kind of theory is more or less the same as that supporting the Gestalt simplicity theory, namely, the tendency for observer to prefer percepts that are simpler, more regular, symmetrical and the like. The question then is whether such evidence is as strong as has been believed to be the case.

I have already given two examples, one on illusory-contour figures and one on interposition, that challenge the belief that the preferred perceptions are based on simplicity or regularity. Recently other evidence of this kind has been presented (Kanizsa, 1975). Thus, for example, where it might be assumed that the interposition-completion effects occuring in Fig. 6-9 are based on the simplicity principle, the parallel cases in Fig. 6-10 show that the same type of effect occurs despite the fact that the outcome is then less regular or less symmetrical than it would be without completion. Thus the regularization that results in the example of Fig. 6-9 seems to be a mere by-product of other factors at work, such as the avoidance of a contour "meshing" solution and organization on the basis of continuity of direction and, I would argue, is governed by the principle of coincidence explanation.

Another example of this kind is shown in Figs. 6-11 and 6-12. In Fig. 6-12 it has been assumed that the outcome when the two patterns in *a* are brought together in *b* is based on the preference for regular forms. But the same result occurs in Fig. 6-12, and here the outcome is if anything less regular than if one continued to perceive the patterns as in *a*. In fact in *b* each figure perceived is composed of some straight and some curved contours, which is not a particularly regular solution. Apparently, then, the outcome is based on continuity of direction and possibly also a preference for convex over concave figures (since in the central region both figures are now convex rather than concave).

The illustrations in Figs. 6-13 and 6-14 are even more impressive. Here when the two regular and symmetrical figures in *a* are brought together in *b*, the result is two new phenomenal figures neither of which is symmetrical or regular in any way. Yet in both cases the symmetry in *a* could be maintained in *b* by perceiving *b* as the two units in *a* placed together. The same factors of continuity of direction and preference for convexity would seem to be responsible for the outcome.

As a final example, consider the claim that the preference to per-

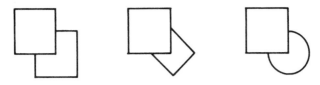

6-9. Examples of interposition that seem to be based on simplicity.
After Kanizsa, 1975.

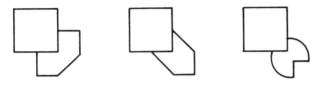

6-10. Examples similar to those in Figure 6-9 in which the interposition
outcome is less regular or symmetrical than would be a "meshing" coplanar
outcome. After Kanizsa, 1975.

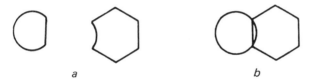

6-11. When the two halves of *a* are brought together in *b*, the perceptual
outcome seems to be based on the preference for regularity. After Kanizsa,
1975.

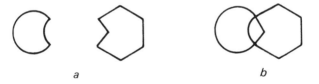

6-12. An example like that in Figure 6-11 in which the same kind of
outcome does not yield more regular shapes. After Kanizsa, 1974.

ceive projections of cubes as either two- or three-dimensional is based
on that outcome which is most regular (see Kopfermann, 1930).
Thus *a* in Fig. 6-15 is perceived as three-dimensional, where the two-
dimensional percept would be very irregular indeed; whereas *b* is
perceived as two-dimensional since, as such, it is perfectly symmetrical. I have mentioned elsewhere that this claim can be replaced by
two plausible hypotheses: (1) the pattern in *a* is seen as three-dimen-

6-13. Two symmetrical figures in *a* yield two asymmetrical figures in *b* when they are brought together, After Kanizsa, 1975.

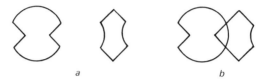

6-14. Two symmetrical figures in *a* yield two asymmetrical figures in *b* when they are brought together. After Kanizsa, 1975.

sional on the basis of past experience with projections of this kind; (2) the factor of continuity of direction along the central contours in *b* is powerful, thereby creating a new organization unlike the familiar one in *a* and thus preempting a past-experience effect (Rock, 1975). A recent demonstration supports this argument but puts it in a somewhat broader perspective. In Fig. 6-16 the pattern is such that a regular cube cannot be achieved in *a* nor a symmetrical two-dimensional configuration in *b* (Kanizsa, 1975). Nevertheless, *a* is seen as three- and *b* as two-dimensional. I would therefore revise my argument as follows: While the figure in *a* is novel as a specific structure, it nonetheless contains components present in Fig. 6-15*a* such as Y vertices that suggest three-dimensionality (Wallach, et al., 1953; Hochberg, 1968; Gúzman, 1965), and the remaining contours support that interpretation. Conversely, the two-dimensional percept achieved in *b* can be explained by the simple fact that there is no reason to invoke a three-dimensional interpretation on the basis of experience because the two crucial vertices of *a*, so important as cluing factors, are here camouflaged and therefore inoperative. With no good information for a three-dimensional interpretation, a two-dimensional one will prevail.

The examples of Figs. 6-15*b* and 6-15*a* are interesting because another factor may be operating. The outcome can be thought of as an illustration of the coincidence-explanation principle. To perceive this pattern as three-dimensional is to leave as unexplained coincidence the collinearity of the front and rear vertices along the line of sight, with the resulting radiating of the six internal contours from a common origin. When the pattern is perceived as two-dimensional,

6-15. The three-dimensional outcome in *a* and the two-dimensional outcome in *b* have been explained on the basis of a preference for regularity. After Kopfermann, 1930.

6-16. Figures very similar to those in 6-15 that yield a three-dimensional outcome in *a* and a two-dimensional outcome in *b*, but whose outcomes are not regular. After Kanizsa, 1975.

these contours are of course also perceived as emanating from such a common origin, but coincidence is no longer a factor.

The critical reader may argue that in many of the examples considered here that contradict the prediction based on simplicity or regularity of outcome, the principle responsible for what *is* perceived is continuity of direction. That principle is one of the Gestalt laws of grouping and has itself been interpreted as illustrating prägnanz. However, I would argue that this very powerful principle of perceptual organization can be best understood in terms of the coincidence-explanation principle. The perceptual system detects continuity of direction among contours. Once doing so, not to interpret two or more elements as parts of one larger entity is to accept that continuity as the result of coincidental placement in space of these elements, that is, of elements that have no intrinsic relationship to one another.

On the other hand, it is no doubt true about continuity of direction that more economical encoding can be given to a contour that does not change its direction or changes it gradually according to some mathematical function, and the same can be said about other Gestalt principles of grouping such as similarity, common fate, symmetry in figure-ground organization, and figure-ground organization in general (although grouping by proximity does not seem to be explicable in terms of this theoretical perspective). The important point to be made, though, is that in many of these examples, in the contest between the achievement of regularity of the whole configuration and the operation of principles such as continuity of direction that pertain only to local regions, it is the latter that wins out. Since it is the whole percept that must be accounted for, it would seem to be unwarranted to explain failure of preference for the most economical description of the whole stimulus on the basis of economy of description of only part of the whole (see Hochberg, 1981).

Some Related Meanings of Simplicity and Good Figure
SINGULARITY

In many cases, there does seem to be a principle at work that suggests a preference for certain unique, singular states or, in the Gestaltist's language, "prägnant steps." Suppose the proximal stimulus consists of images of two forms of the same shape but different size. With no depth cues—as in viewing luminous figures in the dark with one eye and head stationary—this stimulus will be seen as either literally, two circles of different size in the same plane *or* as two circles of the same size at approximately different distances. The stimulus will probably not be perceived as two circles of different size—but of less of a difference than the image-size difference—*and* as at somewhat different distances, although such an outcome is logically possible.

So it would seem that there is a preference for one of two solutions and each entails one dimension with respect to which the units are equal, either equality of size or equality of distance. Therefore, the fact of preference for one of these two solutions might be construed as a manifestation of a simplicity principle. However, another way of looking at this example is that with no information to the contrary, no special cues, the perceptual system assumes that all stimulus units are in one plane, particularly units that are adjacent (Gogel, 1965). But two units of the same shape and different size represents a cue to depth, namely, size perspective, a cue that may very well be learned. When the two units of different size are also of different shape the preference for the depth solution will generally not be manifested. Thus, there is a specific determinant for the two preferred solutions, neither of which necessarily has to do with simplicity, the equidistance tendency and the size-perspective cue.

Recent research supporting the belief in perceptual preference for prägnant or regular outcomes concerns the perception of line drawings (or the equivalent monocular projections) of certain three-dimensional structures. A pattern such as that shown in Fig. 6-17 is ambiguous with regard to the specific three-dimensional shape it represents. Investigators have found that provided the pattern *could be* the projection of a regular cuboid consisting of right angles, there is a strong tendency to perceive it as such (Perkins, 1972, 1976; Attneave and Frost, 1969; Attneave, 1972; Perkins and Cooper, 1980). Similar findings suggest that an ambiguous projection such as that shown in Fig. 6-18 may be perceived as a symmetrical object. The issue here is not the one of main concern in this chapter, namely, which of several qualitatively different perceptual solutions occur. Thus the question is not whether a two- or three-dimensional percept occurs or whether entirely different patterns or events are perceived given the same stimulus but rather the specific three-dimensional shape of an object such as a six-sided solid that will be preferred. Nonetheless it is of interest to consider what kind of case has been made for a simplicity theory in this domain of facts.

6-17. Drawing of a three-dimensional object that is perceived as representing a regular cube.

6-18. Drawing that can be perceived as representing a symmetrical three-dimensional object. After Perkins, 1976.

In some of these examples the specific percept such as the rectangularity of a corner may be a derivative of a tendency to perceive its sides as vertical and horizontal. Such seems to be the case for two-dimensional angles, since a right angle oriented obliquely appears to be more or less indeterminate as to its precise angle and thus is not easily discriminated from a slightly lesser or greater angle (see Fig. 6-19a). Yet the perception of a right angle is immediate when the sides are vertical and horizontal (Fig. 6-19b). Thus one might infer that what is immediately given are verticality and horizontality and that a phenomenal right angle is an emergent by-product of these directions. Precisely the same kind of fact may be true about three-dimensional corners. Thus angle a in Fig. 6-20A immediately appears to be rectangular, but in C (which is A rotated) it does not and in B (another rotation of A) it may or may not appear so (Draper, 1980). The explanation seems to be that in Fig. 6-20A the bottom of the object appears to be resting on a horizontal surface and the vertical lines of the figure are assumed to be vertical edges of the object. Therefore, the intersections of all bottom contours with vertical ones yield, derivatively, rectangular corners. These same corners do not necessarily look rectangular when the figure is rotated so that they no longer are at the bottom.

6-19. (a) The ease in discriminating a right angle when the sides are horizontal and vertical. (b) The difficulty in discriminating a right angle when the sides are oblique. After Goldmeier, 1972.

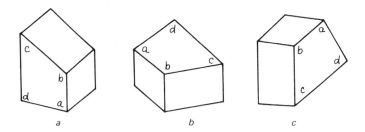

6-20. Three identical figures whose internal angles appear very different as a function of the orientation of the figure. In A, angle a appears to be rectangular, but in C, it does not, and in B, it may or may not appear so. After Draper, 1980.

Therefore, some of the findings suggesting a preference for those specific shapes that are most regular given such ambiguous figures may be instead explicable in terms of how we assign environmental coordinate directions to such figures. However, it is probable that not all the reported findings can be explained in this way. For example, the angle formed at corners *within* a horizontal plane, such as a or b in Fig. 6-20B, cannot be the derivative of sides that are horizontal and vertical, since both are horizontal. Interestingly enough, these angles remain ambiguous, with some observers seeing b as rectangular (and therefore not a), some seeing a as rectangular (and therefore not b), and some seeing neither as rectangular but seeing them as equal so that the top surface is symmetrical (Perkins, 1976).

That one of these three outcomes tends to occur rather than others suggests that they are unique or singular values along a continuum. The preference to perceive rectangular corners in line drawings not derivable from intersecting, phenomenally vertical and horizontal contours, is further evidenced in parallelogram-shaped regions representing horizontal surfaces as in Fig. 6-21. There is a strong tendency to perceive this shape as representing a rectangle. Naturally then, if seen as the top of an object with vertical edges, the object will look like a regular cuboid. So the question arises as to why the preference here is for rectangular shapes. Surely one answer that must be given great weight, unless and until it can be ruled out by experiment, is past experience. Since it is plausible that the very perception of line drawings of this kind as three- rather than two-dimensional is based on experience with actual objects in the environment, it is plausible that the *specific* three-dimensional shape perceived is based on the specific kind of experience we have had.

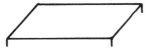

6-21. Parallelograms, even those in a horizontal plane, tend to look like rectangles at a slant.

We certainly have had much experience with regular, rectangular objects, and more particularly, most six-sided solid objects we encounter are rectangular. Therefore, given an ambiguous representation of such an object, rectangularity ought to be preferred on the basis of sheer frequency of past experience or, alternatively, on the basis of the singularity of rectangles that emerges from such experience. It is of interest that although cubes and boxes yield projections in linear perspective, drawings of them either in parallel projection as in Fig. 6-17 or in central projection as in Fig. 6-22 are nonetheless perceived as rectangular. Since such parallel projections of real objects would surely lead to phenomenally distorted cubes rather than to regular ones given the presence of other cues to depth, the acceptance of them in drawings as illustrations of regular cubes suggests a possible role of convention. Expressed differently, where the two-dimensional drawing is the only basis of depth perception, we will regard either converging lines or parallel lines as representing the parallel sides of rectangular surfaces receding in depth. This suggests that parallelism in pictures, being singular, is accepted as representing parallelism in objects even though the perceptual system "knows" that this projection is incorrect.

Returning to the analysis of the top side of Fig. 6-18, if we assume a preference for rectangular corners, only some of the four can qualify. That is because of a reason not yet discussed, that computation and internal consistency enter into the process. Therefore, if b is a right angle, only the supplement of it can also be a right angle, and thus the angle at a in Fig. 6-18 cannot represent it. So one solu-

6-22. Drawing in central projection, as here, as well as those in parallel projection, as in Figure 6-17, tend to be perceived as representing regular objects.

tion is to see one of these two as a right angle, and that occurs frequently. But since both *a* and *b* cannot be rectangular corners, the executive agency may seek still another solution, and one such is symmetry in which neither *a* nor *b* is rectangular but in which they are equal to each other.

In summary, it would seem that singularity may be a determinant of perceptual preference of a certain kind, and I would propose the following explanation. Whenever possible, perception will be specific and not indeterminate. Given the ambiguity in the drawing of the top side of the object in Fig. 6-17 (and in many of the other drawings under discussion) the executive agency seeks one specific solution. With nothing else to serve as a guide, the selection of a singular value such as regularity or symmetry makes a good deal of sense. Thus regular rather than irregular perceptions will occur, but that does not imply a tendency toward simplicity.

PERCEPTUAL SIMPLICITY UNRELATED TO
THE PROBLEM OF PREFERENCE

The concept of unique states illustrated in these last examples is similar to the concept of singularity discussed in Chapter 3. "Singularity" was defined as unique or distinctive values or reference points along some perceptual dimension such as orientation (for which vertical and horizontal are singular values) or curvature (for which straightness is a singular value) and so forth (Goldmeier, 1972; Rosch, 1975). It was suggested that singularity plays a very important role in the description of an object. While this concept is relevant to the question of what makes a figure "good," it does not follow that "goodness" in the sense of singularity illustrates or is subsumable under the category of simplicity. What makes a vertical line perceptually different from a tilted one is not simplicity but rather its distinctiveness in the continuum of possible orientations.

Figural goodness as defined in terms of economy of encoding or informational redundancy (Attneave, 1954; Garner, 1974) can, logically speaking, be a possible cause of preference, and we have discussed this possibility. But it can play other roles. Thus, for example,

Fig. 6-23a is a "better gestalt" than b by virtue of its symmetry. There are various consequences of figural goodness as, for example, easier discriminability of patterns from one another or superior learning and memory. But such effects are not to be confused with a preference to perceive a "good figure" over a less "good figure" given an ambiguous stimulus. It is the latter issue that concerns us here.

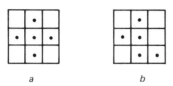

a   b

6-23. a is a "better" figure than b because of its symmetry. After Garner, 1974.

Still another meaning of simplicity, one that characterizes the Gestalt theorizing, is the notion that autochthonous forces are at work in the brain directed toward the creation of a "good figure." However, the presence of the stimulus was held to be a constraint that prevents optimum regularization. Hence it was predicted that under impoverished stimulus conditions such as brief exposure or low intensity, a more regular or simpler percept would result. This same theory led to the prediction that once the stimulus was no longer present, the memory trace of the percept would change in the direction of greater simplicity. As to impoverished stimulus conditions, the evidence for simpler perception has not been impressive, and what evidence there is is more parsimoniously interpreted in terms of past experience or response biases. Thus a briefly exposed incomplete circle may be described as a complete circle because that is a reasonable guess as to what had been presented—given an uncertain perception. As to memory change, the evidence thus far does not support the simplicity prediction, although some very recent research favors an interpretation of memory change in the direction of singular reference points (Goldmeier, 1972). In any event, effects of this kind are not directly relevant to the problem of preference of concern in this chapter.

Finally, there is the sense in which I have used the term "regularity" in relation to the coincidence principle. To briefly review, what I mean is that the perceptual system detects regular features such as continuity of direction or symmetry that are present in the stimulus. This step then governs the process of decision as to how to describe the stimulus; i.e., it influences the choice of a solution. The perceptual solution itself need not be simple, good, or regular, as already noted above. Thus the term "regularity" used to refer to features present in the stimulus is not the same as the use of the term to refer to the perceptual solution.

Past Experience

There remains the possibility of accounting for preferences on the basis of past experience. Some examples of this kind have already been given. The argument would be that we have had specific experience with one solution or much more experience with one solution.

It is certainly possible to argue that experience with rotating figures or experience based on one's own motion has led to the preference for interpreting kinetic image transformations as representing rigid objects undergoing rotation. Similarly, we have had some experience with objects seen only part at a time through narrow apertures; we have had specific experience with objects undergoing momentary occlusion; we have had experience with objects interposed in front of and partially occluding other objects; and so forth. Therefore, it is entirely possible that the very existence of certain potential solutions derives from experience, and the preference for these solutions may be based on the absence of, or limited amount of, experience with the alternative solution in each case.

There are, however, certain difficulties with this view. One is the problem of how the relevant experience is brought to bear on the impinging stimulus. The appropriate memories must be accessed by the stimulus. But memory access is ordinarily based on similarity between a perception and a memory, which means that first some degree of perceptual processing must occur without benefit of that memory. Thus, for example, in the case of interposition, we would have to assume that first the distinctive characteristics of this kind of pattern are perceived entailing T-type junctures of countours, etc. This could correspond to the literal solution discussed in the two previous chapters. Then, via similarity, memories of this kind of pattern are accessed. These memories, to be effective in leading to the interposition effect, must be associated with other memories of perceiving one object behind another. The latter memories then presumably serve to organize the percept along the same lines as in the past.

So this problem is not insurmountable, although it is surprising given the continued popularity of empiricist explanation in some quarters how little serious attention has been paid to precisely how experience can have its effect. The really serious problem flows from the analysis just presented. The perception in the past must be the one that is intended to explain the effect in the present. The argument is therefore potentially circular. How did one achieve the percept in the past? The only logical way out of this dilemma is to assume that the percept was originally achieved on the basis of some other determinant rather than that of experience. Thus, for example, it could be argued that initially the interposition pattern did not itself create a depth impression, but when the appropriate arrangement of objects was encountered, depth was achieved via other, possibly innate, cues, such as binocular disparity. The interposition pattern becomes a depth cue by association and thus ultimately can itself, without the presence of other cues, produce an impression of depth.

There is experimental evidence for just this kind of process. Subjects were first shown novel two-dimensional patterns that did not produce any impression of depth. They were then given experience in which the projection of these patterns resulted from three-dimensional objects but they were provided with cues (via kinetic transformation) that rendered the objects phenomenally three-dimensional. Subsequently the pattern alone (without any cues) looked three-dimensional (Wallach, O'Connell, and Neisser, 1953). Among other effects a process of this kind could account for several of the known pictorial cues to depth as well as for local depth cues such as Y vertices and parallelogram patterns.

This kind of mechanism may explain how past experience could have an effect in certain cases. But the problem then remains of why there is a preference. Logically, the stimulus pattern can be perceived now as it once was, before the acquisition of the relevant experience; or it can be perceived now in accord with that experience. Is it a sufficient answer merely to assert that there is a preference to perceive on the basis of experience? To make this point dramatically clear, consider those cases where the specific stimulus as such is sufficiently novel not to lead us to expect any immediate contact with what is stored in memory. Examples of this would be an illusory contour pattern such as that in Fig. 4-5 or the kind of pattern shown in Fig. 6-24, in which a familiar entity is "hidden." In these cases I believe we are on safe ground in maintaining that at the outset one perceives a meaningless array of fragments. But in time one perceives something familiar, although in such cases the transition may occur only if there is a deliberate search for an alternative solution. Once that occurs, the situation is irreversible. One can no longer perceive these as meaningless, as one did at the outset.

Apparently, then, the sequence is as follows: (1) One perceives first in terms of certain general principles of perceptual organization, which results in a particular description (the literal solution). (2) Some process leads to a perceptual reorganization (e.g., figure-ground reversal in the case of Figs. 4-5 and 6-24). (3) That in turn leads to recognition and identification of something familiar. (4) That

6-24. At the outset the black regions are figural, but once the familiar pattern in the white region is detected, it becomes stabilized as a figure.

in turn leads to stabilization of that familiar percept. If this analysis is correct, it means that prior experience enters in only as a stabilizing, preferential factor once the percept is achieved.

Why should this be the case? I can only try to answer this with a question. Why is recognition in general irreversible? One is not at liberty to choose *not* to recognize a familiar object, sound, or word. Once something is recognized, it means that certain memories are brought to bear on the perception, and except in rare cases, the participation of those memories in the overall experience cannot be eliminated. This same kind of inexorable memory-participation process may then account for perceptual preference whenever one of the alternatives, once perceived appropriately, is familiar.

Such preference may be a manifestation of a general principle operating in *all* of cognition according to which the deepest possible processing is dominant. Thus, for example, in listening to speech, deep structure and semantic content dominate rather than surface structure or perceived auditory properties.

There is one difference between the two kinds of examples just discussed. In the first kind—e.g., interposition—the argument is that the stimulus pattern leads immediately, albeit fleetingly and sometimes unconsciously, to a literal percept that, via similarity, accesses the appropriate memory. In the second kind—e.g., "poor" illusory-contour figures—the percept initially resulting from the stimulus pattern endures somewhat longer and therefore is always consciously experienced. Moreover, it does not lead via similarity to access to the memory. Rather a perceptual reorganization must occur first. In this case, then, the preferred percept occurs without benefit of memory access. Then and then only is there similarity with the memory. The memory here serves to stabilize an already occurring perception. But what the two kinds of examples have in common is that once the memory is accessed it leads inexorably and irreversibly to a percept governed by the content of the memory. In the first case, the memory that has the effect is one associated with the memory accessed via similarity; in the second case the memory that has the effect is accessed directly via similarity. Figure 6-25 illustrates the suggested sequence of events in the two cases.

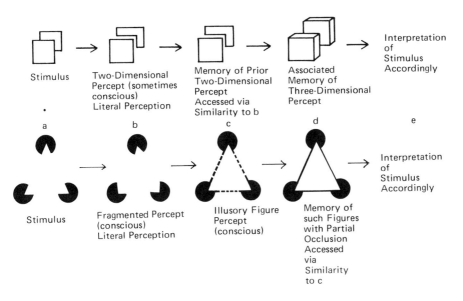

6-25. The sequence of events in two cases in which recognition leads to a preference to perceive in accord with the accessed memories.

The main point I wanted to make about both kinds of examples is that, however it is achieved, once memory access occurs, and thereby recognition, the percept that is in accord with the memory is irreversible. The preference can be said to be based upon the inability of the perceptual system to inhibit the memory reference, so to speak.

An important further question about these effects concerns the precise meaning of the term "familiar." In the examples given above I deliberately chose objects with which one has had specific prior experience, namely, a triangle and circles (Fig. 4-5) and a cursively written word (Fig. 6-24). In the case of illusory contour, however, it is not necessary that the figure be familiar, as can be seen in the illustration in Fig. 2-4b. However, there is familiarity with the general category of "opaque thing occluding parts of other things." Similarly, it is not necessary that we have familiarity with every conceivable three-dimensional object in order to maintain that experience with cuboid objects can play a determining role in the perception of line drawings or other equivalent projections (see Fig. 6-16a). Therefore, it is plausible to conclude that "category recognition" can play the same stabilizing, preference-generating, role as does specific recognition.

Does this analysis apply to all cases of preference? That seems unlikely for a number of reasons. In some cases the perception in queston is so fundamental that determination by past experiences can probably be ruled out. Kinetic transformations would seem to be one of the original sources of depth perception—by association with which certain stationary pictorial patterns may become cues—so that it is unlikely that preference here is based on past experience. Another example of this kind is phenomenal causality. It is difficult to imagine how such perception could possibly result from past experience. Even the great empiricist Helmholtz acknowledged that were it not for an innate predisposition to experience events on the basis of what he called a "law of causation," we would not derive very useful knowledge from our experience.

One might want to argue that the coincidence-explanation principle itself reduces to one concerning past experience because coincidence in the final analysis reduces to a matter of probability. For example, it is highly improbable that a contour of one object produces a retinal image that is contiguous with and collinear with the image of a contour produced by another object. It is improbable because this state of affairs will result only when the eye is in one particular position in space. For all other positions these two contours will not yield that retinal state of affairs. Therefore, if for "coincidence" one reads "improbable object or event" then does this principle not come down to Helmholtz' likelihood principle, namely, that we will tend to perceive those objects that would most likely be there to produce the given proximal stimulus?

However, probability (of a structure's being present or of an event's occurring) is a more all-embracing concept than coincidence, there being many reasons why something is improbable. For example, it is not probable that an object will behave in defiance of the law of gravity, but that has nothing to do with the notion of coincidence as used here. The claim about coincidence is that the literal or nonpreferred solution embodies an unexplained regularity or co-occurrence so that the perceptual system seeks to account for it by a different solution. Therefore, the guidance in the search for a better solution is not probability per se but the specific requirement of explaining the regularity or co-occurrence. Moreover the preferred solution is not necessarily one that is frequently encountered. Thus, for example, transparency conditions may be relatively infrequent as compared with those in which multiple regions of varying lightness values obtain. In principle, there need not be any past experience at all with the preferred solution, since it arises to account for the regularity or covariation, not simply because it is more probable. The kinetic depth effect is a possible case in point.

Concluding Remarks

One problem that any theory of preference must face concerns the selection of the preferred percept from among the competing alternatives. Are the alternatives all produced, i.e., realized psychologically, and do they arise in any particular order before the final solution is made? Different answers to these questions are implied by the different theories. According to the original Gestalt principle of prägnanz, the "good figure" results from a spontaneous process of self-distribution of forces in the neural medium based on a tendency toward equilibrium. Therefore, other less good perceptions would not even arise. According to the information-theory account, however, it would seem necessary to assume that each alternative is encoded and then the most economical one is selected. Otherwise how can it be known which *is* the most economical? Since nothing has been said by advocates of this approach about process, it is not known what arguments would be advanced about this kind of question. If, however, the alternatives must all be achieved before a selection is made, the entire process would hardly seem to be economical. The economy would reside only in the preservation in memory of what is perceived, not in the process of perception itself.

According to the account of preference I have suggested, there is a definite sequence of events that does entail realization of the alternatives. There is an initial stage in which the nonpreferred, literal solution occurs. It does not endure, either because the executive agency searches for a more satisfactory perception that explains the seeming coincidence, or because another such perception is clued that has this characteristic, or because another solution is stabilized by recognition.[3]

Are the major theories of preference considered here mutually exclusive? From the standpoint of logic they need not be, so that in

3. This analysis concerning the sequence of events, in which the literal solution occurs first, applies to most of the examples considered in this chapter. However, a difficulty with it arises in connection with examples that concern perceptual organization, e.g., figure-ground organization, for in such cases, to be consistent, it would have to be maintained that there is a stage of perception prior to the achievement of the organization. Presumably it would be in that stage that the coincidence or covariation is noted by the executive agency and a search for an explanation of it initiated. The difficulty with this claim is that organization is thought to occur at a very early stage of perceptual processing, and I have maintained that the literal perception is itself an organized one.

some cases one account may be correct and in others another account may be correct. Or in some cases the preferred solution may be over-determined by the simultaneous operation of more than one basis of preference.

My view is that the common-cause or coincidence-explanation principle is compatible with an explanation in terms of past experi-ence. Thus, for example, the interposition effect can result both from the rejection of coincidence as suggested earlier and from prior experience with such stimulus patterns.

In fact the two theories dovetail nicely. Given a search for a com-mon cause or a solution that accounts for coincidence in the literal percept, the presence of a highly available schema in memory makes it all the more likely that it will be accessed and accepted. On the other hand, there may be cases where only past experience deter-mines the outcome, as in fragmented figures where perceptual reor-ganization goes hand in hand with recognition. Alternatively, there may be cases where only the coincidence-explanation principle is correct, as in anorthoscopic perception.

The explanation of preference in terms of maintaining the rigidity of objects, i.e., of perceiving objects that themselves do not change, mentioned briefly at the beginning of this chapter, is essentially tele-ological. The description of the preferred outcome as one of un-changing objects is generally correct, but what drives the perceptual system to search for a solution beyond the literal one? Perhaps this principle can be reformulated to hold that the perceptual system abhors object-change solutions and thus searches for alternatives. Stated in this way, such a principle cannot be ruled out, but it would be limited to certain cases of event perception such as the kinetic depth effect or similar effects such as those studied by Johansson (1977).

As to the simplicity doctrine, I am inclined to rule it out on the basis of the evidence considered in this chapter. Also, such a theory is not compatible with the view of perception as problem solving. In essence, the modern information-theory account of simplicity is based on the assumption that the driving force behind preference is the economy of description. But the task for perception is to achieve veridicality. It is not obvious why that description which is most eco-nomical will be most likely to yield a veridical perceptual outcome. On the other hand, the common-cause or coincidence-explanation theory is one that is likely to achieve veridicality because it concerns the relationship between the stimulus and the probable events or configurations in the environment that would yield that stimulus. Therefore, it is a principle that makes sense in the context of percep-tion as a process of problem solving.

7 ⬛

Perception as Problem Solving: IV. Case Studies

THE PURPOSE OF THIS CHAPTER is twofold: to examine in some detail several perceptual phenomena that heretofore have not been considered to be based on a process of problem solving in order to demonstrate the legitimacy and fruitfulness of this approach; and to illustrate the principles of the problem-solving process as developed in the previous chapters.

Apparent Motion

Although we know a good deal about the conditions that produce the illusory impression of motion referred to as apparent movement (or sometimes as stroboscopic or beta movement or the phi phenomenon), we still do not understand why it occurs or, for that matter, why it occurs only under certain conditions. What we know about this effect is that given the sudden appearance of object *a*, its sudden disappearance, followed at just the right time interval by object *b* in just the right new spatial location, one tends to see motion of *a* to *b*. Wertheimer (1912) suggested that a short circuit occurred in the brain between the locus of the projection of *a* and *b* to the visual cortex, a nice example of a spontaneous interaction theory. This idea is no longer taken too seriously. An alternative, more modern explanation is that a motion-detector cell in the visual nervous system will discharge even if the appropriate region of the retina is stimulated discontinuously by two points rather than by a point moving over the retina. Such cells do seem to exist in various species of animals (Grüsser-Cornehls, 1973; Barlow and Levick, 1965).

However, it is not necessarily the case that the condition for apparent motion perception entail stimulation of separate retinal regions. Ordinarily that is the case, since a and b are in separate spatial locations and the eye is more or less stationary. It is possible that what matters is the *perception* of a and b in separate locations.

To get at this question, an experiment was performed in which the observers had to move their eyes quickly back and forth synchronous with the onset of a and b, so that each stimulated the same central region of the retina, rather than as, more typically, two discretely different loci (Rock and Ebenholtz, 1962). Therefore, the conditions for apparent motion might be thought not to exist. Yet the observer does locate a and b in phenomenally discrete places in the environment. The result was that although nothing was said to the observers about motion that might create an expectation of perceiving motion, most observers spontaneously perceived motion. This experiment seems to prove that, in humans at least, it is incorrect to maintain that apparent motion is necessarily determined by a spread of neural excitation from one cortical locus to another or in terms of a cell that detects sudden change of retinal location. There is neither change of retinal nor cortical locus of projection of a and b here.

These findings would seem to demonstrate that an explanation in terms of spontaneous interaction or of a motion-detector mechanism is not necessary, although it may prove to be sufficient under certain conditions of stimulation (see below, p. 176). The phenomenon itself seems to rule out explanation in terms of a stimulus theory because there is a property in the percept that simply is not present in the stimulus, namely, motion. An entirely different view is that the impression of motion is a solution to the problem posed by the rather unusual stimulus sequence. First a inexplicably disappears. Then b inexplicably appears elsewhere. By "inexplicable" I mean that when an object in the world disappears as we are looking at it, it is generally because another object moves in front of it or it is occluded by another object because of our motion. However, when a stationary object suddenly and rapidly moves to another location, it does tend to disappear from one location and to appear in another. Therefore, perhaps this state of affairs in a stroboscopic display suggests the solution of motion. (Such a problem-solving view of apparent motion may be applicable when the spatial and temporal separation between a and b is greater than certain small values, below which a more direct sensory basis of motion may be applicable (see footnotes 1 and 2 and p. 176).)

Given that potential solution, the question arises as to whether it is acceptable. Motion from a to b does account for the brief stimulation by a and b, the first requirement (of stimulus conformity), but is not the absence of any visible object between locus a and b a violation of the second requirement (of stimulus support)? If the solution is "*a* moving across space to *b*" does this not call for stimulus support in the form of continuously visible motion across that spatial interval? Ordinarily that would be true, but it is a fact that has been demonstrated that for very rapid motion of an *actually* displacing object, little more than a blur can be seen in the region between the terminal locations (Kaufman et al., 1971). It was shown that if the terminal locations are occluded, no motion of a moving object is seen. Therefore, when the spatial and temporal intervals between *a* and *b* in a stroboscopic display are such as would correspond with the real motion of a rapidly displacing object, the absence of continuously visible movement need not act as a constraint against perceiving movement. In fact, this analysis may explain why *slow* rates of alternation do *not* lead to the impression of motion. By "slow rate" I mean a condition with a relatively long interval between the disappearance (offset) of *a* and the appearance (onset) of *b*. Such a rate would imply a slowly moving object, and a slowly moving object *would* normally be seen throughout the spatial interval between *a* and *b*. Therefore, the absence of object motion over that interval at slow rates of attention is a violation of the requirement of stimulus support. Hence the movement solution is not acceptable at slow rates even if the offset and onset tend to suggest this solution.

While on this topic of rate, I might briefly comment on the case where the alternation is very rapid, i.e., a zero or only a minimum interval between the offset of *a* and onset of *b*. If the "on" time of *a* and *b* is itself very brief, this state of affairs will result in *a* and *b* being visible simultaneously by virtue of neural persistence. But if *a* is visible when *b* appears, the solution that *a* has moved to *b* is not supported, or one might say, is contradicted. I have tested this deduction by using rates of alternation that ordinarily *do* produce the motion effect but with the following variation: First *a* appears, followed by the usual blank interval; when *b* appears, so does *a* (in its original location). Therefore, the sequence of events is: *a*; *a* and *b*; *a*; *a* and *b*, etc. See Fig. 7-1. If the presence of *a* during the exposure of *b* violates the requirements of the motion solution, observers should not achieve a motion effect under these conditions. Our observers did not. If, however, the display is changed so that the *a* object that appears concurrently with *b* but in the same location as *a* is somewhat different from the *a* that appears alone, observers *do* perceive *a* moving to *b*. The sequence is *a*; *a'* and *b*; *a*; *a'* and *b*; etc. (see Fig. 7-1).

It was noted above that in the typical experiment on apparent motion, *a* and *b* inexplicably disappear and appear. What was meant was that no rationale is provided to the observer of why they appear and disappear, as is the case when things in the environment suddenly

7-1. Left: a sequence that eliminates apparent motion. Right: a sequence in which apparent motion from *a* to *b* occurs.

appear or disappear because another object in front suddenly moves out of the way or in the way. This suggested the following kind of experiment. Suppose we cause the retina to be stimulated by *a* and *b* in just the right places at just the right tempo, etc., but by a method in which we move an opaque object back and forth, alternately covering and uncovering *a* and *b*[1] (Fig. 7-2). As far as other theories of apparent movement are concerned, there is no obvious reason why these conditions should not produce an impression of *a* and *b* moving. But from the standpoint of problem-solving theory, we have now provided an explicable basis for the alternate appearance and disappearance of *a* and *b*, namely, that they are there all the time but undergoing covering and uncovering. Therefore, the perceptual system may prefer this solution, or at least we are offering it a viable alternative not usually available (see Stoper, 1964; Sigman and Rock, 1974).

The subjects rarely perceived motion of the dots here (see Table 7-1). Some may object that the presence of the actually moving rectangle interfered in some way with perceiving apparent motion. It is, after all, an unusual, atypical, way of studying such motion. The rectangle may draw the subject's attention or otherwise inhibit motion perception of the dots. For this reason a slight change was introduced, one that had another purpose to it as well. Suppose the rectangle moves, but a bit too far, far enough no longer to be in front of where the dot had been. But by a method the details of which need not be discussed here, things were so arranged that when the

1. There appear to be two kinds of apparent movement, depending upon the spatial and temporal separation between stimuli *a* and *b* (see p. 176). Therefore, some readers may wish to know what these values were in the experiments under discussion. The angular separation between the objects (dots) in the experiment described in Table 7-1, A and B, and illustrated in Figs. 7-2 and 7-3, was 3.8 degrees, and the duration of exposure of each dot and the interstimulus interval between dots was of the order of 200 to 300 milliseconds. In the other experiments described in Table 7-1, C through G, and illustrated in Figs. 7-4 and 7-5, the angular separation between the dots was either 1.5 or 1.7 degrees, the duration of exposure 250 or 350 milliseconds, and the interstimulus interval between dots, 75 or 107 milliseconds.

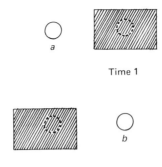

Time 1

Time 2

7-2. An opaque rectangle moves back and forth alternately covering and uncovering dots *a* and *b*. Apparent motion is rarely perceived. After Sigman and Rock, 1974.

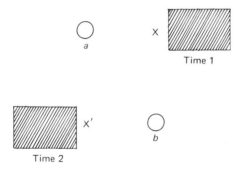

Time 1

Time 2

7-3. A rectangle is moved back and forth as dots appear and disappear but in its terminal positions is not in front of regions where the dots were. Apparent motion is perceived. After Sigman and Rock, 1974.

rectangle is in its terminal location, the dot is nonetheless not visible (see Fig. 7-3).

Now it is no longer a fitting or intelligent solution to perceive *a* and *b* as two permanently present dots that are simply undergoing covering and uncovering. For it can be seen that in fact the rectangle is not covering the spot in its terminal location and yet the spot is not visible (violation of the stimulus-support requirement). Therefore, the best solution is again one of movement, and movement was frequently perceived (Table 7-1). Note that this experiment serves as a control for the objection raised to the first one: the moving rectangle here does *not* interfere with perceiving motion of the dots.

Another variation performed is based on the idea that for the covering-uncovering solution to be viable, the covering object must appear to be opaque. If it does not, it can hardly be covering any-

Table 7-1: Perception of Apparent Movement under Varying Conditions

Condition	N	Number Reporting Apparent Motion†	Median Duration of Perceived Motion, sec‡
A. Opaque Square Covering Dots (see Fig. 7-2)	48*	4	
B. Opaque Square Not Covering Dots (see Fig. 7-3)	48*	27	
C. Rectangular Outline (see Fig. 7-4i)	10		28.6
D. Solid Rectangle with Oblique Lines (see Fig. 7-4ii)	10		5.8
E. Solid Plain Rectangle	10		0.1
F. Illusory Contour Rectangle (see Fig. 7-5A)	11		14.3
G. Control for Condition F (see Fig. 7-5B)	11		48.4

*Combines subjects in four different experiments using either head motion or display motion to alternately cover and uncover the dots.
†Thirty-second viewing period.   ‡Sixty-second viewing period.

thing. This factor was manipulated in the experiments illustrated in Fig. 7-4. The actual stimulus conditions are very similar in the two conditions employed, but in one case, i, because the oblique lines within the rectangle are stationary and aligned with all the others, the rectangle looks like a hollow wire perimeter. In the other case, ii, because the lines inside it move with the rectangle, it looks like an opaque object. The difference in results is very clear: in one case, i, subjects by and large perceive movement, whereas in the other case, ii, they do not (Table 7-1). A hollow rectangle is in contradiction of the property of opacity required by the covering-uncovering solution.

In the final experiment, conditions were such that no physical contours at all moved back and forth in front of the dots. There was, however, a phenomenally opaque object that moved, one based on illusory contour (Fig. 7-5a). Most subjects did not see any movement, and those who did saw it only for brief periods (Fig. 7-5a). In a control experiment the orientation of the corner fragments was changed so that no subjective rectangle was perceived (Fig. 7-5b), and this array was moved back and forth. Now the majority of subjects did perceive movement most of the time (Table 7-1).

It should be noted that in all these cases where a covering-uncovering effect is perceived there is no reason why movement of the dots

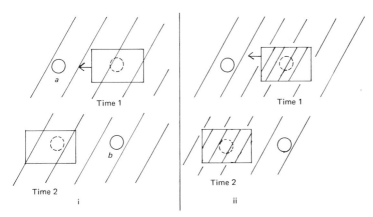

7-4. (i) A moving rectangle looks like an outline perimeter rather than a solid opaque figure. Apparent motion is perceived. (ii) A moving rectangle looks like a solid figure with oblique stripes. Here apparent motion is not perceived. After Sigman and Rock, 1974.

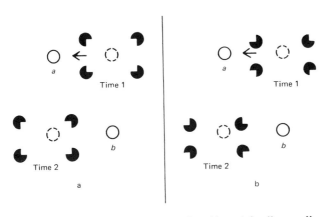

7-5. (a) An illusory contour rectangle alternately "covers" and "uncovers" dots. Apparent motion is not perceived. (b) Control experiment using a similar moving pattern that is not seen as an opaque rectangle. Apparent motion is perceived. After Sigman and Rock, 1974.

could not have been perceived. That is to say, none of the requirements discussed in previous chapters would be violated if the observer were to see an opaque rectangle moving back and forth and, simultaneous with this, a dot stroboscopically moving in the opposite direction. This solution would also account for the stimulus sequence. Conversely everything implied by that solution is represented in the stimulus, and no contradictory perception is occuring. Therefore, the tendency to perceive dots undergoing occlusion and disocclusion rather than dots moving represents a preference for one solution over the other. The preferred solution is obviously related to a very basic characteristic of perception, namely, object permanence, the tendency to assume the continued presence or existence of an object even when it is made momentarily invisible. But given the very strong predilection we have to perceive apparent motion even under the most unlikely conditions, it remains a problem why it is not perceived in this situation and the object-permanence solution is preferred. A possible answer is that the covering-uncovering solution accounts for all stimulus change by one "cause": a moving rectangle covering and uncovering spots that are continuously present. The other solution entails two independent events that are coincidentally and unaccountably correlated: a rectangle moving in one direction and in antiphase to spots moving in the opposite direction.

There is one other line of evidence that, in my opinion, also supports a problem-solving interpretation of apparent movement. If the stimulus consists of more than a single dot or line, the problem of correspondence arises, i.e., the problem of which items in a are seen moving to which in b. To make the point clear, suppose a and b each consists of a set of dots as in Fig. 7-6. What will be seen here is the rectangular grouping moving as a whole (Ternus, 1926). Apparently the perceptual system seeks a movement solution that will do justice to the entire array. Indeed, were this not the case, the motion perceived in moving pictures would be quite chaotic, because it is typically objects consisting of many parts that change location from frame to frame (and often many such objects are simultaneously changing locations in either the same or varying directions). Yet this outcome is not predictable at all in terms of the other kinds of theories mentioned earlier. In fact, in the illustration in Fig. 7-6, based on the principle of proximity that often is relevant in apparent motion, the rightmost dots in a should be seen to move to where the leftmost dots in b are located (but of course in that event the remaining two dots would appear to flash on and off without appearing to move).[2]

A related example is the perception of motion of complex stimuli such as the three-dimensional structures shown in Fig. 7-7 when presented stroboscopically in two different perspectives (Shepard and Judd, 1976). At the appropriate rate of alternation, observers

2. The example given here is not quite the same as one used by Ternus (1926) in which some of the dots overlapped in the two presentations, e.g., a, b, c alternating with b', c', d. In that case the outcome depends upon the duration of the interval between the two presentations and whether they both are presented to the same eye or not (Pantle and Picciano, 1976).

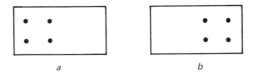

7-6. *a* and *b* consist of a set of dots that change their locations as shown. The entire configuration as a coherent whole is typically perceived to move.

perceive these objects rotating through the angle necessary to account for the change in perspective from *a* to *b*. This effect clearly implies that the perceptual system deals with the problem of accounting for the differences in *a* and *b* by an intelligent motion solution. A further finding of interest is that the optimum rate of alternation for achieving a smooth coherent rotation of a rigid whole object was an inverse function of the angular difference between the two perspective views. In other words, the greater the angle through which rotational motion was seen, the slower the rate of alternation had to be.

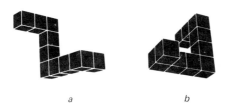

7-7. When apparent movement occurs, the three-dimensional object in *a* appears to rotate through the necessary angle to account for the change in perspective in *b*. After Shepard and Judd, 1976.

This finding can be considered to be in keeping with one of Korte's laws which states that optimum apparent motion is preserved when the spatial separation between *a* and *b* is increased by increasing the time interval between presentation of *a* and *b* (Korte, 1915). This law makes sense if one assumes that the perceived speed of motion is constant. If, therefore, the mental representation of the object has to rotate through a greater angle, more time is required. Further support for this interpretation is provided by an experiment which asked the following question: Is it the retinal separation or the perceived separation that governs Korte's law? Perceived separation was varied by creating conditions in which *a* and *b* appeared at differing distance but were always located so as to project to the eye in the same retinal loci (Corbin, 1942; Attneave and Block, 1973). The experiment demonstrated that it was the perceived spatial separation not the retinal separation that entered into Korte's law. It would seem then that the mentally constructed motion is such as to dovetail with the perceived distances across which the moving object must traverse.

Some recent findings might be taken as evidence against the interpretation of apparent movement perception as a solution that offers a sensible explanation of the *a* to *b* sequence. It was shown that similarity of form does not govern the correspondence of what is seen as moving to what when an ambiguous display such as is shown in Fig. 7-8 is presented (Navon, 1976; Ullman, 1979; Kolers, 1972). For example, the items in *a* are not seen to be moving horizontally to the items in *b* (i.e., Z to Z and E to E) significantly more than they are seen moving vertically (i.e., Z to E and E to Z). One might have thought that in such an ambiguous display, similarity would govern the choice. However, Navon has suggested the plausible explanation that the perceptual system processes the presence of an entity in a certain location before it processes the form of that entity. Thus before the exact forms in *b* are psychologically realized, the perceptual system detects "things" in certain new locations. As soon as these "things" are detected, motion to them from the location of the items in *a* is inferred. Thus it is too late for form to play a role. However, while motion from *a* to *b* will occur despite dissimilarity of form, it is worth repeating a point made earlier (Chapter 5, p. 119), that there is an experience of *a* transforming during its motion so that it turns into *b*, an example of perceptual rationalization (Kolers and Pomerantz, 1971).

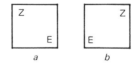

7-8. When *a* and *b* alternate, similarity of form does not govern correspondence, so that Z in *a* will equally often appear to move to E in *b* as to Z. After Navon, 1976.

Based on a similar design, another experiment might be thought to contradict the conclusion stated above concerning the relevance of perceived rather than retinal separation in Korte's law. Following the presentation of a line stimulus in *a*, two such stimuli are presented in *b*. All are seen on a background of a drawn three-dimensional structure such as a cuboid (Ullman, 1979). The location of lines in *b* can thus vary in their proximity to the one in *a* either in retinal locus or in perceived three-dimensional space. It was found that a always appeared to move to the line in b that was more proximal in retinal locus even if both lines in b were equally far away in three-dimensional space; a did not appear to move more often to the line in b that was more proximal in three-dimensional space if both lines were equally far away in retinal location. One flaw in this experiment is that it relies entirely on a picture to create the requisite three-dimensionality. This is inadequate, as can be proved simply by asking observers which stimulus line in b appears nearer to the one in a. Two-dimensional proximity will undoubtedly govern here. The experiment should be repeated using full-depth cues.

Assuming, however, that the results would be the same, how can they be reconciled with those showing that it is perceived separation, not retinal separation, that governs Korte's law? The answer may be that this experiment (and the previously described one on similarity of form) is directed at the correspondence question, whereas those on Korte's law are directed at the occurrence of or smoothness, goodness, or quality of perceived motion where correspondence is not at issue (see Marr, 1982).

If, as seems plausible, correspondence is based on early "thing" processing, such things or units may be localized in two-dimensional space before they can be appropriately localized in three-dimensional space. In other words, depth localization may take more time and the correspondence decision may be made before it occurs. But once correspondence is decided, or in cases where there is only one thing in a and one in b so that the correspondence issue does not arise, factors such as perceived separation in space become relevant. This can be shown using measures such as whether apparent motion occurs or not and the "goodness" or smoothness of motion.

In summary, a problem-solving theory can account for a number of facts about the perception of apparent movement. It offers an explanation of why motion is seen. Unlike other theories, it takes as a point of departure and is quite compatible with the fact that the conditions leading to motion perception entail change of perceived location rather than change of retinal location (an example of a perception—in this case motion—based on another perception—in this case direction). It offers a rationale for the known facts about alternation, i.e., why movement is perceived only within a certain range of middle values of interstimulus interval. It can deal with the kinds of perceived transformations or movements that occur when a and b are more than single dots or lines, such as groupings or forms with subparts. Finally it permits us to predict instances where no motion will be perceived despite the maintenance of the spatial and temporal parameters that ordinarily produce the apparent motion effect.

On the other hand, this theory does not yet explain all the known facts. It does not explain the reported findings that motion is seen more readily if both *a* and *b* are placed so that their projections fall within one hemisphere of the brain rather than, as is more typical when the observer fixates between *a* and *b*, *a* falls in one hemisphere and *b* in the other (Gengerelli, 1948); nor does it explain why the effect is less readily obtained or not obtained of all when *a* stimulates one eye and *b* the other compared with the case where *a* and *b* stimulate one eye (Ammons and Weitz, 1951; Braddick, 1974). And finally a problem-solving theory might be considered to be inappropriate as an explanation of the apparent motion effect that seems to occur in decorticated guinea pigs (Smith, 1940) or newly born lower organisms such as fish or insects (Rock, Tauber, and Heller, 1965).

However, there now seems to be fairly good evidence that there are two kinds of apparent motion (Braddick, 1974; Anstis, 1978; Marr, 1982). One kind, referred to as the short-range process, occurs over very small angular separations of *a* and *b* and of very short interstimulus intervals.[3] There is reason for believing that this kind may be based on motion-detector neurons responsive to a small shift in stimulation on the retina. For example, the effect requires stimulation of the *same* eye by *a* and *b* (Braddick, 1974). The other kind, referred to as the long-range process, occurs over larger angular separations of *a* and *b* and longer time intervals.[4] This process is probably not based on the activation of motion-detector neurons. For example, apparent motion occurs when *a* stimulates one eye and *b* the other (Shipley, Kenney and King, 1945). Most if not all of the evidence discussed in the preceding pages pertains to this long-range process. The short-range process thus seems to have a direct sensory basis, whereas the long-range process seems to have a cognitive basis. In the light of this distinction, it is possible that the findings referred to in the preceding paragraph are explicable in terms of the short-range process.

Anorthoscopic Form Perception

In previous chapters I have referred to the perception of form resulting from viewing a figure only a small part of which is visible at a time as the figure is revealed successively through a narrow slit.

---

3. The spatial separation for this kind of apparent motion must be 15 minutes of arc or less and the interstimulus interval less than 100 milliseconds (with a stimulus duration time of around 100 milliseconds.

4. Of the order of *degrees* of arc and with interstimulus intervals of 200 to 300 milliseconds or more.

In Chapter 3 (pp. 45-47) the concern was with the implication of this anorthoscopic paradigm for the thesis that form perception results from the perception of the set of directions relative to one another that collectively constitute a figure's boundaries. An experiment with a moving point was described, the path of which was perceptible whether its image displaced over the retina (with eyes stationary) or did not (when the eyes tracked the point). One method for presenting such a single-element stimulus is the anorthoscopic procedure. It was noted that when this method is used, and the entire display of slit in an opaque surface in front of a line figure is visible, the observer perceives a figure with extended contours similar to ordinary form perception and not merely the path of a moving point of light, as occurs when the surface containing the slit is not visible.

In Chapter 4 (pp. 108-110) the anorthoscopic paradigm was referred to as an illustration of how an hypothesis can be clued by an unambiguous feature such as the end of a line figure as it moves across the opening of the slit. In Chapter 5 (pp. 124-125) an explanation was suggested as to why an extended figure is not perceived when the surface containing the slit is either not visible or is visible but appears as only narrow strips that surround the slit on both sides. These conditions do not provide stimulus support for the figure-percept solution (or they can be thought of as evidence contradicting that solution). A brief discussion of the importance for sustaining the figure solution of change of slope of the visible element of the figure was included, as was the adverse effect of altering the perception of the slit region from "ground" to "figure."

In this section I propose to discuss more thoroughly the problem of and evidence bearing on anorthoscopic perception (see Rock, 1981). In the 19th century several investigators, including Plateau (1836), Zöllner (1862), and Helmholtz (1867), employed an experimental device called the anorthoscope, consisting of two disks mounted axially one behind the other. The disks could rotate at different speeds and in opposite directions. The observer viewed figures on the rear disk through slits in the front disk, thereby perceiving certain illusory distortions of the figures. They referred to their procedure as anorthoscopic presentation, presumably because it was a nonstandard method of visual stimulation.

This early work was largely forgotten until relatively recently when the phenomenon was rediscovered by Parks (1965). Both in the 19th century and after the rediscovery a controversy arose over how to interpret the effect. Helmholtz and others thought an extended image of the figure behind the slit is always imprinted on the retina. This interpretation has since come to be known as the "retinal painting" hypothesis, since it is based on the assumption that an image is spread over the retina one area at a time. Where the slit moves in front of a stationary figure, retinal painting would require observers to keep their eyes stationary and not track the slit. Where the figure moves behind a stationary slit, retinal painting would require the observers to move their eyes back and forth. Helmholtz argued that observers might be holding their eyes stationary in the first case and moving them in the second case but not necessarily know whether their eyes were still or moving. As a matter of fact, though, it would be an odd and difficult thing to do to hold the eyes still in viewing a moving display or to engage in smooth pursuit movement in viewing a stationary display.

If the retinal-painting hypothesis is correct, the perception of form under such conditions would hardly be surprising. An extended retinal image of a figure would then be present in both the cases cited above, and the only difference between perception in the abnormal viewing situation and in the normal situation would be that in anorthoscopic viewing the image would be created in segments presented successively rather than simultaneously. Moreover, because the sensory cells of the retina tend to continue discharging for a short time after the stimulation has ended (neural persistence), the image presented in successive segments would not be significantly different from an image formed all at once, assuming that the successive presentation was fast enough. The observer would therefore be expected to perceive the entire anorthoscopic image as if it had been established normally.

However, in our laboratory we have been able to demonstrate by eye recordings taken when the observers are viewing a figure moving behind a stationary slit that by and large they do not move their eyes (See also Fendrich and Mack, 1980). Conversely, when they view a slit moving over a stationary figure, they tend to move their eyes along with the slit (Rock and Halper, 1969).

Other experiments done in our laboratory (using the moving-slit condition) and elsewhere indicate that the only way the anorthoscopic effect could result from retinal painting would be if the image of the slit were to move over the retina very quickly. Only at a speed approaching five sweeps per second, or five times the speed we typically employ, could neural persistence account for the impression of a whole figure. Moreover, in the moving-figure condition, retinal painting would have to be based on eye movements, and the eyes would therefore have to move back and forth at that rapid rate. Observers are unable to move their eyes that fast.[5]

5. This research, as yet unpublished, was done in collaboration with Joseph Di Vita.

On the basis of this and other evidence one must conclude that retinal painting is not a sufficiently general explanation of anorthoscopic perception. What then is the basis of form perception in experiments of this kind? Consider again the tracking of a luminous point in a dark room. Although the image of the point does not move over the retina, the perceptual system does receive information about the path of the point, because the eyes must move to track it. The executive agency takes into account the position of the eyes in arriving at the changing location of the point in space. Thus the perceived path of the point is derived from the set of perceived locations of the point as it moves.[6]

The same argument can be made when proper conditions for anorthoscopic perception apply. The executive agency integrates the information about the locations of the parts of the figure as they appear successively through the slit. When the slit moves over a stationary figure, the visible element at one end of the figure is characterized as, say, "at the bottom of the slit and to the left," whereas a moment later the visible element is characterized as "higher in the slit and straight ahead." Integrating these directions leads to the perception of an oblique line sloping upward to the right. Therefore, both anorthoscopic perception and normal form perception can be said to entail an integration of all given locations of parts of a figure with respect to one another into a description of the whole.

Further evidence for this conclusion derives from an effect that we refer to as *induced form* (Rock and Gilchrist, 1975a). It is based on inducing horizontal movement in the opaque surface containing the slit by displacing a textured background so that the slit seems to be moving over a figure. To introduce a vertical dimension to the figure, both the surface with slit and the background are moved together vertically. The element representing the momentarily revealed part of the figure is absolutely stationary (see Fig. 7-9). The theoretical point of this experiment is simply to demonstrate that what matters for the anorthoscopic effect is the impression of viewing sucessive phenomenal parts of a figure.

---

6. Generalizing this argument to all form perception, one can say, as I did in Chapter 3 (pp. 45-47), that when an extended image of a figure is present on the retina, the observer perceives each point of the figure as being in a certain place. Hence one might suppose that the perceived shape is the result of a mental integration of the perceived locations of all the points constituting the shape. This process might be organized hierarchically, with points integrated into lines or contours and the placement of contours with respect to one another integrated into figures, culminating in a description of the whole figure. If it is, it might be the set of perceived locations that is important about a retinal image of a figure. In other words, perhaps the role of the retinal contours of a figure is to establish a set of locations that together yield a form.

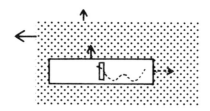

7-9. Induced form. The surface containing the slit appears to move side to side by virtue of the movement of the background. Observers achieve an anorthoscopic form percept although the visible part of the figure is stationary. After Rock and Gilchrist, 1975*a*.

This explanation turns out to be incomplete for several reasons. First, direction with respect to the observer is given directly in the moving-slit condition but not in the moving-figure condition. In the latter case the slit remains stationary and straight ahead. Where then does the information come from that the successively revealed parts of the figure are in different places? Apparently it must first be hypothesized that something is moving behind the slit. Once that idea is entertained, the temporal succession of stimuli can be converted into a spatial configuration. Next, as in the moving-slit condition, the perceptual system can integrate the sequence of stimuli into a shape based on the set of directions of the parts with respect to one another.

There is another reason why the location-integration hypothesis does not tell the whole story. Often observers do not perceive a figure in the anorthoscopic display. This result must be related in some way to the kind of figure we employ, because other investigators have not reported such failures. We have deliberately chosen figures with several distinctive features: they are single lines and are shaped so that only one figure element at a time is visible in the slit; they are fairly smooth curves rather than patterns with abrupt changes in direction; they are continuous lines rather than dotted or broken; they do not depict familiar objects. Other have employed features such as squares, circles, and ellipses or outline drawings of familiar objects such as animals.

Our kind of figure is ambiguous in that the anorthoscopic display of it could logically represent either an element moving vertically in a slit or an extended figure being revealed through the slit. Therefore, one can investigate what factors are important in figure perception, since a figure is not always perceived. The guiding hypothesis has been that figure perception under anorthoscopic conditions is based on a process of problem solving. Even before any location-integration activity begins, the executive agency must hypothesize that there is an extended figure behind the slit and that it is being revealed in successive sections.

To clarify this hypothesis, consider again what would be seen if the figure were made luminous and were viewed in a dark room, so that the slit was not visible. In the stationary-slit condition all the observer would see would be a point of light moving up and down. In the moving-slit condition the observer would see a moving point of light traversing a path. In neither case would one describe the percept as an extended figure. Thus it seems the observer must perceive that the momentary view is through a narrow slit and that the remainder of the figure is hidden by an opaque surface, an example of what I described in Chapter 5 as perceptual support. To perceive a figure anorthoscopically, it is not enough to know one is looking through a slit; the slit must be seen.

Not only must the slit be seen, the visible portion of the figure must also extend fully across it. To investigate this point, Alan Gilchrist and I devised a technique for simulating anorthoscopic presentation. Instead of a figure behind the slit, there was only a small line segment drawn on transparent plastic. The plastic was attached by thin rods to a set of rollers that rode on a cam not visible through the slit; the cam had the shape of the figure to be simulated (Fig. 7-10).

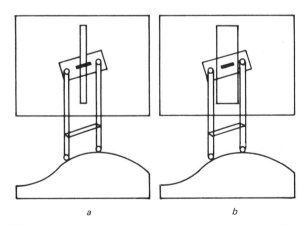

a   *b*

7-10. (a) A method for simulating anorthoscopic perception. The segment representing the visible part of a figure changes its slope as it displaces vertically. (b) The slit is widened so that the visible segment does not entirely fill it. In this case observers do not achieve the anorthoscopic effect.

Under some conditions, simulation with this device leads to figure perception (Fig. 7-10a). In this instance, however, we widened the

slit so that the visible line segment did not fill it but rather was isolated within it (Fig. 7-10b). Although the segment moved vertically
and changed its slope just as it had when the slit was narrower, a figure was never perceived. The stimulus apparently violated the logic
of the solution: that one was viewing a continuous figure being revealed through the slit. A variation of the simulation technique also
made it possible to investigate the effect of holding the slope constant
when the visible line segment did fill the slit. This was achieved by
using only one of the rollers shown in Fig. 7-10. As was noted in a
previous chapter (p. 125), when the slope did not change but the
slit was wide enough for the slope to be detected, a figure was not
perceived. The constant slope does not provide the necessary stimulus support, or otherwise interpreted, it contradicts the solution of a
curved-line figure behind the opaque surface.

Consider next the kind of figure displayed behind the stationary
slit. If the figure is an oblique straight line and the ends do not pass
across the slit (which, let us say, is about 1/16 inch wide and is
viewed from a distance of about 3 feet), the stimulus consists of a
line segment undergoing vertical displacement. This stimulus could
result from either of two physical events: a segment moving up and
down at a uniform speed or an oblique line moving back and forth
horizontally at a uniform speed.

Under such conditions of ambiguity, the shape of the aperture has
an important influence on what is perceived (Wallach, 1935). When
the aperture is square, and oblique lines move behind it, the outcome is ambiguous. The oblique lines can appear to move vertically, horizontally, or obliquely (Fig. 7-11a). But when the aperture
is rectangular, there is a strong tendency to perceive the lines as
moving parallel to its long axis, probably because with such a narrow
opening there is no information to suggest any change in the identity
of the segment (see Fig. 7-11b). Accordingly we have found that
under such conditions in the anorthoscopic paradigm, an extended,
moving figure is never perceived.

Suppose the figure is a curved line but the conditions of presentation are otherwise the same. Here the only new factor is that the
visible segment accelerates and decelerates as it moves vertically
(Fig. 7-12). We have found that this information does not alter the
outcome. All observers perceive a vertically moving segment, not a
figure.

Next suppose the width of the slit is increased to 1/8 inch. Under
these conditions we found that the slope of the visible segment and
the change in the slope can be detected through the slit. Even with
this information, however, and the correlated vertical acceleration
and deceleration of the segment, most observers still do not perceive

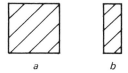

a   b

7-11. (a) When oblique lines move behind a square aperture, the perceived direction of the movement is ambiguous. (b) When a rectangular aperture is used, observers tend to perceive the lines moving in the direction of long axis. This tendency opposes the anorthoscopic effect. After Wallach, 1935.

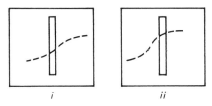

i   ii

7-12. The successive positions of a curved figure moving horizontally behind a narrow slit. Despite acceleration and deceleration of the visible segment as a function of the figure's curvature, the anorthoscopic effect does not occur.

a figure. Hence one might conclude that the tendency noted by Wallach for a segment to maintain its identity is so strong that it will do so even if the segment appears to tilt back and forth as it rises and falls (see Fig. 7-13).

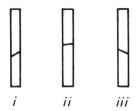

i   ii   iii

7-13. The successive views of a figure's visible segment, using a wider slit. Here the slope and change of slope of the segment is visible, but the anorthoscopic effect is typically not achieved.

Only when the slit is widened still further, so that the curvature and the change in the curvature become detectable through the slit, does the balance shift in favor of figure perception (Fig. 7-14). The explanation of this shift in preference, in line with the principle enunciated in the preceding chapter, may well be that the acceleration of a line segment upward just as its slope is tilting toward the vertical and just as its curvature is changing appropriately would represent a good deal of coincidental covariation. The executive agency seeks an explanation, and one is provided by the solution of a moving figure. However, others may feel that the shift in preference is based on the gain in economy of encoding in terms of a rigid moving figure once the stimulus transformation includes the further complexities of change of curvature.

i   *ii*   *iii*

7-14. The successive views using a slit wide enough to allow perception of the curvature of the visible segment. Here the anorthoscopic effect is generally achieved.

There are other kinds of information in the display that can affect the outcome. As noted earlier, allowing the ends of the figure to be seen through the slit may lead to the hypothesis of a moving figure. Clearly, when the ends are visible, there is a moment of unambiguous information to the effect that something is moving across the slit, not along it. One might think of this information as a clue that suggests the figure hypothesis, but in itself the information does not seem to be adequate; an oblique straight line still tends to be seen as a vertically moving segment except for the brief time when the end points are in view. When such end-of-line information is coupled with change-of-slope information, however, the balance is often shifted toward figure perception. Perhaps the reason is that a perceived change of slope tends to support the hypothesis triggered by seeing the ends of the line. Of course, the kind of unambiguous information given by the end points may be present throughout a figure if it happens to have sharp discontinuities or changes in the direction of contours. But we did not use this kind of figure.

There is another factor we have found to be important. If observers know the display may represent a figure behind a slit, they are more likely to perceive it. Ordinarily merely knowing something does not affect what one perceives, but in this case it does. Even with prior knowledge the conditions must be favorable for form perception. Such knowledge has no effect if the slope of the line segment never changes or if the figure is luminous and viewed in the dark so that the slit is not visible.[7]

7. The research described here on characteristics of the display that govern the anorthoscopic effect was done in collaboration with Ann Corrigan and Fred Halper.

Our research on the characteristics of the display that govern the perceptual outcome bears on the question of whether the anorthoscopic effect is genuinely perceptual when retinal painting is ruled out. Several investigators have contended that when only part of the figure is seen at any moment, the impression one has of the whole figure is more a matter of knowing it is present than a result of true form perception. Only if one sees the whole figure at once, they say, should the experience be described as form perception (see, for example, Haber and Nathanson, 1968).

In my opinion there is a confusion here that can be traced to a theoretical preconception. If one believes form perception presupposes an extended retinal image all of whose parts are present simultaneously, then of course the anorthoscopic effect cannot be perceptual when retinal painting is ruled out. There is no reason, however, to equate form perception with simultaneity. Hearing a melody or a spoken sentence is certainly perceptual, even though what is perceived is extended over time. Only if the figure or the slit were moved very slowly might it be appropriate to say that one fails to perceive the figure although one knows it is there. Analogously, one might block the perception of a melody by separating the tones by extremely long intervals.

The fact is that those who have experienced the anorthoscopic effect in the laboratory are sure it is a perceptual phenomenon. One reason for the certainty is undoubtedly the clear differences that are observed under the different conditions. Hence the failures become very important. Observers may know that a figure is being presented, but they never perceive it unless the conditions allow. In other words, there are cases where it *is* appropriate to say the observer knows a figure is being presented but does not perceive it; these cases, in contrast, make it clear that the other cases are perceptual. Moreover, there are many instances where perception shifts from one possibility to the other during the presentation; such a reversal under ambiguous conditions is one of the hallmarks of the perceptual process.

There is one peculiarity of anorthoscopic presentation not yet mentioned. When the slit is stationary and the figure is moving, the perceived figure is generally distorted; typically it is compressed along the axis of its motion. Thus a circle may look like an ellipse with its longer axis vertical. What is responsible for this effect? Advocates of the retinal-painting hypothesis have suggested that the distortion results from the failure of observers to move their eyes in perfect synchrony with the figure. If the eye movement fell short of either the speed or the amplitude of the figure motion, the image painted on the retina would be compressed, and that could nicely account for the distortion.

An experiment tends to support this hypothesis (Anstis and Atkinson, 1967). The investigators introduced a moving target (a point of light) that the observer had to track back and forth. By varying the speed of the target point with respect to the speed of the figure it was possible to "paint" a retinal image of the figure that varied in shape. For example, if the moving figure was a circle and the tracking target moved at half that speed, the image spread over the retina would be an ellipse whose vertical axis was twice as long as its horizontal axis. If the figure moved to the right as the tracking target moved to the left, the image created would be the reverse of the one yielded by ordinary perception. The observers reported seeing figures whose shapes corresponded precisely with the retinal image established.

These findings are puzzling, if, as I have argued here, there is good reason to doubt that the retinal-painting hypothesis accounts for the anorthoscopic effect or for these perceptual distortions. Ultimately we devised an alternative explanation that seems to fit the facts better. To understand the explanation, one must first consider more carefully the perception of figure motion when the slit is stationary and the figure is moving. The question that then arises is: What determines the perceived speed of the figure?[8] Given the narrowness of the slit, information about the speed of the figure can hardly be conveyed accurately by the brief passage of distinguishable contour components across the slit. Moreover, with the figures we employ there are no distinguishable components except at the ends. Therefore, the speed of the figure is at best ambiguously represented. The perceived length of the figure depends entirely on its perceived speed, at least according to the problem-solving interpretation of anorthoscopic perception. Since the typical outcome when there is no tracking target is one of perceived compression, it would seem that the speed is underestimated. It is not clear why this is so, but it is important to keep in mind that there is no reason to expect accurate speed perception either.

When a tracking target is introduced, the executive agency seems to assume that the figure is moving at the speed of the target. One can formulate a general hypothesis that eye movement is a clue to figure motion under anorthoscopic conditions. Given this clue, the perceived speed of the figure is doubled when the target moves at twice the figure speed and is reduced by half when the target moves at half the figure speed. Since the apparent length of the figure de-

8. According to the retinal-painting hypothesis, what should be seen is the whole figure, simultaneously present, within a large rectangular opening; the rectangle represents the image of the slit, which should also be painted on the retina. The figure should not be seen as moving at all, and thus the question of its apparent speed does not even arise.

pends on how far it seems to move behind the slit during the interval between the appearance of one end and the appearance of the other end, the distortion found by Anstis and Atkinson is explained. It results from a mental construction of length derived from the apparent speed of the figure and not directly from a distorted retinal image (see Fig. 7-15).

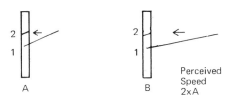

7-15. The effect of perceived speed of a figure on its apparent length. If speed in *b* is perceived to be twice that in *a*, the length of the figure would have to be twice that in *a*.

To provide evidence for this interpretation, we performed an experiment in which observers viewed a curved-line figure moving behind a slit at a certain speed and at the same time tracked a target dot.[9] In effect we repeated the Anstis-Atkinson experiment but with our kind of figure. There was an important addition to the procedure as well. The observer not only indicated the perceived length of the figure (by adjusting a shadow-casting device that varied the length of a replica of the figure while holding its height constant) but also told us whether the speed of the figure appeared to be equal to, less than, or greater than that of the moving target. Observations were made at several target speeds: equal to the speed of the figure, half the speed of the figure, twice the speed of the figure, and the same speed as the figure but in the opposite direction. There was also a condition of free viewing, with no moving target present.

Whenever a target was tracked, all observers perceived a figure, whereas in the free-viewing condition none did. We deliberately made the slit very narrow in this experiment (1/16 inch), which we knew would eliminate the anorthoscopic effect under the more usual no-tracking condition. Therefore, it is evident that tracking is an important determinant of the anorthoscopic figure percept. We believe the major reason for this is that movement of the eyes provides an effective clue that a figure is moving back and forth behind the slit. Precisely why this is the case we do not know. In any event, such a clue

9. The experiment was performed in collaboration with Joseph Di Vita, Deborah Wheeler, and Fred Halper.

specifies the figure's speed, whereas without it the speed is indeterminate. It would be difficult to arrive at a figure percept of a definite length with the speed indeterminate. Virtually all the observers reported that the speed of the figure was the same or almost the same as that of the target regardless of the actual speed of each. As for the perceived length of the figure, if the actual length is assumed to be 1, the perceived length was 0.77 when the two speeds were the same, 1.65 when the target speed was twice that of the figure, and 0.50 when the target speed was half that of the figure.

When the figure moved in one direction and the target in the opposite direction at the same speed, all observers perceived the figure as the mirror image of its true shape. For this test we employed an asymmetrical figure and had observers make a rough sketch of what they perceived. The outcome was what one would predict on the basis of the reversed image painted over the retina, but it was also what we predicted from our eye-movement cluing hypothesis. Not only was the speed of the figure behind the slit ambiguous; its direction was too. For example, if a figure such as the letter E moved to the right, the end points of its three horizontal prongs would be revealed first. If the figure seemed to be moving to the left but the end points of the prongs still appeared first and were followed by the vertical contour of the E, the figure would have to be a left-right reversed figure (see Fig. 7-16). That the direction of motion was mistakenly perceived in this way is borne out by the incorrect response of all those observers who perceived the reversed figure when they were asked its direction of movement.

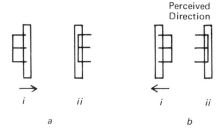

7-16. How misperception of the direction of figure motion will result in mirror reversal of its shape. (a) The E moves toward the right so that the end points of the horizontal prongs are revealed first, followed by the vertical contour. (b) The same sequence of visible parts occurs if a left-right reversed E were to be moving leftward.

In this last experiment the tracking of a moving target has the effect of spreading the image of the figure over the retina. Although we have rejected the hypothesis that the image thus painted is the direct cause of anorthoscopic form perception and of the observed distortions, there is one aspect of the results that suggests an important role of the extended image. The figure percept is clearer and more similar to ordinary form perception under these conditions than it is when the eyes are stationary while viewing the stationary slit. We have found a similar result when, in the moving-slit condition, a stationary point is introduced and observers fix their gaze on it. Here too the image is spread over the retina, whereas in tracking the moving slit there is no such extended image. In both cases, when such an image is present, an observer rarely fails to perceive a figure even if the conditions are otherwise poor for the anorthoscopic effect.

One might call the improvement in anorthoscopic perception that can be attributed to an extended retinal image a *facilitation effect.* Apparently the perceptual system finds it easier to integrate the successive slices of the figure into a whole form when the slices are spread across the retina than when they all fall on one vertical strip. Although the extended image can thereby facilitate the anorthoscopic effect, it does not directly cause it. The evidence for this conclusion has been given above, and in addition it is supported by certain further control experiments.

In one of these experiments the figure was a horizontal straight line, and the observer tracked a target moving at the same speed as the figure. Although an image of the figure was spread over the retina, no observer perceived a figure. Instead the visible segment of the line seemed to be part of the slit and there was no impression of anything moving (except the target dot). One can only conclude that without some vertical displacement of the contour there is no reason for the executive agency to infer that an extended figure is moving behind the slit; hence the extended image, although present, is not integrated into a mentally constructed form.

In another control experiment the figure consisted of a cutout stencil of a curved figure, which was illuminated from behind (Fig. 7-17a). A luminous target dot was also provided, and the display was viewed in an otherwise dark room. When the observer tracked the moving target, an image of the bright line was spread over the retina. Nevertheless, no figure was perceived. Rather, the visible segment of the figure, which was essentially a small point of light, appeared to move up and down, although its path seemed to be slightly tilted from the vertical (Fig. 7-17b). Since tracking has the effect of spreading the image of the visible fragment over the retina, the failure to obtain a figure percept in this case shows dramatically how the anorthoscopic effect depends on the perception of the slit as an opening in an opaque surface. Only then is there the needed support for the mental construction of an extended figure.

In any event there seem to be two factors that combine to make

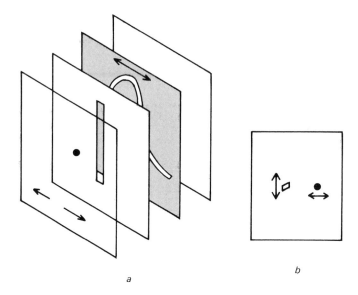

7-17. Control experiment on retinal painting. (a) In a dark room a rear illuminated cut-out of the figure moves side to side behind a slit, and the observer tracks a dot moving sideways. (b) Despite the presence of the image of the figure spread over the retina, a figure is not perceived.

the anorthoscopic perception of form particularly successful when a moving target is tracked. First, eye movement serves as a clue that a figure is moving at right angles to the slit and imparts an unambiguous speed to the figure. Second, the presence of an image spread over the retina facilitates the integration of the figure. Perhaps it is this facilitation that has led some investigators to subscribe to the retinal-painting hypothesis.

In conclusion, it would seem that the perception of form can be understood as a process of integrating information about the location of the parts of a figure with respect to one another culminating in a structural description of the shape. Physical contours or their representations in the retinal image are not necessary as long as some kind of information indicates where the boundaries of a figure are. Consequently anorthoscopic presentation of a figure one part at a time can yield form perception even though no extended image of the whole figure appears on the retina at any one time.

Because the anorthoscopic display is ambiguous and does not necessarily represent an occluded figure, however, the achievement of a form percept in this case entails a process of problem solving. The presence of a region seen as a narrow aperture in a surrounding opaque surface is indispensable, and the stimulus must have certain other properties as well if perception of a figure is to be the preferred solution. The principle of common cause of covarying transforma- tions may be the basis of the preference, although other explanations cannot yet be ruled out. Where a figure moves behind a stationary slit, the perceptual system must also infer the figure's speed and direction in order to reconstruct its length and shape.

If this interpretation of the events that follow viewing an anortho- scopic display is correct, the perception of form is a process much closer to the cognitive level than has heretofore been recognized. It cannot be explained as a direct outcome of the physiological pro- cessing of contours stimulating the retina.

Kinetic Stimulus Transformations

As we move about in the environment, the retinal images of objects undergo continuous transformation. In the laboratory situation, with the observer stationary, these changing patterns have been simulated (Wallach and O'Connell, 1953). Thin wire objects were rotated be- hind a screen, and observers viewed the transforming shadow patterns cast by such objects. They typically perceived three-dimensional ob- jects rather than the logically possible alternative of distorting two- dimensional configurations. This phenomenon is referred to as the kinetic depth effect. The investigators believed that the effect de- pends on the simultaneous change of length and orientation of the figure's retinal projection. Although the presence of orientation change simultaneous with length change is not absolutely necessary, when it does change concomitantly with length, the kinetic depth effect is stronger and more readily achieved.

The question I would like to pose is why does this transforming stimulus pattern generally produce an impression of a three-dimen- sional object? One answer might be that the combined length and orientation change constitutes the stimulus for depth, that is, leads directly to that percept much as a particular frequency of vibration of a sound wave reaching the ear constitutes the stimulus for the per- ception of a tone of a particular pitch.

The answer against which I would like to pit the direct stimulus theory is that the impression of depth results from a process like inference or problem solving. To review, the broad outlines of such a theory would run somewhat as follows: The transforming stimulus poses the problem for the perceptual system as to what event in the world might be producing it. Hypotheses are generated that could do justice to that stimulus; that is, if such and such an event were occur- ring, it would produce just that stimulus. In the present case, two such hypotheses can be considered that would have that capability: (1) There is a line in a frontal plane that is simultaneously changing its length and orientation. This is a literal solution in that the percept correlates perfectly with the stimulus transformations. One might speculate, therefore, that no prior experience is necessary for this hypothesis to be generated and also that, in terms of sequence, it is the first hypothesis to be generated. (2) There is a line of constant length rotating in depth about a particular axis. This is clearly not a literal solution, since it entails the third dimension. It might well arise by virtue of prior experience from daily life in which such transforming images were produced by rotating rigid objects. Alternatively, it is logically possible that the depth hypothesis is available on the basis of evolutionary "experience" rather than on the ontogenetic experience of the individual. In any event, I would argue that this solution occurs only after the literal solution has been entertained. Once the hypothesis is elicited, the second stage of processing consists of comparing stimulus and solution in terms of the adequacy of the match. However, the two hypotheses both are acceptable in terms of the criteria of a stimulus-solution match. In other words, both hypotheses account for the stimulus transformation and both are supported by that transformation.

Of these two possible solutions, the depth solution is preferred, since, given a sufficient period of observation, most observers arrive at it and, once having done so, do not, indeed generally cannot, avoid it and revert to the literal solution. Thus, a fundamental problem here is to explain the preference for that perception given the ambiguity of the stimulus.

Logically there can be no denying that the simultaneous length and orientation change of a line stimulus is ambiguous in that it can be produced in several different ways, either by an object rotating in depth or by a stimulus actually changing length and orientation. In fact, in the experiments to be described here, the transforming image is never produced by an object rotating in depth. But beyond the issue of logical ambiguity is the matter of de facto ambiguity. The transforming stimulus does not always lead to the depth percept, and even when it does, is often preceded by a period when it is not so perceived.

In our laboratory certain changes in the typical kinetic depth display were deliberately introduced to investigate whether the rotation-in-depth outcome would still be preferred (Rock and Smith, 1981). We were predicting that in certain of these cases that perceptual outcome would not be preferred because it no longer constitutes the best or preferred solution to the problem. In these experiments, the transforming image was a luminous line simultaneously changing its length and orientation. The line, in fact, was oscillating in a frontal plane, thus changing its orientation. But it was rotating behind and viewed through a rectangular aperture, thus also changing the length of its image. The transforming image, therefore, was roughly the same as the one that would be produced by a thin rod rotating in depth about a vertical axis at its midpoint. Consequently, it was expected that when only the line was visible, the typical kinetic depth effect would occur.

The question of alternative solutions was investigated by permitting the aperture to be visible. In one experiment it appeared as an aperture. Thus, a solution other than the kinetic depth effect became possible, namely, interpreting the line as oscillating in a frontal plane behind an aperture. In other words, if the ends of the line always remain contiguous with the inner contour of a visible aperture, one interpretation of what is occurring might be that of a line oscillating behind the aperture in a frontal plane. This interpretation may then be preferred over that of a line rotating in depth, although the latter certainly remains a logically possible interpretation.

Subjects viewed the display in a dark room with one eye only. They were several feet from a luminous line that oscillated in a frontal plane. This was accomplished by placing the line on a disk that alternately changed its direction of rotation. The line was viewed under three conditions. In condition 1, the line could be seen through a rectangular aperture, but the aperture itself was not visible because it was not made of luminous materials (Figs. 7-18 and 7-19a). Consequently, the retinal projection of the line concurrently changed length and orientation, thereby fulfilling the essential stimulus requirement for the occurrence of the kinetic depth effect (Fig. 7-19a). Virtually all the subjects perceived the line rotating in depth (see Table 7-2). The typical stimulus requirements for the occurrence of the kinetic depth effect prevailed; so the depth solution is to be expected here. Since the line in fact oscillated in a frontal plane, the perception of depth is illusory and cannot be based on information picked up concerning the actual spatial arrangement.

In condition 2, the only variation was that the rectangle surrounding the aperture was luminous and, therefore, visible (Fig. 7-19b). Prior to the onset of motion, subjects perceived the luminous display here as a line behind a rectangular frame. When the line was oscillated, only one observer perceived rotation in depth (Table 7-2). All others veridically perceived the objective state of affairs, a line of constant length oscillating in a frontal plane undergoing partial occlusion by the aperture.

In condition 3, a substitute aperture was visible. It was a luminous, irregularly contoured frame, similar to that seen in condition 2. However, the upper and lower contours of this frame were not coterminous with the path of the ends of the line (Fig. 7-19c). In other

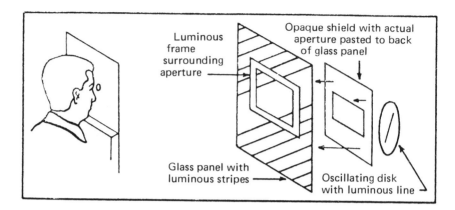

7-18. The illustration of an experiment on kinetic stimulus transformation. A luminous oscillating line is seen through the aperture in a dark room. The luminous frame in front shown here and used in Condition 2 (see Figure 7-19b) is not visible in all conditions. After Rock and Smith, 1981.

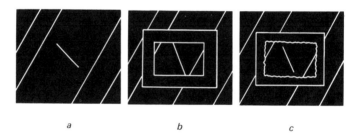

7-19. What observers see in various conditions of the experiment illustrated in Figure 7-18. (a) Condition 1. Oscillating line simultaneously changing length and orientation. (b) Condition 2. Line seen within the aperture. (c) Condition 3. Line seen inside a substitute aperture.

words, the ends of the line did not extend to the inside contours of the frame. This condition was included as a control for the possibility that the presence of a visible aperture in condition 2 might lead to a strong tendency to localize the line in the same frontal plane, via the equidistance tendency (Gogel, 1965) and thus oppose a depth outcome. However, the fact that there is a space between the ends of the line and the inner contours of the aperture makes unlikely the interpretation that the line is rotating behind the aperture in a frontal plane. Before the onset of motion, subjects perceived the luminous line as a line inside an irregular frame. When the line was oscillated, the majority of subjects achieved a depth effect in this condition

Table 7-2: Perception During Kinetic Stimulus Transformation

	Experiment 1: Rectangular Aperture	
Condition	*N*	*Number Perceiving Rotation in Depth*
Condition 1. Line Alone (see Fig. 7-19*a*)	10	9
Condition 2. Aperture (see Fig. 7-19*b*)	10	1
Condition 3. Control (see Fig. 7-19*c*)	10	8
	Experiment 2: Rectangular Figure	
Condition 1. Experimental (see Fig. 7-20*a*)	10	0
Condition 2. Control (see Fig. 7-20*b*)	10	7
	Experiment 3: Illusory Contour Figures	
Condition 1. Aperture (see Fig. 7-21*a*)	10	2
Condition 2. Rectangle (see Fig. 7-21*b*)	10	3
Condition 3. Control (see Fig. 7-21*c*)	10	8

(Table 7-2). This last finding appears to rule out an interpretation of the results of condition 2 simply in terms of a tendency to perceive line and frame in one plane. There is clearly a significant difference between either condition 1 and 3 on the one hand and condition 2 on the other. Thus it would seem that the crucial factor that determines whether or not a depth effect occurs is whether or not the path of the ends of the line is or is not coterminous with the visible inner frame contours.

One might argue that the elimination of the kinetic depth effect in condition 2 is not surprising, at least intuitively. The alternative possibility of perceiving a line of constant length undergoing partial occlusion is readily at hand. An advocate of a stimulus theory might say that we have simply introduced new conditions—those for a different kind of depth, namely, of an object in the frontal plane, but amodally behind an object in a different frontal plane, with the alleged stimulus conditions simply being "occlusion" and "disocclusion" (Gibson, 1979; Kaplan, 1969). If so, this condition can be thought of as representing conflicting determinants, with those favoring the kinetic depth effect losing out to those favoring the occlusion solution.

Therefore, in a second experiment, the line is made to appear *on* a rectangular surface, not behind a rectangular aperture. Under these conditions it can no longer be argued that the kinetic depth interpretation is simply displaced by one that is more appropriate to the total stimulus context, namely, that of occlusion/disocclusion. For now that interpretation is not likely to occur. If so, the elimination of the kinetic depth interpretation cannot be explained in terms of a different prediction, as seems to be possible in the case of the first experiment.

To achieve the desired effect, a display was created with thicker and more closely arranged oblique lines outside a rectangular contour, and the oblique lines were no longer visible inside. Thus, as the reader can see in Fig. 7-20a the conditions now favored perception of a solid rectangularly shaped figural region instead of an aperture region. Consequently, it was assumed that the luminous line would appear to be *on* this rectangular surface.

Two conditions were analogous to those in the first experiment. In condition 1, the line was expected to be seen on the surface of a rectangle whose upper and lower contours were coterminous with the path of the ends of the line (Fig. 7-20a). In condition 2, the path of the ends of the line was not coterminous with the contours of an irregularly shaped rectangular figure (Fig. 7-20b) because the ends of the line did not extend all the way to the borders of the rectangle. In all other respects the apparatus and procedure were the same as in the first experiment.

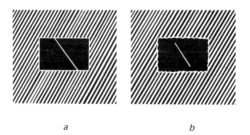

a   b

7-20. A further variation of the experiment illustrated in Figure 7-18. (a) Condition 1. The inner rectangle looks like a solid figure rather than a rectangular aperture. (b) Condition 2. A substitute rectangular figure.

As intended, in both conditions, before motion was introduced, subjects reported perceiving a luminous line lying in front of, or directly on, a solid figural region. It was important to establish this fact because objectively the rectangular region was an opening. During motion, in condition 1, all subjects perceived oscillation in a frontal plane rather than rotation in depth (Table 7-2). No subject had any impression of occlusion/disocclusion. The line seemed to change its length as it rotated on the rectangular surface. In condition 2, the majority of subjects perceived motion in depth (Table 7-2).

In a final experiment, we investigated whether the effect obtained in the first two experiments would still occur if illusory contours of the visible aperture or figural region were substituted for real contours. If so, it would imply that what matters is how the rectangle display is perceived rather than the presence of specific stimulus components. It would suggest that whether or not the oscillating line is perceived in depth depends on the perception of the static display.

In condition 1, the intention was to simulate an aperture (as in the first experiment) by the use of illusory contours. This display is shown in Fig. 7-21. The results were analogous to the previous experiments. All subjects perceived an illusory aperture behind which the great majority of subjects perceived a line oscillating in a frontal plane undergoing partial occlusion. In condition 2, illusory contours were used to simulate a rectangular opaque surface (as in the second experiment) (Fig. 7-21b). All subjects here described the display as containing a solid rectangular region, and the majority perceived a line oscillating in a frontal plane. A third condition was included as a control analogous to that of condition 3 of the first experiment (Fig. 7-21c). The ends of the line did not extend to the borders of the illusory aperture. The kinetic depth effect therefore should be expected to occur. Subjects described the stationary display in the same way as in condition 1, namely, as a hollow rectangular perimeter, and the great majority of subjects achieved a strong depth effect when the line oscillated (Table 7-2). Taking condition 3 as a control, both conditions 1 and 2 differ significantly from it.

How can we explain the various preferences encountered here in terms of a problem-solving theory? In the preceding chapter I have indicated why there would be a preference for the kinetic depth solution under the typical laboratory conditions such as in those experimental conditions in which we predicted it. Although some of these conditions are not pure kinetic depth condition, in that in each of them are certain additional stimulus components, they are not components that should be expected to matter. Thus, in passing, it is worth emphasizing the fact that a new context does not necessarily affect the outcome. In all these cases, the line that simultaneously changes its length and orientation is relatively isolated. Although the transformation is ambiguous, the kinetic depth solution accounts for the covariation of length and orientation change elegantly and without the need to accept what would otherwise be a coincidental

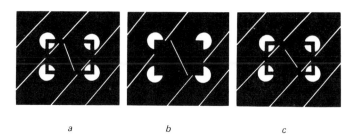

a   b   c

7-21. Illusory contour patterns used in experiments corresponding to those illustrated in Figures 7-18, 19, and 20.

covariation. In other words, with the line rotating about a vertical axis, the line's retinal image would simultaneously change in both length and orientation, by virtue of changing perspective foreshortening, so that this covariation is accounted for by a single cause, so to speak. With the line perceived as oscillating in a plane, however, the change in length correlated with the change in orientation is not at all accounted for. It is inexplicable and coincidental.

Consider next the static display in the first experiment, condition 2, in which a rectangular frame is seen surrounding a central region perceived as aperture or ground in which the transforming line is located (Fig. 7-19b). Given that perception of the central region in the static display, supported as it is by the oblique lines running across the field and through this region, the question to be addressed is why there is a preference to perceive the transforming line as one of constant length rotating in a frontal plane behind the frame. Logically it is possible to perceive the line as rotating in depth (the kinetic depth effect) either behind or in front of the frame. This solution does meet the requirement of stimulus conformity and stimulus support. But either of these perceptions would imply that the path of the ends of the line in three-dimensional space precisely projected to the eye along the upper and lower inner contours of the aperture. That would be a highly coincidental or accidental state of affairs, and thus, I am arguing, the perceptual system rejects it.

This is how I would explain why the kinetic depth interpretation is not preferred in this condition. That the perception of oscillation of a line in a frontal plane with partial occlusion of its ends is preferred over the perception of a line oscillating in a frontal plane and changing its length is also not hard to understand. Change of length would imply that the line was in the same plane as the frame rather than behind it. In the first place, even for the static display, the line would be expected to be—and in fact is—perceived as extending behind the frame. We have here the conditions for interposition or completion. With the line oscillating, the conditions for interposition remain in force, but even if they were not, the occlusion-disocclusion solution should be preferred because the covarying change of line length and orientation is accounted for by the perception of an interposed opaque frame, whereas in the absence of that solution, the co-variation remains unaccounted for.

This analysis makes all the more puzzling the outcome of condition 1 of the second experiment (Fig. 7-20a). For here the line *is* perceived as inexplicably changing length as it oscillates. Thus, the solution here accepts a coincidental state of affairs. Why the perceptual system does not reject this solution in favor of either the kinetic depth or occlusion-disocclusion solution requires an answer. The latter solution would entail contradiction, namely, that the inner region cannot at one and the same time be perceived as both opaque (or figural) and as opening (or ground). Since the conditions were deliberately made effective for the perception of the inner region as figure, the line cannot then be seen as going behind it—unless, I might add, a figure-ground reversal were to occur. But why then is the kinetic depth solution not preferred? I have already explained in the case of the first experiment how that would entail acceptance of the coincidence of the end points of the line remaining coterminous with the contours of the central region. That same reasoning applies to the second experiment. Thus, it would seem to come down to a contest between two kinds of coincidence. Either the line is seen to oscillate in a frontal plane coincidentally covarying in length and orientation, or it is seen as rotating in depth in front of the central figural region with its retinal projection coincidentally terminating along the projection of the contours of the figural region. Apparently, the latter coincidence is taken as more unlikely than the former, and thus the kinetic depth solution is rejected. I cannot at this time account for this ranking by the perceptual system of different coincidences in terms of any formal principle.

As can be seen from this discussion, two meanings of coincidence can be distinguished: unexplained covariation—as in the case of length and orientation change in the typical kinetic depth display—or certain regularities within the proximal stimulus that would occur only by virtue of unique or accidental spatial arrangements of observers vis-à-vis objects—as in the special displays used in these experiments. We saw an example of the latter meaning in the case of a drawing of an irregular wire cube that yields a retinal image such as that shown in Fig. 6-16b, which will occur only if the far and near corners of the cube are both along the line of sight to one eye. For all other positions the retinal image would be more like that shown in Fig. 6-16a. Given the coincidental nature of such a projection, the perceptual system favors a solution that does not entail it, in this case that the object is two-dimensional, whereas the drawing in Fig. 6-16a will typically be perceived as three-dimensional.

In conclusion, one can interpret these experiments as evidence against any theory which maintains that perception is based directly and exclusively on either an absolute or a higher-order attribute of the proximal stimulus. Rather, the experiments support the view that the stimulus is interpreted in terms of what it most probably represents in the world.

Concluding Remarks

The evidence bearing on two of the topics considered in this chapter, namely, apparent motion and kinetic depth, indicates that what is perceived is not the inexorable outcome of certain stimulus sequences or transformations that have been taken to be the necessary and sufficient determinants of these phenomena. The evidence bearing on the anorthoscopic paradigm indicates that an extended retinal image is not a necessary condition for the perception of form. Taken together, these studies reveal the inadequacy of theories based solely on the nature of the stimulus or on the spontaneous interactions to which the stimulus might give rise.

Instead, the evidence in each case suggests that what is perceived is the preferred solution to the problem posed by the stimulus sequence. I have tried to show how one can interpret both the effects as they typically occur given a certain stimulus sequences (for example, apparent motion) as well as the effects of new experiments where something else is perceived, in terms of the various principles developed in previous chapters.

8 ⬡

Perception Governed by Stimulus Relationships

THE MOST STRIKING DEMONSTRATIONS in perception are those in
which the appearance of one entity is a function of the characteristics of neighboring entities. Thus, for example, a disk of a given light
intensity will appear white or gray or even black depending upon the
intensity of light surrounding it. A stationary spot will appear to
move if it is inside or adjacent to a larger moving object. The perceived path of one moving object is a function of the path of motion
of other nearby objects, so that although it may in fact be moving
horizontally it will appear to be moving obliquely or although
moving in a circular path it will appear to be moving back and forth.
A vertical line will appear tilted when seen within a tilted "room" or
within just a tilted rectangle, and so forth.

One might regard these phenomena as illusions, but there is widespread agreement that reliance on these same stimulus relationships
leads to veridical perception, as well. Thus, for example, it is precisely the relationship of the intensity of light reflected to the eye from
one region to the intensity of light reflected from neighboring
regions that generally leads to the correct perception of the lightness
of colors on the black-gray-white coninuum despite the variations
in illumination that occur from time to time. Such intensity relationships or ratios remain constant. The displacement of one object
with respect to others or the absence of it undoubtedly is an important
determinant of the veridical perception of motion or the lack of it
in daily life. That this is true is borne out by the much higher threshold for detecting motion of an isolated point in an otherwise homogeneous surround and by the instability of an isolated stationary
point, the so-called autokinetic effect. The correct perception of an
object as upright or tilted is clearly a function of how it is oriented

with respect to other entities in the visible scene. When a vertical rod is made luminous and it alone is viewed in a dark room by an observer who is tilted, the rod will appear to be somewhat tilted (Aubert, 1861; Müller, 1916). But with lights on, this effect disappears. Therefore, the parallelism of the rod to other vertical contours in the scene serves as important information about its orientation, such that it can offset the failure of complete compensation for body tilt that occurs when the scene is not visible.

Clearly, then, whether the effects are illusory or veridical there can be little question of the central role for perception of relational stimulus information. The question I would like to address is how we should understand this fact. If one object or region in the field affects the appearance of another object or region, it is plausible to believe that this outcome is based on an interaction of some kind. Therefore, it is not surprising that attempts have been made to account for relational determination in terms of interaction theories. However, it was also noted that relationships among stimulus units can be regarded as higher-order features of the stimulus. Therefore, it is also not surprising to find that these phenomena have been regarded by some as explicable within the framework of a modified stimulus theory.

To my knowledge, however, no attempt has ever been made to deal with the facts of relation determination in terms of a cognitively oriented theory of perception. Indeed relational accounts of perceptual phenomena have often been pitted against cognitive theories. For example, if the perception of lightness can be understood in terms of interacting luminances or contrast effects, as first suggested by Hering (1920), there is no need to invoke unconscious inference in which the level of illumination is taken into account as first suggested by Helmholtz (1867). If perceptual phenomena such as contrast or induced motion are relationally determined, one might well ask how they can possibly be explained along the lines of inference or problem solving. Therefore those phenomena as compared to all others in perception would seem to lend themselves *least* to this kind of theory. The discussion in this chapter should therefore be viewed as an attempt to show how such an approach might try to deal with these facts, not as a finished theoretical statement. I will try to show that relational effects cannot be adequately accounted for in terms of either interaction or modified stimulus theories and that instead they can best be understood as the result of cognitive operations based upon stimulus information in which relationships are salient. Toward this end, I will discuss separately several topics where perception clearly is governed by stimulus relationships beginning with the perception of lightness.

The Perception of Lightness

I will begin with the assumption that Helmholtz was essentially wrong in his belief that an object's lightness can be inferred by interpreting the luminance reflected by it to the eye in terms of the amount of illumination falling upon it. Such a process requries unequivocal information about the illumination, whereas the only information directly available is the intensity of light or luminance reflected by each surface in the field. Each such luminance is the joint product of the reflectance property of the surface and the illumination falling on that surface. Rather, I will begin with the working hypothesis that the perceived shade of gray of a surface, its lightness, is governed primarily by the luminance of that surface relative to the luminance of neighboring surfaces, as Hering (1920) suggested and as Wallach (1948) elegantly demonstrated. There is now fairly considerable agreement among investigators on this general principle. If the ratio of luminances of adjacent regions governs lightness perception, we have an instance of relational determination.

But what is the underlying explanation of it? There is great appeal in Hering's suggestion of reciprocal interaction, i.e., that a bright region of the field would have a darkening effect on an adjacent region and a dark region would have a brightening effect on an adjacent region. We now know for a fact that the rate of discharge in one nerve fiber is attenuated when a neighboring fiber is stimulated by light. Thus such lateral inhibition can plausibly be invoked to explain why the apparent lightness of one region is governed by the extent of stimulation of an adjacent region.

In fact, given lateral inhibition as a known sensory effect, one would be able to predict the phenomenon of contrast, even if it had never been observed. Surrounding a gray region by a white one should lead to diminished discharging of retinal fibers stimulated by the gray region; surrounding another gray region of the same value by a black one should lead to increased discharging of retinal fibers stimulated by that gray region because of a release of inhibition. Thus one of these gray regions should look lighter than the other, and so it does. An implicit assumption here is that the phenomenal color perceived in a given region is a direct function of the rate of discharging of fibers stimulated by that region.

The fact of constancy of neutral color can be explained along the same lines. When the illumination falling on a surface changes, the luminance of all adjacent regions rises and falls together. Thus, while the rate of discharging of cells stimulated by a gray region should increase when illumination increases, so too should the rate of discharging of cells from a surrounding white region increase. The latter will increase the inhibition on the former, with the possible net result of little if any change in the absolute rate of discharging of those cells. Therefore, the perceived lightness should remain more or less constant, and so it does. Note again, however, the assumption, here explicit, that the phenomenal color is a direct function of the rate of discharge of the appropriate fibers (see Chapter 2, pp. 34-35).

Underlying this assumption is another assumption about how the visual system works that might be called the photocell theory (see Gilchrist, 1979). Just as the energy yielded by a photocell is a direct function of the light falling upon it, so the perceived lightness of each point in the field is assumed to be a direct function of the rate of dicharging of the cells stimulated by each such point. With the knowledge that has been available about light, about the formation of the retinal image, about photochemical processes and nerve physiology, it is understandable why such a view has become so deeply ingrained as not even to be explicitly recognized as an assumption. Given this assumption, phenomena such as contrast and constancy seem to require an explanation along the lines of lateral inhibition, and the direct laboratory confirmation of the fact of lateral inhibition has reinforced this view.

There is now, however, reason to reject this approach. Evidence has been accumulating to support the theory that the perception of lightness (and chromatic color as well) is based upon information at the edges between regions of differing luminance (or hue). Homogeneous regions between edges then "take on" the lightness value indicated by these edges. There are two opposite lines of evidence for this conclusion. Either artificial edges are created by a steep gradient between extended regions that are otherwise *equal* in luminance or the edges that ordinarily are present between regions that do *differ* in luminance are experimentally eliminated. In the first case, then, the prediction is that regions of equal luminance will be made to appear unequal; in the second case the prediction is that regions of unequal luminance will be made to appear equal. Both kinds of prediction have been confirmed.

In the Craik-O'Brien effect, an artificial edge is created by spinning a disk with a pattern such as that in Fig. 8-1a (Craik, 1966; O'Brien, 1958). What is perceived is shown in Fig. 8-1b. Thus the regions of equal luminance on the two sides of the artificial edge appear unequal. The opposite effect is demonstrated by stabilizing the retinal image of the boundary between two regions. Stabilization of contours on the retina leads to their disappearance. Thus, for example, if a green disk is surrounded by a red ring and the boundary between them is stabilized—but not the boundary between the red ring and its sur-

 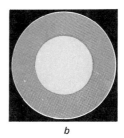

8-1. The Craik-O'Brien effect. When the disk in *a* is spun, it creates an artificial edge. Observers perceive a disk, *b*, that appears uniformly lighter than the surrounding ring, despite an equivalent luminance across the entire region.

rounding—the entire display appears homogeneously red (Krauskopf, 1963). See Fig. 8-2. With the elimination of the red-green edge, functionally speaking the only edge present is the outer red-white one. Thus the stimulation by green light in the central region has no effect on perception. Regions of unequal color here appear equal.

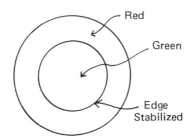

8-2. When the edge between a red ring and a green disk is stabilized on the retina, the entire display appears homogeneously red. After Krauskopf, 1963.

We need not be concerned with the mechanism for detecting the difference in luminance (or color) on the two sides of an edge. But it seems highly probable that what is directly detected is the relative difference or ratio of luminances. A luminance edge is a step, either up or down, of a certain magnitude. Therefore, one might conclude that the information at an edge between a region and its background is the same regardless of the amount of illumination falling on the surface.

If so, there is no need to invoke a concept such as lateral inhibition to explain constancy. One might say that the problem of constancy does not even arise. What about contrast? If all information about lightness is given at edges, what must we predict will be perceived when squares of the same gray are viewed on either a white or black surround? Fig. 8–3. The edge indicates, for the gray square on black, that the square is lighter than the background and, for the gray square on white, that it is much darker than the background. Therefore, the edge information is such as to lead us to predict that the squares will look different, as indeed they do. Again there is no need to invoke lateral inhibition as there would be if the rate of discharge of cells in a given locus rather than edge information were the determinant of perceived lightness. For in that case, the two equal gray squares should yield the *same* rate of discharge unless some mechanism explains why they do not. So much for the moment for an interaction theory.

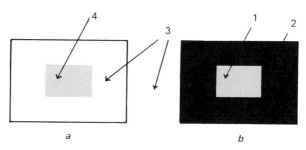

8-3. Simultaneous lightness contrast. Region 4 appears darker than region 1, although the two are equal in luminance.

The facts thus far considered would support a modified stimulus theory. Lightness perception could be assumed to be correlated not with absolute luminance value but with relative luminance values. Thus a given luminance ratio could be the stimulus for a given lightness value. It is more or less irrelevant for this kind of theory how such relational information is "picked up" except that the knowledge that it occurs at edges strongly supports the view that the stimulus *is* relational.

The real problem for this view of lightness perception is that a certain ratio of luminances at a boundary cannot in and of itself be the stimulus correlate for a particular shade of gray. How that luminance ratio is interpreted depends entirely upon other such ratios elsewhere in the field and—as we shall see—how those ratios are interpreted. Consider again the example of contrast, but first under the following special dark-room conditions: one gray square is surrounded by a white square and the other by a black square, the two pairs of squares are spatially separated, and each pair is illuminated by a beam of light viewed in an otherwise dark room. Under these conditions, the gray square on the white background will appear middle gray but the one on the black background will appear either white or possibly even luminous. In other words, there will be a tremendous difference in the appearance of the two gray regions, not merely the slight difference that occurs in the more typical illustration of contrast. This great difference is precisely what the stimulus theory should predict, because not only are the two ratios very different quantitatively, but their signs are reversed; i.e., in one case the gray region has a luminance greater than its surround and in the other case, it has a luminance smaller than its surround.

Why then are the two lightness values only *slightly* different in the more typical case of contrast? The obvious answer is that under these conditions both pairs of regions are presented together and the surrounding black and white regions are adjacent to one another and meet at an edge. If, however, all information is conveyed only at edges, this means that the black-white edge *remote* from the gray-black and gray-white edges is playing a very important role. Further, assuming we can rule out any role of lateral inhibition or other form of neural interaction that might conceivably be invoked to deal with such "remote" effects, there would seem to be only one conclusion to be drawn. The perceptual system *interprets* the gray-black and gray-white edge information differently than would be the case in the dark-room condition because of the presence of the black-white edge. Another way of putting this is to say that the assignment of lightness values to the various regions is the end result of a computational process in whcih the information from all edges present is integrated.

Thus the challenge for a stimulus theory is that the ratio as an example of a higher-order stimulus attribute is not a fixed correlate of any particular perception. The meaning of the ratio depends upon context, so to speak. Therefore, one would have to take account of multiple ratios, and to explain any outcome and make predictions, that would require specifying how each ratio was weighted. Computational processing of this kind is not the sort of thing intended by a stimulus theory.

A dramatic example of such a process is the following: two rings of equal reflectance and lighter than the background are placed on the two sides of a disk with an artificially created circular contour (see Fig. 8-4). (Arend et al., 1971). Since the ratios at the edges of these rings to the background is the same in both cases, one might predict that they will look equal. But, in fact, they look unequal. The presence of the central, Craik-O'Brien edge requires the assignment of different lightness values to the two rings. It is as if the perceptional system infers that if both rings represent reflectance values higher than their backgrounds and if, further, those backgrounds represent unequal reflectance values, then the two rings cannot be equal to each other in reflectance.

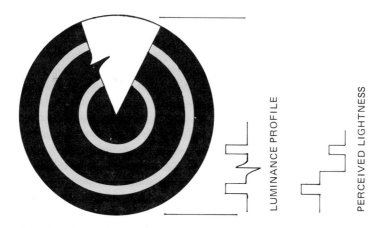

8-4. Two rings of equal lightness are viewed on a rotating disk with an artificial edge created between them. The luminance profile and perceived lightnesses of the several regions are shown on the right. After Arend et al., 1971.

If such computational processes occur and are governed by remote as well as local edge information, then what was said before about the achievement of constancy was oversimplified. Consider the typical case where regions of equal reflectance on the same background are unequally illuminated because one region and its immediate background are in shadow (Fig. 8-5). To say as I did earlier that constancy can be explained on the basis of the equal ratio of each gray region to its background is to ignore any effect of remote edges, which we have just seen, do enter into the equation. The shadow edge in the center, between the two sides of the background, can easily have a ratio as great as a white-black edge and, more probably, even greater. If this is entered into the computation, the equal gray-white ratios here logically cannot signify that the two grays are equal, or so it would seem.

However, perhaps the perceptual system can discriminate between color edges and illumination edges. If so, perhaps illumination edges would not be included in the computation of lightness values. There is now impressive evidence of just such discrimination of lightness and illumination edges (Gilchrist et al., 1979). If observers are permitted to view a display such as that shown in Fig. 8-5, they typically do perceive the two grays as almost equal; i.e., constancy is

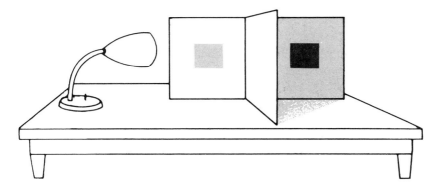

8-5. The lightness constancy paradigm. Rectangles of equal reflectance on backgrounds of equal reflectance are viewed in unequal illumination.

achieved. Moreover, they perceive both sides of the background as white with one side in shadow. Thus the central edge is apparently correctly identified as an illumination edge. If, however, the observers view the display through an aperture that permits only part of the background and the two gray regions to be seen, the grays no longer look equal; i.e., constancy is not achieved (Fig. 8-6). Moreover, the observers now perceive the two sides of the background as of unequal lightnesses. Thus the center edge between them is interpreted as separating different shades of gray, not different illuminations. In this condition only, then, does the central edge enter into the process of computing the colors of the gray regions.

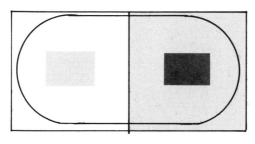

Seen through aperture

8-6. View of the central region of display in Figure 8-5 through aperture. Here constancy is not achieved.

Precisely how the perceptual system discriminates illumination from lightness is not yet fully understood, although Gilchrist has uncovered several sources of information (Gilchrist, 1979). One such source is based on depth. Thus, for example, a luminance difference at a corner (or dihedral angle) will often be interpreted as an illumination rather than a lightness edge (Rock, 1975; Gilchrist, 1977). I discuss this fact in the next chapter (pp. 246–247).

Before continuing, it is worth considering the ramifications of what we have just discussed for the notion of lateral inhibition or any other theory of neural interaction which seeks to explain the important effects of remote edges on what is perceived in regions adjacent to other edges. For now, in addition to other difficulties such a theory faces, in dealing with "remote" effects it would have to be argued that such effects do not occur at all when those remote edges are interpreted as representing illumination rather than lightness differences. In fact, it has been demonstrated that the expected inhibitory effects do not occur even across the *immediate* edge separating regions of differing luminance if that edge is interpreted as stemming from an illumination difference (Gilchrist, 1979). The difficulties for a modified stimulus theory are also significantly magnified by the realization that the perceptual system deals differently with the two kinds of edges. Such a theory might be able to account for the discrimination between them, since presumably there is some stimulus-informational basis for it. But that the system includes or excludes edge information—depending upon type of edge—in its computational processing is another story.

Instead, as Gilchrist suggests, the facts seem to require a theory that assumes the following kind of central events: first, the perceptional system detects or registers all the luminance steps, their magnitude and sign, at all the edges in the scene; second, it discriminates and sorts into separate categories edges that represent reflectance differences from those that represent illumination differences; third, it integrates all reflectance edge steps by computational processing in order to arrive at appropriate descriptions of the lightness (or reflectance value) of each region (simultaneous with this, the perceptual system may engage in a similar integration of all illumination edge steps in order to arrive at appropriate descriptions of the relative levels of illumination of all regions in the field).

By separating out illumination edges and not including them in the computation of the lightnesses values of regions, the perceptual system has only to make use of relative luminance to compute relative degree of lightness or reflectance. With illumination differences eliminated, the fact is that all relative luminance differences at edges will be produced by reflectance differences. That region computed to be the one with the highest luminance in the scene is therefore the one with the highest reflectance, and conversely with respect to the one with the lowest luminance. What we *call* "white" and "black" is essentially just this, regions with the highest or lowest possible relative reflectance value.

According to this view of the process, nothing in the field need be assumed *to affect* anything else as *is* assumed to be the case by interaction theories. Rather, what is crucial, following the registration of the relevant stimulus information that is directly given only locally, at edges, is putting it all together, so to speak. This process has properties that are formally similar to logical operations that entail the relating of one proposition to another and arriving at conclusions. Thus, for example, in the case of contrast (Fig. 8–3), we have (*a*) region 1 (gray square) is eight times more intense than region 2 (black surround); (*b*) region 2 has a luminance one-sixteenth that of region 3 (white region adjacent to black one). Only by transitively relating (*a*) and (*b*) can the system "infer" that region 1 falls somewhere in the middle of the scale of reflectance values because from (*a*) alone it would follow that it falls at the upper end of the scale (see Fig. 8-7).

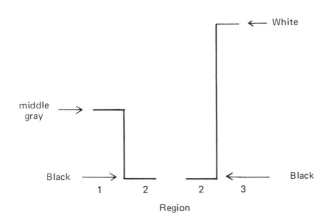

8-7. Luminance profile of lightness contrast display shown in Figure 8-3.

As a matter of fact, the above analysis affords an opportunity to reconsider a matter that has been glossed over. If the logical operation of integrating edge information succeeds perfectly, there should be no contrast effect. Region 1 in Fig. 8–3 should be perceived veridically, i.e., in terms of its relative reflectance characteristics. But so should region 4, the other gray square, following the same kind of transitivity operation. If so, regions 1 and 4 should appear to be exactly the same lightness. Therefore, it must be admitted that the kind of cognitive theory here advocated does not explain the slight difference in lightness that characterizes the two gray squares in the case of contrast. However, it is possible that the basis of the failure is to be understood as a slight failure in the computational process underlying the transitivity operation. The local edge is telling us that region 1 is much lighter than region 2; the remote edge is telling us indirectly that region 3 must be much lighter than region 1. Therefore, our assessment of the relative reflectance of region 1 should be modified downward, so to speak. If this correction is not fully carried out, our description of the relative reflectance value of region 1 will be in error as governed by the partially uncorrected local edge information.

It will be helpful to make explicit here the relevance of the principle of stimulus conformity described in Chapter 5. The percept must do justice to or conform to the proximal stimulus. In the domain of lightness perception it is probable that only stimulus relationships (in the form of edge ratios) are registered, so that the percept must conform only to the total set of such edge ratios rather than to absolute luminance values as well. In the case of the other phenomena discussed in this chapter, such as of motion or orientation, not only must perception conform to stimulus relationships but it must conform to absolute features of the stimulus as well. Disconformity with the stimulus can imply perceiving either more or less than is to be expected. Except for the slight effect in the contrast paradigm—which can be explained as a failure of transitivity based on a dominant conformity to the local edge information at the expense of the correct integration of *all* edge information—all other examples considered here are in accord with the principle. Perception ends up faithful to the entire proximal stimulus distribution of luminance ratios with a set of regions of varying phenomenal reflectance values and illumination transitions.

The separation of lightness from illumination edges can be thought of in terms of perceptual organization where some entities are grouped together and separated from others. We will encounter similar effects of organization, particularly in connection with the perception of motion and direction of motion, and will see that, in these cases as well, computations tend to be *within* certain organized structures, with the perception of the whole then resulting from the integration of the separately computed substructures or groupings.

The Perception of Motion and Direction of Motion

MOTION

Not all cases of motion perception are governed by the changing relationship of one visual object to another. Thus, for example, when a single object in an otherwise homogeneous surround changes its location at a sufficiently rapid rate, it will appear to move. Here the changing angular direction with respect to the observer (subject—relative change) is what matters.

But more typically, a moving object is seen against a differentiated background of stationary objects and texture. Therefore, there are two possible bases for detecting its motion: its angular change vis-à-vis the subject (subject-relative change) and its change relative to other objects. The importance of object-relative change is indicated by several facts: (1) the much lower threshold for motion perception when other stationary objects are present than when they are not; (2) the related fact that when the moving object is below threshold, and a second, stationary object is introduced, it is equally likely for the stationary object to be seen as the "carrier" of that motion as for the objectively displacing object; (3) the phenomenon of induced motion; (4) the effect on the perceived direction of a moving object of other moving objects.

By "induced motion" is meant the inducing of an impression of motion in a stationary object by virtue of the actual movement of a nearby object, the latter typically being larger than or surrounding the former object. In the laboratory, the stationary object is usually a small spot and the surrounding object a rectangular perimeter. Under these conditions, there is a conflict between subject-and object-relative information. The spot, being stationary, does not change its angular direction and the rectangle, which is actually moving, does. Clearly the changing location of the spot relative to the rectangle is a dominant determining factor. These facts then support the conclusion that in daily life, the perception of an object's motion is in part a function of its changing location relative to stationary objects.

What kind of theory can best account for induced movement? A stimulus theory would regard change of relative location as a higher-order stimulus variable that directly leads to motion perception. But since subject-relative, angular change alone can lead to such perception, the theory would have to acknowledge that both higher-order and "lower-order" stimulus features determine perception. As to object-relative change of location as a higher-order stimulus for motion, the problem remains of accounting for *what* is perceived as moving. In induced motion, there is the tendency to attribute the motion to the spot which would seem to be based upon the tendency to regard the rectangle as the frame of reference and, thus, as stationary. This fact is not itself anything that reduces to or is predictable in terms of higher-order stimulus information. There is an inherent ambiguity in the changing stimulus relationship, but some selective principle within the organism leads to the asymmetrical outcome, namely, the tendency to assign the motion to the spot and to regard the rectangle as the frame of reference.

Another theoretical approach to the role of stimulus relationships in motion perception is implicit in the thinking of the Gestalt psychologists. Based on the doctrine of isomorphism, the physiological correlate of perceived motion was assumed to be a change in the distribution of forces within the neural substrate. Thus the flow of electrical energy was thought to be governed by the changing locus of projection of one stimulus entity in the brain relative to that of others. While the concept of frame of reference or framework was central to the thinking of these theorists, no explicit physiological theory of it was formulated. We thus have only the vague outline of a theory, partly physiological and partly psychological. But the essence of the theory is the notion of some neural interaction between the cortical representation of the objects.

As an alternative to these approaches, one might try to explain the facts in question in terms of an attempt by the perceptual system to solve the problem posed by the transforming proximal stimulus. To begin with, I will assume that not only is the perceptual system very sensitive to object-relative change but that this kind of stimulus information is salient. When two equal objects are present and one moves away from the other below the subject-relative threshold, the solution must be that one object or the other is in motion (one, let us say, to the left or the other to the right), but there is no basis for deciding which one is in motion. An alternative is that both are moving apart. When, however, one object is larger than the other and/or surrounds the other, it is interpreted as the stable framework, a representative or surrogate of the environment. Such an interpretation or "assumption" could be the result of past experience in which smaller things typically do move within a stable, surrounding environment. Or it could be an innately given predisposition based on the adaptive value of such a principle of preference in evolution.

Since, in the example under discussion, the rectangle is moving at below-threshold speed, the situation is logically ambiguous as to what is moving so that the preference to interpret the rectangle as stationary is all that is needed to resolve the problem. The solution is rational in that no information contradicts it. But the fact is that induced movement occurs as well when the rectangle moves at an above-threshold speed. Here we do have a contradiction, because by definition of "above threshold," there is information that the rectangle is in motion. Moreover, the perception of the rectangle moving fully accounts for the object-relative change between it and the spot. Why then should induced movement occur?

In fact, if the rectangle's motion is veridically perceived *and* induced motion of the spot occurs, there is more perceived motion than is warranted on the basis of the object-relative change. If the rectangle is displacing at the rate of θ degrees per second and is so perceived and the spot appears to be moving θ degrees a second in the opposite direction, we have a total of 2θ degrees per second of peceived motion. For a theory that explains perceptual phenomena in terms of stimulus interactions, such *excess motion* poses no particular problem. The process has nothing to do with computation or consistency. In fact Duncker explicitly stated that there can be multiple frames of reference simultaneously present and that the perception of any item is governed only by its relationship to that frame of reference in which it is embedded. The item's perceived motion is thus not governed by its relationship to remote frames of reference. This interpretation was referred to as a separation of systems (Duncker, 1929). [See Fig. 8-8a for the case where the rectangle is moving below threshold and 8-8b for the case where it is moving above threshold].

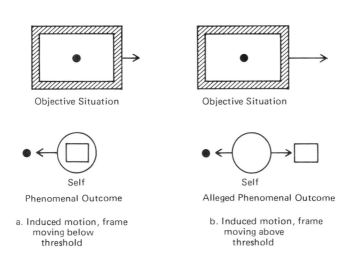

8-8. Induced motion. In this and the subsequent figures, the upper diagrams represent the objective situation in which the arrows give the physical motion. The lower diagrams represent the perceptual outcome (or alleged outcome) in which the self (large circle), the frame (rectangle), and the spot (small dark circle) are all shown. The origin of the arrow represents the entity with respect to which motion is seen, and the arrowhead represents the entity seen as moving. The direction of the arrow represents the left-right, up-down, or oblique direction of the seen motion. (a) The frame moving below threshold. (b) The frame moving above threshold.

But for a theory that regards perception as the result of thought-like operations, there is a difficulty here. Excess motion is irrational and violates the principle of stimulus conformity in that more motion is perceived than is warranted based on the changing stimulus relationship. In propositional form, the following is "known": (1) Spot a and rectangle b are displacing with respect to one another at θ degrees per second. (2) Rectangle b is displacing with respect to the observer θ degrees per second. From these two propositions the conclusion to be drawn is: (3) Spot a is stationary. Another way of putting this is to say that if the perceptual system succeeds in integrating the information available and is seeking to describe whatever the stimulus transformation indicates is occurring in the world, then it is not clear why an illusory motion should be perceived.

There is another reason why induced motion should not be expected to occur when the rectangle displaces at a rate above threshold. Suppose the observer is fixating the spot. As noted above, information is available that there is no angular, subject-relative change in its location. Were it to be moving at the speed of the rectangle (in the opposite direction), the observer would have to be tracking it at that above-threshold speed. The absence of signals from the eye system indicating such tracking motion should serve to oppose any perception of motion in the spot. Here we have a violation of the principle of stimulus conformity in regard to the absolute aspect of the stimulus, namely, its angular direction. Nevertheless such motion is perceived, and moreover the observers experienced their eyes as if they are tracking the spot, although in fact they are essentially stationary.

This last fact suggests a possible resolution of the difficulty. If the observers "feel" their eyes to be tracking the spot, the situation is analogous to the more typical one of tracking a spot actually moving across a stationary background. In that situation the background appears to be stationary: position constancy occurs. If in the induced-motion paradigm, the eyes fixating the spot are interpreted as moving in viewing a phenomenally moving spot, the moving rectangle might appear to be stationary. In that event, the contradiction would be resolved. There would be no excess motion.

The sequence of events might run as follows: (1) The executive agency immediately registers the displacement of spot and rectangle relative to one another. (2) There is a strong preference to interpret the rectangle as representing a stationary frame of reference. (3) There is thus a tendency to attribute the relative displacement to motion of the spot. (4) But for this to be possible without contradiction from other sources of information, the eyes must be interpreted as tracking the spot (as example of visual capture). (5) Thus 2, 3, and 4 are consistent with the interpretation that the frame is in fact stationary.

But the reader will object that we are discussing the case where the rectangle is moving at an above-threshold speed, which implies that its motion *is* perceived. There is no necessary contradiction here because the above-threshold criterion is established for the rectangle alone, when the spot is not present. The presence of the spot changes the equation. In experiments on induced movement in our laboratory we have required observers to report not only about the spot but about the rectangle as well. The rectangle displaces at various speeds, all of which are above threshold, and the display is visible for only a few seconds. Induced movement does not always occur, particularly at the faster speeds of the rectangle, but when it does, the motion of the rectangle is misperceived. Either it appears to be stationary—and this occurs almost half the time—or it appears to be moving more slowly than it does when induced movement fails to occur. The findings suggest a transfer of the rectangle's motion to the spot and support what might be termed the *apportionment hypothesis:* the relative displacement between spot and frame is accounted for by perceiving only the spot moving by that amount, only the frame moving by that amount, or both spot and frame each moving so that the total sums to that amount (Rock, Auster, Schiffman, and Wheeler, 1980).

Thus our findings suggest that the induced-movement effect can be viewed as a rational integration of the relational stimulus information and a reinterpretation of the absolute stimulus information, the latter referring to information as to the angular direction of spot and rectangle. Excess motion is not perceived and the principle of stimulus conformity is not violated. Either all or some of the relative displacement is attributed to motion of the spot and thereby either none or only some of that relative displacement is attributed to motion of the rectangle. The cause of the shift in attribution of motion from rectangle to spot would seem to be the powerful tendency to interpret the rectangle as a stationary frame of reference or, if that is not possible because of conflicting angular-change information, to interpret it as moving more slowly than would otherwise be the case. This shift in attribution can be thought of as a process of perceptual rationalization as a result of the "pressure" resulting from the predilection to solve the problem in the preferred way suggested here.

Before concluding this discussion, brief mention should be made about induced motion of the self. When this effect occurs, either the frame surrounding the observer will appear to be moving more slowly than is warranted by its rate of angular displacement *or* it will appear

to be stationary. In keeping with the principle of stimulus conformity, the sum of phenomenal motion of self and frame will equal the
angular displacement between self and frame. Thus, leaving aside
possible sensory information of a nonvisual kind, either veridical
perception of frame motion (with no induced self-motion) or total
induced self-motion (with frame stationary) or some combination of
these is compatible with the stimulus input. Since nonaccelerating
motion of the body, either rotary or linear, would not be signaled
differentially from nonmotion of the self in the vestibular apparatus,
any of these alternative outcomes is possible. The predominance of
perceived self-motion then indicates a strong preference to interpret
the frame as stationary, once again an example of an assumption on
the part of the executive agency, which must be strong enough to
overcome another interpretation, namely, that in the absence of information to the contrary, the body is stationary.

If now a stationary spot is introduced, how it is perceived will depend upon how the self is perceived. If self-motion is experienced,
the spot will appear to be traveling along with the self, always remaining straight ahead (see Fig. 8-9). If self-motion is not experienced and if, moreover, conditions are not suitable for induced motion of the spot, the spot will appear stationary and straight ahead.
A final possibility is that although induced self-motion is not occurring, induced motion of the spot is. In that event, as noted earlier,
there is a tendency to interpret the eyes as tracking the spot, which
can be thought of as an induced effect of the moving frame on part
of the self, namely, eye position. (See the discussion of these effects
in Chapter 1, Example 1.)

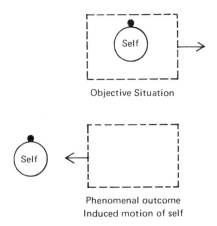

Objective Situation

Phenomenal outcome
Induced motion of self

8-9. Induced motion of the self when a spot is present in front of the
moving frame.

DIRECTION OF MOTION

The dominant role of relational stimulus information is nowhere as evident as in the preception of the direction in which obejcts appear to move. Consider the example illustrated in Fig. 8-9 in which a rectangle moves back and forth. Within it is a spot moving obliquely, but in phase with the rectangle. If perception were in accord with the absolute changes of these proximal stimuli, we would perceive the rectangle moving horizontally and the spot moving obliquely. What we do in fact perceive is a spot moving vertically up and down within a rectangle moving horizontally (Fig. 8-10). Since one might say that the spot does not appear to be moving horizontally (as well as vertically), this demonstration could be regarded as an illustration opposite to that of excess motion, namely, of diminished motion. The spot has a component of horizontal motion, but it is not perceived. That would mean stimulus disconformity.

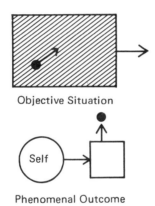

Objective Situation

Phenomenal Outcome

8-10. The perceived direction of motion affected by the motion of other objects.

Relative to the rectangle, the spot changes location only in the vertical direction. Apparently this object-relative change dominates our perception. Still the horizontal component of the motion of the spot is not without some phenomenal representation. We perceive the spot-and-rectangle as a system moving back and forth. Unlike induced motion, effects of this kind are robust; they will occur even at very rapid speeds and often in daylight as well as in dark-field conditions. Thus it seems fair to say that the subject-relative oblique change of location of the spot (or, otherwise expressed, its absolute angular change) is accounted for by the two perceptual vectors: the spot's vertical motion and the horizontal motion of the system "rectangle-with-spot."

But why do we perceive the motion of the spot as we do rather than in a direction directly correlated with the path of its angular displacement? In answering this question it will be helpful to imagine an object in daily life that is moving horizontally with a smaller object on it that is moving vertically with respect to it, for example, a fly on a horse or a person on a moving train waving a hand up and down (Fig. 8-11). While it is true that the change of angular direction of the fly vis-à-vis the observer is oblique, based on the resolution of its two component vectors, the fact is that the vectorial separation of the fly's motion into two components is in a sense the more veridical description of what in fact is occurring. The fly *is* in fact moving only vertically; and the horse is moving only horizontally. In the laboratory analog of this, however, the spot happens to be independent of the rectangle, and, therefore, in fact, the spot must be given an objectively oblique direction of motion as in Fig. 8–9. When we perceive its motion otherwise, therefore, we tend to think of this outcome as illusory. That it is seen as part of or belonging to the rectangle "system" can here be understood in terms of the organizing principle of common fate. In the example of the fly, however, there is other information leading to the perception of it as *on* the horse. In any event, we see here a powerful effect of perceptual organization. The perception of the spot or fly is governed by a description of its behavior vis-à-vis the rectangle or horse, and the perception of either of these frames is governed by a description of its behavior vis-à-vis the observer (see Fig. 8-10, bottom).

8-11. An insect moving vertically on a horse moving horizontally.

Therefore, one can understand the outcome as a plausible solution to the problem posed by the transforming stimulus pattern; a rectangle-with-spot is displacing horizontally, and, in addition, the spot is displacing vertically within the rectangle. We end up with a dual description of the event.

In this example and others like it studied by Duncker (1929) and

Johansson (1950) one can think of the perceptual outcome in terms of a hierarchical organization. The motion of objects within a reference frame is seen relative to that frame and the motion of the frame with its contained objects is seen relative to the observer. But note again that there is no violation of the principle of stimulus conformity. The stimulus considered absolutely leads to perceptual components that *together* fully conform to or account for it; considered relationally there is a salient aspect of the percept that directly conforms to it.

There is a similar display that seems to yield excess motion (Wallach et al., 1978) (Fig. 8-12, top). There the spot moves vertically, not obliquely. This case has features in common with the usual demonstration of induced motion, but it also can be thought of as a variation of the example just discussed. When the rectangle displaces horizontally, the vertically moving spot appears to move obliquely. One might say that induced motion is responsible for a horizontal component of motion in the spot. If, as seems to be the case, this effect occurs for all speeds of the rectangle and if, further, the rectangle's motion is perceived veridically, any induced motion of the spot is excess. It cannot be explained by apportionment based on subtraction of the motion of the frame. In fact, the induced motion appears to be complete, by which I mean that if, for example, the rectangle is moving horizontally at the same speed that the spot is moving vertically, the spot appears to move along a path that is 45 degrees oblique. Is this a contradiction to what I have been saying?

Unlike the simple case of induced motion, the vertically moving spot does have an objective motion, and this seems to make it possible to perceive it as having two components. In addition to the object-relative component already mentioned (e.g., 45 degrees oblique) another component is possible: the spot can seem to be carried along with the rectangle: it partakes of the rectangle's motion. Thus relative to the subject the spot remains in the same direction, straight ahead (along a vertical path). Its perceived oblique direction of motion is only one aspect of its motion. Therefore, what at first seemed to imply excess motion turns out to be fallacious: there are two components to the spot's phenomenal motion, namely, its own relative to the rectangle and the motion it has or partakes of as part of the rectangle.

To make this difficult example clearer, imagine again that the spot is a fly walking on a horse. Let the fly walk at a 45 degree angle upward, toward the left, while the horse walks to the right (Fig. 8-13). Then the direction of motion of the fly's image on the retina will be vertical (assuming we give the appropriate speeds to both

222   CHAPTER EIGHT

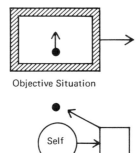

Objective Situation

Phenomenal Outcome

8-12. A spot moving vertically inside a frame moving horizontally. After Wallach et al., 1978.

8-13. An insect moving obliquely upward on a horse moving horizontally, such that the path of the insect's image on the retina is vertical.

fly and horse). We will perceive (veridically) that the fly is walking along an oblique path on the horse and that the horse is walking to the right. We would not describe the percept as entailing excess motion.

What this analysis seems to suggest is that excess or diminished motion must be defined in terms of a single frame of reference so that we can legitimately add and subtract motions. If the observer is that frame of reference, excess motion means that more motion with respect to the observer is perceived and diminished motion means that less is perceived than is predictable on the basis of stimulus motion. In simple induced motion the meaning is clear enough, but the evidence cited above on apportionment suggests that excess motion does not occur. Thus separation of systems and the consequent excess or diminished motion seems not to be valid if motion perception is referred to the self as a single system of reference. In the other examples considered here where the spot is in motion and its perceived direction is investigated, the foregoing analysis suggests that what at first might look like excess or diminished motion is not. The error is in failure to take account of all aspects of the motion of the critical object (the spot) with respect to the single, proper sytem of reference for evaluating whether or not motion is excessive or diminished, the self. When this is done, there is no reason for maintaining that there is excess or diminished motion.

However, when the concept of separation of systems is defined appropriately in terms of hierarchical organization, it is valid and necessary to understand these examples bearing on the perception of direction. We tend to organize moving configurations hierarchically in terms of structures and substructures. The perceived motion of any item is governed by its changing relation to that structure, which serves as frame of reference for it, so that the item's motion is characterized phenomenally, i.e., described, in relation to that structure. The perceived motion of that structure in turn depends upon its changing relation to the reference frame for it. The observer will be the reference frame for the most encompassing externally visible structure. But this apportioning of motion is governed by the principle of stimulus conformity. All perceived motion collectively exactly accounts for the proximal stimulus displacements. As we have seen, this kind of organization will generally yield veridical perception because things in the world often displace within the structure of which they are a part. In the laboratory this same organization will yield what at first appear to be illusory outcomes, but that is because we are describing the stimulus input in terms of angular change relative to the observer rather than in terms of hierarchical organization.

One unresolved problem, however, is the case of simple induced motion. It is logically possible for the observer to perceive the spot moving across its rectangular frame at exactly the speed that the rectangle is moving in the other direction. That solution would be in keeping with the principle of stimulus conformity. It would not entail excess motion provided that the perceived motion of the spot were object-relative. Then the spot would also partake of the motion of the rectangle, thus nullifying any subject-relative change. This hierarchical organization might occur if the spot seemed to *belong* to the rectangle (for example, if the rectangle were a surface and not a perimeter and the spot were an entity such as a fly). But this typically does not happen. An isolated luminous spot within a luminous perimeter yields a retinal image that does not adequately support a belongingness solution. Therefore, only if the spot seems to move *relative to the observer* will induced motion readily occur, and for this to happen, I have suggested that the rectangle's motion must be misperceived. When it is, the combined perceived motion of spot and rectangle meets the requirement of stimulus conformity.

However, when the spot has some motion of its own, it of course will be seen to move, and if a rectangle is moving around it, let us say in a direction orthogonal to the spot's motion, the direction of the spot's motion is the resultant of the two relative motions, in this case oblique. But here, to repeat, the spot is perceived as part of or belonging to the rectangle, so that this oblique motion is phenomenologically speaking, object-relative. Because the spot also partakes of the rectangle's motion, its resultant subject-relative motion is vertical. Real motion of the spot, therefore, seems to be important to achieve such a hierarchically organized effect, but the reason for this is not yet clear. Since, however, the spot is moving and will necessarily be seen as moving, it is not surprising that the *direction* in which it appears to move will reflect both aspects of its object-relative change, vertical and horizontal.

The Perception of Orientation in the Environment

There is general agreement among investigators that there are two independent sources of information that enable us to perceive how objects are oriented in the environment. Whether an object appears upright or tilted in space is governed by its relation to the directional pull of gravity *and* by its relation to the horizontal and vertical coordinates given by various visual structures in the scene. That information dependent on the pull of gravity alone determines perceived orientation in the environment is easily shown by experiments in which only the test object, typically a luminous rod, is visible. Observers can judge when the rod is vertical with great accuracy when they are in an upright position and with a fair degree of accuracy even when they are in a tilted position. In the latter case one refers to this achievement as constancy of orientation, since the orientation perceived as vertical (or horizontal) remains more or less constant and veridical despite the varying orientation of the retinal image of the object seen as vertical. Here the percept is not relationally determined but rather must be based on taking account of nonvisual information about the direction of gravity in assessing the orientational significance of the retinal image of the object.

That *visual* information can affect perceived orientation is indicated by the tendency to accept the main directions such as the vertical and horizontal axes of a visible room as defining the vertical and horizontal of space. Thus even when such a room is in fact tilted with respect to gravity—as in the case of a cabin of a listing ship or a banking airplane or a tilted room in an amusement park—it tends to be seen as upright by an observer within it. Consequently a plumb line within the room that is known by observers to be vertical will nonetheless appear to be tilted, and observers will perceive themselves as tilted as well. Thus we have here another example of relational determination. When the observer is inside a tilted room, there can be no disputing the conclusion that the coordinate directions of that room serve as frame of reference with respect to which the orientation of other objects in it including the self is judged. Needless to say, the visible terrain and objects such as trees, buildings and telegraph poles must play this same role, but it is difficult to do experiments in which the physical orientation of such structures can be varied (although "natural experiments" are possible, as when vertically aligned trees often appear tilted when we see them on a hill).

Experiments have been performed with specially constructed tilted rooms or rooms made to appear tilted by optical devices that are viewed by observers either inside them or outside (Wertheimer, 1912; Gibson and Mowrer, 1938; Asch and Witkin, 1948a, b; Witkin, 1949; Singer, Purcell, and Austin, 1970). When observers are inside a room, not only do vertical objects in it appear quite tilted but upright observers experience themselves as tilted. When the observer views such a room from outside, there is still an appreciable effect which can be measured by the actual tilt of a rod that the observer judges to be vertical. A similar but typically smaller effect occurs when a luminous rectangular perimeter (or frame) is substituted for the room and the observer judges when a luminous rod within it appears vertical (or horizontal), now referred to as the rod-and-frame effect (Witkin and Asch, 1948; Ebenholtz, 1977; Gogel and Newton, 1975; Wenderoth, 1974).

Experiments of this kind create a conflict situation, since gravity information is available and therefore should be expected to lead to veridical perception, particularly when the observer is upright. The frame is, however, tilted from the direction of gravity. Were the rod to be set parallel to one axis of the frame, it would no longer be aligned with the direction of gravity. As a consequence of the conflicting determinants, observers typically achieve a compromise solution: they judge the rod to be vertical when it is in fact in an orientation somewhere between the true vertical and that axis of the frame considered to represent the vertical.

Somewhere along the line, in research on this problem, the original idea of Wertheimer according to which the axes of the visible scene become the frame of reference in relation to which orientation is then judged has been cast aside. There are several probable reasons for this development, one of which is the emergence of other hypotheses about the rod-and-frame effect, such as induced ocular torsion of the eyes (Hughes, 1973; Goodenough et al., 1979) or a contrast effect entailing overestimation of angles (Wenderoth, 1974; Blakemore, Carpenter, and Georgeson, 1970), which need not concern us here. Suffice to say, the magnitude of the effect obtained based on these hypothesized mechanisms is of the order of 1 or 2 degrees and thus is too small to explain the rod-and-frame effect, which typically is about 6 degrees or more.

This leads directly to a question that, by and large, has been neglected, namely, how is the frame itself perceived in these experiments? The implication in Wertheimer's thinking is that the tilted scene tends to "right itself" psychologically speaking, so that after some short period of exposure to this scene, it tends to appear upright. There was some evidence along this line in the research of Asch and Witkin (1948). But it also seems that when a tilted frame is used, it appears to be tilted even while it is exerting a strong effect on the appearance of the rod within it. If the frame appears to be as tilted as in fact it is tilted, what is the meaning of the effect it has on the rod? One can hardly argue that the frame serves as a surrogate for the environment and is thus taken to be upright if, in fact, it is seen to be tilted.

The situation here is quite analogous to the situation in induced motion. Can one invoke separation of systems? According to this principle, the rod would be affected only by its immediately surrounding frame, the rectangle, whereas the frame's orientation would be a function of either another more all-encompassing external frame or of the observer as frame of reference. Since information derived from the pull of gravity is available, the frame would then presumably be perceived veridically, as tilted. According to this view, it is irrelevant how the frame is perceived. Excess tilt occurs analogous to excess motion. In my opinion, this approach leaves the rod-and-frame effect completely unexplained, since all we can say is that some asymmetrical interaction between the internal representation of the rod and frame occurs.

A different view of the rod-and-frame effect stems from a problem-solving perspective based on Wertheimer's concept of frame of reference and the notion of apportionment as outlined in the previous discussion of induced motion. The task for the observer is to arrive at the orientation within the rectangle that appears vertical in the environment. If the rectangle is seen veridically as tilted by as much of an angle as it is tilted, the observer should set the rod to the true vertical. There would be no error induced by the frame. If a small frame, of let us say 10 degrees of visual angle is used, as sometimes is the case in such experiments, there is little reason to expect it to have the capability of serving as a surrogate of environmental directions. For that to occur a much larger frame must be viewed, one that in some sense "surrounds" the observer. In point of fact, when such small frames are used, the rod-and-frame effect is quite small or entirely absent (Ebenholtz and Benzschawel, 1977; Wenderoth, 1974). Moreover, in the one experiment where measures were taken of the perceived orientation of the frame itself, such a small rectangle was used and its orientation was apparently veridically perceived (Gogel and Newton, 1975). Such small effects of the frame on the rod that are sometimes obtained with this size of frame are quite possibly caused by the factors referred to above, such as ocular torsion and contrast entailing overestimation of angle.

When, however, a larger frame is used, such as 30 degrees or more, there will be a tendency for it to serve as world surrogate. However, information based on gravity is available, so that a conflict exists. Only if observers are inside a tilted room is there reason for expecting such information to be completely overpowered by visual information (visual capture), in which case observers feel that they are tilted by an amount close to the full tilt of the room and in the opposite direction. Consequently, in a manner of speaking, one might say that a conflict no longer exists psychologically even though it is potentially present. For now even if observers rely entirely on their felt body position to judge the upright, they should err in the direction of the tilted room.

But in the more typically employed condition of a large tilted rectangle seen from outside, the conflict that does exist leads to two predictions: (1) a tendency to perceive the frame as less tilted than it is and (2) a consequent tendency to perceive the rod as tilted when vertical, leading to an error in judging its upright position by an amount equal to the misperception of the frame as suggested in 1. Thus, for example, if the frame is in fact tilted by 20 degrees it may appear to be tilted by only 15 degrees. This "righting" effect of 5 degrees leads to the prediction of a 5-degree error in judging the upright orientation of the rod (see Fig. 8-14). Otherwise expressed, the magnitude of the error in setting the rod to the perceived vertical exactly equals the error in the perception of the frame's orientation. The perception of both together accounts for the proximal stimulus input to the retina; i.e., the angular relationship between rod and frame is veridically perceived and fulfills the requirement of stimulus conformity.

It would be expected that a frame capable of serving as an environmental surrogate for a rod would also be one capable of affecting observers' perception of their own body (or head) orientation. Therefore, in such cases, observers should be expected to misperceive their own body or head orientation, i.e., to perceive it as tilted by

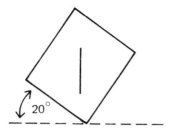

8-14. Rod-and-frame paradigm. If the frame is tilted 20 degrees from the upright but is misperceived as tilted by only 15 degrees, then a vertical rod within it will appear to be tilted by 5 degrees in the opposite direction.

(in this example) 5 degrees. Such an effect occurs (Sigman, Goodenough, and Flannagan, 1978, 1979; Ebenholtz and Benzschawel, 1977). Whether the magnitude of this feeling of self-tilt is precisely what should be predicted based on the magnitude of righting of the frame is not yet known, but in my opinion, it is difficult to obtain measures of such perceived self-tilt with any precision. In any event, the induced feeling of head or body tilt provides a further rationale for the orientation of the retinal image of the frame. In other words, its tilt of 20 degrees on the retina is accounted for by the sum of its perceived tilt in the environment (15 degrees) plus the perceived tilt of the observer from the upright (5 degrees). Thus the perceptual solution also fulfills the requirement of conformity with the stimulus considered in absolute terms.

Based on this theoretical perspective, experiments were undertaken in our laboratory in order to ascertain how the frame appeared when it induced an error in the perception of a rod within it (Di Lorenzo and Rock, 1982). We employed a somewhat indirect method to measure the perceived orientation of the frame. The observer set the frame to the vertical, in the absence of a rod, from some initial starting orientation. The presumption was that to the extent that observers misperceived the frame in an initial tilted orientation because of a "righting" tendency, to that extent they would evidence a strong starting-position effect. Thus if the frame appeared fully upright in its starting orientation of 20-degree tilt, observers would accept it in that orientation; if it appeared almost upright, observers would require it to be tilted back toward the vertical slightly before regarding it as upright, and so forth.

In one experiment a large frame was used, subtending a visual angle of 54 degrees. The average error obtained in judging the vertical orientation of a rod, the rod-and-frame effect, was approximately 10 degrees. The perceived tilt of the frame, reflecting a righting effect, was somewhat less than 8 degrees. A high and significant positive correlation between these two measures was obtained. This correlation means of course that when observers erred appreciably in their judgments of the rod, they also tended to accept the frame as upright or close to upright in its initial tilted orientation. Conversely those who tended to resist the effect of the frame on the rod also tended to see the frame more or less veridically as tilted in its starting orientation. These results would seem to validate the method used for assessing the degree of righting of the frame.

Since it is known that when observers are tilted their reliance on gravity is weakened, following an earlier procedure of Asch and Witkin (1948), we repeated the previous experiment with the observer viewing the frame with head tilted by 45 degrees. Here the average rod-and-frame effect increased to an average of approximately 13½ degrees and the righting effect increased to roughly 14 degrees. Many observers achieved a complete righting of the frame; i.e., they regarded it as upright in its initial position. These same observers also yielded very large rod-and-frame errors.

In further experiments, two frames surrounded the rod. Consider the case where an outer frame is upright but an inner frame is tilted (Fig. 8-15). According to a separation of systems analysis, the rod-and-frame effect should be expected to occur, presumably undiminished in comparison with the typical single-frame paradigm. But from the perspective of a theory that places all the emphasis on the righting of the frame, the outermost, upright rectangle would serve as world surrogate and thus eliminate any effect on the rod. The results were as follows. The inner frame seen within the upright outer frame was perceived veridically as tilted and there was no error to speak of in setting the rod within it to the vertical.

What would be the effect of tilting the outer frame and leaving the inner one in the upright position (Fig. 8-16)? Here we were predicting that the perception of the inner frame would be a function of the degree of righting of the outer frame. Consequently the appearance of the rod within the inner frame would also be a function primarily of how the outer frame appeared. The result was a rod-and-frame effect of about 6 degrees despite the upright position of the inner frame. Significant correlations were also obtained between this measure and a measure of the righting of the outer frame. This is a rather striking finding, since one might have supposed that the presence of the inner upright frame would either eliminate or substantially lower the rod-and-frame effect.

To summarize the arguments and findings, it appears that there are striking parallels between relational determinants of perceived orientation in the environment and of perceived motion. In both cases observers' perception of their own bodies will be governed by

8-15. Double-frame experiment. The outer frame is upright, the inner frame tilted. After Di Lorenzo and Rock, 1982.

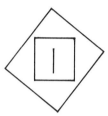

8-16. Double-frame experiment. The outer frame is tilted, the inner frame upright. After Di Lorenzo and Rock, 1982.

the body's relation to the surrounding structure that serves as frame of reference provided they are within that structure. Thus observers will experience themselves as in motion or as tilted when the surrounding framework is either moving or tilted and will tend to perceive the framework as either stationary or upright. The framework is assumed to represent the stationary, upright environment and serves as a surrogate of it. Under such conditions, an object will also be perceived in relation to the framework in the same way as the self.

When the observer is outside the structure, similar effects will occur, but to a lesser extent. Still the tendency to interpret the moving or tilted structure as a stationary or upright world surrogate is manifest if it is large enough, with the result that its motion or tilt is either not perceived or is underestimated. Therefore, the perceptual righting or stabilization of the framework results in a misperception of the object (rod-and-frame effect or induced motion). This effect will be accompanied by certain induced misperceptions of the self, namely, body tilt in the one case and eye movements in the other.

Therefore, the perceptual otucome conforms to the stimulus input considered both relationally and absolutely and does not entail excess or diminished motion or tilt. Specifically, it is not the case that the frame's orientation in relation to the environment or its motion in relation to the self is veridically perceived while at the same time the rod's orientation in the environment or the spot's state in relation to the self is misperceived just because the rod or spot is governed by its relation to the framework. Separation of systems in this absolute sense, where the orientation or motion in question is gauged with respect to the same origin or reference frame, does not seem to occur.

But as regards orientation, should there not be a kind of separation of systems effect analogous to many of those in motion perception where hierarchical organization leads us to perceive the rod's orientation in relation to the frame and the frame's orientation in relation to the self? Effects of this kind have apparently not yet been achieved, perhaps because belongingness would be crucial. One exception is the effect not on a rod but on a figure such as is shown in Fig. 8-17 (Kopfermann, 1930). Here it is clear that a diamond will tend to look like a square and a square like a diamond by virtue of their relation to the surrounding frame. Since ordinarily the different appearance of this kind of figure as a square or diamond is a function to its orientation, the change in its phenomenal shape when it belongs to a tilted frame is clearly based on its *altered* phenomenal orientation.

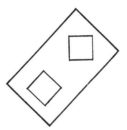

8-17. Hierarchical organization effect. The phenomenal shapes of the inner figures are determined by their perceived orientation relative to the frame, while the orientation of the frame in the environment is perceived veridically. After Kopfermann, 1930.

Do we have here an example of stimulus disconformity? Not at all. The inner figures also partake of the frame's orientation. Thus the inner figure on the left in Fig. 8-17 that looks like a square (implying vertical and horizontal sides) partakes of the tilt of the frame so that its net orientation in relation to the observer is one in which its sides are oblique, and this corresponds to the oblique retinal images of these sides. In principle, the same kind of effect should be possible in a rod-and-frame display. We are now exploring this possibility. Thus it is possible that the same kind of hierarchical organization can occur with respect to perceived orientation as we have seen occurring with respect to direction of perceived motion.

Size

Since objects are always seen in particular contexts, the question arises as to the possibility of a determining effect of size relationships on perceived size. In fact, were such relationships to govern phenomenal size, the problem of size constancy would have a simple solution. The size of one object, for example, a person, in relation to a background object serving as a frame of reference, for example, a house, remains invariant despite changes of distance between observer and objects. Or one might think of the background in terms of its texture, and consequently an object on the ground would cover the same number of units of texture regardless of the distance of the observer (Gibson, 1950). Thus such proportions or invariances logically could serve as the basis of perceived size and of constancy of size.

To test this hypothesis, we performed an experiment in which objects within frames were compared with one another while the distance to the two frames was equal (Rock and Ebenholtz, 1959). A vertical line within one rectangular perimeter served as the standard and another such line within its rectangular perimeter served as the comparison object (see Fig. 8-18). The lines and frames were luminous and viewed in a dark room by observers who sat midway between the two so that they had to swivel around by 180 degrees to see the other rectangle. The instructions were to indicate when the variable-length comparison line appeared to be equal to the standard line. When the comparison frame was three times the size of the standard, the average length of the line within it selected by observers was more than twice the length of the standard. This means that a line longer than 6 inches was judged to be equal to a 3 inch line. In a control condition where the frames were removed, observers had no difficulty in accurately matching the standard.

Thus a very considerable relational effect was obtained. Others who have repeated this experiment (with certain variations) have found smaller effects (Wenderoth, 1976) or no effect at all (Gogel and Sturm, 1972).[1] The possibility that the effect was based on a misperception of the distances of the two frames was considered in

1. In the experiment by Gogel and Sturm (1972) the observers were shown each line and frame display successively and asked to judge the length of line and frame and their distances in linear units. Such a task would tend to minimize or eliminate entirely any relational effect. Moreover the task may have elicited judgmental rather than perceptual reports.

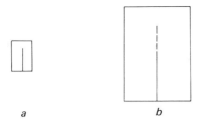

8-18. Size-proportionality effect. The two luminous displays 180 degrees apart were viewed in the dark by an observer midway between them. The observer selected the length of line in the larger frame which appeared equal to the standard line in the smaller frame. After Rock and Ebenholtz, 1959.

these experiments. The difference in size of the frames might be expected to lead to an impression of two rectangles of the *same* size but at different distances. Size perspective is a cue to depth. Were that the case, the outcome would not be particularly surprising. If the rectangles were seen as the same size, naturally the lines within them would appear equal when they stood in the same proportion to the rectangles. However, the separation of the rectangles by 180 degrees should eliminate or lessen this depth cue, and other control conditions in the original experiment indicated that such an effect was not occurring.

Assuming then that the strong illusion (or a lesser illusion but still appreciable if one of the repeated experiments is correct) is not an artifact, how can it be accounted for in terms of cognitive theory? Given the equality of distance to the two frames perceived by the observer, the two lines should look equal only when their visual angles are equal, or at least one might ask why the inequality of visual angles when the observer matches on the basis of proportion does not enter in as a constraining factor. Stimulus conformity to the relational information here implies disconformity to the absolute information. To this one might answer that the frames surrounding the lines tend to insulate the lines from one another and thus make it difficult to compare them directly. But if that is so, what about the comparison of the frames with one another? Assuming that these can be easily compared, the observer then perceives the degree of their inequality. Perceiving the lines as equal on the basis of proportionality is therefore irrational. If premise 1 is that rectangle A is 3 × rectangle B and premise 2 is that line A is in the same proportion to rectangle A as line B is to rectangle B, then the inference must be that line A is 3 × line B rather than that line A equals line B.

Against this conclusion of irrational perception are the following considerations: (1) The average setting of the comparison line is midway between a prediction made on the basis of visual angle equality and proportionality determination (or less if the subsequent studies are correct). When the difference between the sizes of the rectangle is increased beyond the 3:1 ratio, the compromise is all the closer to a visual angle match. Thus the inequality of the rectangles *is* playing a constraining role. (2) The transitivity operation implied above requires comparison of rectangles quite spatially remote from one another. Were they to be side by side, only a very small illusion would occur (Künnapas, 1955).

Still, it is important to note that the size difference between the rectangles is undoubtedly perceived veridically (as indicated by the control experiment with lines alone). Therefore, it would not seem to be the case here that the frames are misperceived (in this case their relative size) as is true for frame orientation and motion. Were that to be the case (as could result from the misperception of the relative distances of the frames), the strong relational effect becomes explicable without any implication of stimulus disconformity. But this kind of effect is not possible here because a frame does not serve as a surrogate of an environmental structure of some particular size. There is no singular or normative size corresponding to the singularity of uprightness or stationarity for which internal "assumptions" can be invoked.

Finally: (3) The observers undoubtedly react to the configuration as a whole in the sense that only when the lines stand in the same proportion to their frames do they "look alike." The display can be thought of in terms of size transposition in that the shape of the whole figure is independent of size. Observers may confuse similarity of configuration based on relative size with equality of absolute size, instructions to the contrary notwithstanding. Given this fact and the difficulty referred to in (2), the outcome becomes understandable. This last point can be restated in a form paralleling the argument made about hierarchical organization in connection with the other topics considered in this chapter. A line's apparent size can be governed by its relationship to its context so that the two lines may look equal when they stand in the same proportion to their respective frames. But since they "partake" of the size of their frames, e.g., ¾ of 4 vs. ¾ of 12, their absolute size is also simultaneously perceived. If this reasoning is correct, it suggests that the instructions to match size absolutely represent a bias against a separation of systems effect much as would instructing observers to report how a spot was moving relative only to themselves in some of the motion-display conditions described earlier. With different instructions an even stronger proportionality effect might have been obtained, but it would not entail stimulus disconformity for the reason here suggested.

The implications of this kind of experimental result for the problem of size constancy will be addressed in the next chapter, but, as I will show, there are good reasons for concluding that invariance of proportion of object to background can at most play a subsidiary role. Still the kind of effect obtained does show once again the saliency of relational stimulus information in perception.

Implications

How do these facts about relational determination fit the kind of cognitive theory of perception presented in the previous chapters? Some specific comments about this have already been made here and there in this chapter, but it will be helpful now to review the more general implications.

One important question is how relational determination relates to the principle of stimulus conformity (see Chapter 5). There are several new problems that emerge in connection with relationally determined perception. As we have seen, there is good reason for believing that the perceptual system is particularly sensitive and responsive to stimulus relationships. Thus the descriptions will always center around and conform to such relationships. Few students of perception would disagree with this formulation. But then the further question arises whether and, if so, how the description will deal with aspects of the proximal stimulus that must be defined in more absolute terms. In some cases, it may be that this kind of information is not available, as may be true for absolute luminance. But more generally such stimulus information is registered, as is the case for above-threshold motion of objects or the orientation of an object with respect to the observer.

In my view, not only does such information lead to some corresponding perception but that perception must be one that is consistent with what is perceived on the basis of the relational information. Thus the solution must conform to both aspects of the proximal stimulus. The current belief seems to be that since perception has nothing to do with rationality or internal consistency, there are no constraints of this kind on whether the perception of all objects in the field considered collectively conforms to the stimulus input. Accordingly, a rectangular frame that induces motion in a spot within it or that induces a tilt of a line within it may itself be seen veridically as moving or tilted.

However, I have argued against diminished or excess motion and orientation. This is where perception considered in relation to the stimulus defined absolutely enters the picture. The principle of stimulus conformity must apply to this aspect of perception as well. Thus, if an object is tilted such that its retinal image is tilted, the observer being upright, one should expect it to be perceived as tilted. Here again few students of perception would disagree. The disagreement would arise when one relates absolutely based perceptions to relatively based perceptions. In my view they must be consistent with one another. Thus, if a vertical rod in a tilted frame appears tilted with respect to the environment (let us say by a magnitude equal to the angular difference between rod and frame), the frame cannot be perceived as tilted with respect to the environment by a magnitude equal to the tilt of its retinal image. That would imply the perception of excess tilt because the only tilt in the proximal stimulus is that of the frame. I have argued and presented evidence in support of the claim that the apparent tilt of the rod depends upon a misperception of the tilt of the frame.

But, one may ask, is not the misperception of the tilt of the frame a violation of the conformity principle? After all, the tilt of the frame is given directly by the orientation of its retinal image. At this point we must consider how observers perceive themselves. While the orientation of the image must always lead to a corresponding perceived orientation of the object producing it, we are now talking about perceived orientation in relation to the self. But suppose observers misperceive their own orientation in space. That is an outcome compatible with the principle of stimulus conformity for vision which requires only that we perceive veridically the orientation of the object to self. Therefore, the solution entails the perception of an upright or less tilted frame and a tilted self viewing a tilted rod parallel to the self. As noted earlier, just such misperception of one's own body (or head) tilt occurs in these situations.

Exactly the same reasoning applies to the phenomenon of induced movement when the frame moves above threshold. The absolute motion of the rectangle's image must lead to some conforming perception of it. This is apparently accomplished by feeling that one's eyes are tracking the (stationary but phenomenally moving) spot. If that were occurring, a motion of the rectangle's image over the retina would be present, although the rectangle would then be stationary. It is true in this case and the one above on orientation that information from some nonvisual stimulus is suppressed or reinterpreted in the process, namely, information based on eye position and on gravity, respectively.

Then there are the cases of perceived direction where several objects are moving in differing directions. As already noted, a description of what the objects are doing in relation to one another is in center stage. But the requirement that their absolute retinal motions also be accounted for is clearly demonstrated by an additional component in what is perceived. This generally takes the form of a component of motion of the entire display. The motion defined relationally and the motion defined absolutely vectorially summate to equal the motion over the retina.

Various other seeming departures from the principle of stimulus conformity result from the effect of organization. Stimulus motions, contour orientations, visual extents, or luminance ratios at edges are grouped together or segregated, as the case may be. Thus how a particular item will appear depends, first, upon its relation to the structure of which it appears to belong. If this were all there was to the perception of that item, stimulus disconformity would prevail. But the item also partakes secondarily of the phenomenal property of the larger structure, such as its motion or orientation, and the sum of this perceived property and the first, relational one does correspond to the stimulus input.

In the case of the perception of lightness and illumination, it seems probable that information about absolute luminance is not picked up, at least if, as seems to be the case, the new hypothesis about edge informtion is correct. Therefore, perception of lightness and illumination can be and is based entirely on relative luminance without the problem arising of a potential conflict with absolute stimulus information. In any event the overall solution conforms to the stimulus considered in its entirety, in that an array of lightness and illumination regions is perceived that is grounded in and correlated perfectly with the proximal stimulus.

There are a few exceptions to this rule, as, for example, the small illusion referred to as simultaneous brightness contrast (better called simultaneous lightness contrast) (see Fig. 8-3). One might think of this kind of effect as excess or diminished lightness of color because it should not occur if computations across all edges in the field are accurate. The illusion seems to imply that somewhat more weight is given to the immediate edge (e.g., gray-white or gray-black) than to a remote edge (e.g., white-black). It is possible that a similar small effect occurs in the case of induced motion, size perception, or the perceived orientation of a rod in a tilted frame. In other words, there may be some slight failure in the transitivity operation that leads to the assessment of what the lightness of a square or motion of a spot or tilt of a rod is by taking account of what the remote edge is or what motion or tilt of the surrounding frame is. Cognitive operations need not always lead to correct answers even when the premises are valid. Evidence from our research does not reveal any such effect in induced motion or the rod-and-frame effect, but others report effects which can be interpreted in this way.

So much for an analysis of the principle of stimulus conformity. What about the principle of stimulus support? That is most clearly revealed in the discussion of the perception of lightness. To perceive regions of differing shades of gray or differing illuminations, certain luminance differences at edges must be present. One cannot perceive an isolated black surface as black if it is locally illuminated in an otherwise dark room. One cannot perceive an edge as resulting from differing illuminations rather than from differing reflectances unless some stimulus information such as penumbra or depth information or the like is present.

But we also ran across factors relevant to stimulus support in the other topics considered in this chapter. For a region to serve as frame of reference or world surrogate it must be sufficiently large or surround the object being judged. For a region to be seen as belonging to another region in the case of motion perception, it is probable that the display must have stimulus characteristics such as surface color or texture or the display must be one in which the object judged shares some common motion with the moving background. That may be why the case of induced motion with a luminous spot inside a luminous perimeter fails to yield the kind of hierarchically organized effect achieved with many other displays.

As far as preference is concerned, the examples of relational determination considered here do not seem to come under the principle of common cause or common explanation (coincidence avoidance) discussed in Chapter 6. Rather another kind of principle seems to be responsible for the outcomes. In the case of induced motion, the tendency to interpret the frame as stationary can be thought of as an "assumption" on the part of the perceptual system. As mentioning earlier, such an "assumption" might result from prior experience in daily life, where typically it is the smaller or enclosed object that moves, or from evolutionary "experience." Similarly, the tendency to interpret the frame as defining the horizontal and vertical coordinates can be viewed as an "assumption." Certainly in daily life the visual scene with ground and structures perpendicular to the ground would be important in defining the horizontal and vertical of space, particularly in the light of the fact that sensory information based on gravity alone is relatively weak and imprecise. Thus to "assume" that in a dark room a large luminous rectangle, in the absence of any other visible structures, defines the vertical and horizontal is plausible.

There also seem to be certain "assumptions" occurring in the perception of lightness, e.g., that with no information to the contrary, all edges in a display are reflectance edges or, otherwise expressed, that illumination throughout is the same; or with good information such as in the case of a dihedral angle, that the luminance edge is based on illumination differences.

Finally, it should be noted that the kind of problem solving occurring in the examples considered here is different in certain respects from that considered earlier. Unlike the earlier examples, it does not seem appropriate to speak of a literal solution that is then superseded by a preferred solution following a period of search. Rather the justification for speaking of problem solving in these cases of relational determination is that computational or inference processes occur based on the stimulus information and on "assumptions" that arise that disambiguate the stimulus information and on the effort toward achieving an internally consistent solution that seems to occur.

By way of summary, I have argued that relational determination is based on cognitive or thoughtlike operations. The perceptual system emphasizes proximal stimulus relationships in seeking to describe objects and events. These descriptions tend to conform to such stimulus relationships but also are constrained to be consistent with stimulus information defined in absolute terms. Assumptions or preferences such as those in which certain structures are taken to be world surrogates guide the interpretation of potentially ambiguous stimulus input. Organization, particularly hierarchical organization entailing belongingness of an object to a certain structure and sorting of qualitatively different kinds of luminance edges, leads to a decomposition of the input into separate or subsidiary perceptions, but the sum of these adds up to an accurate representation of the stimulus as a whole. Computational or inference processes utilize all relevant information in arriving at perceptual descriptions.

To the extent that processes of this kind do in fact occur, it is clear that a direct or higher-order stimulus theory does not provide a sufficient explanation of relational determination. As to the difference between the account I am suggesting and an interaction type of theory, the essential points are, first, that there is *no* implication that any stimulus representation affects or changes another. Rather the relationships are simply cognitively registered and evaluated. And, second, there *is* an implication that what is perceived is rationally consistent with the stimulus input as a whole.

9 ⬛

Unconscious Inference

THUS FAR I HAVE CONSIDERED two categories of perceptual process, namely, form construction and perceptual problem solving. In the case of form I have argued that the percept is based upon a process of description. In the case of problem solving I have argued that the percept is the preferred solution to the problem posed by the ambiguous proximal stimulus and that the process entails some degree of creativity in finding or selecting solutions, i.e., the final descriptions. Relationally determined perception, a third category of process, is in a class by itself in that the final description seems to reflect a rational solution that conforms to and is supported by the proximal stimulus and that depends upon certain "assumptions" or preferential interpretations. However, it does not seem appropriate to describe the process in such cases as one of searching for a hypothesis.

There is another broad category of process where much the same thing is true, i.e., phenomena that can be understood as the end result of a process of inference and ultimate description but where there is no search for the appropriate solution. Foremost in this category are the various cases of perceptual constancy. I will argue that the process of achieving constancy is one of deductive inference where the relevant "premises" are immediately known. That is to say, in the case of a specific constancy such as that of size, two aspects of the proximal stimulus are most relevant, one being the visual angle subtended by the object and the other being information about the object's distance. The executive agency "knows" that these are the relevant aspects and therefore proceeds to relate them to one another.

Two Theories of Constancy

Two different kinds of explanation have been proposed for constancy in perceptual experience, the origins of which date back to Helmholtz and Hering. Both start with the fact that the proximal stimulus representing the object under consideration cannot by itself be the basis of what is perceived because it is subject to variation. Because an object's image will change as a function of the object's distance, slant, or illumination or of the observer's movement or orientation, any particular image considered alone is ambiguous as to what it might represent in the world.

According to one explanation (Helmholtz), the perceptual system takes account of factors such as distance or illumination in arriving at a perceptual judgment of what the retinal image represents in the world. There are two aspects of this theory that distinguish it from the other:

1. The information (or cue) taken into account derives from a source separate from the retinal image of the object, for example, cues to distance or illumination.
2. The view that the process is a cognitive operation or an unconscious inference, which in turn seems to imply a determining role of experience.

It will be helpful in the discussion to follow first to separate these two aspects and to put the emphasis on the first as the major defining characteristic of this theory. It essence, then, is the notion of a combinatorial process (Epstein, 1973) in which the percept results from combining a property of the retinal image of the object with other information concerning the location and orientation of the object or the state of the observer. Stated in this way, the theory reduces to a testable hypothesis; whereas if the second aspect is also included in the statement, far more is implied concerning the origin and nature of the combinatorial process. Therefore, it is best to postpone discussion of this second aspect.

According to the other kind of explanation the information that leads to constancy is given in the retinal image, but we must look beyond the local stimulus representing the object itself; for example, in the perception of lightness it is not only the intensity of the image of the surface under consideration that matters but the intensity of the images of neighboring surfaces as well (Hering). Another way of stating this is to say that it is not the absolute property of the local proximal stimulus of the object that determines perception but the relationship of that stimulus to other neighboring proximal stimuli.

There are several variations of this kind of theory that I propose to group together, at least for the moment. Thus, for Hering (1920), the basis for the important role of neighboring images in the perception of "brightness" was what he referred to as opponent processes in the nervous system, anticipating what is now called lateral inhibition. The emphasis here is on interactional neural events determined by extended patterns of stimulation. More recently J. J. Gibson (1950, 1966) argued that all the information necessary for constancy is available in the proximal stimulus; therefore, it suffices to specify the attributes of the proximal stimulus correlated with particular perceptions. Gibson's claim was that hitherto unrecognized features of the proximal stimulus (e.g., visual angle relations deriving from perspective transformations in the formation of the image), which are directly correlated with constant features of perception, entail a higher-order level of analysis. Therefore, in the critique that follows the higher-order stimulus theory and the interaction theory will be considered together, as slightly different versions of an explanation based on ratios or relationships.

In the preceding chapter, I discussed the problem of lightness constancy. Logical considerations and evidence favor the interpretation that this constancy is based upon the invariant ratio of luminance values given at edges between regions in the field. Changes in overall illumination in the scene will not alter this ratio. Although this conclusion would seem to support either a modified stimulus theory or an interactional theory, further evidence made it clear that computational processes based on processes of organization and certain "assumptions" occur. At this point some further discussion including additional evidence is warranted.

LIGHTNESS CONSTANCY

The ratio principle explains anomalous illusions such as the Gelb effect in which an isolated black surface suspended in midair by a string in a dark room, looks white when only it is illuminated or the Kardos effect in which a white surface looks dark gray when only it is shadowed (Gelb, 1929; Kardos, 1934). The principle also explains the departure from constancy obtained in experiments when the surfaces to be compared, each under different illumination, are viewed through openings in a reduction screen. The reduction screen represents a new surround for each surface and because its color is uniform and is in uniform illumination throughout, the ratio for the surfaces under comparison, each to its respective surround, is no longer preserved.

Not only does this principle have great explanatory power but the alternative theory of constancy based on a process of taking account of illumination is weak. The major difficulty of the latter concerns the question how information about illumination can be obtained (see Chapter 8, p. 203). Unless the reflectance were already "known," there would be no way of "knowing" the incident light received in order to take it into account. However, there are certain instances in daily life in which the notion of taking account of illumination on a surface seems to make sense and when it is not obvious how the ratio principle could apply. Consider the best-known example of this kind, namely, the situation in which surfaces are oriented differently with respect to the source of light. A surface orthogonal to a light source receives more intense light per unit of area than one slanted with respect to that source. This is conveniently illustrated by an dihedral angle, opening either toward or away from the observer (i.e., where the walls of a room meet at a corner) in which both surfaces are the same shade of gray. One surface will typically receive more light than the other. How do these surfaces appear? Were they to look alike, we might say that constancy obtains.

There is some disagreement about how to describe this kind of experience. Suppose both surfaces are white. A few observers will say that the two surfaces appear quite different—one light, the other dark. However, most will say they look different, but both appear to be white—one intense or "bright" and the other "dim." In other words, we experience a difference in illumination. If, however, the corner is subjectively flattened out, either by closing one eye or by blocking from view the junction points of the corner with ceiling and floor, then all observers will agree that the two surfaces now look different in lightness—one white, the other some shade of gray. In fact, after seeing the corner thus flattened, the observers who until then described the two surfaces as "light" and "dark" may now realize that they should have said "brightly and dimly illuminated."

What do the two theories predict? It is not obvious how any tendency toward constancy can be accounted for by the ratio principle, which refers to the ratio of luminances between the retinal images of the surfaces in question. The surfaces meeting at the corner and receiving different amounts of illumination give rise to images at the eye of different luminance. They should look as different from one another as two surfaces of different lightness in the same illumination. Yet for most observers both look white. Although the perception of different lightnesses that occurs with subjective "flattening" is predictable by the ratio principle, *the change* in perception that definitely does occur purely as a result of a change in depth perception is not at all predictable. Actual luminance relations are not affected by subjective reorganizations of depth perception.

How can the taking-into-account theory of constancy explain facts of this kind? The logical difficulty of independent access to information about illumination can be overcome, at least in part, in this example. Here depth and attached shadow clues that signify the direction of the source of light are available. Given that information and the "knowledge" of the relationship between the orientation of the surface to the light source and the proportion of light received, the perceptual system can then consider that orientation in arriving at the perception of the surface's lightness value. By taking account of the different amount of light received by the surfaces meeting at the corner, a tendency toward constancy is to be expected, but if the two surfaces are perceived to be in one plane the illumination can be assumed to be equal and the different luminances of the surfaces must then signify different lightness values.

In the preceding chapter, following Gilchrist's analysis (1979), I indicated that the dilemma posed here for the ratio hypothesis is resolved if we assume that the perceptual system sorts edges into two categories, those representing lightness differences and those representing illumination differences. Thus, in the case in point, it is probable that the depth information at the corner edge leads the system to categorize that edge as one formed by illumination difference. When the apparent depth is eliminated, the system categorizes that edge as one formed by lightness difference.

Recent experiments indicate that the manner in which edge ratios are interpreted depends upon whether or not the edges are perceived to be in the same plane. Figure 9-1 illustrates an experiment on parallel planes (Gilchrist, 1977). The point of the experiment was to determine the effect on perceived lightness of localizing a target surface in a far or near plane. In the far plane it appears to be adjacent to a square surface of much higher luminance and in the near plane to a square surface of much lower luminance. The change in localization is achieved by making use of interposition as a depth cue and so arranging things that the target square appears to overlap a square in the near plane (near condition) and thus appears in the near plane, or it appears to be overlapped by that square as well as by the distant square so that it appears in the far plane (far condition). This target is, in fact, in the near plane in both conditions, partly covering the adjacent square in the near condition and partly covered by it in the far condition. By cutting out a notch in the upper left corner of the target square and correctly positioning it, it was made to appear to be in the far plane partly covered by the adjacent square in the far condition (Fig. 9-1c). The target was white cardboard. The adjacent square in the far plane was also white cardboard, but the square in the near plane was black. The far plane was much more highly illuminated than the near plane (by hidden light sources). As a result the relative luminance values were as follows (see Fig. 9-1c for the absolute values in foot-lamberts): the near adjacent black square was assigned a value of 1; the target square being white and in the same illumination, 30; the far adjacent white square, being in a much stronger illumination, approximately 2167. The subject matched the target square to one of a series of 16 values on a Munsell achromatic color chart.

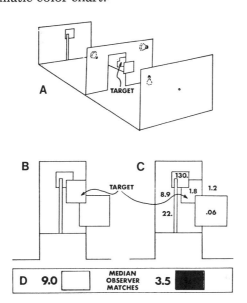

9-1. Illustration of an experiment on parallel planes. (a) Three-dimensional arrangement illustrating the far condition. (b) and (c) The display as seen by the observer, giving the relative luminance values of the various surfaces in c. (d) The median observer matches in the two conditions. After Gilchrist, 1977.

Before examining the results, it will be helpful to consider what might be predicted in such an experiment. From the standpoint of the retinal image there is only a negligible difference between the near and far conditions, as shown by a comparison of the two lower configurations in b and c. Therefore, there is no basis for predicting a difference in the perceived lightness of the target in the two conditions. Beyond that it is difficult to predict precisely what lightness value that should be. The image of the target is near several images of different luminances, some of which are greater and some lesser. If, however, the belongingness to a specific plane governs the outcome, it should be predicted that in the near condition the target will look white because it stands in the ratio of 30:1 with respect to the phenomenally adjacent black square in the near plane. Because the target *is* white, that outcome perhaps will not occasion much surprise. In the far condition it should be predicted that the target will look black, because it stands in the ratio of 30:2167 (or 1:72) with respect to the white phenomenally adjacent square in that plane. The results were as follows: the median match for subjects in the near condition was 9.0, which is white; the median match for subjects in the far conditions was 3.5, which is a dark gray, almost black. Thus, as a result of a change in phenomenal depth localization only (interestingly enough created by a pictorial cue to depth), a target surface changes its phenomenal shade of gray from one end of the scale almost to the other.

Another experiment was concerned with planes meeting at one edge and forming a 90-degree dihedral angle. In each of the two planes two regions of different luminance values are introduced. The basic idea is illustrated in Fig. 9-2. One plane is horizontal and receives stronger illumination than the other. The inner squares or tabs are the target surfaces whose lightnesses are to be judged. As will be made clear, in this experiment prediction in terms of relationships between luminance values of regions considered in terms of the retina *is opposed* to prediction in terms of relationships between regions perceived to be in the same plane. The plan of the experiment can be readily grasped by examining Fig. 9-2. The observer views the array from above. In the binocular condition the figure on the left illustrates what the subject sees, namely, tabs (the targets) attached to the background surfaces in which their edges meet. If what matters for perceived lightness is the ratio formed between a target surface and another surface in that plane, one prediction follows, but if the ratio that governs perception of lightness is between adjacent retinal images an entirely different prediction follows. This is so because the retinal images of the tabs are surrounded on three sides by stimulation deriving from the surface *not* in the plane of the tabs (Fig. 9-2, right).

The horizontal plane receives 30 times as much illumination as the vertical plane. Given the actual reflectances of tabs and background, as shown in Fig. 9-2 (right), the relative luminance values of the regions are 1:30:900. Note that the difference in illumination compensates exactly for the difference in lightness of the two tabs (one white, the other black) such that the two are of equal luminance. These tabs are trapezoidal in shape. When the array is viewed monocularly, they look like squares in the planes of the background surfaces, but the background surfaces are perceived veridically as meeting at a right angle. That being the case, the hypothesis that only ratios within perceived planes govern the outcome predicts that the ratio formed by each tab to the surface perceived to be in that

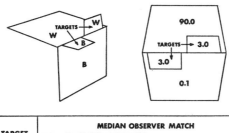

TARGET	MEDIAN OBSERVER MATCH	
	MONOCULAR	BINOCULAR
UPPER TAB	3.75	8.0
LOWER TAB	7.75	3.0

9-2. Illustration of the display in an experiment on planes meeting at an edge. After Gilchrist, 1977.

same plane will determine its apparent lightness. Because the background luminances are so different from one another, the horizontal one being 900 times as intense as the vertical, the phenomenal lightness of each tab should undergo rather drastic change if the effective ratio for it entails the horizontal *or* vertical background surface.

The median matches for subjects in each condition in Munsell units were as follows (see Fig. 9-2, bottom): binocular condition, upper tab, 8.0 (or almost white), lower tab, 3.0 or black; monocular condition, upper tab, 3.75 (almost black), lower tab, 7.75 (almost white). Thus the outcome for both conditions is exactly what the hypothesis predicted. The results of the binocular condition are particularly striking, for in this case it is the surface on that fourth side, that is, on one side of the tab only, that completely governs the outcome because only on that one side is the background in the phenomenal plane of the tab. It does so despite the fact that the prediction based on luminance ratios for the other three sides of the tab goes in the opposite direction. The fact is that the phenomenal lightness of each tab changes from almost black to almost white simply as a function of change in depth perception.

Thus the hypothesis concerning depth organization is one that explains many of the known facts concerning the perception of lightness. Which of the two kinds of theory of constancy does it support? In some sense it is compatible with both theories and in another sense it is incompatible with them. As a principle concerning ratios rather than absolute stimulus values it clearly fits the higher-order stimulus theory, but it is not simply the retinally given ratios that govern the outcome. Yet that theory refers to relations within or derivable from the retinal image. On the other hand, to the extent that the perceived spatial structure of the array is relevant, the hypothesis fits the idea of an internal process of sorting edge information into the categories of lightness and illumination. Later in this chapter I will take up the problem of why.

OTHER CONSTANCIES

If this conclusion is correct, the ratio type of theory of constancy has been seriously challenged in the domain in which it has always been considered basically correct and therefore in which the strongest case can be made for it, namely, the perception of lightness. What about the other constancies? With respect to constancy of direction, position, and orientation, a rather good prima facie case can be made in favor of the taking-into-account theory.

The phenomenal direction of a point in the field (its egocentric location with respect to the observer's mideye position as origin) clearly depends on combining information about the retinal locus of the image of the point with information about the position of the eyes in the head (see Hill, 1972). It is difficult to see how a theory based entirely on retinal stimulation is possible in this case. A similar argument holds for the related fact of position constancy, the apparent stability of the visual world despite eye or head movement. Here, too, such movement must be taken into account by the perceptual system in order to assess the implications of change of the object's angular direction. In the case of head or observer movement, the distance of the object has to be taken into account as well. That is because the angular displacement of a stationary object is a function of its distance.

It has been suggested that the shifting of the entire retinal image is the stimulus for phenomenal stationarity (and the simultaneous experience of one's own movement) (Gibson, 1966). In this view eye or head motion need not be considered. This explanation, however, is incorrect. If the entire visible array is suddenly moved, it will appear to move and will not yield an induced impression that the eye or body is in motion in the opposite direction. It is true that under the appropriate conditions movement of the surrounding visual field gives rise to the impression that the field is stationary and we are moving (induced movement of the self). This fact is the source of Gibson's hypothesis. But the sudden motion of the entire field is not a good condition for such induced self-motion. The visual field appears to move during head movement in patients with vestibular dysfunction. The entire array appears to move when one pushes one's eye with a finger. Conversely, it appears to move when one tries to move one's eyes, but when, in doing so, the eyes are prevented from moving, (Brindley and Merton, 1960). Moreover, position constancy is manifested even for a single object in an otherwise homogeneous field when the eyes are moved normally. Therefore, the evidence is strong for a process of taking head movement or eye movement (or, more carefully stated, intended eye movement) into account.

By orientation constancy is meant the constancy of the perceived orientation in the environment of an extended object, such as a line, regardless of head orientation. Such constancy occurs, within certain limits of accuracy, for a single line in a dark field so that it clearly depends on a process of taking account of head orientation in assessing the perceptual significance of an image in a given orientation. With the entire scene visible it is true that constancy is now complete; that is, the orientation in the environment is perceived veridically, regardless of the observer's posture. Hence we might argue that relationally defined stimulus information is relevant as well. The line is now seen to be parallel to those contours of the room taken to be vertical, and this parallelism is no doubt a source of information that is utilized by the perceptual system. Information of this kind, however, is not sufficient, for when a conflict is created by tilting a room or a rectangular frame of reference, a compromise occurs (rod-and-frame effect). The line does not look upright for most observers when it is parallel to the edges of the rectangle. Gravity information is taken into account.

SIZE CONSTANCY

Thus it seems fair to say that for these constancies there can be little doubt that the mechanism is one of considering information from other sources in interpreting the perceptual significance of the retinal image. What can we say about size constancy that has been the subject of so much research in the last 50 years? It is well known that size perception is intimately related to distance perception. Perceived size is a function not of the object's visual angle alone but of the distance at which the object is perceived to be as well.

It is possible, however, to argue that size perception is not a direct function of a process of taking account of distance but a function of certain information contained within the retinal image that happens to covary with distance. One hypothesis is that phenomenal size is determined by the size of the retinal image of an object in relation to that of neighboring object images, that is, a size ratio or proportionality principle. Because the size of object A in relation to that of neighboring object B (both at the same distance from the observer) remains constant for all distances of the pair of objects, such a principle could also explain size constancy, and it would not depend at all on taking account of distance. This kind of proportionality effect was discussed in the preceding chapter.

Consistent with the overall theory that the information for all aspects of perception is contained within the proximal stimulus, it has been proposed that information exists for phenomenal size, regardless of an object's distance. The very texture-density gradient that is said to be the stimulus for the perceived slant of a plane in the third dimension is also held to be the basis of size perception. All objects of equal size at any distance on this plane will cover the same number of texture elements (at least this is true for objects lying entirely *on* the plane; it is not true for objects rising vertically *from* the plane) (Gillam, 1981). Therefore, this equivalence of number of subtended textural elements is said to be the information that directly leads to veridical size perception or constancy (Gibson, 1950).

The argument is that the texture-density gradient directly leads to an impression of a plane at a given slant or slope in *which all texture elements are perceived on the average as equisized and equidistant from one another*. The *scale* within the plane is said to be constant, for if the underlined phrase is not part of the claim, size constancy does not follow at all. If, instead, the argument is only that the texture-density gradient is the stimulus for a plane receding into depth, why should equality of the number of texture elements subtended determine equality of size of the object? Information concerning distance or depth relations is not ipso facto information about size; it is only information that can potentially be used in assessing size.

Therefore, this hypothesis differs from a simple proportionality hypothesis described above. It links size with distance perception, whereas the proportionality hypothesis makes no reference whatsoever to the perception of distance. If, for whatever reason, a texture-density gradient failed to lead to an impression of a plane at a slant (but instead to the perception of a frontal plane), this hypothesis should not predict that equality of number of texture elements subtended by objects would determine equality of size of the objects. The phenomenal scale within the plane would no longer be constant.

In a recent experiment, this prediction was tested by presenting a slide of a textured grassy field under conditions where it was not always recognized (Rock, Shallo, and Schwartz, 1978). In one condition the sky and horizon were eliminated. Subjects who failed to recognize the scene had no impression of depth and perceived a square placed near the top of the scene as equal to one of the same size placed near the bottom. In other words, there was no tendency toward size constancy. Those who did recognize the scene did have an impression of depth and, of the average, perceived the upper square as roughly 10 percent larger than the lower one.

In another condition, the slide was tilted 90 degrees and viewed by subjects whose heads were tilted in the same direction by 90 degrees. For subjects in one group a set was created by means of several other prior figures to the effect that the top of the grassy field figure would be the region uppermost on the screen, which was not the case. As a result, these subjects failed to recognize the scene and showed no tendency toward constancy. For another group, the appropriate set was created to the effect that the critical figure was tilted. Consequently these subjects did recognize the scene and did show a significant compensatory effect toward constancy. Thus these experiments indicate that it is not the texture gradient per se that matters but the recognition and recognition-based construction of the scene as representing the third dimension of space. Only then can one say that a scale is present within the plane that is constant (see Fig. 9-3).

9-3. Picture of textured grassy field tilted 90 degrees clockwise used in experiment. Depth perception and a size illusion for the two white squares depend upon recognition. After Rock, Shallo, and Schwartz, 1978.

In any event, there are strong arguments and evidence against both versions of the higher-order stimulus theory of size constancy.

1. It is not a necessary explanation because it is easily shown that constancy is present under dark field conditions in which only a single isolated object is visible. Distance cues such as accommodation and convergence are enough to achieve constancy, at least at distances within which these cues are effective. Here only the taking-into-account kind of theory can be applicable. Along the same lines is an experiment done in our laboratory in which texture and perspective information were eliminated by a method that simulated a

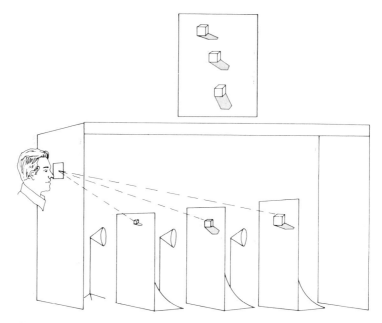

9-4. Illustration of arrangement used in an experiment on construction of a receding plane, based on three-dimensional objects and their cast shadows. After Rock, Wheeler, Shallo, and Rotunda, 1982.

horizontal plane (Rock, Wheeler, Shallo, and Rotunda, 1982). The observer viewed a display of vertical planes that contained only figures of cubes with attached and cast shadows. The visual angles of the cubes were equal, so that size perspective was not a factor (Fig. 9-4). This display created an impression of cubes resting on a surface receding in depth, with the further consequence that the uppermost cube appeared to be substantially larger than the lowermost one. The receding surface or plane is the resultant of a process of construction. Here again only a theory in which distance information, in this case location in the perceived plane, is taken into account can explain the results.

2. The higher-order stimulus theory is not a sufficient explanation because, with distance held otherwise constant, the proportionality effect achieved falls far short of what would be necessary to explain the constancy that obtains in daily life, or in experiments permitting distance cues (for details, see pp. 232–235 and Rock and Ebenholtz, 1959). Moreover while experiments performed on the texture-gradient explanation of depth perception focused on the perceived inclination of the plane rather than on the perceived size of objects in the plane, we do know that in these experiments the perceived inclination of the plane falls considerably short of the predicted

inclination, and this means that constancy would have to be far from complete.

3. Logically the higher-order stimulus theory cannot explain the perception of absolute (or specific) size. By these terms I mean that we have an impression of the linear size of an object at a distance specifiable in units such as inches or feet. For this to be possible we must "know," that is, have the information, about the object's absolute distance from us. What the higher-order stimulus can explain, however, is the equivalence of an object at one distance with that at another distance. This is very clear in the case of the proportionality principle, but I believe it is also true for Gibson's hypothesis. Texture-density gradients do not convey information about absolute distance. Therefore, on purely a priori grounds a higher-order stimulus theory cannot provide a sufficient explanation of size perception.

4. Then there is the question of ecological validity; for example, for the size proportionality principle to lead to constancy, the size of an object relative to neighboring objects must be invariant for all distances. Thus, if an automobile is next to a small tree at a distance but next to a larger tree nearby, the prediction must be that it will *not* appear to be the same size. In this case the nearby car would have to appear *smaller*. To what extent does the environment contain such necessary invariants? It seems doubtful that it does to an extent sufficient to explain the prevalence of constancy. Moreover, the relationship is not reciprocal in that the size of the larger object (or frame of reference), for example, the rectangle in our experiments, is not at all a function of its size in relation to the smaller one, the line in our experiments. This leaves size constancy unexplained for the largest objects in any given grouping of objects in the environment, as the tree in the foregoing example.

For a higher-order stimulus theory, uniformity of texture in the plane is an ecological prerequisite for veridical depth and size perception. Although such uniformity is certainly frequent, the question is whether texture is always visible. Thus beyond a short distance the texture of snow, ice, sand, or the water in a lake is undoubtedly below the acuity threshold.

In summary, formidable arguments and evidence challenge a theory of size constancy based on higher-order attributes of the proximal stimulus and, ipso facto, support a theory based on a process of taking account of distance. In the laboratory, the effect of manipulating perceived distance on perceived size is common knowledge, as, for example, when a three-dimensional wire object is perceptually reversed. The apparent sizes of the objects' faces then change exactly in accord with the changes in their apparent distances. There is, however, reason for believing that proportionality or the invariant occlusion of texture elements can play an important role in size perception. In an experiment not yet mentioned conditions were first created in which cues to distance were relatively poor but not entirely absent, i.e., luminous objects at differing distances viewed in an otherwise dark room with both eyes. Only a partial effect of distance on size occurred. But when the objects (lines) were then surrounded by objectively equal luminous rectangles, full constancy was achieved (Rock and Ebenholtz, 1959). It would be plausible to assume that similar effects occur frequently in daily life and also that objects perceived to be at differing distances seen on textured backgrounds or within converging lines of perspective look more nearly equal in size than they would were the background without stimulus content.

Dual Aspects of Perception

One major fact concerning all constancies which has been more or less neglected is relevant to the discussion of the two kinds of theory of constancy. Although it is true that perception is generally in agreement with the objective properties of things and events rather than with absolute features of the proximal stimulus, one aspect is correlated with these features. I refer to these two aspects of perceptual experiences as the world mode and the proximal mode, respectively. Some investigators have recognized this dual aspect of perception, but it seems not to play any role in contemporary theorizing (Brunswik, 1956; Gibson, 1950; Mack, 1978). I believe that the presence of proximal mode experience is not merely of interest as a phenomenological nicety but rather has important ramifications for a thoroughgoing theory of perceptual constancy. It will be helpful first to examine some different examples.[1]

Consider size perception. Although an object at varying distances does appear to be the same objective size, its changing visual angle is by no means a fact without representation in consciousness. We are aware of, even if not attending to, the fact that at a greater distance the object does not fill as much of the field of view as it does when it is nearby. One might refer to the aspect of an object's size that is a function of its visual angle as perceived *extensity*. This fact has been

---

1. Insofar as the proximal mode is highly correlated with the proximal stimulus—as will be made clear by many examples—the concept is very close in meaning to that of literal solution as used in previous chapters. However, there are certain differences between the two concepts that would seem to warrant a distinction. Hence I will reserve the term "proximal mode" to refer to an aspect of perceptual experience that does not pertain to the objective properties of things or events in the way the world mode of perception does, as illustrated in this chapter. See the further discussion on p. 260. The term "world mode" is of course an apt description of the nature of the preferred or constructed solution discussed in previous chapters.

demonstrated in experiments on size perception when the instructions are to match on the basis of visual angle (in whatever way this is explained) rather than in terms of objective size or simply the size that the objects spontaneously appear to be (e.g., Gilinsky, 1955; Epstein, 1963). Typically, matches obtained under such instructions are more nearly in correspondence with visual angle than those obtained under the customary instructions. That size matches nevertheless still depart from visual angle equivalency in the direction of constancy suggests that it is often difficult to isolate extensity from objective size experience under daylight conditions when information concerning distance is adequate.

Another approach has been to require observers to match the sizes of objects at different distances under reduction conditions, that is, in a dark field in which no information whatsoever about distance is available (Holway and Boring, 1941; Hastorf and Way, 1952; Rock and McDermott, 1964; Epstein and Landauer, 1969). There is no question that this task can be achieved with fair accuracy. Because a definite objective size can arise in experience only when distance is determinate, such findings would seem to prove directly that the perception of extensity is possible and a function of visual angle. However, a controversy has developed concerning the meaning of these findings. One investigator has asserted that accurate matches under reduction conditions are based not on the perception of pure extensity, which he considers to be impossible, but rather on the assumption by the observer that both objects are equidistant. If equidistant, distance can be equally taken into account and can provide the basis for size judgments along more traditional lines (Gogel, 1965, 1969).

It is difficult to resolve the issue experimentally. There is evidence for and against this position. In one study we tested the equidistance hypothesis directly by including measurements of perceived relative distance. The subjects viewed two reduction triangles successively, separated from one another by 90 degrees. One was the standard and the other the triangle that appeared equal in size to the standard for that subject. The task was to indicate the relative distances of the two triangles by positioning two luminous beads, each of which slid along strings over luminous lines at right angles to one another. Among all the judgments of the relative distances of the triangles thus obtained, few indicated equality or near equality (Rock and McDermott, 1964).

We also demonstrated that a comparison object can be equated with the standard reduction object when cues to distance are provided for the comparison object but not for the standard. The reduction triangle was 14 inches high at 32 feet and viewed with one eye through an artificial pupil. When the comparison triangle was viewed at a distance of 2 feet with binocular vision, it was set on the average to 1.16 inch in height, which is quite close to a visual angle match, namely, 0.87 inch. When, however, the comparison triangle was at 8 feet, a group of different subjects set it on the average to 3.08 inches in height; this is quite close to a visual angle match for these distances, namely, 3.5 inches. These findings suggest that we can compare objects on the basis of extensity even though we are simultaneously aware of objective size. After all, the subjects appreciate the objective size of the comparison object, and in a control experiment it was shown that they correctly matched a binocularly seen triangle at 8 feet with one seen at 2 feet. A further condition of the experiment indicated that the visual angle matches obtained were not based on an impression of equidistance between standard and comparison objects. Subjects were asked if they had any definite impression of the relative distances of the two triangles when comparing their size. Many did not and, overall, the triangles were rarely described as equidistant.

Logically, a tendency to perceive reduction objects as equidistant can only explain the *equivalence* of size perception; that is, the objects will appear equal in size. What is the phenomenal size of such equated objects? My impression and that of our subjects is that it is indeterminate as far as linear size is concerned. True, one might invoke the notion of specific distance tendency to respond to this question. In the absence of absolute distance information objects tend to appear at the specific distance of 6 to 7 feet (Gogel, 1969, 1977). However, this answer clashes with the central fact that under reduction conditions objects appear *indeterminate* in linear size, yet produce an impression of a certain extensity. Regardless of how this controversy concerning reduction objects is resolved, the simple fact is, as already noted, that in daily life we can clearly distinguish between perceived objective size and perceived extensity. A tree a hundred yards away may appear as large as another of the same size nearby, but we certainly are aware it fills far less of our visual field. The facts concerning the other constancies to be reviewed also add great weight to the claim that in the case of size we perceive in the proximal as well as in the world mode.

Consider next the perception of shape. A circle seen from the side, let us say at a 45-degree angle, may in one respect be said to continue to look circular, shape constancy, but its elliptical retinal image is not without some perceptual representation. Again instructions to match in accord with the "projected shape" rather than the objective shape will result in matches that are closer to the shape of the retinal image than to the object shape. Although it is difficult to describe the nature of this aspect of shape perception, perhaps the term *extensity relations* will suffice. We are aware that one diameter of the circle has a greater extensity in our field of view than the other while nevertheless simultaneously experiencing the objective sizes of these diameters as equal.

Turning now to the perception of movement, it is a fact that when we move, or when only our eyes move, stationary objects do not appear to move Yet this angular motion is in some sense perceived because we are aware that objects are changing their location in the field of view. Now the chair is to my left, now straight ahead, now to my right, as I swing my head around sharply to the left. It is true that the chair does not look as if *it* is moving; therefore, the designation position constancy is certainly a correct one. Nevertheless, there is (or can be) some experience correlated with a changing angular direction at least in the case of head motion, and that can be termed "field movement" or "pseudo-movement" (Carr, 1935). In some situations this type of experience is more directly noticed, as when we move rapidly in a vehicle. We say then that the trees and road markings are "sweeping by," although surely they are not seen as moving in the objective sense; that is, they do not appear to be in actual motion.

It is also relevant in this connection to consider the question of perceived velocity. The apparent speed of an object moving across the field is more or less constant with variations in the distance of the object from us. Are we unaware of the difference in rate of angular displacement of the object? I think not. Although in one respect we perceived the distant automobile to be moving rapidly, in another respect we are aware that it displaces across our field at a slower rate than when it is seen nearby.

Closely related to these facts about movement are others about perceived direction. Does the perceived constancy of radial direction, despite changes in the location of the retinal image with changes in eye position, mean that retinal locus has no unvarying significance for perceived direction? No, because we can speak of perceived field location. By field location I mean the apparent location of a point within the *momentary visual field*, that is, whether central, left, right, up, or down; for example, a foveal stimulus will always appear in the "center" of a momentary field of vision, regardless of how the eyes are positioned and despite the changing radial direction of the object. An object directly in front of the observer's head and torso will continue to appear in that same direction even when viewed with eyes turned sharply to the side, *but* the observer is then aware that the object is in the extreme periphery of the momentary field of view.

Less well known are the experiences that occur in the perception of orientation. To be sure, we continue to perceive a vertical line as more or less vertical, whether we view it from an upright posture or with the head tilted. Is there any perceptual awareness correlated with such changing retinal orientations? Yes. The line is perceived as having varying orientations in relation to ourselves. Thus, for example, when the head is tilted 90 degrees to the side, an objectively vertical line is perceived to be egocentrically "horizontal," by which I mean that observers are aware that the line is parallel to the horizontal axis of their heads. As in the other examples given of proximal mode perception, observers may not realize they are aware of this egocentric aspect of orientation, but a question would immediately elicit evidence of its phenomenal reality.

The perception of egocentric orientation can be conveniently isolated from the perception of environmental orientation by requiring an observer to view a line that rotates in a horizontal plane. Thus, supine observers who view a luminous horizontal rod in the dark, which rotates about a vertical axis above their heads, can make fairly accurate judgments about its egocentric orientation (Rock, 1954). Under these conditions the line never changes its orientation with respect to the direction of gravity; it remains horizontal. Therefore, we see that perceived egocentric orientation is directly correlated with retinal-image orientation, whereas perceived environmental orientation, that is, whether an object appears vertical, horizontal, or tilted in space, is a joint function of retinal-image orientation and other information about body position.

The dual aspects of perceived orientation are also revealed by the facts concerning form perception and recognition. Figures can generally be adequately described and recognized even when they are viewed by the observer from a tilted position. However, this description requires a process of correction in which the figure (or observer) is rotated mentally so that the figure assumes an upright egocentric orientation. If the figure is of a certain complex kind, such correction is difficult to achieve. But if the figure's image is retinally upright, no such correction is necessary as long as the subject is aware of the location of the figure's top, bottom, and sides. Apparently, then, upright egocentric orientation based on retinal orientation is the "natural" condition of uprightness (see Chapter 3, pp. 89–91, and Rock, 1973).

As a final example consider the perception of lightness. To be sure, a surface will continue to appear white, gray, or black, regardless of the illumination it receives. Therefore, it would seem that the absolute intensity of reflected light or luminance is not correlated with perception. The fact is, however, that a white object in bright sunlight does look different from one in dim room light in one respect; namely, it appears *more intense*, or as in stronger illumination. Therefore, changes in the absolute intensity of reflected light are in some sense directly correlated with changes in this aspect of perception. Presumably the perception of lightness and the perception of illumination summate and yield an impression of "brightness" that correlates with absolute luminance.

There are other examples than those pertaining to constancy in which dual aspects of perception can also be distinguished; for example, in the case of interposition as a depth cue we say that we perceive one rectangle behind another and the rectangle behind is seen as completed (Fig. 6-3). This is the dominant, spontaneous impression. We certainly are also aware that we do not perceive parts of the completed rectangle, or to put it differently, we are in some sense aware of the L shape corresponding to that rectangle's actual image. In the case of linear perspective we experience the converging lines as parallel and receding into depth but we are also aware of the convergence. In the case of motion parallax the relative shifts in the retinal images of points at different distances may or may not lead directly to an impression of depth, but we are also often aware of these optical changes.

Perhaps the most dramatic example of all that reveals the presence of a proximal mode of perception is one in which three-dimensional wire objects were employed. When these objects are first viewed from one perspective and are subsequently rotated 90 degrees about their vertical axes, observers naive to the fact of this rotation often fail to recognize them (Rock, DiVita, and Barbeito, 1981). Since these wire objects are viewed with binocular vision from a close distance, we assume that the three-dimensionality is perceived veridically. Moreover, because they are made of wire, parts of these objects are not occluded as is the case for all solid objects (see Fig. 3-34). Therefore, if the executive agency were to achieve a description of such an object in terms of its internal geometry there is no obvious reason why it should not be recognized when rotated. There is no change of what is at the top, bottom, or sides with the kind of rotation under discussion, so that the effect of orientation in the environment should not be relevant. I believe instead that the explanation lies with the great *qualitative* change in the retinal projection of these objects yielded by the 90-degree rotation in question, as the reader can see in Fig. 3-34. Apparently a description is achieved directly based on the retinal projection (an egocentrically governed description) rather than only one based on the recovery of objective shape, and it is the great change in this description with the rotation that renders the test object phenomenally different.

So much for the facts concerning these dual aspects of perception. The phenomenal reality of the proximal mode of perception to which I have called attention here has been denied or considered to be an insignificant epiphenomenon which emerges only under special or artificial conditions. It remains to be seen what role if any these experiences play in perception in daily life. However, the emphasis I have given to these attributes in the above survey is not intended to argue against the fact that the world mode of perception is not only salient in experience but most relevant to guiding behavior. It has an objective character in that it characterizes the physical properties of things. Conversely, the proximal mode is not salient in experience, it is not in any obvious way relevant to behavior, it is often hard to describe and phenomenally has a subjective or egocentric character; that is, it is experienced as stemming from the relation of the object to the self or to the momentary conditions of observation. Compare phenomenal size and perceived extensity, phenomenal movement and pseudo-movement, or environmental orientation and egocentric orientation.

With the many examples now given it may be useful at this point to compare the meaning of the term "proximal mode" of perception as used here with the term "literal solution or description" as used in earlier chapters. They are obviously similar concepts because both refer to perception that closely parallels features of the proximal stimulus. For example, in the case of interposition, in referring earlier to the *literal solution*, the percept corresponds fairly directly with the stimulus in that both can be said to contain an L-shaped region as one component (see Fig. 6-3). In referring here to the *proximal mode*, the percept also corresponds with the stimulus in that we are aware of this L-shaped region rather than a completed rectangular region.

However, there is this difference. In the literal solution, we have a distinct two-dimensional perception, e.g., a rectangle meshing together in mosaic form with an L. But in the proximal mode of perception we have simply the awareness of a nonvisible region of the far rectangle or an awareness that what is visible could be described as L-shaped. In other words, the proximal mode of perception reflects the subjective vantage point, whereas the literal percept has the same objective character as does the preferred or constancy solution in the world mode. As a consequence, the proximal mode can accompany the world mode experience, in the present example of two overlapping rectangles. Or, to give another example, the literal solution to the kinetic depth transformation is of a two-dimensional rod changing length while changing orientation; the proximal mode percept, on the other hand, is of an awareness of a rod changing its extensity while it rotates as an aspect of the world mode experience of a rigid rod rotating in depth. This awareness of extensity change is not tied to a two-dimensional organization as in the case of the literal solution.

An important point here, then, is that the proximal-mode experience can occur as an accompaniment to the salient world mode experience, whereas the literal solution, when it occurs, albeit often only for short durations, stands alone. This point was not brought out in previous chapters in discussing problem solving. When the preferred solution occurs, the literal solution ceases to be entertained, but a proximal mode of experience remains as an accompaniment of the world mode character of the preferred solution.

FACTORS FACILITATING OR IMPEDING PERCEPTION
IN THE PROXIMAL MODE

There would seem to be certain conditions in which the proximal mode of perception becomes more accessible. Whatever facilitates comparison between one image and another facilitates such perception; for example, in the case of extensity, when the objects to be compared are adjacent, the differences become obvious. Who is not aware of the smaller size of field subtended by a window of a building seen across the street through one's own window, although in terms of objective size, constancy may prevail? Similarly, the awareness of the ever-diminishing extensity of the ties of a railroad track with distance is perfectly clear. The fact that the ties are parallel to one another probably also facilitates awareness of extensity differences. Yet if we compared one such object in one direction with another in a different direction and at a greater distance, we would be far less aware of the extensity difference and would be primarily aware of the objective size quality. The obviousness of extensity changes in the case of expanding and contracting images leading to what is now called the "looming effect" may also derive from the adjacency of the successive images. The dominant impression is of an object approaching and receding, but we are also simultaneously aware of expansion and contraction. The similarity between objects may also facilitate proximal mode comparison.

Conversely, adjacency can facilitate the perception of *equality* of proximal stimulation as when regions of unequal lightnesses are in unequal illumination such that they produce images of equal luminance. In the experiment described earlier (Fig. 9-2) we can be aware that the two tabs look equal in a certain sense, in phenomenal intensity, although one appears to be white, the other black.

Great differences in the proximal stimulus also facilitate awareness of the proximal mode. Thus it is difficult to note differences in extensity between identical objects at different distances within a room (unless their images are adjacent). Yet objects outdoors at very great distances are readily seen in terms of their reduced extensity. People look diminutive and houses look like toys at a distance of a mile or so. I believe these descriptions refer to phenomenal extensity and not to perceived objective size. Rapid movement in a vehicle makes field displacement of objects (or pseudo-movement) evident in comparison with slow movement, as in walking.

Finally, under reduction conditions, the proximal mode of perception moves into the center of the stage. There is no longer a dominant objective percept that supersedes it.

On the other hand, proximal mode attributes are not so readily or directly available when contextual and relational factors affect the way these components are perceived; for example, in movement perception, whenever the outcome depends on relational information, it would seem that we do not experience or are not capable of experiencing the behavior of an object as a *direct* function of the behavior of its retinal image. For example, as we have seen, the perceived path of moving objects depends to a great extent upon their displacements relative to one another and not upon their absolute retinal-image displacement. However, the behavior of the retinal image of each point is fully accounted for if we consider *all* the vectorial components of the motion perceived, as argued in the previous chapter.

The geometrical illusions represent another set of phenomena in which there does not seem to be a proximal mode of perception distinct from the dominant perception. Perceived extent, direction, or curvature is not perceived correctly in such illusion patterns. It does not seem appropriate to speak of dual aspects of perception in the case of these illusions. If the geometric illusions result from a process of misapplied constancy, as some have suggested (e.g., Gregory, 1968; Gillam, 1980), it ought to follow that the proximal mode of perception would be present. If so, with the appropriate attitude, it should be possible *not* to perceive the illusions by emphasizing the perception of extensity and the like. Yet this is not easily achieved. However, we do not yet know the extent to which proximal mode perception is "veridical" to the retinal image under ordinary conditions, so that the force of the argument made here remains to be assessed.

There are other situations not relevant to constancy in which the proximal stimulus attributes are not accessible to conscious awareness. The difference between the two retinal images in binocular disparity, although producing impressions of depth, is not itself experienced. The binaural difference between time of arrival of an auditory stimulus is not experienced, although it leads to sound localization.

The movement of the retinal image when the eyes move saccadically from one position to another is not directly experienced.

Despite these examples in which it is difficult or impossible to perceive in the proximal mode, such perception does occur in connection with all the constancies and in certain other situations as well. It remains now to consider the implications of the existence of the dual aspects of perception for a theory of constancy.

Implications of the Existence of the Proximal Mode in Perception

CHARACTERIZATION OF PHENOMENAL EXPERIENCE

First and foremost, we cannot properly describe sensory experience without including reference to the proximal mode of perception. Consider again the example of the railroad track. How shall we describe its appearance? Are the tracks parallel or do they seem to converge toward the horizon? Both descriptions are true, a fact that has been referred to as the paradox of converging parallels. If we stress constancy of size, as has been true in the literature since the Gestalt revolution, we cannot explain the vivid impression of convergence that observers will tell you they have. By the same token, the texture-density gradient in a plane can be said to be perceived, even though the plane appears to recede into the distance and the spacing between the texture elements is perceived to be the same everywhere.

Consider again the circle seen at a slant. Many students in introductory classes in psychology are likely to shake their heads when the instructor points out that the circle looks circular and not elliptical. They often say "it looks elliptical but I know it is circular." In saying this, they are advocating the classical thesis the Gestaltists opposed so vigorously and successfully that perception is in accord with the proximal stimulus and that constancy is a fact of interpretation, not of perception. In this I believe they are mistaken. We do *perceive* the circle at a slant as circular, but we *also* are aware that its projected extensity relations are "elliptical." The point is that we would be seriously distorting the phenomenal facts if we chose to speak *only* of the constancy aspects of perception. In this respect the students have been right and we have been wrong.

It is difficult to imagine what the phenomenal world would be like if these proximal stimulus attributes did not enter our awareness. Objects at varying distances, slants, and the like would look as much alike as the same objects seen at identical distances and slants. The fact is, however, that even when constancy is present a distant or slanted object does not look exactly like a near or unslanted object of the same size and shape.

THEORETICAL IMPLICATIONS

As far as I can see there is no basis whatsoever for the proximal mode of perception according to the higher-order stimulus theory of constancy. Therefore, the phenomenal experiences that I have referred to as in the proximal mode have no basis in such a theory. To put it differently, the theory is designed to explain one mode of perception, not two.

As far as the taking-into-account theory is concerned, again viewed solely as a combinatorial process, it would seem that there is no place in the theory for proximal-mode perception. The presumption would seem to be that the information concerning the proximal stimulus is fused with the information that is taken into account and that the conscious experience of the attributes of the proximal stimulus is simply not available. A modern version of the combinatorial hypothesis is that neural units that "detect" features such as size or orientation are modified by feedback from other neural units that "detect" distance or body orientation (see Spinelli, 1970; Richards, 1967; Horn and Hill, 1969). Therefore, the size or orientation detectors are in effect tuned to the distal stimulus rather than to the proximal stimulus; that is, they are constancy detectors. If so, there is then no basis for detecting the proximal stimulus feature per se (at least not in that particular detector mechanism). In any event, even if some basis is found for explaining proximal-mode perceptions, such perceptions would remain irrelevant as far as constancy is concerned, or they are viewed as epiphenomena, requiring special conditions, attitudes, or instructions to become manifest. They do not constitute a necessary stage in the achievement of constancy.

By contrast the earlier, classical view of constancy was that such proximal-mode experiences are the fundamental sensations. Constancy is the result of interpreting these sensations on the basis of further information. This view was, of course, strongly and effectively criticized, chiefly by the Gestalt psychologists. Thus historically we have witnessed a complete reversal of viewpoints regarding the role of perception correlated with the proximal stimulus, from one in which they *are* the perceptions, the only true perceptions, to one in which they are either artifacts or epiphenomena. I believe the classical view is closer to the truth, that proximal-mode experiences are fundamental, but the sensation-interpretation dichotomy need not be reintroduced. Proximal-mode experiences are best thought of as perceptions rather than as sensations. Constancy is clearly perceptual rather than merely a fact we have learned about an object. The notion may well be correct, however, that constancy perception is based on a stage of prior detection of a feature directly

correlated with the proximal stimulus and a central process of interpretation of that perceptual experience by the perceptual system on
the basis of other relevant information. Otherwise the existence of
the proximal mode would seem to be a curious, redundant, unexplained phenomenon.

There is now new evidence for the reality of a stage of processing
in a constancy situation in which the proximal mode of perception
occurs. Experiments have shown that if a masking pattern is presented
a fraction of a second after an object is presented, constancy is not
achieved and instead the percept conforms with the retinal projection (Epstein and Hatfield, 1978a, 1978b). An ellipse rotated in
depth was viewed binocularly. When the masking pattern was not
presented, constancy occurred but when it followed the ellipse either
immediately or after a brief interval (25 to 50 milliseconds), observers
perceived an elliptical shape that correlated with the shape of the
retinal image. The investigators have tentatively concluded that the
outcome is based on failure to achieve the appropriate depth perception in the limited time available. Whatever may be its basis, the finding indicates that there is a stage prior to the integration of depth
information with the relevant retinal stimulus in which only a percept
based on the retinal stimulus occurs.

Thus the concept of proximal mode fits the kind of cognitive
theory defended here, namely, that the proximal input is scanned by
and is available to an executive agency and is ultimately interpreted
in terms of what object or event it represents in the environment.

EXPERIMENTAL IMPLICATIONS

A further implication has to do with the results of all empirical
investigations of constancy in the laboratory. As is well known, the
result is often one of compromise, of "regression to the real object,"
of less than complete constancy (Thouless, 1931). The usual interpretation of such findings is to say that the information necessary
for constancy is inadequately registered. Thus in the case of perceived position some motion of stationary objects is experienced
when we track a moving point, an effect that is probably the result
of inadequate registration of the actual rate of eye movement (Mack
and Herman, 1973). In size perception we say that we fail to register
the true distance and that, predictably, phenomenal size cannot be
veridical.

This explanation is no doubt correct under certain conditions; for
example, when we view an airplane in the sky, its diminutive phenomenal size is to some extent the result of poor cues to distance.
After all, if the sky is cloudless and the head stationary, only accommodation and convergence would seem to be operating in such a

situation, and these cues are ineffective at great distances. The small perceived size of the elevated moon can be explained in the same way. More typically, such quasi-reduction conditions do not obtain. In viewing an object across the terrain, in which pictorial cues such as texture gradients and perspective are presumed to be present, is there any reason why information about distance should not be accurate?

There is another possible explanation of the results of constancy experiments. Given the dual aspects of perception, a potential conflict is always present. Observers are aware of the discrepancy between the proximal-mode appearance of the standard and comparison object. They are then no longer sure how they should match the objects. Should they concentrate on objective size or shade of gray and ignore extensity or "brightness"? What they actually do is to make a decision, and this decision may be to compromise between the two aspects. Instructions are therefore extremely important, and it follows that if the instructions could make sufficiently clear that the observer is *not* to be concerned with extensity or "brightness," that constancy would then indeed be complete. Some early investigations point in this direction. Another approach to eliminating the ambiguity would be to change the task for the observer so that, for example, in matching a distant and nearby object visual angle would be held constant as the objective size of the comparison object varies. This was accomplished in our laboratory by moving the nearby comparison object along a track (Begelman, 1966). The object became physically larger as it receded. Both normal and schizophrenic subjects were easily able to match sizes in this way and, incidentally, did not differ from one another in degree of constancy achieved. (The converse procedure for varying visual angle without varying objective size was also employed. Here the comparison object moved back and forth along a track but remained constant in size.)

Research on size perception in recent years has reflected an increased sophistication concerning these dual aspects of phenomenal experience. In fact, even in the earliest experiments the objects to be compared were separated from one another, thus reflecting the realization that extensity relations are more readily perceived when objects are adjacent and that such proximal-mode perception would interfere with constancy perception. Instructions to match on the basis of spontaneous impression of size (rather than on the basis of visual angle or inferred objective size) do result in more or less perfect constancy. However, research on the perception of lightness has often been naive with respect to this issue. Either the instructions fail to make clear whether one is to match on the basis of perceived lightness of color or of perceived "brightness" or they incorrectly call for brightness matching when lightness is the phenomenon the investigator wishes to study.

It is as legitimate and desirable to study the perception of proximal-mode attributes as it is to study the perception of constancy, but only confusion can result if we fail to distinguish which of these is under study or, worse, if we intend to study one while creating conditions in which the other is necessarily what is being measured.

A related problem in experiments on the constancies concerns the effect of increasing the difference between the proximal stimuli of the objects under comparison; for example, in experiments on size perception we can increase the distance of one of the objects; in experiments on shape perception we can increase the slant of one of the objects; in experiments on lightness perception we can increase the difference in luminance of the regions under comparison by increasing the difference in illumination. In many earlier experiments on size and shape perception it was found that constancy "falls off" as distance or slant increases. In some experiments on lightness perception it was found that constancy holds for middle ranges of absolute luminance differences but "falls off" at extreme differences. In later, more sophisticated experiments on size perception it was found that constancy holds up under instructions to match in terms of spontaneous impression of size but that overestimation occurs (overconstancy) under instructions to match in terms of objective equality, with the distant object being judged increasingly large as a function of its distance.

The traditional interpretation of the "falling off" of size constancy is that the information which necessarily must be taken into account is the more inadequately registered, the greater the distance of the object. Thus it is believed that cues to distance become increasingly ineffective the greater the distance of the object judged. As noted above, there are conditions of observation in which this is no doubt true, but under typical conditions it is not obvious why this should be the case. At great distances one would think that the pictorial cues are of primary importance. If so, why should one think that perceived distance would fall off as a function of objective distance?

Another way of looking at data of this kind is that the greater the difference between the proximal stimuli of the objects under comparison, the more the differences between the correlated proximal mode of perception obtrude on our consciousness (see the discussion of this point on pp. 261-262). Thus, for example, we can hardly help noticing that people seen at a great distance subtend miniscule extensities in our visual field; we can hardly help noticing that a circle at an angle of 80 degrees to the frontal plane subtends a much smaller extent along one axis than the other. That being the case, it is not surprising that effects of such extreme differences in proximal stimulation would show up in experiments. The potential dilemma for the subject between matches on the basis of objective properties and proximal stimulus properties is exacerbated. If, however, pains are taken to eliminate the dilemma by careful instructions or an unambiguous task, perhaps little if any "falling off" of constancy will occur.

As to "overconstancy," it seems unlikely that such experimental findings reflect facts concerning perception. It simply is not the case that an object at a great distance looks larger than when it is nearby. Nor is it the case that distance is increasingly overestimated, which is what would be theoretically required to explain such findings were they genuinely perceptual in nature. Therefore, overconstancy is clearly an artifact of the experimental situation and, as noted, seems to occur under the "objective match" instructions to which the subjects seek to get the "right answer." They seem to be applying this rule: "An object far away looks smaller than it is in fact; therefore, to be correct I must compensate by judging it larger." In applying this rule, they err by judging the distant object too large.

How do we come to know that "objects far away look smaller than they are" if size constancy does not fall off with distance? One investigator suggested that we know this from experience with pictures and photographs (Carlson, 1960). Another answer is that "looks smaller" refers to the extensity aspect of size perception. Therefore, the more this aspect becomes salient within the experimental situation, the more such errors of judgment will tend to occur, and it becomes salient with great differences between the proximal stimuli.

As a test of this reasoning, we conducted an experiment in our laboratory in which we duplicated the proximal stimulus differences between standard and comparison objects of a well-known study (Gilinsky, 1955). In that study an object at 100 feet was compared with another at 100, 200, 400, 800, 1600, and 4000 feet. It was found that under the objective match instructions, the greater the distance of the distant object, the more its size was overestimated. At these distances the ratios of image sizes of equal-sized objects were 1:1, 2:1, 4:1, 8:1, 16:1, and 40:1, respectively. In our study these same ratios were created, not by placing the distant object at increasingly greater distances but by placing the nearby object at increasingly closer distances (Posin, 1962). Although one object was always at 20 feet, the other was at 20, 10, 5, 2.5, or 1.25 feet. Under these conditions the subject should be more inclined to be aware of the differences in extensity the greater the difference in visual angle, although both objects are always well within the range of distances in which complete constancy almost always obtains. The more aware the subject is of the extensity differences, the more this will lead to a tendency to make overestimation judgments of the distant object. The results more or less paralleled those of the earlier study indicating increasing overestimation of the object at 20 feet, the closer the other object was to the observer.

One other result of experiments on the constancies may be explicable in terms of the presence of dual aspects in perception. Typically, individuals differ from one another in their judgments and consistently so. There is evidence also that age is a factor, young children presumably perceiving objects as less constant than older children or adults. Why, according to prevailing theory, should individuals differ in such perception? Do some individuals perceive distance or slant more accurately than others? Or is it not this difference that is relevant but the extent to which they apply such information in assessing objective size and shape?

Perhaps individuals do not differ in such perceptions. There is no evidence that they do so in daily life, although admittedly it can be argued that they do, but it can be revealed only by careful measurement. At any rate, I propose that the differences obtained in experiments are artifacts resulting from the presence of the dual aspects under discussion. Some observers choose to give more weight than others to the proximal mode. This might conceivably result from the greater attention paid to this attribute by some individuals for reasons not yet understood. If true, to that extent we might wish to characterize the differences as perceptual, although that is not what is usually implied by the individual differences in constancy experiments. However, the difference might also be one of attitude or interpretation of instructions, particularly when they are not made explicitly clear.

As to the findings with children, the fact is that their judgments of size differ from those of adults only beyond a substantial distance, (Leibowitz, Pollard and Dickson, 1967; Brislin and Leibowitz, 1970). Evidence from our laboratory suggests that even this difference disappears when the task for the child and adult is such that a *choice* between visual angle or objective size matching is eliminated as in the manner referred to above (Shallo, 1983). The evidence is pointing toward the tendency of children to be as responsive as adults to visual angle, if not more so, i.e., to the proximal mode of perception.

Physiological Explanations of Constancy

Ultimately the explanation of perceptual constancy, as for all perception, will be in terms of neural mechanisms. If the analysis to be offered here is correct, these will be mechanisms mediating inference processes. Of course, we have no knowledge of what such neural mechanisms would be like. Alternative physiological explanations have been suggested that have already been mentioned, namely, matching signals in the case of position constancy (p. 33 of Chapter 2), feature-detector mechanisms in the case of some of the spatial constancies (p. 264 above), and lateral inhibition in the case of lightness constancy (pp. 203–212). Some further comment about these suggested explanations is in order in light of the arguments and evidence presented in this chapter.

Neural units responsive to the proximal state of affairs, such as those triggered by contours in a particular orientation (Hubel and Wiesel, 1962), cannot of course, do justice to constancy phenomena. But units tuned to the distal state of affairs can, in principle at least, be invoked to explain constancy. One difficulty is that constancy is a function of taking account of various kinds of information, not only of the kind rooted in known physiological mechanisms. Although it is at least possible that feedback from accommodation of the lens or from convergence of the eyes could modify the nature of the receptive field of a neural unit, it is not at all obvious and seems unlikely that such a mechanism could explain size constancy based on pictorial information about depth relations.

Moreover, size perception can change without the introduction of a specific "cue" merely by a change in perceived depth. The perspective reversal of a drawing of a wire rectangle will often result in certain concomitant changes in phenomenal size of the different faces of the rectangle. Even more striking than this example are the dramatic size transformations that occur when one succeeds in reversing a three-dimensional wire cube. It is simply inappropriate to speak of "cues" here. Rather it is quite clear that a central change in one perception (depth) without any change in stimulation or other sensory information brings about a change in another perception (size) (see Hochberg, 1974). One implication of these effects is that the perceptual system is indifferent to the source of information that is taken into account (see Epstein, 1973). What seems to matter for size perception is the perception of a particular distance, not the particular source of information (or, I would add, whatever central reorganization) that leads to that perception of distance. In the light of this implication it seems unlikely that at this stage of our knowledge a physiological theory based on feature detectors is defensible.

Earlier I alluded to another difficulty with the attempt to explain constancy in terms of constancy detector units, namely, the problem of explaining proximal-mode perceptions. Of course, one might argue that two kinds of unit exist—one responsive to the proximal state of affairs, for example, orientation of retinal contours (mediating perceived egocentric orientation), size of retinal image (mediating perceived extensity), and the like, and one responsive to the distal state of affairs; for example, object orientation and size. Together these units could be said to account for constancy and proximal-mode perceptions.

No one to my knowledge has suggested this possibility, but if it were to be seriously entertained it is important to be clear that what has to be explained is not merely the dual aspects of perception but the *relationship* between them. The proximal mode of perception remains as an essential ingredient of the overall experience. Perceived extensity is an important feature of the overall impression of an object's size. A distant object is perceived as one of a certain physical size, *at* a distance, and of *small* extensity. A shade of gray is simultaneously a gray in a certain illumination. Therefore, in order to explain both aspects of perception the detectors of proximal features would have to be thought of as inputs to the detectors of distal features.

Still another problem with explanations of this kind concerns the origin of constancy. Matching afferent and efferent neural signals or distal feature detectors imply innateness and immutability of constancy. While this question is still unresolved, there is certainly evidence that experience can alter the equation. Thus, for example, position constancy is at first eliminated, but then reestablished when the angular displacement of the scene contingent upon observer movement is experimentally altered (see below, pp. 276-278). This kind of finding is more in keeping with an explanation based on the application of (learnable) rules than on fixed neural-signal cancellations.

As for the mechanism of lateral inhibition as an explanation of lightness constancy there is no need to repeat here what was said in the preceding chapter. In addition to the difficulties noted there that this theory faces, there is the following problem. Given the assumption that lightness is a function of rate of discharge of neurons in the critical region, there would seem to be no basis for explaining the differing phenomenal appearances of two surfaces in differing illuminations that have the same phenomenal lightness. If lateral inhibition leads to the same rate of discharging neurons from the critical region in the two cases, that region should look exactly the same in *every respect*, but it does not.

Therefore, it is probable that lateral inhibition is not the mechanism that explains why constancy is a function of ratios of differing luminance values. Until now, however, it has been impossible to separate lateral inhibition from determination by ratio, for whenever the latter would apply, so would the former. However, the research described earlier and in the preceding chapter does seem to provide a basis for separating the two kinds of explanation (Gil-christ, 1977, 1980). Lateral inhibition is based on the spatial rela-tionship of regions within the retinal image; that is, it is the activity in the cells in the retina stimulated by light that inhibits the dis-charging of ganglion cells stimulated by adjacent retinal cells. With this in mind, consider the experiment illustrated in Fig. 9-2. The critical tabs shown on the left yield images surrounded on three sides by images whose luminance values are shown on the right. Yet it is not these luminance ratios that govern the outcome, at least when veridical depth is achieved. In fact, this experiment can be viewed as a contest between what is to be expected on the basis of lateral in-hibition and what is to be expected on the basis of ratios within phe-nomenal planes. At least it is if we make the plausible assumption that the effects of lateral inhibition on three sides of the target would dominate the effect on the fourth side. Therefore, the two principles here lead not only to different predictions but to opposite predictions. According to lateral inhibition, the upper tab should look darker than the lower; in fact, the upper tab is seen as almost white and the lower one as black.

These findings suggest that it is the luminance ratio itself, not the rate of discharge from one region as modified by that from neighbor-ing regions that governs lightness perception. These ratios are then interpreted in relation to all other ratios present taking account of whether they result from reflectance or illuminating edges.

In Defense of Unconscious Inference

So far I have presented evidence and arguments against the higher-order stimulus theory and a spontaneous interaction theory in favor of the taking-into-account theory of constancy. In discussing the latter earlier in this chapter, I deliberately restricted its definition to the notion of combination of retinal-image information with infor-mation from other sources. Some of the suggested mechanisms just considered are consistent with the combinatorial meaning of this theory. Thus, for example, a hypothetical detector tuned to distal size would depend upon information about distance. As noted at the outset, however, there is the further implication that the process of taking-into-account is a cognitive operation, an unconscious infer-ence. The question I should now like to address is whether there is reason for favoring a deeper interpretation of this theory beyond the acceptance of the combinatorial hypothesis. By unconscious infer-ence I mean that the process of arriving at the percept is one much like reasoning in which conclusions are drawn from premises, except that in perception the process is not conscious and the outcome is a percept rather than a conclusion. I do *not* argue as Helmholtz did that such a process is necessarily a direct result of experience. That is a separate question.

Consider the case of orientation constancy. We view a luminous line in the dark with head tilted and perceive its orientation in the environment more or less veridically. We also perceive its orientation relative to ourselves. It makes a good deal of sense therefore to view the achievement of constancy as resulting from a process analogous to reasoning:

1. The perception of the line's egocentric orientation on the basis of its image's orientation (proximal mode). (As noted earlier, observers may not realize that they are perceiving or detecting the line's egocentric orientation, although they would be able to report about it if questioned.)

2. Information available concerning the orientation of the head (or body) in the environment.

3. The interpretation of the line's orientation in the environment by the executive agency on the basis of 1 and 2 (world mode percept).

A concrete example may be helpful. If the observer is laterally tilted 50 degrees clockwise and achieves perfect constancy, the image of a line judged to be horizontal in the environment is retinally oblique. Therefore, in terms of our analysis we have the following:

1. The line is perceived as egocentrically oblique at a 40-degree clockwise angle with respect to the head (proximal mode).

2. Information is available that the head is tilted 50 degrees clockwise with respect to gravity.

3. Therefore, the line in the environment producing the image must be 90 degrees from the direction of gravity, or horizontal (world mode percept).

The process is a form of reasoning that can be formalized according to general predicate logic, for the premises and conclusions entail relations. (By contrast, inference for Helmholtz meant reaching a conclusion based on a syllogism. The major premise, derived inductively from experience, was of the form "retinal image a always results from object A in the world"; the minor premise was of the form "Retinal image a is now present." The conclusion was of the form "This retinal image a represents object A"). In the example of the line we might say that the process has the form of a transitive deductive inference. (A is tilted 40 degrees clockwise from B; B is tilted 50 degrees clockwise from C; therefore A is tilted 90 degrees from C.) This analysis assumes that the executive agency "knows" how body orientation affects image orientation, a point to which I return shortly.

A similar process may underlie size constancy. The perceived extensity correlated with visual angle is interpreted by the executive agency as signifying a particular objective size on the basis of information available concerning the object's distance. The components here would be as follows:

1. A particular extent is perceived based on the visual angle (proximal mode).

2. Information is available that the object producing that visual angle is at a certain distance.

3. "Therefore," the object must be a particular size (world mode percept).

Again, however, this analysis presupposes that the perceptual system "knows" how visual angle changes as a function of distance. Therefore, so far in the analysis certain additional principles that must be "known" have not been made explicit.

Other spatial constancies such as that of shape can be understood in much the same way. In the preceding chapter I dealt with the problem of lightness constancy. The process is not parallel to other constancies because the proximal information is in the form of edge ratios to begin with (see Chapter 8, pp. 203–212). To that discussion I would only add the following comments.

That information concerning reflectance value depends on the *relative* luminance of two or more regions should not be surprising, given the fact that the reflectance characteristic of a surface is itself a relative fact. A surface reflects a certain proportion of the light it receives, and what matters is whether it reflects more or less light than other surfaces. What phenomenal whiteness "means" is that this proportion is high in relation to another surface. It is this property that must be detected if we are to achieve a perception correlated with it. How could that relational property be picked up by the perceptual system? Relative luminance between surfaces at their edges seems to be the direct source of that information. This information is valid if and only if it can be assumed that the surfaces receive the same amount of illumination. According to the explanation offered here, lightness and lightness constancy is not determined by a neural correlate based on the *interaction* of the regions of differing luminance in which, regardless of absolute luminance levels, that correlate remains invariant. Rather the luminance differences are simply detected (i.e., perceived as light intensity differences) and are *interpreted* as signifying lightness differences when there is no information to suggest that illumination edges are present.

To summarize the argument concerning lightness perception, the first stage is the stimulation of the retina by regions of differing relative luminance. These differences or ratios at edges are then detected. We can consider perception at this stage to be in the proximal mode. If the regions are phenomenally coplanar, without a penumbra along the boundary separating the regions or other information suggesting illumination edges, they are assumed to be receiving equal illumination. Consequently they are interpreted as differing in lightness. Precisely what those inferred (or computed) lightness values are will depend upon the magnitude of all the relative luminance differences in the array. If the regions are not phenomenally coplanar, the situation is ambiguous. In any event, the phenomenal lightness of a region is achieved as a result of taking account of equality or inequality of illumination in assessing the perceptual meaning of luminance differences.

"Knowledge" of the Rules of Proximal Stimulus Change and the Role of Experience

"Unconscious inference" for Helmholtz and others since has meant that what we infer to be present in the environment is based on experience. Through such experience we presumably learn that objects at a distance are much larger than they at first appeared to be, that objects receiving weak illumination are lighter in color than they at first appeared to be, and so on. A generalization arrived at inductively in this way then would constitute the major premise in the subsequent inference process. (The specific proximal stimulus and relevant cues would constitute the minor premises.) Of course, it makes sense to believe that such premises, referring as they do to certain characteristics of the environment, are acquired by commerce with the environment, but it is not logically necessary to assume that they are acquired.

There are difficulties with the view that constancy is based on learning. The argument seems to assume some kind of direct access to the veridical state of affairs under some privileged conditions of observation; for example, when we approach the distant object, we find that it is large, not small. This presupposes that no learning is required for the perception of the size of a near object, for if there were how could we perceive its size when it is near? A possible resolution of this problem is that we can compare a nearby object with other familiar objects at the same distance, particularly with the body itself. Thus we can learn that a visual angle created by an object at a given distance is the same as that of one part of the body (e.g., the size of a foot) and different from other parts (e.g., larger than a hand); it is the size of a magazine, but smaller than a newspaper, and so on. This would seem to be all that absolute size can possibly mean.

One way of formulating the learning hypothesis is to say that what we learn *is how the proximal stimulus changes* as a result of our behavior. Thus we could learn that visual angle is a function of distance, that image orientation is a function of head orientation, that image motion is a function of eye, head, or body motion, and so on. In order for such learning to have any useful meaning, it must be presupposed that the proximal stimulus transformations do not result from simultaneous object transformations. Hence the learning hypothesis presupposes an a priori cognitive assumption about the nature of the environment, namely, that stimulus changes resulting from our behavior are not caused by object changes; that is, under such circumstances things remain constant. Given that assumption, however, we could in principle learn precisely *how* the proximal stimulus varies as a function of change in our vantage point. In the special dynamic case in which the observe is *in* motion, such an assumption may be based on the rejection of coincidence on the part of the perceptual system. The stimulus change begins and ends with the observer's movement, and the rate of change is perfectly correlated with the rate of movement. Therefore, it is plausible for the executive agency to conclude, "I am causing this stimulus to change rather than any change in the environment." Otherwise it must be acknowledged that the perfect correlation is pure coincidence.

However, the fact is that whenever we move in space or only move our heads, the image of the stationary environment sweeps over the retina in a *particular direction* and at a *particular rate*. Thus it is possible that the perceptual system has acquired the rule "image displacement to the right at α degrees per second during head rotation to the right at α degrees per second implies that the objects imaged are stationary." The proof that this rule does in fact govern perception is that when the relationship is altered by means of optical devices or the equivalent, the scene appears to move during head rotations in a predictable manner. For example, Stratton in his famous experiment with inverting lenses—which had the effect of reversing the direction of image displacement during head motion— noted that at first the scene appeared to rotate in the direction of his movements, but faster. However, he also reported that this illusory motion diminished and, after several days, completely disappeared. Most convincing was the fact that, when the lenses were removed, the scene appeared to move during head rotation in the direction opposite to the one initially experienced, a negative aftereffect. Similar results have since been obtained with optical and other methods of altering head-contingent image motion such as reducing the rate of image motion (Posin, 1966; Wallach and Kravitz, 1965a and b). Therefore, we can conclude that a new rule can be acquired and govern perception. The fact that such rules can be learned and then determine perception is very convincing evidence that they are internally represented.

Since no unequivocal information is available to subjects in this kind of experiment that the scene is not in motion during their movements, it seems probable that the basis of adaptation is the coincidence principle. In other words, at the beginning of the experiment two factors are at work: the coincidence principle, which should lead immediately to perceiving all observer-contingent or reafferent stimulus changes as signifying a stationary scene; and the internalized rule, which should lead to perceiving the scene as in motion. Given enough experience, a new rule concerning the contingent changes is established on the basis of the coincidence principle, and when this rule displaces the old one, adaptation is complete.

These experiments concern the general topic of adaptation to optical distortion such as to prismatically altered direction and orientation. There is now considerable evidence that adaptation of various kinds to these optical changes occurs. For example, one kind of adaptation that has been well documented is to prismatic displacement. The perceived direction of objects viewed through a wedge prism is systematically displaced by a particular angle. Consequently, when an observer first looks at the world through such a prism, objects appear to the side of their true location, with predictable effects on reaching or pointing. But after observers wear the prism goggles for some period of time, in which they walk and move around in the environment, a perceptual adaptation occurs in addition to a behavioral adaptation. On removing the prisms, the observer misperceives what direction appears to be straight ahead.

There is agreement about the mechanism that produces this perceptual change. Normally, an object whose image falls in the fovea will appear straight ahead only when the eyes are directed straight ahead. The executive agency must take account of eye position in assessing the directional significance of a given retinal locus to achieve constancy of visual direction. Thus the system knows a rule concerning eye position, namely, with "eyes straight ahead, foveally represented points are straight ahead and with eyes turned by an angle α, the foveally represented point is located off to the side by the angle α."

In viewing through the prism, however, the eyes must be turned to view an object that in fact is straight ahead. Given perceptual information during the adaptation period that objects so viewed are in fact straight ahead, a new rule is learned, namely, "with eyes turned by angle $\propto$, a foveally represented point is straight ahead." Proof that the system operates according to this new rule is the finding that when asked to look straight ahead in a dark room after the prisms have been removed, subjects turn their eyes in the predicted direction. Thus they now feel their eyes to be straight ahead when in fact they are not (Kalil and Freedman, 1966; McLaughlin and Webster, 1967). Another way of stating the result of the adaptation process is that the significance of eye position for the perceived angular direction of foveal objects is recalibrated. The "zero position" of the eyes signifying objects as straight ahead is no longer the actual straight ahead position of the eyes but one in which the eyes are turned by a specific angle and all other positions take on an appropriate new signification. But once again, the fact that such perceptual learning occurs makes the assertion more convincing that a rule is internally represented. The utilization of a rule of this kind can then be regarded as a process of inference.

In order for the perception that is achieved to be veridical, the perceptual system must take account of the relevant information in a manner that is *quantitatively correct*; for example, it is not enough to say that the perceptual system operates on the basis of the rule that visual angle is a function of distance. Assuming for the moment that the distance of the object is correctly registered, the mental computation requires that the correction be appropriate to the law of the visual angle. In other words, because visual angle varies inversely with distance, the computation requires a process equivalent to multiplication of visual angle by distance. This suggests that the perceptual system in some sense "knows" the law of the visual angle.

In stereoscopic-depth constancy the perceived depth relation between a pair of contours remains more or less constant despite the absolute distance of the pair (at least at near distances) and thus despite variation in the magnitude of retinal disparity (Wallach and Zuckerman, 1963; Ono and Comerford, 1977). Distance is taken into account, but retinal disparity varies inversely with the *square* of the distance. To correct for the lessened disparity as a function of distance, the computation must entail a process equivalent to multiplying the disparity by the square of the distance. Therefore, to achieve veridical perception of the depth relation by stereopsis, the perceptual system must in some sense "know" this inverse square law.

There has been some dispute about this claim. That some such process occurs is easily demonstrated by viewing an anaglyph at varying distances. An anaglyph is a picture containing two colored representations of the same objects viewed through an appropriate filter over each eye. Here, because the disparity is *in the display*, regional disparity varies inversely with distance but not with the square of the distance. When the distance to the anaglyph display is increased, the depth perceived among the parts of the display should remain constant if distance is taken into account in the same way as for size constancy. In fact, the perceived depth of these parts *increases* with the distance of the display.

Thus it would seem necessary to assume that the organism "knows" various rules concerning proximal stimulus change and that these rules constitute the major premises from which constancy is inferred. Despite some of the examples just given, it does *not* seem to me to be necessary to assume that all such rules are learned. The evidence is not yet decisive on the origin of constancy and in fact is somewhat contradictory (Bower, 1966; Heller, 1968; Day and McKenzie, 1977; Rock, 1975). Whether or not the rules derive from learning does not preclude a theory that asserts that constancy results from a process of inference. In other words, the process of inference itself need not be thought of as deriving from experience, regardless of the origin of "rules" and "assumptions" utilized by the perceptual system.

To illustrate with a concrete example of size perception, the inference would be of the following form:

Major premise: An object's visual angle is inversely proportional to distance.

Minor premise: Visual angle is 1 degree (producing a particular perceived extensity); distance is 50 feet (producing a particular perceived distance).

Conclusion: Object is equivalent to one that would yield a visual angle of 25 degrees at 2 feet (or 5 degrees at 10 feet, etc.).

What about the case of lightness perception? The rules in this case are not so much concerned with the observer's locations or orientations as with conditions of illumination. For a cognitive theory of the kind I have proposed to be viable, the organism would have to "know" the following: (1) that luminance differences are caused by reflectance-property differences or by illumination differences, (2) that illumination tends to be equal for nearby regions in a plane unless a penumbra or certain other information is present along the border of a region, and (3) that illumination is unequal for adjacent planes that are not parallel. Given the psychological reality of such premises, the major facts concerning the perception of lightness can be explained.

The most convincing kind of evidence for the existence of internally represented rules is the occurrence of "errors" or illusions that stem from the application of such rules. Errors of this kind occur often in the perception of properties of objects such as size, shape, and motion. The aftereffects of adaptation can be viewed in this light. But there are other examples. For instance, suppose visual angle remains constant instead of diminishing with distance as it usually does. An afterimage, whose visual angle of course remains constant, when projected out into the scene will yield perception of changing size as a direct function of the distance of the surface on which it appears. This relation is known as Emmert's law. It is an outcome or corollary entirely predictable on the basis of the application of the law of the visual angle. The moon illusion, in which the moon or other celestial object or extent when seen over the horizon appears to be much larger than when seen in the elevated sky, can be thought of in terms of this corollary. The visual angle of the moon is roughly the same in any of its locations in the sky. Seen over the horizon, however, with the rich depth information present in the visible terrain, it is located at a greater psychological distance than when seen against the homogeneous elevated sky. Thus the same law applies (Kaufman and Rock, 1962; Rock and Kaufman, 1962).

Analogous effects occur for other perceptual properties. An afterimage will appear as a different shape depending upon the perceived orientation of the surface on which it is projected. Such an effect is predictable on the assumption that a law is internally represented relating the width of the visual angle to the slant of the surface of the object producing the image, the same law that ordinarily yields shape constancy, wherein the width of the image varies with the slant of the surface. In the same way, an afterimage, which of course is stationary, will lead to the impression of a moving entity when the eyes move (Mack and Bachant, 1969). If the rule is known that stationary objects yield moving images when such motion is contingent upon eye movement, it follows as a corollary that images that remain stationary during eye movement must represent moving objects.

Another example of illusory perception based on knowledge of rules was considered in the first chapter under the general heading of false-depth parallax anomalies (Example 2, p. 5). In viewing a wire cube, if a perceptual reversal is achieved, the observer's movement leads to an illusory impression of rotation of the cube (Fig. 1-3). This phenomenon was explained in terms of a contradiction between the parallax changes that occur and the depth achieved by the reversal. But then the rules of parallax change must be known. They are in fact rather complex and have the following form: Given contours A and B (Fig. 9-5) with head motion to the right, if the images a and b separate, B is behind A; if the images a and b come together, B is in front of A. With head motion to the left, the opposite relations hold.

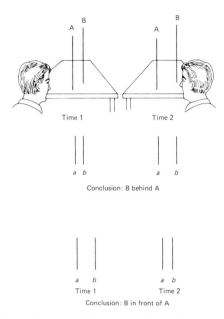

Time 1   Time 2

a   b   a   b

Conclusion: B behind A

a   b   a   b
Time 1   Time 2
Conclusion: B in front of A

9-5. Illustration of some of the rules of parallax based on observer motion. Retinal images of contours at differing distances approach or recede from one another as a function of which contour is farther away and the direction of observer movement.

Whether or not these rules can lead to depth perception when all other information about depth is eliminated is not yet entirely clear. But that the rules are known (possibly on the basis of visual experience in daily life when the depth relation is already perceived on the basis of other information) seems to be established by the paradoxical case under discussion. For in this case, head motion to, let us say, the right leads to a parallax change, let us say, of a and b separating, and that change is associated with the percept "B behind A," whereas A is perceived behind B. The contradiction forces the solution of the cube rotating enough to explain the actual parallax change in the light of the depth perceived so that the two kinds of information can be consistent with the external object and event.

In suggesting that constancy can be explained by logical inference, as in the above examples, I obviously do not mean to imply that the process is one in which each premise is explicitly present in awareness or even that the process producing it always occurs as an explicit state or that the order of events follows the formal logical order. After all, we do not even say that about thought itself. We say only that thinking can be translated into a form of logical inference, as *if* it occurs in precisely that way, not that it does follow that form. A related matter is the fact that in thinking we do not believe that we must go through the same process each time the same problem comes up. Analogously in perception, it is possible that the process runs off more or less directly by virtue of repeated instances of the same kind of situation, based on memory of the earlier solution.

10 ⬚

Perceptual Interdependencies

IN THE PRECEDING CHAPTERS, scattered examples have been given where perception is some function of another perception. Although I listed this kind of effect as a characteristic of perception that any theory would have to explain (Chapter 2, pp. 27–28), the fact is that, with a few notable exceptions, little attention has been paid to it (Hochberg, 1974; Epstein, 1982; Gogel, 1973). Yet to the extent that relations of this kind do characterize perception they are of great theoretical significance. Thus if one perception depends upon another perception, is affected by another, or is determined by another, a stimulus theory is inadequate. Logically, a stimulus theory can account for any one perception or even several co-occurring perceptions but not for influences of one on another. That is because the perception having the influence is a mediating event or central representation. Similarly, a spontaneous interaction theory, paradoxically enough, is not equipped to explain such possible perception-perception interactions.

But many would say that one cannot explain perception by perception. Explanation of phenomenal facts must be in terms of constructs that are not themselves phenomenological. Even those who avoid physiological explanation as premature would maintain that in the long run their explanatory concepts, be they memory traces, schemata, hypotheses, or whatever, must be translatable into phsyiological events. To be sure, any one perception can in principle be explained by its underlying neural concomitants. Therefore, why not simply say that the final perception is determined by a sequence of neural events which in some cases is somewhat more extended temporally than in other cases? Or why not simply say that the neural events determining one perception interact with those determining another simultaneous perception?

There are several reasons why it would be either misleading or extremely uneconomical to deal with the cases I have in mind in this way. It would be misleading because the meaning of perceptual interdependency is that one particular description occurs as to what is present in the world and that description is crucial for what happens next or for what happens with regard to another description. Therefore, while in principle perception is translatable into neurophysiological langauge, the kind of neural events that would account for an interdependency must be unique or different from the sum of the neural events that are the correlates of each perception taken separately. Until we know what such differences are we would be losing sight of a psychological fact of the first importance if we were to blur over or fail to emphasize the importance of the kinds of effect under discussion. It would be uneconomical because there may be many possible determinants of the one perception and each of these would have its own specific neural correlates. Therefore, all these would have to be separately listed as potential determinants of the subsequent or of another perception. For example, suppose that the perception of a given arrangement of objects as three-dimensional is a prerequisite for some other perception. What is important for that other perception is not necessarily disparity depth information but any adequate depth information, i.e., any information that leads first to the three-dimensional percept. Various optical inputs are functionally equivalent or intersubstitutable (Epstein 19). The fact is that it is the perceptual description of the array as three-dimensional (however that may be achieved) that leads to the final percept.

There seem to be different kinds of examples where one might say that perception is a function of another perception. Rather than lump them all together, therefore, I will, if for no other reason than convenience of exposition, divide them into separate categories. One category covers examples where a particular perception is a precondition for another one. A second category refers to cases where one percept affects another, although they may occur at the same time. Finally, there are cases where perception is based upon or is an emergent property of the integration of perceptions at a lower level. This organization of different kinds of perception-perception relationships is tentative, and it is probable that there are no such sharp boundaries separating these different effects.

The Dependence of One Perception upon Another

Perhaps the most theoretically important category of a perception-perception relation consists of cases where one perception depends upon the achievement of another. In this kind of effect a given perception must occur temporally before the other, although the time difference might well appear to be minimum. The following examples will make clear what I have in mind here.

In the stereokinetic effect a disk is rotated on which are drawn circles surrounding other circles but eccentrically rather than concentrically positioned (Fig. 10-1a). If when the disk begins to rotate the observer veridically perceives these circles rotating, no depth effect will be achieved. The dot on the small circle in Fig. 10-1a was included in the illustration to make clear what is meant by perceiving rotation. (It is not present in the actual display.) At

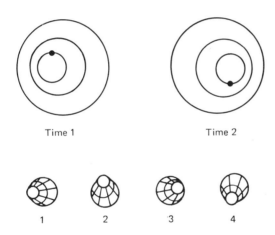

Time 1   Time 2

1   2   3   4

10-1. (a) Successive views of stereokinetic display. A disk with eccentrically positioned circles rotates about its center, leading to the perception of a three-dimensional wobbling structure such as shown in (b).

time 2, the circle appears to have rotated by 180 degrees, and thus the dot is now at the bottom. But after a while most observers no longer perceive the circles as rotating. They appear to shift their locations sideways and vertically but not by virtue of rotation. In this case it is as if the dot always remains at the top of the circle. This phenomenon is a special case of a larger category of effects discussed earlier (pp. 119–120), where the direction of motion of straight or curved lines is misperceived because each part of such a contour is identical to or similar to each other part. In the present example, any portion of a circle can be substituted for any other.

Therefore, the rotating circles need not be seen as rotating. However, they necessarily must be seen as changing their positions. There seems to be a preference to perceive them as unchanging in orientation (Wallach, Weisz, and Adams, 1956). Once that perception is achieved, it will soon be followed by a visual depth impression, in this case of a truncated cone pointed toward the observer or, reversibly, of a hollow cylinder into which the observer is looking. The object appears to be wobbling in an up-down and left-right direction (see Fig. 10-1b). This is the stereokinetic effect proper first demonstrated by Benussi (Musatti, 1924).

It seems to be the case that this effect will occur if and only if it is preceded by the perception of the circles as maintaining their orientation rather than as rotating. In our laboratory we have observed this stage of perception occurring prior to the final perception of the depth effect. The reason why this sequence is necessary is perhaps besides the point here but I believe it is because a problem calling for a solution arises only once the circles are seen as inexplicably shifting around, changing their left-right-up-down locations relative to one another. If, then a wobbling three-dimensional object is perceived, all stimulus changes are elegantly accounted for. We have been able to demonstrate in our laboratory that if rotation perception can be maintained by the expedient of making the circles out of dots instead of continuous lines, so that the true rotary motion of each dot is now unambiguously given, the stereokinetic effect never develops.

This is an important example. It means that the stereokinetic effect cannot simply be explained on the basis of the transforming proximal stimulus. With no change of that retinal input, this powerful, vivid depth effect—one directly comparable with the phenomenally vivid depth achieved by stereopsis—will occur only if first a certain prior perception occurs.

There is another example in which the perception of a configuration as maintaining its orientation rather than as rotating also can lead to a depth effect. When a spiral is drawn on a disk and the disk is rotated, the spiral will generally be perceived from the very beginning as circular regions moving either inward toward the center or outward from the center (depending upon the direction of rotation of the disk) (Fig. 10-2). Although this fact is well known (since the rotating spiral is often used to generate an aftereffect of motion), it is surprising that few realize that the impression of inward or outward movement of the curved contours is itself a problem. Why is the display not simply seen veridically as a rotating spiral? The answer is that the preference for nonrotation is manifested here. Thus, to illustrate with Fig. 10-2, suppose one fixates point i in a and that the disk is rotating clockwise. If one perceives rotation, a while later (after 90 degrees rotation) i would be seen to be at the bottom of the disk as shown in *b* and ultimately (after 360 degrees rotation) back where it was at the outset. But if one perceived nonrotation, the region one had psychologically identified as i would, after 360 degrees rotation, be at ii, therefore implying inward motion of this (and all other) segments.

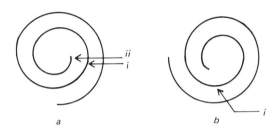

10-2. Successive views *a* and *b* of spiral rotating clockwise. After 90 degrees of rotation, the region i in *a* will be at the bottom in *b* and back where it started from after 360 degrees of rotation. But because rotation is not perceived, the region i appears to have moved to ii after 360 degrees of rotation. Therefore, the spiral as a whole appears to be moving inward with clockwise rotation (and outward with counterclockwise rotation).

For many observers, this impression is dominant and does not change. But for some, an impression of circles moving into the third dimension occurs. This is not surprising given the well-known fact that the contraction or expansion of a pattern is a strong cue to depth. But such a depth effect here is completely dependent upon the prior perception of the pattern as maintaining its orientation. Otherwise stated, perceived depth depends upon *perceived* contraction or expansion of the pattern not simply on the physical transformation of the retinal image.

A second example: in the first chapter I described cases where false depth perception led to certain illusory effects during motion of the observer because the parallax change was not appropriate to that perceived depth. In one case the depth was stereoscopically produced (Example 2, pp. 5–11) so that with head motion the object appeared to rotate. Logically, unless false depth perception is occurring, there is no reason at all why the zero parallax change should lead to any illusion. In fact veridical depth perception here—i.e., of a flat two-dimensional array—is perfectly congruent with zero parallax change. In our laboratory we have shown that prior to the emergence of the stereoscopically-derived depth—since this often takes a while to emerge—no illusion of rotation is perceived. Therefore, the claim would seem justified that the illusory perception of rotation depends causally upon the prior achievement of the illusory depth perception.

As a third example, consider the various experiments described in previous chapters where an array that yields a figure percept with illusory contours leads to other perceptions (e.g., object permanence rather than apparent motion (pp. 170–171); oscillation of a line in a plane rather than the kinetic depth effect (pp. 197–198). Such illusory figure percepts have been shown to have other consequences, such as yielding geometrical illusions (Farnè, 1970; Gregory, 1972). Since we know that a figure with illusory contours is a perceptual construction, not anything simply given in the stimulus, these examples illustrate that certain other perceptions are completely dependent upon that prior perceptual achievement.

In a number of other examples the common denominator is that perception is at first of the kind I have called "literal" (pp. 101–102) in that it is highly correlated with the stimulus input. Then the perception changes to one that is more constructive in character and less directly correlated with the stimulus. All these cases are illustrations of perceptual problem solving. The reason I now discuss them is that, unlike the examples in the previously described category, there is no logical necessity for assuming that the literal percept must precede the constructed percept, although I have argued that it does.

These examples have all been described earlier. To review briefly, therefore, consider first the kinetic depth effect paradigm. Before a rigid object is perceived as rotating there is typically the prior literal perception of a pattern whose components change in length and orientation. In the anorthoscopic paradigm, before an extended, constant form is perceived there is typically the prior literal perception of an element moving up and down the slit while simultaneously changing its orientation. In an illusory-contour paradigm, before the figure with contours is perceived, at least with the type of pattern shown in Fig. 4-5, there always is the prior perception of the dark fragments as figural with the white region, later to become figural, as ground. In the fragmented figure paradigm (Fig. 1-4), for naive observers, there always is the prior perception of the configuration as a meaningless, two-dimensional jumble of fragments corresponding closely to the retinal image. In the case of phenomenal transparency (Fig. 4-1), if such a figure is viewed by naive observers it is more than likely that it will first be seen as an array of black, white, and gray rectangular regions all part of one surface. This is the literal percept.

So much for examples that constitute the subset where it seems appropriate to speak of problem solving. To review what was said in previous chapters about such examples, the constructed percept is generally, but not necessarily, veridical, is in certain respects a better solution to the problem, and is preferred once it is realized, to the extent that it is difficult if not impossible to revert to the literal percept once it has been achieved.

The really interesting question about this category of effect is whether there might be a reason why the literal perception *must* occur first, granted that it is understandable why it often would occur first. [1] I would argue that the literal solution is the first to occur because it requires only the achievement of organization followed by a fairly straightforward description of the thus organized proximal input. Moreover it is the literal solution with its implicit coincidences and regularities that poses the problem and leads to the search for a better solution. Therefore, I am inclined to believe that the preferred perception depends upon the prior occurrence of the literal perception.

Perceptual Interactions

I have not included the perceptual constancies in the examples thus far considered. Yet to the extent that the constancy percept is based on inference from known rules, one might be inclined to list it under the category just considered. To refer to the argument made in Chapter 9, I suggested that there is first a perception corresponding closely to the attributes of the proximal stimulus (proximal mode), followed by a perception in the world mode. There is now evidence based on masking that supports this claim about the sequence of events (pp. 265).

There is also another perception to be considered here, namely, the one that provides the specific information to be taken into account in applying the rule, for example perceived depth and distance in the case of size constancy or perception of body orientation in the case of orientation constancy. Thus the constancy percept depends upon another co-occurring perception (see Hochberg, 1974). There has been disagreement and the issue is not yet settled whether information such as that of distance or body orientation must be

1. In cases where a temporal transformation occurs, at least some time must elapse before the system can appreciate just what the proximal stimulus transformation is. If, as in the kinetic depth effect, what is crucial is the change in length and orientation of the parts of the figure, some minimum time is required before that change can be detected (some temporal threshold for this change). During that time, therefore, one might argue that the perception must be of the literal kind. But one trouble with this argument is that once the change is detected the perception could well be retroactive, so that the phenomenal experience was never of the literal kind. (An example of this kind of effect is apparent movement perception where, logically, there is no basis for perceiving motion of *a* until *b* appears, but when it does, the motion is retroactively experienced as in progress before *b* appeared.)

consciously experienced, i.e., perceived, before it can be taken into account by the system or simply must be registered without any necessity of accompanying conscious experience. But the fact is that what matters for, let us say, size constancy is an internal representation of depth—or whatever information must be taken into account in the case of other constancies—not simply a particular cue to depth. Different cues are intersubstitutable as long as they lead to the same representation of depth. If they do, they will presumably have the same effect on perceived size.

In any event, however, there is one case where there can be no question that a constancy-like, rule-following percept is logically dependent upon another perceptual achievement. Given an ambiguous depth pattern, whether in the form of a line drawing such as a Necker cube or an actual three-dimensional wire cube viewed monocularly, with one depth organization certain size relations are perceived, but with a depth reversal, different size relations are perceived. Thus in Fig. 10-3, which is a deliberately modified version of the Necker cube, if the larger rectangle is perceived as nearer, the smaller rectangle at the other end will tend to appear equal or almost equal in size to the larger one. But if the smaller rectangle is perceived as nearer, the figure looks like a truncated pyramid. With a real wire cube, the effect is similar: when it is perceived veridically, it looks like a cube but when it is phenomenally reversed in depth, it looks quite distorted, like a truncated pyramid, because the rules concerning distance are applied inappropriately, in reverse so to speak. Obviously, whatever occurs in size perception in these examples is unequivocally determined by what happens in depth perception. Here one cannot maintain that registered depth information is all that matters, since there is no change in the proximal input. What matters is the perceptual organization in depth achieved and/or its sudden reversal.

Another relationship between perceptions that falls under the category of an interaction is that between absolute and relative distance. Thus binocular disparity in itself provides information only about the relative distances of objects. Accommodation and convergence considered jointly provide absolute distance about any particular object. But when they are all acting together—as is typical in daily life—it is quite probable that the relative distances are converted to absolute distances. The logic is as follows: (1) B is y distance behind A. (2) A is x distance from the observer. Therefore, (3) B is $x + y$ distance from the observer. (This is a good example of a deductive perceptual inference.) As a matter of fact, in the case of binocular disparity, the degree of relative depth depends upon abso-

10-3. Modified Necker cube. When the larger rectangle is seen in front, the object looks like a cube or an almost regular box. When the smaller rectangle is seen in front, the figure looks like a truncated pyramid.

lute distance perception. Logically the precise depth signified by a given amount of binocular disparity is ambiguous. Thus if A and B are only slightly separated in depth and both are near the observer, the amount of disparity can be the same as when A and B are appreciably separated in depth but both are farther from the observer. To repeat what was said in Chapter 9, it has been demonstrated that the absolute distance is taken into account by the system in evaluating the magnitude of depth given by disparity (stereoscopic depth constancy) (Wallach and Zuckerman, 1963; Ono and Comerford, 1977).

There are many other examples showing that how something is perceived is a function of how something else is perceived. Consider the effect of orientation on perceived form (pp. 48–51). The specific phenomenal shape of a figure depends very much on which regions are taken as top, bottom, and sides. The evidence is quite decisive in support of the conclusion that it is the psychological act of assignment of these directions that matters, not their up-down, left-right retinal coordinates. Therefore, perceived orientations profoundly affect perceived shape. Many different sources of information can either separately or cooperatively determine the perceived orientation of the figure, such as gravity, the visual coordinates of the environment, egocentric orientation, or set, but regardless of how achieved, it is the perceived orientation that is causally linked to the perceived shape.

Another example of this kind relates to Korte's third law governing apparent movement. To review, an important parameter of such perception is the spatial separation between a and b. With the interstimulus temporal interval and other factors such as luminance held constant, a change in the separation between a and b will either improve or disrupt the impression of motion. However, the question can be raised as to whether the meaning of "separation" here refers to the retina or to the perceived distance from a to b. As noted in Chapter 7 (p. 173), it was found that what matters here is the perceived distance between the two stimulus objects (Corbin, 1942; Attneave and Block, 1973). Thus one perception, of phenomenal distance, affects the specific quality of another, apparent motion.

Then an increasing number of effects are being discovered each year all of which point to the importance of perceived depth relationships with respect to other perceptual effects. Most of these reduce to the finding that certain well-known phenomena depend upon the localization of all components of the display in the same rather than in different planes. For example, if the inducing lines in the pattern such as the converging contours in Fig. 10-4 are seen in a plane different from that of the horizontal test lines (i.e., nearer or farther), this well-known Ponzo illusion of extent will either

10-4. When the inducing lines and the test lines of the Ponzo illusion are perceived to be in different planes, the illusion is much reduced. After Gogel, 1975.

be much reduced or will fail to materialize (Gogel, 1975). Even the phenomenon of masking, in which spatially adjacent contours detrimentally affect the perception of other contours just presented, is much reduced if the masking pattern appears farther away than the target figure (Lehmkuhle and Fox, 1980). It was shown earlier that optimum masking occurred not when the target figure's image occupied a region adjacent on the retina to that of the masking pattern but when it occupied a region *perceived* as adjacent to the masking pattern (White, 1976). Or if the moving rectangle in an induced motion experiment is localized as nearer or farther than the spot inside it rather than in the same plane, much less motion of the spot will be induced (Gogel and Koslow, 1971). Or if a surface of a given reflectance is localized in one plane—and therefore seen as adjacent to certain other surfaces—it can appear as a lightness value very different from how it will appear if it is localized in another plane—and therefore as adjacent to entirely different surfaces (see pp. 244–247). A change in the appearance of a region as great as from white to black can occur as a result, with little change in the retinal image, by the simple expedient of manipulating the pictorial depth cue of inter-position. (Gilchrist, 1979; 1980). Apparently perceived lightness depends upon ratios of luminance among regions all of which can be assumed to be under one illumination, which is generally true when they all are localized in the same plane but not necessarily true when they are not.

Higher-Level Perceptions Based on Lower-Level Perceptions

One sense in which it would seem appropriate to say that percep-tion depends upon perception is where a given kind of perception can arise only by the integration of lower-level perceptual data. What is the perceptual "output," given certain stimulus information, be-comes the "input" for higher-level analysis.

MOVEMENT

Consider the problem of the perception of motion With the possible exception of one phenomenon, the aftereffect of movement [also referred to as the waterfall or spiral illusion or aftereffect, which can probably be explained in terms of known physiological mechanisms (Barlow and Hill, 1963)], all other examples of motion perception can be explained on the basis of change of perceived direc-tion. Direction is defined either subject-relatively, in terms of angular location with respect to the observer's mideye position as origin, or object-relatively, in terms of its location relative to other objects. In either case, it is a valid generalization that whenever perceived direc-tion changes above some threshold rate, motion will be perceived; otherwise not. Viewed in this way, movement is an emergent property, since it is not present in the moments of time where we can speak only of perceived direction or location.

This is not the place for a full discussion or recapitulation of earlier discussions of the topic of movement perception, but a few illustra-tions that support the above claim are in order. Perceived angular direction (sometimes referred to as egocentric or radial direction) is a joint function of retinal locus and eye position. Thus, for example, if the object is straight ahead of observers and they fixate it, the con-dition "foveal image, eyes straight ahead" leads to the impression that the object is straight ahead. But then with the eyes turned to the right, the combination "foveal image, eyes 10 degrees to right" now leads to the impression that the object is off to the right by that angle. Similarly for each intermediate location of the eyes. In other words, in each position of the eyes, the object appears to be in a different place. Therefore, given our knowledge of perceived angular direction under static conditions, it would seem gratuitous to invoke any new

concept to explain why the object appears to move under dynamic
conditions. There is a change of perceived direction and, therefore, an
impression of movement. Thus in tracking a single luminous point in
the dark or moving the eyes with an afterimage present, movement
will be perceived.

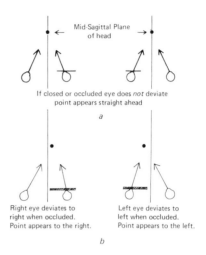

10-5. Apparent movement from alternate occlusion of the eyes. (a) A
point in a sagittal plane is viewed successively by the left and right eye. If
the closed (or occluded) eye does not deviate, the point will continue to
appear straight ahead. (b) When the occluded eye does deviate, based on
heterophoria, the point will appear to change direction. After Ono and
Gonda, 1978.

A recent experiment illustrates the argument here and at the same
time clears up a previously unsolved problem. When we alternately
open and close each eye, i.e., left open, right closed followed by right
open, left closed, a point straight ahead will appear to move stroboscopically back and forth. This occurs even in an otherwise dark field,
so that the effect cannot entirely be explained on the basis of the
shifting parallax location of the point relative to background objects.
What can one say about the perceived direction of a point that is
straight ahead but viewed with one eye closed? See Fig. 10-5. Suppose
the closed eye, instead of maintaining its position symmetrical with
the open eye, shifts somewhat based on heterophoria (a slight im-
balance of the muscles of the two eyes). That combination of positions of the two eyes would no longer signify that the point was
straight ahead but rather that it was shifted slightly in the direction
of the deviated eye. When the closed eye opens simultaneous with

the closing of the other eye, the direction of the point is now seen incorrectly on the other side of the straight ahead. Therefore, there is a change in the perceived direction of the point each time the alternation of eyes occurs. That this is the cause of the apparent motion effect was shown in experiments in which the observer's eyes were alternately occluded or disoccluded by opaque shields as they viewed a single point of light in the dark. A high correlation was obtained between the direction and magnitude of phoria for a given observer under either near or far viewing conditions and the direction and magnitude of apparent movement perception (Ono and Gonda, 1978).

Apparent movement has been shown to be a function of alternation of the perceived direction of the flashing objects rather than of the changing locations of their retinal images. The experiments on which this conclusion is based were described earlier (pp. 165-166). In the case of induced movement, the spot appears to change its location with respect to the observer, but in more complex displays entailing motion of more than a single object, the kind of motion seen can be described phenomenally as object-relative. In other words, the objects appear to change their locations with respect to a frame of reference (see pp. 219-224).

FORM

Any two points can be said to define a simple form, a configuration, provided the executive agency relates them to each other. The relationship is one of relative direction. This is true whether the points are seen simultaneously or successively and whether in different retinal loci or the same. In the latter case there would have to be some other basis for a difference in perceived direction between the points, such as change of eye position in tracking a moving point. Therefore, it seems correct to say that form perception depends upon the perception of relative direction of the units constituting the form.

This is not to say that form is *nothing but* the collective apprehension of a set of directions, for several reasons. One is that organization is relevant. For example, in Figure 10-6 while there is a directional relation between the upper point in the triangle configuration and the lower left point in the square configuration, no phenomenal form is spontaneously realized between them (although it can be, with the intention to relate them). Another reason why phenomenal form is more than the perception of a set of directions is that properties emerge with the perception of the form that have no psychological existence prior to that, such as symmetry or asymmetry, sharpness or smoothness, compactness or elongation.

10-6. The potential configuration defined by the direction of the lower left point in the square grouping relative to the direction of the upper point in the triangle grouping does not exist phenomenally, because these two points are not organized into a unit.

Once lines or borders are generated by the relation of the directions of the points constituting them, these are related to one another. Then, for example, given the apprehension of two lines in a display, the manner in which they relate to one another—whether parallel, diverging, or the like—is central to the form perceived. Therefore, this would be another example of a higher-order perception based on a lower one, namely, certain perceived properties based on the perceived orientation of its components relative to one another when the components are no longer merely points. It is interesting in this connection to note again that a right angle is perceived appropriately only when its side are perceived as vertical and horizontal; when the sides are oblique their perpendicularity is not apparent (Goldmeier, 1972). See Fig. 6-19. Thus the perceived angle depends upon the perceived orientation of its sides and how these then relate to one another. Such hierarchical processing does not stop with line or border relations because, once regions or subunits of form emerge, they are related to each other as regions. This would obviously be true in the case of three-dimensional figures but is no doubt true for two-dimensional ones as well.

Therefore, it seems correct to say that form perception is a function of the perceived relative direction and orientation of its constituent parts. These are necessary albeit not sufficient determinants of phenomenal form. There is no need to repeat here the argument and evidence marshaled for this view of form perception in Chapter 3. However, it may be worth mentioning briefly again the case of form perception achieved anorthoscopically. Here at any moment all that is perceived is a small element, and over time it alters its direction relative to the one it had before. Therefore, in this special case the dependency of form on the relative direction of its constituent parts seems particularly clear. There is no extended retinal image generated as long as the element remains foveal, and in the case of the moving-figure condition, there is not even any change in the perceived angular direction of the visible element (at least along the axis of the figure's motion). The aperture remains in a fixed direction. But given the correct hypothesis, the direction of each successively viewed element within the aperture is interpreted in relation to the one seen a moment before. Out of such relative directions—which no doubt also build hierarchically into extended line components whose orientations to one another are then perceived—form is synthesized.

GROUPING

The organization of units into larger wholes seems to be based on certain principles such as proximity and similarity. But as noted in Chapter 3 (pp. 75–76), it also seems that it is the *perception* of proximity, not simply the physical proximity of units to one another retinally, that matters. Moreover it is relative, not absolute proximity that matters, so that it is only after arriving at the perception of what units are closer together than certain others that the decision about what units to describe as belonging together can be made by the executive agency. Some evidence along the same line suggests that grouping on the basis of similarity is at least in part a function of the perceived rather than the objective properties of the stimulus units. Therefore, such grouping must be a two-stage process, in which the final organization (the higher-level perception in this case) depends upon a prior or lower-level perception.

Concluding Remarks

Enough examples have been given to make it evident that perception is often based upon, preceded by, or at least affected by another perception. In fact, if we consider all the categories analyzed here, virtually all the phenomena of object and event perception would seem to have been included. The question then remains whether there are *any* cases that *do not* entail such perceptual interdependency and, if so, what, if anything, these cases have in common. It is probably premature to attempt to resolve this question at this time.

The phenomena discussed in this chapter are entirely compatible with a cognitive theory of the kind developed in the previous chapters. Solving the problem of what object or event is producing the proximal stimulus takes time and generally entails a sequence of steps. In that respect the theory subscribes to the major tenet of the contemporary approach of information processing. There is no difficulty with instances in which one step in the sequence itself has the status of a percept. That the final perceptual description would depend upon a prior description is in fact dictated by the requirement of internal consistency in the final description. Or, to state this differently, the final description must conform to and be supported by prior descriptions of the stimulus input, should such earlier descriptions happen to be intermediate in the sequence (see Chapter 5). More generally, if a percept is the conscious representation of an underlying description and if a description has the status of propositional knowledge, the integration of such knowledge in a final percept is precisely what we should expect.

In the case of perceptual problem solving, where the stimulus is ambiguous, while literal solutions are a logical alternative to constructed solutions, I believe that they occur first. It is not necessary to repeat the arguments and evidence in favor of this conclusion, but to the extent it is true, a sequence of two perceptions, with the latter in a sense predicated on the former, is entirely understandable. The literal percept is a description characterizing the proximal stimulus and the constructed percept is a preferred reinterpretation of it. An analogous statement can be made about perceptual constancy in which the proximal-mode description characterizes the proximal stimulus and the constancy percept is a reinterpretation of it. Thus the proximal-mode description is transformed, on the basis of other information, into a world mode description, although in this case I have argued that the proximal-mode description remains in the fringe of awareness.

The "other information" that is taken into account by the perceptual system itself has the status of a perception. Therefore, constancy can be thought of as a lawful relationship between perceptions, for example, perceived size as a function of perceived distance (see Gogel, 1973). However, it is an asymmetrical relation, since the percept that is taken into account is not a function of the constancy percept; for example, we would not say that perceived distance is a function of perceived size. (The special case where *familiar* size has been held to determine perceived distance, even if established as true, does not alter the generality of this statement.) In any event, it is clear that constancy entails relationships between perceptual variables. In that sense we can include it among the many other cases where one perceptual attribute affects another.

That such would be the case is entirely plausible if perception is understood as an effort after a solution to the problem of what is present or occurring in the world. Luminance ratio as an indicator of surface reflectance can be valid if and only if the regions generating the ratio are in the same illumination. They are likely to be so if and only if they are in the same plane. Relative displacement of an object with respect to a potential frame of reference is likely to be a valid indicator of object motion if the object belongs to or is part of the frame system. That will be true when they both are in the same phenomenal plane but not necessarily true when they are not.

As to higher levels of perception entailing emergent properties as a consequence of the integration of lower-level perceptions, this too makes perfect sense. Thus, for example, given the apprehension of an object first in one perceived location and then in another location, the inference of "motion" is precisely what we should expect. Given the perceived orientation and placement of two lines, if organized as parts of one unit, the apprehension of their geometrical relationship to one another is also precisely what we should expect.

Referring to the category where I have argued that the final, constructed, percept is preceded by a prior, literal, percept, some readers may have felt that this analysis is simply a restatement of the classical sensation-interpretation doctrine usually identified with thinkers such as Wundt and Titchener. There are, to be sure, certain formal similarities between that doctrine and the analysis I am making. They have in common, first, the notion of a two-stage sequence of events; second, the notion of the final stage as the result of cognitive processing; and third, the attempt to deal with the departure of the final percept from strict correlation with the proximal input and, in fact, thus to explain its veridicality.

But these similarities should not mask the differences. In the classical view (from which I exclude Helmholtz, who did not make this mistake), the final interpretation was not a perception. It was rather a judgment about what was actually present in the world based on a combination of the sensation and past experience. In my analysis, the final construction is a *perception*. I need not repeat the arguments and data upon which I base this claim, since they appear virtually throughout the book. Moreover, in the classical view, the sensation was presumed to be the direct manifestation in consciousness of the neurally encoded representation of the stimulus. What I am calling the literal perception, as just noted, itself depends upon at least some level of cognitive processing. And whereas the sensation for Wundt and Titchener was the only true perception, which could be accessed by the appropriate analytical introspection, in my way of thinking the literal percept is generally only a stage in arriving at what is the more characteristic, salient, and objective percept. It is true that one can attend to the proximal mode perception even after the constructed one has been achieved, so that it remains actually or potentially as part of the overall phenomenal experience. But at the same time, the constructed percept does not simply vanish as the "interpretation" of Wundt and Titchener supposedly does once we train ourselves to avoid the so-called stimulus error. Finally, I should point out again that I would not simply identify the final construction with past experience in the way that the "interpretation" was by these thinkers.

11

Knowledge and Perception

IN THIS CHAPTER I will try to clarify the relationship between knowledge and perception. I will argue that if knowledge is defined as conceptually based, consciously apprehended information one has about an object or event, by and large it does not affect the perception of that object or event. Some might consider this a critical paradox for a constructionist theory of perception. We will therefore have to inquire about why perception is not affected by such knowledge. However, there are exceptions to this rule, so that I will try to make clear what the common denominator is of these exceptions. I will also argue that certain kinds of past experience, as distinct from those that simply produce conceptually based knowledge, can affect perception. Therefore, I will explore what kinds of past experience can and what kinds cannot affect perception. Finally, I will examine the general question of nativism vs. empiricism, since it does not follow from the fact that certain kinds of experience *can* affect perception that all or even most perception in any way depends upon such experience.

When Knowledge Does Not Affect Perception

It is very important for those who do not work in the field of perception to understand why investigators who do, consider perception to be independent of and isolated from what we may know factually about objects or events. The best way to drive this important point home is by many examples.

To begin with the most obvious example, the geometrical illusions all illustrate this fundamental fact. Naive observers of course do not know they are suffering from an illusion, but when they are informed of it—or, even better, when allowed to make their own measurements—things are not altered at all. In fact this is precisely what delights and intrigues people, particularly children, about illusions. But wherever one looks in perception one finds other kinds of illusion, although they are not well known outside the field. And in these cases as well, to know they are illusory, to know the true state of affairs, is not to alter the effect in the slightest.

In the realm of movement, there are many such effects. In induced movement a stationary object (including the self in some cases) seems to move in a direction opposite to that of a surrounding object as with the moon through the clouds; in the autokinetic effect, an isolated stationary point of light in an otherwise dark room often seems to glide through many degrees across the field; apparent motion is of course illusory; and so forth. None of these phenomena with the possible exception of the autokinetic effect are altered by knowing what actually is taking place.

In the realm of lightness perception, among the many illusory effects are two particularly instructive examples that fly in the face of knowledge: a black surface that is the only region in an otherwise dark room to be illuminated will appear white or light gray (the Gelb effect); a white surface that is in the shadow of a hidden object and which shadow falls only on that surface will look black or dark gray (the Kardos effect). In these cases, it does not matter whether the room lights are periodically turned on so that the observer is allowed to see the actual surface lightnesses and the special conditions responsible for the illusions. The moment the appropriate conditions are established again, the illusory effects return.

There are many examples of illusions of size. I mentioned earlier the examples that go by the name of Emmert's law: an afterimage changes its apparent size as a function of the distance of the surface onto which it is projected. A related example is the moon illusion. The moon over the horizon appears much larger than when it is elevated in the sky, although its visual angle is roughly the same in all positions.

A particularly compelling illusion of size occurs in viewing the well-known Ames distorted room (see Ittelson and Kilpatrick, 1951). The rear wall is slanted away from the frontal plane, but observers viewing it with one eye from the appropriate position perceive it as a normal wall. When people stand in each corner, they are in fact at unequal distances and thus project quite unequal images to the eye. According to the inference process concerning size, unequal visual angles localized at equal distance from the observer will yield percepts of unequal size. Therefore, the people appear to be very different in size, as will the same person who walks from one corner to the other. Thus the knowledge that such perceptions are unlikely to be true or are impossible has no effect.

These examples can be multiplied ad infinitum, and in earlier chapters a variety of anomalies and illusions were described. The kind of knowledge I am considering here, which has no effect on what is perceived, is simply that which refers to the fact of the matter, such as can be ascertained by measurement or viewing under ideal conditions or by authoritative statements. What has been said here about illusions is equally true about veridical perception except that then there is no contradiction between what is seen and what is known. In other words, the same principles that yield all these illusions yield constancy and veridicality, and here too, perception is generally impervious to and does not benefit from knowledge. Some might wish to quarrel with this statement because there seem to be cases in daily life where we improve in perceptual judgment. Thus the sailor soon learns to judge distance over water, which for most of us is difficult. Such learning would seem to be based on knowledge. Or, to take an experimental fact, adults not only achieve full constancy in outdoor scenes with very distant objects, they generally achieve what is referred to in the literature as overconstancy. Children typically do not achieve full constancy at such great distances.

In my opinion these facts refer to judgment on the level of thought and not to perception. What sailors learn is to modify their judgment based on inexact or underperceived distance although continuing to perceive in the same way. What adults learn is that very distant things appear diminutive and, therefore, if the answer is to be correct, they must compensate for this fact. Interestingly enough, overconstancy occurs primarily when the instructions to the subject stress objectivity, e.g., "what size *is* that distant triangle." It is probably judgment rather than perception that underlies observers' reports of an object's distance that are at odds with the distance cues known to be operating.

Why is it that knowledge as defined here generally has no effect on perception? The answer must surely be that perception depends upon the stimulus on the one hand and on unconsciously represented categories of description, rules, and solutions on the other. Consider the case of Emmert's law. The rule concerning size is that the image of an object is inversely proportional to distance. Therefore, applying this rule automatically, the greater the perceived distance of the image, the larger must be the object. Perceived distance itself depends upon sensory information, not upon factual information. Hence once a particular impression of distance obtains, the inference based on the rule takes over irresistibly, inflexibly, and inexorably.

Consider the case of the Gelb effect. The rule here (oversimplifying for present purposes) is that the lightness of a region is a function of its luminance relative to other regions within the same perceived plane. If it is relatively high, it must be white or light gray; if it is relatively low, it must be black or dark gray; etc. Therefore, when the isolated black surface is the sole one directly illuminated, its luminance becomes very high relative to the dimly illuminated other surfaces in the room. Therefore, it must look white or close to white. That one knows the surface is black is simply not information that can play any role because the perceptual system is inflexibly governed by a rule that pertains to relationships among *visible* regions of the field. There is no stimulus support for the perception of the surface as black. The Gelb effect can, however, be abolished by the simple expedient of placing a white surface next to the black one both of which are now in the beam of light. This change means that the black surface will reflect a much lower luminance to the eye than the white surface so that now, following the rule, it *will* look black. In fact now changing the overall room illumination will have no effect on its perceived lightness. Constancy is achieved.

As a final example, one that falls under the category of problem solving, consider the anorthoscopic mode of presentation when the figure is luminous and viewed in a dark room. Permitting observers first to see what is going on and to experience a line figure through the slit before the lights are turned out will have no effect whatsoever. In the dark, observers will see a luminous spot moving vertically (in the case of the moving figure–stationary slit condition) or a luminous spot traversing a particular path (in the case of the stationary figure–moving slit condition) but they will never see an extended figure. Given the prior exposure in the light and the knowledge about what is actually present, we must conclude that the difficulty here is obviously not one of finding the appropriate solution. The difficulty is one of accepting or maintaining it. This in turn, I have argued, is based on the lack of a fit between the suggested solution and the stimulus input (or certain perceptions to which the stimulus gives rise). The solution requires that visible objects be present with properties that can support the figure-uncovering solution (a sufficiently extended opaque surface with a narrow aperture). It is as if the executive agency will accept as usable information only that which it can see for itself!

However, I should add that when the stimulus conditions in a problem-solving situation are less artificial, there are more degrees of freedom. More than one solution is possible and thus there is greater flexibility.

Exceptions to the Above Rule, Where Knowledge Can Affect Perception

Suppose in viewing the anorthoscopic display under typical conditions with room lights on, the observer does not experience an extended figure. If the slit is so narrow as to eliminate detectable change of curvature of the element visible within it, most naive observers will perceive the element displacing vertically behind the slit. But now if one hints at what is actually happening or if, before this presentation, observers saw the display with a wider slit where they did have an impression of a figure, many will achieve the figure percept. Is this not a case of knowledge affecting perception?

There seem to be many cases analogous to this one. When conditions are not ideal for detecting a figure with illusory contours (e.g., Fig. 4-5), a hint that there is one "there" will often suffice. When observers cannot recognize a fragmented figure, a hint about the category of object will often suffice. However, it may be necessary to be far more precise, pointing out exactly what the perspective is and what many regions represent before recognition will occur. Yet when it occurs, there is a genuine perceptual change so that regardless of the manner of arriving at the solution the observer ends up with the same perception as others do.

Still another example of this kind is the special case of the kinetic depth effect when only length changes (Fig. 4-13). This often does not spontaneously lead to the perception of an object of constant length rotating in depth but rather to the perception of an object changing length. However, a hint is often all that is needed to change from the latter to the former percept.

In the case of transparency shown in Fig. 4-1, the initial impression is often that of an array of white, black, and gray rectangles. But when told that this figure represents a semitransparent surface covering part of a white and black display behind it, most people now achieve a new perception, a transparency type of impression, not realized until this suggestion was given. In fact once realized, the new nonliteral impression will be the preferred or dominant one, a fact that is true about all these examples.

In our laboratory we have found a similar effect in the case of pictorial depth perception (see pp. 250–251). Normally a photograph of almost any scene is easily recognized and is accordingly perceived as three-dimensional. But we have found that under certain conditions, a picture of, let us say, a grassy field will often not be recognized. The presence of horizon and sky seems to be important so that, if these are absent, many observers do not recognize what the picture represent. Also if we tilt the picture without informing the observer of this, so that its top is now to the side, this deception also often eliminates recognition. But in either case, all that is necessary is some information either about what the picture is or where its top in fact is, for recognition to occur immediately. That this step entails a genuine perceptual reorganization is supported by the finding that illusory size effects for small objects inserted into the picture occur if and only if the picture is recognized for what it is. Only then do the rules about taking account of *differences* in distances enter into the equation.

Many other examples of this kind can be found, but we have already given enough of them to make it perfectly clear that we have to deal here with a generalizable phenomenon. What all these examples have in common is this: The stimulus array or transformation is in some way improverished or less adequate than it might be in order to bring to mind a particular, in fact the preferred, solution. Therefore, only the literal solution arises. However, the stimulus and certain subsidiary perceptions to which it gives rise can support the preferred solution (as outlined in Chapter 6). This is the essential point. Therefore, given any hint or clue that suggests that solution, it can immediately occur and be maintained. Thus knowledge can have an effect here because (1) it is needed to suggest a solution that would not occur without it and (2) once the solution is suggested, the rest of the process unfolds just as it would without any role of knowledge because the fit between stimulus input and solution is adequate. Therefore, knowledge can have an effect in these cases because it is not called upon to create a percept out of whole cloth or to modify one without adequate stimulus support or to replace inferential processes on the basis of relevant rules. Under the conditions suggested here, then, knowledge can bring about a transformation from literal description to world mode description.

One other type of effect based on knowledge must be considered here, namely, the determining role that knowledge of a figure's reversibility can play on its actual reversal (see Chapter 3, pp. 77–80). Contrary to the widely held opinion about the phenomenon of reversal as one that is spontaneous and inexorable, we have found that subjects completely naive about the possibility of reversal will often not experience a change. Since in this case the initial percept is as "good" as the alternative, there is no reason to expect a change to occur on the basis of preference. Therefore, it would seem that the reversals that do occur under typical instruction have much to do with the knowledge that the figure can be seen in another way. So in certain respects this kind of effect conforms to the reasons suggested above for other cases where knowledge affects perception. Knowledge is necessary to suggest a possibility that otherwise would not come to mind, in this case not because of inadequacies in the stimulus, but because of the adequacy of the first solution. Once suggested, the fit between the stimulus and the new solution is more or less as good as between the stimulus and the first solution.

Related to this kind of effect are cases where attention affects perception by influencing *what* we choose to describe. The point is that knowledge may affect attention and thus, indirectly, it may affect perception.

Past Experience vs. Knowledge

RECOGNITION

The reader might object to the example given above of the perception and recognition of fragmented figures by pointing out that knowledge must always enter in here, whenever these figures are recognized, not merely in the special case where recognition is difficult and the observer is told what the figure represents. We must have previously seen the object represented and have memory of it. Is this not knowledge? It is, of course, but I feel it is important to distinguish knowledge given in the linguistic or conceptual form "this object or event I am now viewing is a such-and-such" from knowledge in the form of stored past perceptual experience. Obviously the latter is necessary for recognition (by definition), and it seems to be necessary in certain cases of perception apart from the question of recognition, whereas, as I have just argued, the former is generally not only *not* necessary (except in special cases) but typically can have no effect on perception.

As to recognition and the associated identification of the category and/or function of the object, it must be presumed that the first stage of processing proceeds without any contact with stored memories. For it is only on the basis of similarity between what is now perceived and what had been perceived that recognition can occur. To make this point crystal clear, I will describe an experiment once performed by Rubin that has the following design (Rubin, 1921). Suppose in a training exposure the ambiguous pattern of Fig. 11-1 is shown and that the observer perceives the white region as figure. Then in a subsequent test, the same pattern is briefly exposed and the observer now, for whatever reason, perceives the black region as figure. Despite the identity of the physical contours as retinal images, no recognition will occur. That is simply because the form described now is totally different from the one described in the training exposure. Conversely, if the white region is the one described in the test, recognition undoubtedly will occur. So recognition here (and in general) depends upon the prior stage of perception.

What kind of process explains recognition? Following the first stage of perceptual description of form, what happens thereafter can be thought of as problem solving. The executive agency asks, "What is this object (or event)?" The solution here simply consists in finding something in memory that is very similar. When something in

11-1. Dependence of recognition on perception. If the white region is perceived as a figure at Time 1, and the black region at Time 2, then recognition will not occur.

memory is found the properties of which fit reasonably well those of the percept as form, that is the solution. The executive agency compares percept with memory and "decides" that the match is acceptable. At that point, the form is redescribed in terms of the properties of the category of object in question. Thus the percept is enriched. But that does not mean that the final description no longer dovetails with the initial form description. The final description is constrained by and must continue to do justice to the form description, which in turn is constrained by the proximal stimulus. Thus it is not just "horse" that is described when one sees one, but one of a particular shape as governed by the particular perspective and the like. This point seems to have been either overlooked or misunderstood by theorists anxious to explain perceptual identification (referred to as pattern recognition in the literature), as if the latter completely overshadows and supersedes the form perception upon which it is based.

However, the recognition process is probably more active and searching than is implied in what was said above about recognition beginning where perception leaves off. When an object is seen under somewhat improverished conditions or when an object has distinguishable parts, the story seems to be more complicated. Under impoverished conditions, such as brief exposure, low level of illumination, blurred contours, or "noisy" background, uncertainty as to what is present leads to hypotheses (Bruner, 1957). Conversely, mental sets can lead to such hypotheses or expectancy in the first place. The degree of prior experience with a category can be relevant. Under certain conditions, misrecognitions can occur on this basis. Thus to use current jargon, recognition is both data-driven and hypothesis-driven; it results in part from bottom-up processing and in part from top-down processing.

The point is even more clearly illustrated with objects that have distinguishable and potentially recognizable parts or with an entire scene that has many recognizable things in it. In such cases, a part can be inadequately represented (as in a sketch) but will nonetheless be recognized by virtue of the whole in which it is embedded or a part will be more quickly recognized in the appropriate context (Palmer, 1975a; 1975b; Biederman, 1972; Tulving and Gold, 1963) (see pp. 84-85). Therefore, it must be the case that memories or schemata are accessed on the basis of global similarity and that these memories now facilitate the perception of parts. The converse can also be true, namely, that we recognize the whole object only by virtue of the initial perception of its parts based upon the very accurate representation of such parts in the proximal stimulus. These observations lead to the next topic.

RECOGNITION-PERCEPTION

So much for recognition per se. The fact is, however, that there are cases where perception itself is at least in part determined by and influenced by past experience stored in the form of specific content. It has been demonstrated in one experiment that whereas a form such as that in Fig. 11-2 will normally look two-dimensional, for those observers who have previously experienced this pattern as but one projection of an actual three-dimensional object, it will appear three-dimensional (Wallach, O'Connell, and Neisser, 1953). From this finding and other considerations it is hardly much of a leap to believe

11-2. Two-dimensional projection of three-dimensional object that will normally look two-dimensional. It will appear three-dimensional to observers who have had prior exposure to the object when other depth cues were available. After Wallach, O'Connell, and Neisser, 1953.

that many drawings, photographs, and objects themselves under certain conditions look three-dimensional on the basis of experience with the objects they represent in daily life (see the discussion on pp. 11-14) and on pp. 91-92).

What distinguishes these cases from others where we would not invoke past experience as a perceptual determinant, and how is it possible for it to be so if, as I have argued above, perceptual description of form must precede access to memory? As to the first question, one distinguishing characteristic of these cases seems to be the fact that there is no basis in the stimulus per se that could lead to the final form description, which is a three-dimensional one. Another is that the "solution" is one that fulfills all the requirements for its acceptance discussed in Chapter 5. In these cases, then, more than just recognition is involved. The final perceptual description is one that is different from what it would have been if no relevant prior experience were available. The form itself is now (in these cases at least) three- rather than two-dimensional. We have here a transition from a literal to preferred world mode description.

This brings me to the second question, how this is possible. The answer, logically, must be that recognition first occurs on the basis of a prior description governed exclusively by the proximal stimulus. For example, Fig. 11-3 might be described as a "square with adjacent parallelograms on top and at right . . . " or the like. That description is similar to those that must have occurred in prior experience with cubes. Therefore, that description leads to the accessing of memories that are associated with memories of cubes. In this way the appropriate solution is found which results in the final description of a three-dimensional cube (seen from the perspective represented in the drawing). Note that if this analysis is correct, past experience can influence perception only if something is first perceived that is *not* in any way based on such experience.

11-3. A prerecognition, two-dimensional description of a drawing of a cube: "Square and two parallelograms joined together at their edges."

A similar effect must occur in the reorganization of fragmented figures that occurs with recognition. Here again there is a definite perceptual change that goes along with recognition, when it occurs. Parts that seemed unrelated a moment ago are now grouped together; certain "ground" regions may become figural; and, most important, regions take on particular depth values as the entire array becomes three-dimensional. The simplest description of the new form description that occurs with recognition is in terms of the object recognized (but again from the appropriate perspective). For example, the array of fragments now looks like an elephant viewed from the side. Prior to recognition, the array did not look like that. As a convenience, therefore, I have suggested that the nature of the percept in these cases where experience enters in be referred to as "recognition perception."

KNOWLEDGE AS RULES

In earlier chapters I have given various examples of rules that the perceptual system seems to "know" and follow. In fact, if a rule be thought of as a form of knowledge,which it surely is, then one reason why conceptual knowledge in the form of "this is a such and such" generally has no effect on perception is that perception is so often governed by the rule type of knowledge. It is possible that many of these rules are learned, and if so, their status as knowledge is all the more clear. But it is also possible that they do not have to be learned, i.e., that they are available from the beginning of our lives, and in that case one would have to refer to them as a form of innate knowledge. The "learning" would then be evolutionary, i.e., the rules acquired by species by virtue of their adaptive value.

We do know that some of these rules are learnable, whatever may have been their origin. For example, as discussed in Chapter 9, whenever we move in the environment, all objects in the environment change their angular direction. This does not lead to any perception of motion in the scene, so that we refer to it as position constancy. Therefore, one might say that the perceptual system knows the following rule: "Rotation of the head in a particular direction at a particular rate produces a change in the angular direction of all objects in the scene in the opposite direction but at the same rate." But this state of affairs is subject to unlearning, and a new rule can be substituted for the original one. At that point the old rule no longer governs perception and the new rule does. That new rule might be something like "Rotation of the head in a particular direction and rate produces a change in the angular direction of all objects in the scene in the *same* direction as the head motion and at *twice* the rate."

This is not the place for a complete survey of all the different kinds of rules that the perceptual system "knows" (but see Chapter 12, pp. 325-328) or for an examination of whether there is reason for believing any or all of these were initially acquired or are acquirable on the basis of experience. Some of these rules refer to various kinds of adaptation to distorting optical devices, some to depth information such as parallax and stereopsis, and some to the laws of perspective as in the perceptual constancies. The point I want to make is that to the extent that some or all of these rules do derive from experience—i.e., are learned—to that extent it is legitimate to consider them as examples of a form of knowledge affecting perception. If "knowledge," however, the content is not conscious and if "learned" the process of acquisition is not conscious either. How such learning occurs through experience is not understood. While there is ample opportunity for the proximal-stimulus transformations embodied in the rules to be encountered, it is far from clear how the perceptual system inductively arrives at the generalization that constitutes the rule and does so unconsciously. It is also difficult at this time to imagine what the substantive nature or language of such rules might be, since they clearly are not in the form of natural language. But the fact that they are represented symbolically in some form is what leads me to speak of them as "rules" rather than simply to say that the system behaves lawfully, "as if" it knows how to apply certain rules but in fact does not "know" anything.

KNOWLEDGE IN THE FORM OF AVAILABLE SOLUTIONS

In discussing perception as problem solving, I have spoken repeatedly of "solutions." For example, if as I have argued, the perception of apparent motion is a solution that comes from *within* and is not simply given by stimulus information, one might ask where that solution comes from. It could derive from prior experience. We have much experience with really moving objects, and as I noted earlier (pp. 166) there is a similarity between the stimulus produced by an object that rapidly moves from one position to another and the stroboscopic stimulus sequence. Therefore, given such stored experience with real motion, the process of solution to the stroboscopic problem could be considered to be much like recognition-perception. The solution thought of as a content in memory is brought to mind on the basis of its similarity to the perceived proximal-stimulus events (i.e., onset of a, sudden disappearance, brief interval, onset of b, etc.). The perception then accordingly changes to one of motion.

In the example of the display of a rectangle moving back and forth and the spots alternately appearing and disappearing (Fig. 7-2), the preferred solution was of the dots being uncovered and covered rather than as moving. This solution too could derive from past experience. The number of occasions in our prior experience in which objects have been occluded and revealed by other objects in front is very great indeed. The characteristics of the display are essentially like those in such prior experiences, so that again one might say that a process of recognition results in the perceptual interpretation which constitutes the solution. (But it is important to recall that for this suggested solution to be viable it must fulfill the requirements described in Chapter 5, so that although it comes to mind, it will be rejected if the occluding object is in the wrong place at the wrong time or appears hollow rather than opaque.)

There is another important role that knowledge about a solution can play. Suppose the stimulus conditions that constitute a particular problem are repeatedly encountered, as is surely the case for stroboscopic alternation or for the kinetic transformation of contours. Similarly the stimulus conditions for a particular inference based on known rules such as lead to constancy occur not just once but all the time. Consequently it is safe to assume that, based on such repetition, the achievement of the preferred solution or of the appropriate inference becomes increasingly more automatic. The same is undoubtedly true about problem solving and inference in the domain of thought.

Cognitive Theory and Innate Determination

Historically there seems to have been a merging of cognitive approaches to perception on the one hand and empiricism on the other. The great influence of Berkeley and Helmholtz is no doubt the major source of this identification. For Helmholtz, unconscious inference was simply an interpretation of what a stimulus represented now on the basis of what it represented in the past. I believe it is a mistake to fuse or confuse the two issues. Cognitive processing, be it symbolic description, rule following, or problem solving, is one thing; the origin of the units of description, the rules, the premises, and the solutions is another thing. As a matter of fact, as the Gestalt psychologists emphasized, thinking itself is not reducible to past experience, although we may draw upon such experience in the process of thinking. Thus, for example, grasping the requirements of a problem by a chimpanzee such as how to obtain food that is out of reach need not itself be dependent upon a prior encounter with that same problem. To argue that it is, is only to push the question back in time. How was the problem solved in the first encounter, if it was? If it was not, of what use was that experience? The empiricist case here makes sense only if thought is denied altogether and blind trial and error and the law of effect (reinforcement) are substituted in its place.

The chimpanzee undoubtedly understands that the food is out of reach and may arrive at the functional solution "find an object to reach it with." In fact, the animal may have a model of search in mind, i.e., the kind of object required (Duncker, 1945). At that stage experience with rigid objects such as sticks may enter in so that either such an object is sought or, if one is present, its suitability is grasped. But it is possible that the problem could be solved even without such experience with objects. In the problem where the food is attached to the ceiling of the cage, what is sought is something to climb upon, and here it is quite likely that an object of the right height such as a box could be seen to have the potential of serving the purpose without any relevant past experience. Again, however, having had the relevant experience such as climbing on boxes might facilitate solution finding at this stage.

This is the type of argument I would make about cognitive processes in perception. The kinds of processes I have tried to isolate are not themselves the product of experience, but in every case certain mental contents acquired in the individual's experience may be drawn upon. For example, the basis cf form perception in a process of description cannot be reduced to prior experience. I would go further and argue that the conceptual categories employed in such description do not derive from experience. For if they did and if I am correct that form perception depends upon description, how could form perception ever get started? But this is not to deny the possibility that, with development, the organism may not later employ as units of description configurations that have become familiar. Thus one might ultimately describe a parallelogram as a "rectangle with slanted sides" or the like, an "ideal form" with variation.

The fact that form perception presupposes organization leads to the same conclusion. If past experience were a prerequisite for organization, not only could no entities be perceived at the outset but, without such perception, no useful memories could be laid down the existence of which are supposed to provide the learned basis of subsequent organization. This argument has been made before, and there is no need to dwell on it here (Köhler, 1940; Wallach, 1949; Zuckerman and Rock, 1957). The Berkeleyan notion of tactual perception providing the basis of visual learning is also not defensible, particularly in the light of recent findings of the dominance of vision over touch, of visual "capture" when a conflict between the two modalities is created, and of the recalibration of tactual (or haptic) perception to conform to vision in studies of adaptation to optical distortion rather than the other way around (Rock and Harris, 1967). In any event, there is now considerable evidence pointing to the innate basis of form perception (e.g., Fantz, 1957; Zimmerman and Torrey, 1965).

It is true that I have claimed earlier in the chapter that there are cases where form perception is a function of past experience. But it is important to understand that in every such case the first stage in the process is the perception (based on description) of what is given in the proximal stimulus and that that stage cannot itself be determined by past experience. Therefore, there are strict limits to the role of experience in perception. It can only enter in to enrich or modify a preexisting percept and then only under certain conditions.

As to the origin of rules that the system must "know," I have already noted that they may be acquired on the basis of prior experience. But "may" does not mean "must." In some cases, logical considerations would seem to rule out learning. For example, if the system follows the rule that the region in an array of several discrete regions with the highest luminance is white and other regions with relatively lower luminance values are gray or black, how could this be learned? Interestingly enough, no theorist in the entire history of philosophy or psychology has, to my knowledge, ever argued that the perception of chromatic hues (or other sensory qualities for that matter) is based on learning.

Unfortunately the evidence thus far available to us is not yet decisive. There is evidence that new rules are learnable in some cases, such as in the one mentioned above of adaptation to the optically altered direction or rate of motion of objects during observer motion. There is good evidence that we can adapt to prismatically displaced angular direction. On the other hand, the evidence from research on some forms of adaptation to optical distortion points more to intractability than to educability. For example, optically altered curvature seems to produce only a bare minimum of change in the shape of an image contour that appears straight, even after weeks of exposure (Pick and Hay, 1964). But whatever the evidence from studies of this kind, it does not necessarily mean that the original rules had to be learned in infancy. There is some evidence for the presence of size and shape constancy in human infants but also contradictory evidence from other species (Bower, 1966; Day and McKenzie, 1977; Heller, 1968). Therefore, we cannot yet say whether the rules of optical projection based on distance and viewing perspective, which I have argued are utilized in achieving constancy, are innately given or acquired by experience.

Finally, to come back to the origin of potential solutions to perceptual problems, it is not necessarily the case that they are the products of past experience. For once again we have to ask how they could be acquired. The first time an infant encounters an object disappearing behind another object, the learning hypothesis must maintain that it is not perceived as undergoing covering but simply as (inexplicably) disappearing. Perhaps so. Piaget certainly believes that the phenomenon of object permanence—which is part of the overall impression of the "covering" solution—is not present in the infant and develops only over a period of time. (Piaget, 1954). The evidence on this question is still equivocal (Michotte, 1955; Bower, 1967, 1974; Gruber, Girgus and Banuazizi, 1971). But the question I would ask is the same one I raised about form perception and organization. How does one achieve a change in perception if the earliest perceptions are of a different kind? Perceiving the object as inexplicably disappearing will not establish a memory that can be useful in perceiving the same event differently in the future. The argument here, that the tendency to perceive in a particular way could not be learned, is roughly equivalent to the Kantian argument that certain modes of perception must be innate.

Concluding Remarks

The main point I have tried to make in this chapter is that while perception is thoughtlike it is nonetheless autonomous. Therefore, by and large, it is not directly affected by consciously respresented knowledge. That perceptions known to be false can occur and persist does not mean that they are unintelligent or irrational, only that they are generally impervious to knowledge of the kind that influences thought. There are two reasons for the autonomy of and difference of perception from thought. One is that it is stimulus-bound or, otherwise expressed, constrained by the requirement of conformity to and support by the stimulus. The other is that the kind of knowledge that does affect or determine perception is in a form very different from the knowledge utilized by and governing thought. It takes the form of memory content from prior perceptions or of unconsciously represented rules or of other unconsciously and nonverbally represented categories and the like.

To summarize, knowledge of the kind we are most familiar with, namely, that which is conceptually based and consciously apprehended, can influence perception only in the special case where a perceptual solution is possible as regards all the requirements discussed previously but does not come to mind spontaneously. In that case, knowing about that solution, however the knowledge is acquired, will generally lead to that solution.

However, knowledge in the form of past experience, specifically memories of prior perceptions, governs recognition and certain cases where recognition affects perception. But in such cases, some degree of perceptual processing *not* governed by past experience must occur first, since a bridge to the accessing of the relevant memories must be provided.

Knowledge in the form of unconsciously represented rules governs perceptual inference whether these rules have been acquired through the past experience of the individual or through evolutionary "experience." Knowledge in the form of unconsciously represented categories and solutions governs description and problem solving. Here again it is not known whether some or all of these categories and solutions are acquired ontogenetically or phylogenetically. Knowledge of a somewhat different kind, based on repeated descriptions, inferences, and solutions in daily life when the same kind of stimulus occurs, undoubtedly changes the processes underlying perception in the sense of making them less discursive and more automatic.

In any event, a cognitive theory of perception should not necessarily be identified with an empiricist theory. The mental processes that enter into description, inference, and problem solving are not any more synonymous with experientially based processes in perception than they are in thinking. This is not to deny a major role of experience in providing memorial content that will affect perception. However, the difficulties with a *totally* empiricist approach have been pointed out.

12 ▢

Criticisms, Clarifications, and Conclusions

MANY PROBLEMS WITH THE KIND of theory advocated here remain. A number of phenomena seem to pose difficulties for the theory. Some of these difficulties turn out to be based on a misunderstanding of what the theory implies or does not imply (that I myself or others have not been clear about), while some are not and thus seem to present a more serious challenge. Therefore, in this chapter I describe these potential difficulties and suggest the direction in which I believe they can be resolved. I also take the occasion of this final chapter to try to make explicit the axioms and assumptions that I believe provide the background upon which perceptual processing stands. Finally I reconsider the case against perceptual intelligence that was outlined in the introductory chapter.

Perceptual Phenomena That Entail Contradiction

The phenomenon that often is mentioned as one that does not fit a theory of perception as logical or rational is the so-called impossible figure. Many of these drawings have been created, but one of the best known is that illustrated in Fig. 12-1 (Penrose and Penrose, 1958). Since all these cases have features in common, it will suffice here to consider just this one. The crux of the matter in Fig. 12-1 is that each of the three corners yields a depth impression that collectively cannot be integrated into a possible object in the world. Thus, for example, one corner, a, yields an impression that the leg above it is receding in depth, but at the other end, at corner b, that leg joins together with the leg from corner c, which is seen as rising vertically in the frontal plane. Thus no such physical structure is likely to exist or is logically possible, at least none where all the corners do join together and the sides of which are straight.

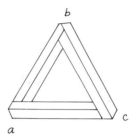

12-1. Impossible figure. After Penrose and Penrose, 1958.

Since earlier I maintained that solutions that entail perceptual con-
tradictions do not occur (Chapter 5, pp. 125–128), how can we explain
this case? There are several points to be made. Since anything can be
drawn, the question is how the perceptual system deals with drawings that are self-contradictory or represent impossible structures. It
is the object represented, not the drawing or the percept, that is impossible. The fact is that when the perceptual system recognizes the
impossibility, it does not accept it. The difficulty we have in arriving
at a coherent perceptual interpretation of the object is testimonial to
the effort at rational solution. The basis of the difficulty derives
from the local depth information, each corner and adjacent sides
representing a particular perspective view of one part of a three-
dimensional triangle.

But some will say that according to a cognitive theory the perceptual system should make an effort to undo the impossibility of
interpretation by altering the percept to one that *is* possible (Gogel,
1978). It has been shown that there is a possible object that would
yield such a picture (see Fig. 12-2; Gregory, 1970). The three legs of
this object are not in one plane, but seen from a particular vantage
point it nonetheless projects the image of Fig. 12-1. However, for
such a percept to occur, certain strong principles of organization
operating with respect to corner *b* would have to be overcome, namely,
a particular combination of good continuation and interposition and
possibly other factors. It is perhaps asking too much to suppose that
these principles can be overcome. A more legitimate expectation
would be whether or not the leg between corner *a* and *b* would appear to recede in depth when its upper end is detached from the
corner at *b* (see Fig. 12-3). This would represent an attempt to rationalize the overall percept. As the reader can see, now that leg does
seem to recede. An effort to undo the impossibility does occur. Presumably no such effect would occur if corner *a* were altered or
blocked from view, and that would constitute a control condition.

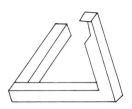
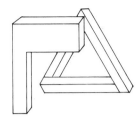

12-2. An object that would yield the projection shown in Figure 12-1 if viewed from an appropriate station point. After Gregory, 1970.

12-3. An effort to undo impossibility. The upper part of the leg between corner *a* and *b* of Figure 12-1 is occluded so as to eliminate strong organizational effects at corner *b*. The remaining part of the leg may then be perceived to recede in depth, rather than to remain in the same plane as corner *b*.

Another case that might be considered to contradict the theory is the effect of the Ames' distorted room on the perceived size of people or of one and the same person walking from one rear corner to the other. Surely this illusion flies in the face of much that we know, not only about the size of people but about the possibility of change of such size. That is true, but I have already dealt with this issue in the preceding chapter. Perception is not affected by knowledge of this kind, so that in following its own inner logic it will countenance such illusions.

A more serious difficulty for the theory is a particular variation of the trapezoidal window illusion (Ames, 1951). In this illusion, a trapezoid appears to oscillate back and forth through an angle of less than 180 degrees when it is in fact rotating through 360 degrees. Without entering into a discussion of the basis of this illusion, I will instead focus on the further effect of viewing a tube or rod thrust through the window and rigidly attached to it. Observers generally perceive the rod veridically rotating through 360 degrees while at the same time perceiving the window oscillating. These two outcomes might be said to contradict one another, but they are nonetheless sustained perceptually. The fact is, however, that there are strong reasons for the perception of the window as oscillating and strong reasons for perceiving the tube as rotating. Perspective information for the trapezoid is such that the image of the taller side always remains larger than that of the shorter side even when the latter is in front. Therefore, the taller side never appears to be farther away than the shorter side, although it is for half of its cycle. But perspective information for the tube including sight of each of its ends is appropriate to its actual motion throughout. Thus each object is seen on the basis of its own information. The chief difficulty for perception is the moment when the tube must seem to go through the window. However, this occurs instantaneously so that it is not entirely clear how to describe what one sees at this moment, and the conflicting evidence from interposition is visible only briefly.

In any event the issue here is whether the perceptual system can do anything to avoid the contradiction. The only thing it can do is to perceive the trapezoid as rotating instead of oscillating or possibly to perceive the tube as oscillating rather than as rotating. Either change would make for overall consistency. But for either of these changes in perception to occur, the information considered locally for each object would have to be suppressed or discarded. However, there is no conflict until the critical moment (since there is no reason why each object cannot turn independently of the other), so that the perceptual change would have to occur only then, instantaneously. One might say that the conflict emerges and disappears before the perceptual system has a chance to deal with it. This analysis suggests an experiment in which the conflicting information is brought more to the fore by employing a surface wider than a tube and by slowing down the rotation. In that case the window may no longer appear to oscillate.

How do these various examples differ from those given earlier where contradiction is avoided? In those cases (Chapter 5, pp. 125–128) ambiguous displays yielded perceptions that were consistent with the perception of a region in front or behind as either opaque or transparent. Thus, for example, if the region in which a figure with illusory contours might appear was seen to be transparent because other contours were seen as behind it (Fig. 5-8), that illusory figure was not perceived. However, it is not the case that there is contradictory information to the effect that the triangle is both opaque and transparent, but only that were the figure to be constructed it would entail this contradiction. So the executive agency can resolve the matter by not perceiving such a figure. Or, to give another example, if the region surrounding the slit in the anorthoscopic paradigm was not perceived as opaque, the figure solution did not occur. In these examples, given the ambiguous stimulus, alternative perceptions are possible which, although not preferred, do fulfill other requirements for a solution. Therefore, contradiction can be avoided by perceiving the display in some other way.

Do these differences between examples mean that when the stimulus information for each of two contradictory percepts is strong and the contradiction cannot be avoided, it will be tolerated, so that one ends up perceiving an impossible state of affairs? Suppose that disparity in the images to the two eyes calls for the perception of an object as behind another surface which is opaque. One can see such an effect in stereoscopic displays. Parts or all of an object may appear to be behind the surface on which the stereogram is printed. To the extent that the surface initially appears opaque, that perception should not be possible, but it nonetheless appears to occur. However, it is also true that the surface directly in front of the object appears to be transparent. This transparency solution is possible because the texture or grain of the surface is not such as to necessarily occlude things behind it. By contrast, consider the situation where information to the effect that the object that is stereoscopically behind is opposed by strong information that it is in front, as when the object is the occluding portion of an interposition pattern. In the conflict between interposition and binocular disparity, as is created with a pattern such as Fig. 12-4d and e, where disparity calls for perceiving the vertical rectangle in front of the horizontal one, either of two outcomes will occur: The binocular depth is not achieved because of its contradiction by the configuration or the horizontal rectangle that should appear behind via stereopsis but in front via interposition does both by appearing to bend (see Fig. 12-4f) (Zanforlin, 1982). The reader can observe this effect by fusing d and e in Fig. 12-4. By doing the same for Figure 12-4a and b, the reader can compare the case where stereopsis and interposition are congruent. This last effect and the transparency effect just described are good examples of how the executive agency will attempt to rationalize a contradition.

Much depends on the relative strength of the conflicting cues. Thus, for example, in Fig. 12-5a, the interposition cue calls for the perception of the upper figure as solid and completed but the hollow center of the lower figure ought to oppose that perception. One can, however, perceive the inner region in the lower figure as an opaque region. That rationalizes the effect. But in Fig. 12-5b the information concerning the hollow opening is too good and, therefore, the upper figure will not necessarily appear to be completed despite the continuing "pressure" toward that outcome.

One final case concerns the conflict between visual and tactual information. Suppose one holds the stem of a three-dimensional wire cube (Fig. 12-6). If the cube is perceptually reversed so that the far side is seen in front and vice versa and if, moreover, the cube is now rotated by twirling the stem between one's fingers, a contradiction is experienced between the seen and felt direction of rotation. The conflict can be simply avoided by perceiving the cube's perspective veridically. The misperception of its depth brings in its wake, so to speak, the misperception of direction of rotation, so that is not a problem requiring explanation. In fact there is an inner consistency here between these two visual percepts. The problem is why the

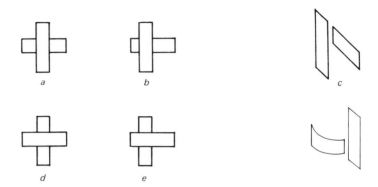

12-4. (a) and (b): Stereogram yielding an impression of a vertical rectangle in front of a horizontal one, as shown in c. Here interposition is congruent with stereopsis. (d) and (e): Stereogram in which stereopsis is in conflict with interposition. One possible resolution is shown in f. After Zanforlin, 1982.

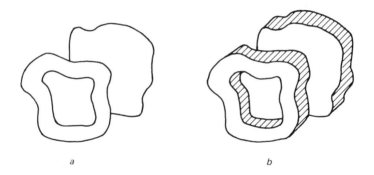

12-5. (a) The inner region of the lower figure, if perceived as an opening, contradicts the completion of the upper figure suggested by the interposition pattern. (b) When the inner region is unambiguously an opening, completion of upper figure may not occur.

tactual information does not lead to the re-reversal of the cube's depth, particularly in the light of the fact that the misperceived depth also leads to various distortions of size and shape. The latter effects are fully predictable in terms of the relationship between size and shape on the one hand and perceived depth on the other, as discussed in Chapter 9.

Since all these unlikely changes and the intersensory conflict itself can be avoided by a perceptual depth reversal, why does it not occur? Gogel (1978). An experiment simila to the one described here was performed by Shopland and Gregory (1964). I would propose

12-6. A conflict between visual and tactual information. The cube is perceptually reversed as its stem is twirled.

an answer in three parts: (1) The percept achieved has a tendency to persist (see Chapter 3, pp. 77–80) at least for a while unless powerful *visual* information contradicts it. (Thus if the wire figure is not properly silhouetted and the observer happens to fixate the region where the image of a far and near wire intersect, the appropriate interposition will immediately bring about a reversal.) (2) Given that persistence, the size and shape transformations must occur by virtue of the inexorable operation of the inference process based on perceived depth. That these transformations are not likely physical events is of no consequence (see below, pp. 324–328). That these are not likely is represented as knowledge in a form that does not affect perception. (3) Information via modalities other than vision seems to have no effect on what is perceived visually because it is either transformed (visual capture), suppressed, disregarded, or interacting with visual information at a higher level where it can no longer affect it. (In this particular example the tactual information is apparently not transformed, since we remain aware of a contradiction. That may be because the *visual* information concerning the direction of rotation of the *stem itself* is poor and thus does not conflict with how the stem feels to be rotating. The visual information that does contradict the tactual derives from another region, namely, the cube itself.)

This last point, (3), calls for further discussion. That tactual (or other nonvisual) information does not affect what is seen is admittedly not a fact that is a priori predictable from the theory proposed here. Nonetheless it *is* a fact. However, the statement is in need of qualification in one respect. Information concerning gravity provided by the vestibular apparatus clearly affects the visual perception of the orientation of objects in the environment, and information concerning the position of the eyes in the head clearly affects the visual perception of angular direction of objects with respect to the observer (although under certain circumstances even these kinds of nonvisual information can be captured). So stimulus information that is not directly visual can affect visual perception. But the kind of perception statement 3 above refers to is one where an externally visible object is also grasped or touched or heard and where the issue concerns the object's spatial properties.

Laws of Geometrical Optics and Laws of Physics

In discussing the example of the rotating wire cube I said that the perceived transformations of size and shape did not constitute a difficulty for the theory. Such changes are not likely to occur, and one might say that they violate certain rules we have abstracted about material things. Things do not usually undergo such transformations, at least not without some observable cause such as something else stretching or pressing them. But the knowledge we have about this concerns the laws of physics. It seems to me that the perceptual system, at least the visual system, is not concerned with the laws of physics and has no internalized rules about such laws. It is concerned with the rules governing the propagation of light or optical projection to the eye, and while the analysis of light is a branch of physics, the knowledge we have about it is selective. It is concerned primarily with spatial relationships and not with many other characteristics or phenomena of light.

Thus neither the laws of gravitational attraction, nor Newton's laws relating mass and acceleration, nor those concerning mass and momentum, inertia, electromagnetic phenomena, molecular structure, and the like play any role in strictly visual perception. (However, knowledge of some of the principles of physics may play a role in *behavior*, as, for example, in visuomotor coordination, where catching a ball may make use of inertia and gravitation.) Depending on our degree of sophistication, we may know more or less about these physical phenomena and their lawful regularities (although we also know about them on an intuitive level), but whatever we may know about them is of the nature of the kind of knowledge that does not affect perception. By way of contrast, we do seem to have internalized rules or laws about the projection of light to the eye.

If this generalization is correct, it means that we need not concern ourselves in perception with possible violations of laws of physics. That an object can appear to be suspended in midair or to rise against the pull of gravity or to penetrate an impenetrable surface[1] or to

---

1. There seem to be two meanings of impenetrability that should be distinguished, one concerning physics and one concerning geometrical optics. That

suddenly move without any observable cause may surprise us or puzzle us or amuse or or delight us as seemingly magical because we do know about gravity and mechanics even without formal education, but none of these violations of the laws of physics is relevant for visual perception.

What are the principles about the behavior of light that have been internalized and that are relevant for perception? Most of these have already been discussed in earlier chapters. Several of these reduce to the principle of central projection and are illustrated in Fig. 12-7: the visual angle of objects of the same size is inversely proportional to distance (law of visual angle); the size of objects subtending the same visual angle varies directly with distance (corollary or Emmert's law); surface extents yield visual angles that are reduced as a direct function of the angle of their plane with respect to the frontoparallel plane (foreshortening); parallel lines in planes other than the frontoparallel yield converging image lines (linear perspective). Corollaries of these rules in which object motion occurs are no doubt also internalized (for example, those pertaining to motion perspective or kinetic depth transformation).

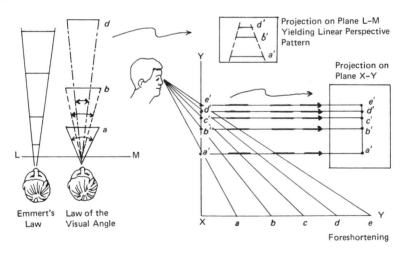

12-7. Illustration of some principles of central projection that seem to be "known" by the perceptual system.

one object might appear to penetrate another known to be solid and impenetrable, such as a surface in the example of stereoscopic transparency given above (p. 321), does *not* create a potential conflict for perception. But that one object appears to penetrate another despite visual information that it remains in front of it, such as in the example of the conflict between interposition and stereopsis given above (p. 321), *does* create a potential conflict for perception.

Several other internalized rules concern the effect of movement of the observer of one kind or another: with rotation of the eyes the retinal image of stationary objects displaces and with rotation of the head the angular (radial or egocentric) direction changes by the same angle as the head in a particular direction and at the same rate; with tilting of the head or entire body the retinal image (or the egocentric orientation) of objects changes as a function of the angle of such tilt; with linear displacement of the observer the angular direction of objects displaces as an inverse function of their distance (absolute motion parallax), and the relative separation between the images of two or more objects changes as a function of their separation from one another and distance from the observer (relative motion parallax); with forward or backward movement of the observer image expansion and contraction occur in accord with the rules relating visual angle and distance. In addition to these rules, there is one concerning the degree of disparity between the images to the two eyes as a function of the separation between contours in depth and the absolute distance of them from the observer, namely, that it varies with the square of the distance (see p. 278).

Then there would seem to be internalized knowledge concerning the occluding properties of opaque surfaces, namely, that objects behind such surfaces are not visible and the size of the occluded objects would increase with distance between surface and object; i.e., the rule about occlusion probably ties in with known rules of visual angle and distances. There may also be internalized knowledge of the effect of surfaces that transmit some but not all of the light (phenomenal transparency).

Finally there are internalized rules about reflectance and illumination that enable us to distinguish between the two kinds of edges and to infer lightness values and illumination in the scene (see pp. 208–212).

This list is not necessarily complete, but it will suffice to make clear the kind of knowledge the perceptual system has available and makes use of. It is with respect to *this* realm of knowledge that perception tends to be internally consistent. It is these rules that the perceptual system applies regardless of the violations of other kinds of knowledge about the world that we may have.

There is one phenomenon that seems to contradict the claim that laws of physics are not known or relevant in visual perception, namely, phenomenal causality (see p. 137). This effect would appear to be relevant to the direct perception of mechanical causation, as in the case of one billiard ball hitting another and causing it to move. While we do have this kind of experience and while it is maintained that it requires very specific stimulus conditions, the fact is that almost any independent events or stimulus onsets appear to be causally related if they coincide in time. The coincidence-explanation principle may be the most powerful determinant in such cases (see Chapter 6). Thus it is questionable in my opinion whether we have internalized rules about mechanical or any other kind of causality or at least that such rules are relevant to the visual domain. Therefore, it is best to leave the question open for the present. One can simply say that certain visual sequences give rise to an impression of causality whatever may be the origin of this kind of effect. But violations, where causality is not experienced, constitute no problem, as when a visual object is seen to move without apparent cause or where a moving object reaches a second object that does not move or moves at an inappropriate angle. In other words, such percepts are not of a kind that we should regard as illogical, irrational, or entailing internal inconsistency.

An important but unanswered question about the rules listed above that *do* govern perception is the form in which they are internally represented. The form in which I listed them was propositional, but it is not necessarily the case that that is their actual form. An alternative that is plausible is that we have an analogic internal representation of three-dimensional space with ourselves at the center (Fig. 12-8). From such a representation one can "read off" various spatial relations. In other words, just as one can directly infer a new relation not directly given by the premises in a transitivity paradigm by representing the premises in visual imagery, one can do the same thing for other kinds of spatial relation. For example, if told that a is north of b and c is east of b, I can "read off" from a cognitive map established on the basis of these given relations what the directional relation is of a to c (Duncker, 1945; Levine et al., 1982).

Something like this could account for perception that is governed by the spatial relationships in the propagation of light. Thus, for example, one can "read off" that the length of ab in Fig. 12-8 is greater than its retinal projection, or one can "read off" that the distance of an object affects visual angle. There is evidence for the belief that we do represent space internally in a form such as this (Attneave, 1974; Attneave and Block, 1973; Cooper and Shepard 1978; Kosslyn, 1980; Kosslyn and Pomerantz, 1977; Rock and Ebenholtz, 1962).

Regardless of how they are represented, these rules are not easily accessed on a conscious, abstract level. Only trained artists, draftsmen, and the like can state them. While the rules are directly reflected in the proximal mode of perception and while internal representation of them is essential for the world mode of perception, the proximal mode is difficult to access under ordinary circumstances. Thus it is difficult to learn about the rules because their manifestation in perception is submerged by virtue of the dominant world mode. The dif-

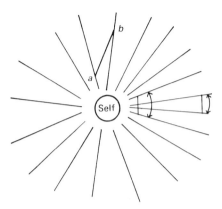

12-8. Illustration of one possible form of internal representation of the rules shown in Figure 12-7. Projections to the eye can be "read off" from an analog map of self in a three-dimensional manifold.

ficulty most people have in drawing three-dimensional objects or scenes, despite the fact that the task is simply to copy the retinal "picture," is precisely that that "picture" is relatively inaccessible because it is blocked by world mode or constancy perception.

Axioms and Assumptions

Besides rules and specific memory content there are internal background factors that surely are fundamental for an understanding of perception, namely, implicit axioms and assumptions. The difficulty in making such factors explicit is that it requires introspection not merely about the content of perceptual experience but about the very character of it, with the realization that it could be other than what it is. The act of perception presupposes or assumes certain characteristics about its objects and about its subject, the perceiver. A general description might run as follows: There is a stable, tangible, enduring world of objects within which perceivers know themselves to be located in a distinct place at any given moment. Moreover, perceivers know that they are viewing this world of objects in the sense that they have a particular vantage point that changes over time and that things exist and tend to remain where they are whether the perceiver moves away or they are momentarily occluded. This implies knowledge that afferent change in a flow of time is based on the perceiver's behavior and it thus implies the capability of distinguishing such change from afferent change produced by external events.

This is what perception is like, and therefore, in my opinion, such aspects can neither be fully explained by a process of learning, by the specification of direct stimulus information, or in fact by any theory designed to explain how a particular object or event is perceived. Not only is visual perception characterized by its inherent spatiality and temporality as Kant has taught but also by object tangibility, stability, and permanence and by a localized self, viewing or sampling the world. According to this account, no specific mental act occurs that yields these characteristics of perception. The following discussion considers some of these characteristics without pretending to provide an exhaustive catalog.

OBJECT PERMANENCE AND THE EXTERNAL
REPRESENTATION OF THE WORLD

A very fundamental characterization of perception is that objects seem to continue to exist and, unless there is evidence of their motion or transformation, to remain as is for some period of time during occasions when we look away, close our eyes, or they are momentarily occluded by another object. The very nature of perceptual experience is that it consists of a world of segregated entities (one important one of which is the self) each in a separate spatial location. This description is more or less a definition of or starting point for the investigation of perception. The observer (animal or human) is a naive realist. All these phenomenal entities exist, independent of our perception of them, and have therefore some assumed degree of permanence at least within the kind of time span pertaining to the present. The phenomenon of position constancy is relevant to the fact of object permanence. We do not see things in the environment move simply because we move, and this effect relates to the assumption of object permanence. After all it is only a matter of the degree of our own movement whether the object displaces to the periphery of vision or goes beyond that to a point where it is not visible at all.

So the only issues about object permanence that are subject to investigation are (1) the manner in which an object disappears, i.e., by displacement derived from our own movement, by closing our eyes, by occlusion by another object, or by inexplicable sudden (e.g., tachistoscopic) vanishing; and (2) the duration of time over which an observer will continue to believe that the object no longer visible is still where it had been. Unlike the other more natural causes, inexplicable vanishing will no doubt lead all, infants *and* adults, to believe the object is in fact no longer present, and this is relevant to the interpretation I have offered about apparent movement under varying conditions (see p. 167-172). The time during which an occluded object will continue to be regarded as still present may have more to do with memory and attention than with any difference in the perception of infants and adults. For the infant, an object out of sight ceases to exist, while for the older child or adult, it is known to be present, but this difference is based on cognitive factors higher than the level of perception. On a perceptual level, at the moment of visual disappearance, infants and adults alike may experience permanent objects undergoing occlusion. Thus insofar as object permanence is defined as the experience at the moment of object disappearance, it is probable that it does not have to develop or be learned (Piaget, 1954; Bower, 1967; Gruber, Girgus, and Banuazizi, 1971).

OBJECT RIGIDITY

It is not too great a step from the claim that object permanence is a fundamental "given" of perceptual experience to the further claim that it is of the nature of perception to assume that objects retain their intrinsic properties. Otherwise object permanence would only mean that a thing as a blob in space tends to be seen as remaining there but it need not retain its shape or size. Suppose, therefore, we do conclude that object permanence incorporates or includes object rigidity. But under what conditions? The most plausible answer is that we assume objects to remain rigidly unchanging during our own motion. However, we can also account for this perceptual rigidity in terms of specific mechanisms like those that yield position constancy. Just as we can say that angular displacement is discounted during observer motion so that we perceive the object as stationary, we can also hypothesize that objects will not appear to change their size or shape or other properties during such motion (see von Holst, 1954). In other words, stimulus change of all kinds, not merely that bearing on location, tends to be discounted during our own motion. Does this mean that object rigidity is overdetermined, it being the result of the very nature of perception in the form of an implicit axiom but also of a specific constancy-like mechanism? The answer is that both factors are relevant, because not *any* apparent change during motion is discounted. If the angular displacement is in the "wrong" direction or rate or if the expansion of the image is inappropriate with respect to the rate of the observer's forward motion, things *will* appear to move or enlarge during observer motion. Thus the predisposition toward thing constancy is present in the form of an axiom, but the outcome depends upon the specific rule that is relevant.

Moreover there are the cases where *the object* changes its distance or rotates when the observer is stationary. In such cases, the constancy mechanism is not directly applicable, but the "axiom hypothesis" is. The fact is, of course, that object motions do tend to yield constancy (i.e., rigidity) as, for example, in the expansion of a pattern in the retinal image or screen as an object approaches us, e.g., the "looming effect" (Schiff, Caviness, and Gibson, 1962) or in the kinetic depth effect with shadow patterns or in many of the more complex moving displays studied by Johannson (1977).

solving. If, for example, the kinetic depth effect can be understood as the inevitable outcome of a fundamental tendency of the perceptual system to interpret such transformations in terms of rigid objects rotating (as part of the broader category of object permanence), is it necessary to view it as a problem based on an ambiguous input with a preferred solution? Certain facts, such as the delay period before a rigid percept is attained or the different outcome with a contour that transforms in length but not in orientation, suggest that the problem-solving analysis is not inappropriate. The fact is that stimulus transformations are ambiguous and sometimes are brought about by nonrigid object transformations (see also the experiments described on pp. 191–200). Yet the preference for the kinetic depth solution may well be based upon the axiomatic character of object rigidity.

One final point on this subject is that the phenomena of constancy under static conditions are not directly derivable from the broader categories of object permanence or object rigidity. A thing at a distance could logically be smaller than it appears unless it is observed while the observer (or it) is in motion or where that motion has just ended. Thus the rules and inferences on which I have argued that constancy is based under such static conditions remain unchallenged by this analysis. However, it is possible that the rules were learned under the dynamic conditions.

So much for a brief consideration of some of the implicit axioms that underlie perception. As noted, we need not assume that a mental act must occur in which at a given time such an axiom is stipulated. But there would seem to be another category in which it is plausible to suppose that such unconscious mental acts do occur. Here I refer to assumptions.

FRAME OF REFERENCE

Various examples considered in previous chapters suggest the tendency to perceive objects in relation to a structure to which they belong. We have seen examples of this kind of effect in the perception of motion, of direction of motion, of orientation, and of size. Insofar as orientation affects shape and orientation is governed by a spatial coordinate system, shape can be added to the list.

The essential fact about frame of reference is that it serves as the zero point or baseline with respect to which the nature or behavior of other visual objects is gauged. Thus things seem to move or to have a direction of motion or to have an orientation or size with respect to it. In many cases that means that the frame itself is taken to be stationary or to define the vertical and horizontal coordinates of the environment. When this happens, it seems appropriate to speak of an assumption. It would seem that such an assumption has enough force to overcome information to the effect that the frame is not stationary or not upright. In other cases the frame is not misperceived but still serves as a baseline with respect to the perception of entities localized within it. The frame itself may be embedded in larger, more encompassing reference frames. Thus we have here a powerful principle of perceptual grouping that should rightly be included among other such principles but rarely is.

Undoubtedly organization that entails reference frames is in the service of achieving veridicality because the world itself is hierarchically organized; e.g., the spokes of a wheel do rotate with respect to the wheel's axis, insects do move over surfaces that themselves are in motion, and we move our fingers with respect to our hands while our hands move in relation to our arm. It is important to perceive an action or event in relation to its immediate reference frame rather than, more absolutely, in relation to ourselves. In fact the latter kind of perception would be thoroughly misleading.

But the question remains how assumptions about frames of references are internally represented. Thought of as a principle of grouping one might say that the perceptual system makes a decision in any given situation to organize the array in such a way that one structure is the reference for other objects. "Frame of reference" would then have the status of "principle of organization," and it would be invoked when it seemed more probable to the executive agency that the array or events are so organized. This description seems appropriate for cases such as multiple objects in motion (Johannsson, 1950; and pp. 219–224). But when the frame is taken to represent or be a surrogate of the environment and thus by definition, so to speak, is seen as stationary or upright, something else seems to be involved. "Assumption" seems like the correct designation. It could be based on an internalized axiom to the effect that the environment *is* stationary or that the directional axes of the environment *define* the vertical and horizontal coordinates of space. In a particular case, then, when the frame has the appropriate properties, it is assumed to represent the environment.

PARSIMONY

There are examples where perception seems to be governed by a principle of parsimony. Thus it seems to be true that with no information to the contrary we tend to perceive an array of objects or all parts of the same object as *equidistant*. For example, if we were to view a luminous three-dimensional wire figure in the dark with one eye and head stationary from a distance of several feet, we would perceive it as a flat, two-dimensional configuration. There are many examples of this kind of fact in perception. The essential feature about Ames' distorted room is that we see the far wall as in a frontal plane rather than as it is, namely, slanted backward toward one side. The principle referred to by its proponent as the equidistance tendency has been convincingly demonstrated in a variety of ways and with evidence also supporting the further principle that the strength of the tendency is inversely related to the separation between objects (Gogel, 1965). The effect can even be strong enough to occur despite countervailing information about distance. It surely is an all-pervasive tendency in the perception of everyday life. We localize a distant object at the distance at which its base intersects the ground plane, although there is no unequivocal information that requires this. Logically, that object could be anywhere along the line of sight between it and the observer (Gibson, 1950).

On what is this tendency based? There could well be an internalized rule or assumption to this effect, whether learned or not, but one might want to argue that the tendency is not based on an assumption at all but occurs by default. That is, the perceptual system may simply be designed to perceive depth between objects only when specific depth information is provided. After all, in the absence of such information, what depth between objects should we expect to be perceived? The main argument against this interpretation is that, as noted above, the tendency can even overcome information that things are at different distances or at least that a compromise will result between the two factors. Moreover, as just noted, the tendency seems to be a function of the proximity or adjacency of the objects.

Another example of this kind is the tendency under certain conditions to perceive contours as stationary rather than as translating along the direction of their own axes. A straight line will not appear to slide along its own direction when seen through an aperture and curved figures such as circles or ellipses will not appear to rotate, although such perceptions are logically possible alternatives (see pp. 119-120 and 285-287). A simple explanation of these effects is that, by default, in the absence of stimulus information attesting to translation or rotation, no such perception should be expected to occur. But even if correct, an explanation of this kind, of perception by default, is of interest. It implies that one principle governing perception is this: When the proximal stimulus is compatible either with a perception entailing no change or no event or with one entailing a change or an event, the former will be preferred.

The preference for nontranslation of lines or nonrotation of figures is strong enough to overcome information that might be expected to lead to a different outcome. An ellipse rotating around a disk will, after a while, look like a deforming figure *not* rotating around its own axis (while it revolves around the axis of the disk). Since rotation would eliminate this perceptual distortion, we can conclude that nonrotation is strongly preferred.

The difficulty of achieving the anorthoscopic effect can be understood along the same lines (see pp. 182–184). With a single-line figure, the anorthoscopic effect is, roughly speaking, an impression of a figure moving in the direction of its own axis. Therefore, a good deal of information is required to overcome the tendency to perceive the element as moving only at right angles to its own length, up and down the slit. Even change of slope of the element is not a sufficient counterindication, at least for naive observers. A possibly related fact is that even when the anorthoscopic effect occurs, the speed of the figure's motion is underestimated.

One can think of these various examples in terms of the concept of stimulus support. To overcome the rule of parsimony suggested above, there must be support in the stimulus (or literal perception to which it gives rise) in favor of the nonparsimonious solution. Moreover that stimulus support must be local. For example, if an ellipse revolving on a disk is constituted of dashed lines, that *is* local stimulus support for perceiving rotation. Otherwise there is no *local* support and the global transformation of orientation of the ellipse does not suffice. That transformation is compatible with a shape-transformation solution. It is interesting that the preference for nonrotation here occurs in spite of the violation of the axiom of object rigidity.

ILLUMINATION AND SHADOW

A well-known fact illustrated in many books on perception is that a picture of a region with attached shadow will tend to appear elevated, convex or in bas-relief if that shadow falls at the bottom and recessed, concave, or in intaglio if the shadow falls at the top. Therefore, one has only to invert the picture to reverse the apparent depth. Since light in the environment typically comes from above, regions on vertically oriented surfaces follow this rule of shadow location.

Therefore, it is plausible to suppose that the utilization of shadow location as a cue to depth is based on an unconscious assumption that light comes from above. A possible alternative interpretation is that this cue is learned. Given the simultaneous presence of attached shadows and other depth information in daily life, shadow location becomes, via association, an independent sign of depth. But there is now evidence that chicks utilize shadow location as an indicator of convexity or concavity much as we do and do so even if raised with all light coming from below (Hershberger, 1970).

Another possible assumption concerning illumination has been suggested earlier. With no information to the contrary, adjacent regions of differing luminances are perceived as regions of differing lightness. But they could of course as well be produced by differing illumination on a region of uniform reflection. In the laboratory (or in a slide of a scene projected on a screen) where such regions are produced in this way, they will be misperceived accordingly. Hence one might legitimately maintain that ordinarily the executive agency assumes equal illumination on neighboring regions in a plane. Further information, such as given by a penumbra, a very high ratio of luminances across the edge, or cues to change of depth, will then suspend this assumption.

COMMON CAUSE AND COINCIDENCE

The preference for certain solutions to perceptual problems may be rooted in the tendency to prefer and search for a common cause or single explanation of covarying stimulus transformations, correlated events, or apparent regularities in the literal percept. Stated negatively, there is an implicit aversion to unexplained or coincidential variation or regularity. In the earlier discussion of this principle (pp. 134–138) the perception of causality was considered to be a special case of it. If this principle is correct, we can add it to the list of assumptions that are here being enumerated. Alternatively we might consider the preference for solutions that satisfy this principle as manifestations of a background characteristic of perception (or axiom) rather than as the result of a mental act.

These examples of axioms and assumptions will suffice to illustrate the reality of such background factors and to indicate just how fundamental they are for an understanding of perception. No doubt there are other such factors that should properly be included here, and conversely, it is possible that some of those that are included either should be thought of differently—for example, as known rules—or have an ontological status different from what I have implied.

The Case against Perceptual Intelligence Reconsidered

In the first chapter, under the above heading, I mentioned a variety of reasons why it was understandable that not all investigators in the field believe that perception is the outcome of intelligent processes analogous to reasoning. While they are aware that there are instances where perception seems to be intelligent, they might prefer the term "intelligent-like" or prefer to say that the instances seem as if they reflect intelligence but that in fact the internal operations that lead to them need not have anything in common with the operations of thought.

One such reason is the apparently instantaneous character of perception. This does not seem to me to be a serious objection at all. If we have learned anything from the current work on information processing, it is that many complex mental events do occur within a matter of milliseconds. In fact just on the basis of logical considerations alone this kind of objection can be ruled out. Phenomenal impressions of time have no necessary implications for real time or for the processing that can occur within a period that seems, phenomenally, to be immediate. To give just one example, we have the impression that recognition is instantaneous, but yet it must be the case that perceptual processing and some kind of memory search must occur for recognition to be possible. I might add, however, that in some kinds of perceptual activity more time does in fact elapse, although in no case does it approach the time usually required for problem solving in the domain of thought.

The second reason considered was the absence of any awareness of thought or thoughtlike process taking place in perception. There are a number of good answers to this objection. It is by no means clear to what extent we are aware of thought processes in the domain of thinking. We are of course aware of certain contents of our thought and we are aware of a long discursive process, including confusion, attempts to verbalize the difficulty and to think of solutions. But one can make out a good case for the proposition that we are not aware of the crucial processes that underlie our understanding of the problem and the transition from one stage of solution to another or to the final solution. A more general claim recently enunciated that rings true to me is that in general in psychology we are not aware of process (Shallice, 1972; Nisbett and Wilson, 1977). In the domain of thinking, however, the hypothesis of unconscious thought has been around for a long time and apparently gaining adherents.

While, originally, unconscious inference was regarded as a contradiction in terms, that conclusion was based on a biased definition of inference and perhaps a narrow view of the role of the nonconscious in human experience and behavior. In any event many nonperceptual attainments that are universally considered to be products of cognitive or thought processes are not represented as such in awareness. So why should the cognitive underpinning of perceptual attainments be questioned on this score? Consequently, I see no special problem with the doctrine of unconscious processes underlying perceptual description, inference, or problem solving.

The third reason given was that perception is autonomous of or independent of knowledge about the prevailing state of affairs so that perception then seems to be inflexible or stupid rather than thoughtlike or intelligent. This kind of objection has been discussed at length in the preceding chapter. It is true that perception is to a great extent autonomous with respect to knowledge of the conceptual kind that often enters into thinking. Perception in this sense *is* inflexible and could be regarded as unintelligent. But nonetheless it can be based upon inference and creative processes in which the domain of relevant knowledge is specific, unconscious, and isolated. Thus "intelligent" must be defined in terms of the kind of process entailed, not necessarily in its flexibility or adaptability or accuracy of conclusion.

The next objection concerned the basis of perception in innate rather than learned factors. The argument was that since reasoning is based on prior experience and learning, to the extent that perception is not, it cannot be explained in terms of reasoning-like mental processes. I have already addressed this question at length, so that little more need be said about it here. The linkage of or identification of thinking with past experience has been a fallacy of the first order or magnitude.

Then there is the argument that if animals and infants or even young children perceive much as human adults do and if it is improbable that *their* perception would be based upon thoughtlike processes, it would seem to be gratuitous to assume that adult perception is based on such processes. There are two possible kinds of answer to this argument. One is that it is possible that for some species of animal other kinds of mechanism account for certain of their perceptions. For example, in some species, the eyes do not move. Therefore, the locus of a stimulus on the retina could directly indicate the angular direction of the object with respect to the animal. This would eliminate the need for a more complex mechanism in which eye position has to be taken into account before angular direction could be known. Another example concerns apparent movement. Evidence now favors the view that there are two kinds, one based on a short-range and one based on a long-range spatial and temporal shift of stimulation (see pp. 176). The motion effect in some animal species might be based only on the short-range shift and thus be explained in terms of known sensory mechanisms rather than in terms of a process of problem solving. On the other hand, all animals have to discriminate stimulus change created by object movement from that created by their own bodily movement, so that much the same mechanism as for humans of discounting afferent change based on self-motion would have to mediate position constancy. In general, though, it is possible that less complex or less cognitive kinds of mechanism might mediate many perceptions for lower species. This remains an empirical question.

The other answer to the argument is that there is no a prior reason why the same kinds of intelligent processing we find in humans cannot mediate perception in animals and infants. Since I have maintained that the kind of processing at issue is not verbal, not conscious, and not based on conceptually represented knowledge, there is no obvious reason why it should not be found in lower species. In fact, since the kind of perceptual processing in humans must have evolved, it would be strange indeed if we did not find somewhat similar processing in animals. Finally, I would reiterate a point made at the beginning of this book, that the kind of intelligent processing we find in perception quite possibly has been the evolutionary link between phylogenetically earlier, less intelligent, more reflex-like sensory processes and the higher mental processes of thought.

A sixth objection concerned those aspects of perception that a priori would seem not to be explicable in terms of thoughtlike operations, namely, the perception of sensory qualities such as chromatic hues, tastes, and odors, the so-called secondary qualities. If so, the argument goes, is it not parsimonious to try to deal with all of perception in the same way? There are several things to be said about this point, perhaps the most obvious being that we still know very little about the processes responsible for the experience of these qualities. Even if we have rather good knowledge about the sensory mechanisms responsible for transmitting the different information about, let us say, the chromatic hues deeper into the brain, we know nothing about how this information ultimately is transmuted into the differential color experiences. However, it is possible that whatever be the ultimate mechanism underlying the experience of sensory qualities, it has little to do with inference or problem solving. That may be because we do not have the problem of stimulus amgiguity in these cases that we do for other aspects of perception. We therefore are not faced with the problem of what object or event in the environment could be yielding the stimulus. One might think of sensory qualities such as hue, including qualities such as "brightness" based on the differential luminance of neutral light as well, as the sensory basis, input, or building blocks out of which objects and events are constructed, so that these qualities are thus not to be thought of as percepts in the same sense as are objects and events. However, if we broaden the problem beyond that of sensory quality per se to one concerning the perception of surface color or illumination, of contrast and constancy with respect to hue, of course we do have problems very similar to those concerning object perception.

The seventh and last argument was based on Lloyd Morgan's canon never to seek explanation of psychological facts on a higher level if they can be explained on a lower level. This is a reasonable philosophy for all of science, not only for psychology, and I certainly subscribe to it. Thus in those cases where such a lower-level mechanism can explain a percept, we would be well advised to accept it. One concerning perceived direction and one concerning apparent motion were just mentioned. I would accept the explanation of the after-effect of motion (spiral or waterfall illusion) on the basis of the differential adaptation of neuron mechanisms responsible for motion of contours over the retina. The explanation deals adequately with the relevant facts as far as we now know. But it is precisely because it does not seem probable that such lower-level mechanisms can explain most other facts of motion perception to say nothing of all other facts of perception that we must look for more complex explanations. It is not enough to say that in time other examples of this kind of mechanism will be found to deal with all aspects of perception. The characteristics of perception such as stimulus ambiguity, constancy, and all those others I have been at pains to point out seem to militate against that *kind* of explanation and in favor of the kind I have here explicated and defended. There are times in science when the data necessarily drive us away from simple, lower-level explanations.

Final Comments about Perception and Thought

In summary, then, how are perception and thought alike and how do they differ? Purely on the level of observable characteristics, the two domains share certain features. Both entail the representation of external objects and events. Both perception and thought entail organization, although how it is achieved and the substance of what is organized differ. Both are influenced by context. Perception sometimes reveals the same sudden insightful reorganization of content as does thought, and in both cases it may arise out of a preceding period of rigid adherence to a different organization. Both show the influence of past experience or rapid learning. Sometimes, although perhaps not often, perception entails the same kind of continued, even conscious searching for a solution as does thought. In both cases instances of imagining or visualizing can be observed.

On a theoretical level, at least according to the theory presented here, both perception and thought entail reasoning. In some cases, generalizations or rules are arrived at in perception by induction. These rules are then used deductively as premises from which inferences are drawn. Perception in some cases can be characterized as the result of creative problem solving, in the sense of searching for the grounds (or internal solution) from which a specific interpretation follows. Solutions in perception must fulfill the requirements of the problem, just as must solutions in thought. Perception entails decisions, just as does thought. Perception can be characterized as based on a description which has the same properties as does a conscious verbal description in the domain of thinking—and it makes use of internalized categories in the process.

But perception differs from thought primarily because it is rooted in and constrained by the necessity of accounting for the proximal stimulus. In my opinion dreaming is the cognitive event most similar to perception in that phenomenologically the content of dreams is so much like perception. Things and events are experienced as external in dreams just as in perception, but the dream process is unconstrained by the necessity of conforming to or of accounting for a stimulus. Despite the centrality of imagery in dreams, we can hardly doubt the thinking that enters into it.

The other major difference between perception and thought is that perception is based on a rather narrow range of internalized knowledge as far as inference and problem solving are concerned. However, form description, recognition, and perceptual effects of past experience have a broader base in internal knowledge. Perception must rigidly adhere to the appropriate internalized rules, so that it often seems unintelligent and inflexible in its imperviousness to other kinds of knowledge. I should add another central difference between the two domains, namely, that the inference or description achieved in the one case has the status of a percept, whereas in the other it has the status of a proposition or of an idea.

Perception is typically quite rapid and nondiscursive, although, as I have pointed out, a sequence of internal events are nonetheless occurring. However, the moment of solution in thinking would seem to be just as rapid. What takes the time in thinking has to do with getting clear about the problem, wrestling with how to deal with it, and a gestation period in which often nothing much is happening at all. The processes in perception are entirely unconscious, whereas much in thinking in conscious. Again, however, as I pointed out above, the *processes* underlying thought are probably unconscious too. Some aspects of thought are of course verbal, whereas no aspects of perception are. It is rare that perception has to be deliberately motivated to achieve its end, and in that respect it is quite different from sustained thought.

Another dimension of difference concerns individual variation. By and large people hardly differ in their perceptions (although there may be room for speculation about differences in style). All people perceive on the basis of constancy, all perceive form in much the same way, all achieve the same solutions in the kinds of conditions I have called problem solving, and so forth. By contrast, in the domain of thought, we are inclined to speak of great differences in intelligence, in the ability to reason or to think creatively. Yet when it comes down to specifying the cognitive functions that lead to such differences it is far from clear what they might be. Perhaps we have underestimated the role here of noncognitive factors such as motivation and attitude.

To come back to the beginning, then, I have tried to show by evidence and argument that perception is thoughtlike and, in that sense, is intelligent. The claim has been that operations that culminate in perceptual experience are of the same kind that characterize thinking. Thought itself is not always as intelligent as it might be (by the criteria of degree of flexibility, valid inferences, creativity, and the like), but when we say of *another* domain that it is governed by operations of the kind that govern thought, we are attributing intelligence to that domain.

References

Ames, A., Jr. 1951. Visual perception and the rotating trapezoidal window. *Psychological Monographs, 65,* Whole No. 324.

Ammons, C. H., and Weitz, J. 1951. Central and peripheral factors in the phi phenomenon. *Journal of Experimental Psychology, 42,* 327-332.

Anderson, J. R., and Bower, G. H. 1973. *Human Associative Memory.* Washington, D. C.: Winston.

Anstis, S. M. 1978. Apparent movement. In R. Held, ed., *Handbook of Sensory Physiology, 8,* New York: Springer-Verlag, 655-673.

Anstis, S. M., and Atkinson, J. 1967. Distortions in moving figures viewed through a stationary slit. *American Journal of Psychology, 80,* 572-585.

Arend, L. E., Buehler, J. N., and Lockhead, G. R. 1971. Difference information in brightness perception. *Perception and Psychophysics, 9,* 367-370.

Arnheim, R. 1954. *Art and Visual Perception.* Berkeley: University of California Press.

Arnheim, R. 1969. *Visual Thinking.* Berkeley: University of California Press.

Asch, S. E., and Witkin, H. A. 1948a. Studies in space orientation: I. Perception of the upright with displaced visual fields. *Journal of Experimental Psychology, 38,* 325-327.

Asch, S. E., and Witkin, H. A. 1948b. Studies in space orientation: II. Perception of the upright with displaced visual fields and with body tilted. *Journal of Experimental Psychology, 38,* 455-477.

Attneave, F. 1954. Some informational aspects of visual perception. *Psychological Review, 61,* 183-193.

Attneave, F. 1968. Triangles as ambiguous figures. *American Journal of Psychology, 81,* 447-453.

Attneave, F. 1971. Multistability in perception. *Scientific American, 225,* 62-71.

Attneave, F. 1972. Representation of physical space. In A. Melton and E. Martin (eds.), *Coding Processes in Human Memory,* Washington: Winston.

Attneave, F. 1974. Apparent movement and the what-where connection. *Psychologia, 17,* 108-120.

Attneave, F., and Block, G. 1973. Apparent movement in tridimensional space. *Perception and Psychophysics, 13,* 301-307.

Attneave, F., and Frost, R. 1969. The determination of perceived tridimensional orientation by minimum criteria. *Perception and Psychophysics*, 6, 391-396.

Aubert, H. 1861. Eine scheinbare bedeutende Drehung von Objekten bei Neigung des Kopfes nach rechts oder links. *Virchows Archives*, 20, 381-393.

Bahnsen, P. 1928. Eine Untersuchung über Symmetrie und Asymmetrie bei visuellen Wahrnehmungen. *Zeitschrift für Psychologie*, 108, 129-154.

Barlow, H. B., and Hill, R. M. 1963. Evidence for a physiological explanation of the waterfall phenomenon and figural after-effects. *Nature*, 200, 1345-1347.

Barlow, H. B., Hill, R. M., and Levick, W. R. 1964. Retinal ganglion cells responding selectively to direction and speed of image motion in the rabbit. *Journal of Physiology*, 173, 377-407.

Barlow, H. B., and Levick, W. R. 1965. The mechanism of directionally selective units in rabbit's retina. *Journal of Physiology*, 178, 477-540.

Beck, J. 1966. Perceptual grouping produced by changes in orientation and shape. *Science*, 154, 538-540.

Begelman, D. 1966. Size perception and schizophrenia. Ph.D. Thesis. Yeshiva University.

Berkeley, G. 1709. *An Essay Towards a New Theory of Vision*. New York: E. P. Dutton, 1910. First published in 1709.

Berko, J. 1958. The child's learning of English morphology. *Word*, 14, 150-177.

Biederman, I. 1972. Perceiving real world scenes. *Science*, 177, 77-80.

Blakemore, C., Carpenter, R. H. S., and Georgeson, M. A. 1970. Lateral inhibition between orientation detectors in the human visual system. *Nature*, 228, 37-39.

Börjesson, E., and Von Hofsten, C. 1972. Spatial determinants of perceived depth in two-dot motion patterns. *Perception and Psychophysics*, 11, 263-268.

Boring, E. G. 1930. A new ambiguous figure. *American Journal of Psychology*, 42, 444-445.

Bower, T. G. R. 1966. The visual world of infants. *Scientific American*, 215, 80-92.

Bower, T. G. R. 1967. The development of object permanence: Some studies of existence constancy. *Perception and Psychophysics*, 2, 416-418.

Braddick, O. 1974. A short-range process in apparent motion. *Vision Research*, 14, 519-528.

Brandt, T., Dichgans, J., and Koenig, E. 1973. Differential effects of central versus peripheral vision on egocentric and exocentric motion perception. *Experimental Brain Research*, 16, 476-491.

Bregman, A. S. 1977. Perception and behavior as compositions of ideals. *Cognitive Psychology*, 9, 250-292.

Brindley, G. S., and Merton, P. A. 1960. The absence of position sense in the human eye. *Journal of Physiology*, 153, 127-130.

Brislin, R. W., and Leibowitz, H. 1970. The effect of separation between test and comparison objects on size constancy at various age levels. *American Journal of Psychology*, 83, 372-376.

Bruner, J. S. 1957. On perceptual readiness. *Psychological Review*, 64, 123-152.

Brunswik, E. 1952. *Systematic and Representative Design of Psychological Experiments*. Berkeley, Cal.: University of California Press.

Buffart, H., Leeuwenberg, E., and Restle, F. 1981. Coding theory of visual pattern completion. *Journal of Experimental Psychology: Human Perception and Performance*, 7, 241-274.

Bugelski, B. R., and Alampay, D. A. 1961. The role of frequency in developing perceptual set. *Canadian Journal of Psychology*, 15, 205-211.

Carr, H. 1935. *An Introduction to Space Perception.* New York: Longmans, Green.

Carlson, V. R. 1960. Overestimation in size-constancy judgments. *American Journal of Psychology*, 73, 199-213.

Clowes, M. B. 1967. Perception, picture processing, and computers. In N. L. Collins and D. Mickie, eds., *Machine Intelligence.* Edinburgh: Oliver and Boyd.

Clowes, M. B. 1971. On seeing things. *Artificial Intelligence*, 2, 79-116.

Cooper, L. A., and Shepard, R. N. 1978. Transformations on representations of objects in space. In E. C. Carterette and M. P. Friedman, eds., *Handbook of Perception*, Vol. 8, New York: Academic Press.

Corbin, H. H. 1942. The perception of grouping and apparent movement in visual depth. *Archives of Psychology*, No. 273.

Craik, K. J. W. 1966. *The Nature of Psychology.* Cambridge, England, Cambridge University Press, 94-97.

Day, R. H., and McKenzie, B. E. 1977. Constancies in the perceptual world of the infant. In W. Epstein, ed., *Stability and Constancy in Visual Perception: Mechanisms and Processes*, New York: Wiley-Interscience, 285-320.

Di Lorenzo, J. R., and Rock, I. 1982. The rod-and-frame effect as a function of the righting of the frame. *Journal of Experimental Psychology: Human Perception and Performance*, 8, No. 4, 536-546.

Dinnerstein, D., and Wertheimer, M. 1957. Some determinants of phenomenal overlapping. *American Journal of Psychology*, 70, 21-37.

Draper, S. W. Reasoning about depth in line-drawing interpretation. Ph.D. Thesis. University of Sussex.

Dretske, F. I. 1981. *Knowledge and the Flow of Information.* Cambridge, Mass.: Bradford Books/The MIT Press.

Duncker, K. 1929. Über induzierte Bewegung. *Psychologische Forschung*, 12, 180-259. Trans. and condensed in W. Ellis, ed., *Source Book of Gestalt Psychology*, New York: Humanities Press, Selection 12.

Duncker, K. 1945. On problem solving. *Psychological Monographs*, 58, 1-112.

Ebenholtz, S. 1977. The constancies in object orientation: An algorithm processing approach. In W. Epstein, ed., *Stability and Constancy in Visual Perception: Mechanisms and Processes*, New York: Wiley-Interscience, 71-89.

Ebenholtz, S. M., and Benzschawel, T. L. 1977. The rod and frame effect and induced head tilt as a function of observation distance. *Perception and Psychophysics*, 22, 491-496.

Epstein, W. 1963. Attitude of judgment and the size-distance invariance hypothesis. *Journal of Experimental Psychology*, 66, 78-83.

Epstein, W. 1973. The process of "taking-into-account" in visual perception. *Perception*, 2, 267-285.

Epstein, W. 1982. Percept-percept couplings. *Perception*, 11, 75-83.

Epstein, W., and Hatfield, G. 1978a. Functional equivalence of masking and cue reduction in perception of shape at a slant. *Perception and Psychophysics, 23,* 137-144.

Epstein, W., and Hatfield, G. 1978b. The locus of masking shape-at-a-slant. *Perception and Psychophysics, 24,* 501-504.

Epstein, W., and Landauer, A. 1969. Size and distance judgments under reduced conditions of viewing. *Perception and Psychophysics, 6,* 269-272.

Fantz, R. L. 1957. Form preference in newly hatched chicks. *Journal of Comparative and Physiological Psychology, 50,* 422-430.

Farnè, M. 1970. On the Poggendorff illusion: A note to Cumming's criticism of Chung Chiang's theory. *Perception and Psychophysics, 8,* 112.

Fendrich, R., and Mach, A. 1980. Anorthoscopic perception occurs with a retinally stabilized stimulus. *Suppl. Invest. Ophthal. and Vis. Sci., 166.*

Garner, W. R. 1974. *The Processing of Information and Structure.* Hillsdale, N.J.: Erlbaum.

Gelb, A. 1929. Die "Farbenkonstanz" der Sehdinge. In A. Bethe, G. V. Bergmann, G. Embden, and A. Ellinger, eds., *Handbuch der Normalen und Pathologischen Physiologie, 12,* New York: Springer, Part I, 594-678.

Gengerelli, A., 1948. Apparent movement in relation to homogeneous and heterogeneous stimulation of the central hemispheres. *Journal of Experimental Psychology, 38,* 592-599.

Gibson, J. J. 1933. Adaptation, after-effect and contrast in the perception of curved lines. *Journal of Experimental Psychology, 16,* 1-31.

Gibson, J. J. 1950. *The Perception of the Visual World.* Boston: Houghton Mifflin.

Gibson, J. J. 1962. Observations on active touch. *Psychological Review, 69,* 477-491.

Gibson, J. J. 1966. *The Senses Considered as Perceptual Systems.* Boston: Houghton Mifflin.

Gibson, J. J. 1979. *The Ecological Approach to Visual Perception.* Boston: Houghton Mifflin.

Gibson, J. J., and Gibson, E. J. 1955. Perceptual learning: Differentiation or enrichment? *Psychological Review, 62,* 32-41.

Gibson, J. J., and Mowrer, O. H. 1938. Determinants of the perceived vertical and horizontal. *Psychological Review, 45,* 300-323.

Gilchrist, A. 1977. Perceived lightness depends on perceived spatial arrangement. *Science, 195,* 185-187.

Gilchrist, A. 1979. The perception of surface blacks and whites. *Scientific American, 240,* 112-126.

Gilchrist, A. 1980. When does perceived lightness depend on perceived spatial arrangement? *Perception and Psychophysics, 28,* 527-538.

Gilchrist, A., Delman, S., and Jacobsen, A. 1983. The classification and integration of edges as critical to the perception of reflectance and illumination. *Perception and Psychophysics,* in press.

Gilinsky, A. 1955. The effect of attitude on the perception of size. *American Journal of Psychology, 68,* 173-192.

Gillam, B. 1980. Geometrical Illusions. *Scientific American, 242,* 102-111.

Gillam, B. 1981. False perspectives. *Perception, 10*, 313-318.

Gogel, W. 1965. Equidistance tendency and its consequences. *Psychological Bulletin, 64*, 153-163.

Gogel, W. 1969. The sensing of retinal size. *Vision Research, 9*, 1079-1094.

Gogel, W. C. 1973. The organization of perceived space: I. Perceptual interactions. *Psychologische Forschung, 36*, 195-221.

Gogel, W. C. 1975. Depth adjacency and the Ponzo illusion. *Perception and Psychophysics, 17*, 125-132.

Gogel, W. C. 1978. Size, distance, and depth perception. In E. C. Carterette and M. P. Friedman, eds., *Handbook of Perception*, IX, New York: Academic Press.

Gogel, W. C. 1979. The common occurrence of errors of perceived distance. *Perception and Psychophysics, 25*, 2-11.

Gogel, W. C. 1981. Perceived depth is a necessary factor in apparent motion concomitant with head motion: A reply to Shebilske and Proffitt. *Perception and Psychophysics, 29*, 173-177.

Gogel, W. C., and Koslow, M. 1971. The effect of perceived distance on induced movement. *Perception and Psychophysics, 10*, 142-146.

Gogel, W. C., and Newton, R. E. 1975. Depth adjacency and the rod and frame illusion. *Perception and Psychophysics, 18*, 163-171.

Gogel, W. C., and Sturm, R. D. 1972. A test of the relational hypothesis of perceived size. *American Journal of Psychology, 85*, 201-216.

Goodenough, D. R., Sigman, E., Oltman, P. K., Rosso, J., and Mertz, H. 1979. Eye torsion in response to a tilted visual stimulus. *Vision Research, 19*, 1177-1179.

Goldmeier, E. 1972. Similarity in visually perceived forms. *Psychological Issues, 8*, No. 1, 1-135.

Goldmeier, E. 1982. *The Memory Trace: Its Formation and Its Fate.* Hillsdale, N.J.: Erlbaum.

Gottschaldt, K. 1929. Über den Einfluss der Erfahrung auf die Wahrnehmung von Figuren, II. *Psychologische Forschung, 12*, 1-87.

Gregory, R. L. 1968. Visual illusions. *Scientific American, 219*, 66-76.

Gregory, R. L. 1970. *The Intelligent Eye.* New York: McGraw Hill.

Gregory, R. L. 1972. Cognitive contours. *Nature, 238*, 51-52.

Gruber, H. E., Girgus, J. S., and Banuazizi, A. 1971. The development of object permanence in the cat. *Developmental Psychology, 41*, 9-15.

Grüsser, O. J., and Grüsser-Cornehls, U. 1973. Neuronal mechanisms of visual movement perception and some psychophysical and behavioral correlations. In R. Jung, ed., *Handbook of Sensory Physiology, Vol. VII/3A: Central Processing of Information.* New York: Springer.

Gúzman, A. 1969. Decomposition of a visual scene into three-dimensional bodies. In A. Grasselli, ed., *Automatic Interpretation and Classification of Images*, New York: Academic Press.

Haber, R. N., and Nathanson, L. S. 1968. Post-retinal storage? Some further observations on Park's Camel as seen through the eye of a needle. *Perception and Psychophysics, 3*, 349-355.

Hastorf, A. H., and Way, K. S. 1952. Apparent size with and without distance cues. *Journal of General Psychology, 47*, 181-188.

Hay, J., Pick, H. L., Jr., and Ikeda, K. 1965. Visual capture produced by prism spectacles. *Psychonomic Science, 2,* 215-216.

Hebb, D. O. 1966. *A Textbook of Psychology.* Philadelphia and London: W. B. Saunders.

Heller, D. 1968. Absence of size constancy in visually deprived rats. *Journal of Comparative and Physiological Psychology, 65,* 336-339.

Helmholtz, H. von. 1867. *Treatise on Physiological Optics,* Vol. III. Trans. from the 3rd German edition, J. P. C. Southall, ed. New York: Dover Publications, 1962. First published in the *Handbuch der physiologischen Optik,* 1867, Voss.

Hering, E. 1920. Grundzüge der Lehre vom Lichtsinne. In *Handbuch der Gesampten Augenheilkunde,* ed. Graefe-Saemisch, Springer. Translated by L. Hurvich and D. Jameson, *Outlines of a Theory of the Light Sense,* Harvard University Press, 1964.

Hershberger, W. 1970. Attached shadow orientation perceived as depth by chickens reared in an environment illuminated from below. *Journal of Comparative and Physiological Psychology, 73,* 407-411.

Hill, A. L. 1972. Direction constancy. *Perception and Psychophysics, 11,* 175-178.

Hochberg, J. 1968. In the mind's eye. In R. N. Haber, ed., *Contemporary Theory and Research in Visual Perception,* New York: Holt.

Hochberg, J. 1970. Attention, organization, and consciousness. In D. I. Mostofsky, ed., *Attention: Contemporary Theory and Analysis,* New York: Appleton-Century-Crofts.

Hochberg, J. 1974. Higher-order stimuli and interresponse coupling in the perception of the visual world. In R. B. Macleod and H. L. Pick, *Perception: Essays in Honor of James J. Gibson,* Ithaca: Cornell University Press, 17-39.

Hochberg, J. 1981. Levels of perceptual organization. In M. Kubovy and J. R. Pomerantz, eds., *Perceptual Organization,* Hillsdale, N. J.: Erlbaum.

Hochberg, J., and McAlister, E. 1953. A quantitative approach to figural "goodness." *Journal of Experimental Psychology, 46,* 361-364.

Holway, A. H., and Boring, E. G. 1941. Determinants of apparent visual size with distance variant. *American Journal of Psychology, 54,* 21-37.

Holst, E. von. 1954. Relations between the central nervous system and the peripheral organs. *British Journal of Animal Behaviour, 2,* 89-94.

Horn, G., and Hill, R. M. 1969. Modifications of receptive fields in the visual cortex occurring spontaneously and associated with bodily tilt. *Nature, 221,* 186-188.

Hubel, D. H., and Wiesel, T. N. 1962. Receptive fields, binocular interaction, and functional architecture in the cat's visual cortex. *Journal of Physiology, 160,* 106-154.

Huffman, D. A. 1971. Impossible objects as nonsense sentences. In B. Meltzer and D. Michie, eds., *Machine Intelligence 6,* Edinburgh: Edinburgh University Press.

Hughes, P. C. 1973. The influence of the visual field upon the visual vertical in relation to ocular torsion of the eye. Ph.D. Thesis, University of Oklahoma, 1973. *Dissertation Abstracts International, 33,* 468B. University Microfilms, No. 73-91, 58B.

Ittelson, W. H. and Kilpatrick, F. P. 1951. Experiments in perception. *Scientific American, 185*, 50-55.

Jastrow, J. 1900. *Fact and Fable in Psychology*. Boston: Houghton Mifflin.

Johansson, G. 1950. *Configurations in Event Perception*. Uppsala, Sweden: Almkvist and Wiksell.

Johansson, G. 1977. Spatial constancy and motion in visual perception. In W. Epstein, ed., *Stability and Constancy in Visual Perception: Mechanisms and Processes*, New York: Wiley-Interscience, 375-419.

Julesz, B. 1971. *Foundations of Cyclopean Perception*. University of Chicago Press.

Julesz, B. 1975. Experiments in the visual perception of texture. *Scientific American, 232*, 34-43.

Kalil, R. E., and Freedman, S. J. 1966. Persistence of ocular rotation following compensation for displaced vision. *Perceptual and Motor Skills, 22*, 135-139.

Kanizsa, G. 1955. Margini quasi-percettivi in campi con stimolazione omogenea. *Rivista di Psicologia, 49*, 7-30.

Kanizsa, G. 1974. Contours without gradients or cognitive contours? *Italian Journal of Psychology, 1*, 93-112.

Kanizsa, G. 1975. The role of regularity in perceptual organization. In G. F. d'Arcais, ed., *Studies in Perception: Festschrift for Fabio Metelli*. Milan: Martello-Gianti.

Kanizsa, G., and Gerbino, W. 1976. Convexity and symmetry in figure-ground organization. In M. Henle, ed., *Vision and Artifact*, New York: Springer.

Kaplan, G. A. 1969. Kinetic disruption of optical texture: The perception of depth at an edge. *Perception and Psychophysics, 6*, 193-198.

Kardos, L. 1934. Ding und Schatten. *Zeitschrift für Psychologie*, Ergb. No. 23.

Kaufman, L., Cyrulnik, I., Kaplowitz, J., Melnick, G., and Stoff, D. 1971. The complementarity of apparent and real motion. *Psychologische Forschung, 34*, 343-348.

Kaufman, L., and Rock, I. 1962. The moon illusion, I. *Science, 136*, 953-961.

Koffka, K. 1935. *Principles of Gestalt Psychology*. New York: Harcourt Brace Jovanovich, 187-190.

Köhler, W. 1929. *Gestalt Psychology*. New York: Liveright.

Köhler, W. 1940. *Dynamics in Psychology*. New York: Liveright, 125-144.

Köhler, W., and Wallach, H. 1944. Figural after-effects: An investigation of visual processes. *Proceedings of the American Philosophical Association, 88*, 269-357.

Kolers, P. A. 1972. *Aspects of Motion Perception*. Oxford: Pergamon Press.

Kolers, P. A., and Pomerantz, J. R. 1971. "Figural change in apparent motion." *Journal of Experimental Psychology, 87*, 99-108.

Kopfermann, H. 1930. Psychologische Untersuchungen über die Wirkung Zweidimensionaler körperlicher Gebilde. *Psychologische Forschung, 13*, 293-364.

Korte, A. 1915. Kinematoskopische Untersuchungen. *Zeitschrift für Psychologie, 72*, 193-206.

Kosslyn, S. M. 1975. Information representation in visual images. *Cognitive Psychology, 7*, 341-370.

Kosslyn, S. M., and Pomerantz, J. R. 1977. Imagery, propositions, and the form of internal representations. *Cognitive Psychology, 9,* 52-76.

Krauskopf, J. 1963. Effect of retinal image stabilization on the appearance of heterochromatic targets. *Journal of the Optical Society of America, 53,* 741-744.

Künnapas, T. M. 1955. Influence of frame size on apparent length of a line. *Journal of Experimental Psychology, 50,* 168-170.

Leeper, R. 1935. A study of a neglected portion of the field of learning: The development of sensory organization. *Journal of Genetic Psychology, 46,* 41-75.

Lehmkuhle, S., and Fox, R. 1980. Effect of depth separation on metacontrast masking. *Journal of Experimental Psychology: Human Perception and Performance, 6,* 605-621.

Leibowitz, H., Pollard, S. W., and Dickson, D. 1967. Minocular and binocular size-matching as a function of distance at various age levels. *American Journal of Psychology, 80,* 263-268.

Levine, M., Jankovic, I. M., and Talig, M. 1982. Principles of spatial problem solving. *Journal of Experimental Psychology: General, 111,* 157-175.

Lindsay, P. H., and Norman, D. A. 1972. *Human Information Processing.* New York: Academic Press.

Lotze, H. 1886. *Outlines of Psychology.* Trans. and ed. from the 3rd German edition by G. T. Ladd. Boston: Ginn.

Mack, A. 1978. Two modes of visual perception. M. H. Pick, ed., *Modes of Perception.* Hillsdale, N.J.: Erlbaum.

Mack, A., and Bachant, J. 1969. Perceived movement of the after-image during eye movement. *Perception and Psychophysics, 6,* 379-384.

Mack, A., and Herman, E. 1973. Position constancy during pursuit eye movements: An investigation of the Filehne illusion. *Quarterly Journal of Experimental Psychology, 25,* 71-84.

Maier, N. R. F. 1931. The solution of a problem and its appearance in consciousness. *Journal of Comparative Psychology, 12,* 181, 194.

Marr, D. 1982. *Vision.* San Francisco: Freeman.

McLaughlin, S. C., and Webster, R. G. 1967. Changes in straight-ahead eye position during adaptation to wedge prisms. *Perception and Psychophysics, 2,* 37-44.

Metelli, F. 1974. The perception of transparency. *Scientific American, 230,* 90-98.

Metzger, W. 1953. *Gesetze des Sehens.* Frankfurt-am-Main: Waldemar Kramer.

Michotte, A. 1963. *The Perception of Causality.* New York: Basic Books. Originally published under the title *La Perception de la causalité,* L'Institute Supérior de Philosophie (Etudes de Psychologie), III, 1946.

Michotte, A. 1955. Perception and Cognition. *Acta Psychologica, 11,* 69-91.

Michotte, A., Thinès, G., and Crabbé, G. 1964. Les compléments amodaux des structures perceptives. *Studia Psychologica* (Universitaires de Louvain, Louvain).

Minsky, M. 1975. A framework for representing knowledge. In P. H. Winston, ed., *The Psychology of Computer Vision*, New York: McGraw Hill.

Morgan, C. L. 1894. *An Introduction to Comparative Psychology.* London: W. Scott.

Müller, G. E. 1916. Über das Aubertsche Phänomenon. *Zeitschrift für Psychologie und Physiologie der Sinnesorgane, 49,* 109–244.

Musatti, C. L. 1924. Sui fenomeni stereocinetici. *Archivio Italiano Psicologia, 3,* 105–120.

Narasimhan, R. 1969. On the description, generation, and recognition of classes of pictures. In A. Grasselli, ed., *Automatic Interpretation and Classification of Images*, New York: Academic Press.

Navon, D. 1976. Irrelevance of figural identity for resolving ambiguities in apparent motion. *Journal of Experimental Psychology, Human Perception, and Performance, 2,* No. 1, 130–138.

Neisser, U. 1967. *Cognitive Psychology.* New York: Appleton-Century-Crofts.

Nisbett, R. E., and Wilson, T. D. 1977. Telling more than we can know: verbal reports on mental processes. *Psychological Review, 84,* 231–259.

Oatley, K. 1978. *Perceptions and Representations.* New York: The Free Press.

O'Brien, V. 1958. Contour perception, illusion, and reality. *Journal of the Optical Society of America, 48,* 112–119.

Olson, R. R., and Attneave, F. 1970. What variables produce similarity grouping? *American Journal of Psychology, 83,* 1–21.

Ono, H., and Comerford, J. 1977. Stereoscopic depth constancy. In W. Epstein, ed., *Stability and Constancy in Visual Perception: Mechanisms and Processes*, New York: Wiley-Internation, 91–128.

Ono, H., and Gonda, G. 1978. Apparent movement, eye movements, and phoria when two eyes alternate in viewing a stimulus. *Perception, 7,* 75–83.

Palmer, S. E. 1975. The effects of contextual scenes on the identification of objects. *Memory and Cognition, 3,* 519–526.

Palmer, S. E. 1975. Visual perception and world knowledge: Notes on a model of sensory-cognitive interaction. In D. A. Norman, D. E. Rumelhart, and the LNR Research Group, eds., *Exploration in Cognition*, San Francisco: W. H. Freeman.

Palmer, S. E. 1977. Hierarchical structure in perceptual representation. *Cognitive Psychology, 9,* 441–474.

Palmer, S. E. 1978. Structural aspects of visual similarity. *Memory and Cognition, 6,* 91–97.

Palmer, S. E. 1980. What makes triangles point: Local and global effects in configuration of ambiguous triangles. *Cognitive Psychology, 12,* 285–305.

Palmer, S. E. 1982. Symmetry, transformation, and the structure of perceptual systems. In J. Beck, ed., *Organization and Representation in Perception*, Hillsdale, N. J.: Erlbaum.

Pantle, A. J., and Picciano, L. 1976. A multi-stable movement display: Evidence for two separate motion systems in humans. *Science, 193,* 500–502.

Parks, T. E. 1965. Post-retinal visual storage. *American Journal of Psychology, 78*, 145-147.

Penrose, L. S., and Penrose, R. 1958. Impossible objects: A special type of visual illusion. *British Journal of Psychology, 49*, 31-33.

Perkins, D. N. 1972. Visual discrimination between rectangular and nonrectangular parallelopipeds. *Perception and Psychophysics, 12*, 396-400.

Perkins, D. N. 1976. How good a bet is good form? *Perception, 5*, 393-406.

Perkins, D. N. 1982. The perceiver as organizer and geometer. In J. Beck, ed., *Organization and Representation in Perception*, Hillsdale, N.J.: Erlbaum.

Perkins, D. N., and Cooper, R. 1980. How the eye makes up what the light leaves out. In M. Hagen, ed., The Perception of Pictures, Vol. II: *Dürer's Devices: Beyond the Projective Model*, New York: Academic Press.

Piaget, J. 1954. *The Construction of Reality in the Child*. New York: Basic Books.

Pick, A. D. 1965. Improvement of visual and tactual form discrimination. *Journal of Experimental Psychology, 69*, 331-339.

Pick, H. L., Jr., and Hay, J. C. 1964. Adaptation to prismatic distortion. *Psychonomic Science, 1*, 199-200.

Plateau, J. 1836. Anorthoskop. *Bulletin de l'Académie de Bruxelles*, III, 7 and 364.

Posin, R. 1962. Size overestimation and the disparity of retinal image size. Unpublished paper. Yeshiva University.

Posin, R. 1966. Perceptual adaptation to contingent visual-field movement: An experimental investigation of position constancy. Ph.D. Thesis. Yeshiva University.

Reed, S. K. 1974. Structural descriptions and the limitations of visual images. *Memory and Cognition, 2*, 329-336.

Restle, F. 1979. Coding theory of the perception of motion configurations. *Psychological Review, 86*, 1-24.

Reynolds, R. 1981. Perception of an illusory contour as a function of processing time. *Perception, 10*, 107-115.

Reynolds, R. 1983. The role of object hypotheses in the organization of fragmented figures. Manuscript submitted for publication. Personal communication.

Richards, W. 1967. Apparent modifiability of receptive fields during accommodation and convergence and a model for size constancy. *Neuropsychologia, 5*, 63-72.

Rock, I. 1954. The perception of the egocentric orientation of a line. *Journal of Experimental Psychology, 48*, 367-374.

Rock, I. 1973. *Orientation and Form*. New York: Academic Press.

Rock, I. 1975. *An Introduction to Perception*. New York: Macmillan; London: Collier-Macmillan.

Rock, I. 1981. Anorthoscopic perception. *Scientific American, 244*, 145-153.

Rock, I., and Anson, R. 1979. Illusory contours as the solution to a problem. *Perception, 8*, 665-681.

Rock, I., Auster, M., Schiffman, M., and Wheeler, D. 1980. Induced movement based on subtraction of motion from the inducing object. *Journal of Experimental Psychology: Human Perception and Performance, 6*, 391-403.

Rock, I., and Brosgole, L. 1964. Grouping based on phenomenal proximity. *Journal of Experimental Psychology, 67*, 531-538.

Rock, I., DiVita, J., and Barbeito, R. 1981. The effect on form perception of change of orientation in the third dimension. *Journal of Experimental Psychology: Human Perception and Performance, 7*, 719-732.

Rock, I., and Ebenholtz, S. 1959. The relational determination of perceived size. *Psychological Review, 66*, 387-401.

Rock, I., and Ebenholtz, S. 1962. Stroboscopic movement based on change of phenomenal rather than retinal location. *American Journal of Psychology, 75*, 193-207.

Rock, I., and Engelstein, P. 1959. A study of memory for visual form. *American Journal of Psychology, 72*, 221-229.

Rock, I. and Gilchrist, A. 1975a. Induced form. *American Journal of Psychology, 88*, 475-482.

Rock, I., and Gilchrist, A. 1975b. The conditions for the perception of the covering and uncovering of a line. *American Journal of Psychology, 88*, 571-582.

Rock, I., Girgus, J., and Egatz, R. 1977. The effect of knowledge of reversibility on the reversibility of ambiguous figures. *Perception and Psychophysics, 22*, 550-556.

Rock, I., and Gutman, D. 1981. The effect of inattention on form perception. *Journal of Experimental Psychology: Human Perception and Performance, 7*, 275-285.

Rock, I., and Halper, F. 1969. Form perception without a retinal image. *American Journal of Pscyhology, 82*, 425-440.

Rock, I., Halper, F., and Clayton, T. 1972. The perception and recognition of complex figures. *Cognitive Psychology, 3*, 655-673.

Rock, I., and Harris, C. S. 1967. Vision and touch. *Scientific American, 216*, 96-104.

Rock, I., and Kaufman, L. 1962. The moon illusion, II. *Science, 136*, 1023-1031.

Rock, I., and Leaman, R. 1963. An experimental analysis of visual symmetry. *Acta Psychologica, 21*, 171-183.

Rock, I., and McDermott, W. The perception of visual angle. *Acta Psychologica, 22*, 119-134.

Rock, I., Shallo, J., and Schwartz, F. 1978. Pictorial depth and related constancy effects as a function of recognition. *Perception, 7*, 3-19.

Rock, I., and Sigman, E. 1973. Intelligence factors in the perception of form through a moving slit. *Perception, 2*, 357-369.

Rock, I., and Smith, D. 1981. Alternative solutions to kinetic stimulus transformations. *Journal of Experimental Psychology: Human Perception and Performance, 7*, 19-29.

Rock, I., Tauber, E. S., and Heller, D. 1965. Perception of stroboscopic movement: Evidence for its innate basis. *Science, 147*, 1050-1052.

Rock, I., and Victor, J. 1964. Vision and touch: An experimentally created conflict between the senses. *Science, 143*, 594-596.

Rock, I., Wheeler, D., Shallo, J., and Rotunda, J. 1982. The construction of a plane from pictorial information. *Perception, 11*, 463-475.

Rosch, E. 1975. Cognitive representations of semantic categories. *Journal of Experimental Psychology: General, 104*, 193-233.

Rubin, E. 1921. *Visuell Wahrgenommene Figuren.* Glydendalske.

Schiff, W., Caviness, J. A., and Gibson, J. J. 1962. Persistent fear responses in rhesus monkeys in response to the optical stimulus of "looming." *Science, 136*, 982-983.

Shallice, T. 1972. On the dual functions of consciousness. *Psychological Review, 79*, 383-396.

Shallo, J. 1983. Size perception in children: Evidence for dual mode processing. Ph.D. Thesis. Rutgers University.

Shepard, R. N., and Judd, S. A. 1976. Perceptual illusion of rotation of three-dimensional objects. *Science, 191*, 952-954.

Shipley, W. G., Kenney, F. A., and King, M. E. 1945. Beta-apparent movement under binocular, monocular, and interocular stimulation. *American Journal of Psychology, 58*, 545-549.

Shopland, C., and Gregory, R. L. 1964. The effect of touch on a visually ambiguous three-dimensional figure. *Quarterly Journal of Experimental Psychology, 16*, 66-70.

Sigman, E., Goodenough, D. R., and Flannagan, M. 1978. Subjective estimates of body tilt and the rod-and-frame test. *Perceptual and Motor Skills, 47*, 1051-1056.

Sigman, E., Goodenough, D. R., and Flannagan, M. 1979. Instructions, illusory self-tilt, and the rod-and-frame test. *Quarterly Journal of Experimental Psychology, 31*, 155-165.

Sigman, E., and Rock, I. 1974. Stroboscopic movement based on perceptual intelligence. *Perception, 3*, 9-28.

Singer, G., Purcell, A. T., and Austin, M. 1970. The effect of structure and degree of tilt on the tilted room illusion. *Perception and Psychophysics, 7*, 250-252.

Smith, K. U. 1940. The neural centers concerned in the mediation of apparent-movement vision. *Journal of Experimental Psychology, 26*, 443-466.

Spinelli, D. N. 1970. Recognition of visual patterns. In D. A. Hamburg, K. H. Pribram, and A. J. Stunkard, eds., *Perception and Its Disorders*, chapter VIII, Baltimore: Williams and Wilkins.

Stoper, A. E. 1964. The effect of the structure of the phenomenal field on the occurrence of stroboscopic motion. Paper delivered at the 1964 meeting of the Eastern Psychological Association.

Sutherland, N. S. 1968. Outlines of a theory of visual pattern recognition in animals and man. *Proceedings of the Royal Society, 171*, 297-317.

Sutherland, N. S. 1973. Object recognition. In E. C. Carterette and M. P. Friedman, eds., *Handbook of Perception*, vol. 3, New York: Academic Press.

Tauber, E. S., and Koffler, S. 1966. Optomotor responses in human infants to apparent motion: Evidence of innateness. *Science, 152*, 382-383.

Ternus, J. 1926. Experimentelle Untersuchungen über phänomenale Identität. *Psychologische Forschung, 7*, 71-126. Trans. and condensed in W. Ellis, ed., *Source Book of Gestalt Psychology*, Selection 11, New York: Humanities Press, 1950.

Thouless, R. 1931. Phenomenal regression to the real object: I. *British Journal of Psychology, 21*, 339-359.

Titchener, E. B. 1926. *A Textbook of Psychology.* New York: Macmillan.

Tulving, E. and Gold, C. 1963. Stimulus information on contextual information as determinants of tachistoscopic recognition of words. *Journal of Experimental Psychology, 66,* 319-327.

Ullman, S. 1979. *The Interpretation of Visual Motion.* Cambridge, Mass., and London, England: The MIT Press.

Verville, E., and Cameron, N. 1946. Age and sex differences in the perception of incomplete pictures in adults. *Pedogogical Seminary, 68,* 149-157.

Wallach, H. 1935. Über visuell wahrgenommene Bewegungsrichtung. *Psychologische Forschung, 20,* 325-380.

Wallach, H. 1948. Brightness constancy and the nature of achromatic colors. *Journal of Experimental Psychology, 38,* 310-324.

Wallach, H. 1949. Some considerations concerning the relation between perception and cognition. *Journal of Personality, 18,* 6-13.

Wallach, H., Bacon, J., and Schulman, P. 1978. Adaptation in motion perception: Alteration of induced motion. *Perception and Psychophysics, 24,* 509-514.

Wallach, H., and Kravitz, J. H. 1965. The measurement of the constancy of visual direction and of its adaptation. *Psychonomic Science, 2,* 217-218.

Wallach, H., and Kravitz, J. H. 1965. Rapid adaptation in the constancy of visual direction with active and passive rotation. *Psychonomic Science, 3,* 165-166.

Wallach, H., and O'Connell, D. N. 1953. The kinetic depth effect. *Journal of Experimental Psychology, 45,* 205-217.

Wallach, H., O'Connell, D. N., and Neisser, U. 1953. The memory effect of visual perception of three-dimensional form. *Journal of Experimental Psychology, 45,* 360-368.

Wallach, H., Weisz, A., and Adams, P. A. 1956. Circles and derived figures in rotation. *American Journal of Psychology, 69,* 48-59.

Wallach, H., and Zuckerman, C. 1963. The constancy of stereoscopic depth. *American Journal of Psychology, 76,* 403-412.

Waltz, D. 1975. Understanding line drawings of scenes with shadows. In P. H. Winston, ed., *The Psychology of Computer Vision,* New York: McGraw Hill.

Wenderoth, P. 1974. The distinction between the rod and frame illusion and the rod and frame test. *Perception, 3,* 205-212.

Wenderoth, P. 1976. The contribution of relational factors to line-length matches. *Perception, 5,* 265-278.

Wertheimer, M. 1912. Experimentelle Studien über das Sehen von Bewegung. *Zeitschrift für Psychologie, 61,* 161-265.

Wertheimer, M. 1923. Untersuchungen zur Lehre von der Gestalt, II. *Psychologische Forschung, 4,* 301-350. See a condensed trans. in W. Ellis, *A Source Book of Gestalt Psychology,* Selection 5, New York: Humanities Press, 1950; see also the condensed trans. in D. C. Beardslee and M. Wertheimer, *Readings in Perception,* Selection 8, Princeton, N.J.: Van Nostrand Reinhold, 1958.

White, C. W. 1976. Visual masking during pursuit movements. *Journal of Experimental Psychology: Human Perception and Performance, 2,* 469-478.

Witkin, H. A. 1949. Perception of body position and the position of the visual field. *Psychological Monographs, 63,* No. 7.

Witkin, H. A., and Asch, S. E. 1948. Studies in space orientation: IV. Further experiments on perception of the upright with displaced visual fields. *Journal of Experimental Psychology, 38,* 762-782.

Winston, P. H. 1975. Learning structural descriptions from examples. In P. H. Winston, ed., *The Psychology of Computer Vision.* New York: McGraw Hill.

Woodworth, R. S. 1938. *Experimental Psychology.* New York: Henry Holt.

Zanforlin, M. 1982. Figure organization and binocular interaction. In J. Beck, ed., *Organization and Representation in Perception,* Hillsdale, N.J.: Erlbaum.

Zimmerman, R. R. and Torrey, C. C. 1965. Ontogeny of learning, in A. M. Schrier, H. F. Harlow, and F. Stollnitz, eds., *Behavior of Nonhuman Primates,* Vol. 2, New York: Academic Press, chap. 11.

Zöllner, F. 1862. Über eine neue Art anorthoskopischer Zerrbilder. *Annalen der Physik und Chemie (Poggendorfs Annalen), 117,* 477-484.

Zuckerman, C. B., and Rock, I. 1957. A reappraisal of the roles of past experience and innate organizing processes in visual perception. *Psychological Bulletin, 54,* 269-296.

Index

Abstraction, 68

Accommodation, 24, 252, 265, 270, 290

Adams, P., 286

Adaptation: to visual distortion, 310, 313, 314; of neural mechanisms of motion perception, 339

Aftereffect of movement, 293, 339

Afterimage, 24, 280, 294, 301; perceived motion of, 33, 37

Alampay, D., 66

Alignment, 105, 106, 113, 143

Ambiguity, 1, 22-23, 29, 36, 65, 66, 73, 75, 77, 81, 109, 111, 119, 133-134, 174, 177, 180, 182, 185, 188, 190, 197, 213, 240, 241, 268; of depth pattern, 290; dimensional, 23, 24, 30; of local stimulus, 36, 320, 331, 338; logical, 25, 192; qualitative, 23, 30, 100

Ambiguous figures, 111, 154; stabilization of, 160

Ames, A., 4, 319

Ames distorted room, 301, 319, 333

Ammons, C., 176

Anaglyph, 278

Anderson, J., 53

Anisotropy, spatial, 63

Anorthoscopic perception, 46, 47, 97, 108-110, 113, 115, 124, 128-129, 136, 164, 176-181, 183, 184, 185-188, 190-191, 200, 288, 296, 303, 320, 333

Anson, R., 105, 125, 126

Anstis, S., 176, 185, 187

Apparent depth, 244; length, 186, 187; lightness, 203; location, 257; motion, 14, 26, 33, 119, 124, 165-176,

288, 289n, 291, 294, 295, 301, 329, 337, 338; long-range process of, 176, 337; short-range process of, 176, 337; size, 30

Apportionment hypothesis, 217

Arend, L., 207, 208

Arnheim, R., 4, 143

Artificial intelligence, 41, 42, 53, 110, 143

Asch, S., 225, 226

Assumptions, 328-335

Atkinson, J., 185-186, 187

Attention, 39, 51, 56, 57, 58, 59, 60, 85, 95, 102, 168, 305-306, 329

Attitude, 340

Attneave, F., 66, 75, 77, 147, 153, 156, 173, 292, 327

Aubert, H., 202

Auster, M., 217

Austin, M., 225

Autochthonous forces, 157

Autokinetic effect, 201, 301

Autonomy: of cognitive processes from sensory input, 2; of perception from thought, 19, 315

Axioms, 328-335

Bachant, J., 280

Bahnsen, P., 144

Backward masking, 115

Banuazizi, A., 314, 330

Barbeito, R., 87, 88, 89, 259

Barlow H., 14, 41, 165, 293

Beck, J., 74

Beselman, D., 266

Benussi, ., 286

Benzschawel, T., 227, 228

Berkeley, G., 32, 312